First Among Equals
Outstanding Senate Leaders of the
Twentieth Century

When Everett McKinley Dirksen first envisioned the Dirksen Center, he pictured an institution where citizens could learn more about American government and politics, especially the role of congressional leadership. His interest grew naturally from a career of national public service that began in 1933 in the House of Representatives. Sixteen years in the House and eighteen more in the Senate, including ten as minority leader, convinced Dirksen that neither the public nor members of Congress fully understood the significance of legislative leadership.

Established in 1965 and located in Dirksen's hometown of Pekin, Illinois, the Everett McKinley Dirksen Congressional Leadership Research Center conducts many programs to foster an interest in congressional leadership. A not-for-profit, nonpartisan organization, the Center sponsors conferences and seminars, awards research grants, administers an archives and exhibit hall, and prepares educational materials about Congress for schools. It is the nation's only research center devoted to the study of congressional leadership in the United States.

First Among Equals

Outstanding Senate Leaders of the Twentieth Century

Richard A. Baker & Roger H. Davidson, *Editors*

The Dirksen Congressional Center

Congressional Quarterly Inc.
Washington, DC

Acknowledgments

1	2	3
4	5	6
7	8	9

Cover photographs:

(1) John W. Kern, *U.S. Senate Historical Office*
(2) Henry Cabot Lodge, *Library of Congress*
(3) Joseph T. Robinson, *Library of Congress*
(4) Charles L. McNary, *Architect of the Capitol*
(5) Alben W. Barkley, *U.S. Senate Historical Office*
(6) Robert A. Taft, *U.S. Senate Historical Office*
(7) Lyndon B. Johnson, *U.S. Senate Historical Office*
(8) Everett McKinley Dirksen, *U.S. Senate Historical Office*
(9) Mike Mansfield, *U.S. Senate Historical Office*

Interior photographs:

*Architect of the Capitol, 98; C.G. Bowers, The Life of John Worth Kern (1918), 7; Collection of Steve Neal, 117;
Dirksen Congressional Center, 253; Georges Tames, 214, 264; Library of Congress, 38, 113, 148, 187, 283;
Martin Luther King Library, 250; U.S. Senate Historical Office, 63, 127, 144, 163, 178, 199, 236, 268.*

Text design by Kachergis Book Design, Pittsboro, N.C. Cover design by Dan Royer with Kachergis Book Design.

Library of Congress Cataloging-in-Publication Data
First among equals / Richard A. Baker, Roger H. Davidson, editors.
    p. cm.
  Includes bibliographical references and index.
   ISBN 0-87187-581-0 (hard) — ISBN 0-87187-586-1 (pbk.)
    1. Legislators—United States—Biography. 2. United States.
Congress. Senate—Biography. 3. United States. Congress. Senate—
Leadership. I. Baker, Richard A. II. Davidson, Roger H.
JK 1161.F57 1991
328.73'092'2—dc20
  [B]   91-17019

CONTENTS

FOREWORD

I have had the privilege of viewing Senate leadership up close. I learned much from my father-in-law, Everett McKinley Dirksen, who, as my friend Mike Mansfield once said, ran the U.S. Senate from the minority leader's chair. I, too, have had the honor of serving as minority leader and then as majority leader. Later, I gained a slightly different, and more distant, perspective on the Senate leadership when I served as chief of staff to the president. My fascination, appreciation, and respect for the offices of majority and minority leader have only grown. As a consequence, I have often wondered if my fellow Americans—and even my former friends and colleagues in the Senate—really understand the role of Senate leader.

The leadership of the U.S. Senate is an institution in and of itself. In many cases it is an independent force in the creation and development of public policy. Yet, its importance aside, the office of leader is of comparatively recent origin, and it continues to evolve. Although the leader is highly visible, the powers and prerogatives of the office are not enumerated. Wielding these powers effectively often depends on the skills and abilities of the individual leader. Many Americans assume that the primary role of a senator is to represent the views of his or her state. Indeed that is so. But someone must speak for the party. Someone must speak for the Senate. Someone must create an intelligible position out of one hundred contending voices. Someone must make sure that the Senate functions.

The U.S. Constitution did not provide a speaker for the Senate as it did for the House of Representatives. The rules and precedents that undergird the House leadership simply do not exist in the Senate. While the vice president presides over the chamber, he does not lead it, nor do those who occupy the presiding officer's chair in his absence.

Power resides in the leaders. How it got there is really a story about the modern Senate: how tradition, circumstance, and a few singular men invented an office.

John Worth Kern of Indiana held a slim majority of Democrats together in 1913 to propel through Congress President Woodrow Wilson's progressive legislative initiatives in spite of a divided opposition. Six years later circumstances and personalities had changed dramatically when Henry Cabot Lodge of Massachusetts and his Republican majority fought the same president over America's role in the world. Both of these men helped to establish the role of Senate leader.

I have fond recollections of Everett McKinley Dirksen. He was a remarkable man. My earliest experiences with him left me impressed with many things, but I will always remember the resonance of his voice and the linearity of his thinking (although the resonance sometimes overwhelmed the linearity). He wielded his rhetorical skill with great effectiveness in his dealings with presidents and senators alike. He contributed something of enduring value to the role of Senate leader.

This book will examine the unique contributions of nine senators who have left a legacy of leadership to those of us who study or practice legislative politics.

Howard H. Baker, Jr.

PREFACE

After his retirement from the Senate in 1985, former majority leader Howard H. Baker, Jr., became senior adviser to the Everett McKinley Dirksen Congressional Leadership Research Center. One of his first suggestions to the board of directors and staff was that the Center undertake a long-term study of the origins, evolution, and operation of leadership in the U.S. Congress. The Center responded by assembling a steering committee of experienced scholars and seasoned observers of Congress to develop a plan for such a study. This committee included Richard A. Baker of the U.S. Senate Historical Office, Richard E. Cohen of the *National Journal*, Roger Davidson of the University of Maryland, Alan Ehrenhalt of Congressional Quarterly, Susan Webb Hammond of the American University, Thomas Mann of the Brookings Institution, Charles O. Jones of the University of Wisconsin, Norman Ornstein of the American Enterprise Institute, Richard Sachs of the Congressional Research Service of the Library of Congress, and Barbara Sinclair of the University of California at Riverside.

Frank Mackaman, former executive director of the Dirksen Center and current director of the Gerald R. Ford Library, and Merle Glick, then-president of the board of directors of the Dirksen Center, served as staff directors during these initial discussions and the early stages of the project that followed.

In early 1987, the Ford Foundation provided $150,000 to support what came to be called the Congressional Leadership Research Project.

This project has three components. The first was designed to find out what is known about congressional leadership. To accomplish this, the Center, with the Congressional Research Service, held six dinner meetings between 1987 and 1988 in Washington, D.C., to discuss leadership issues. Members of Congress, congressional staffers, Capitol Hill journalists, and legislative scholars all attended these dinner meetings. The dinner presentations, each on some aspect of congressional leadership, and subsequent discussions were then transcribed and reviewed.

The second component of the Congressional Leadership Research Project focused on research. Barbara Sinclair was commissioned to write a paper summarizing the status of congressional leadership research and to suggest a research agenda. This paper, along with the six dinner presentations, became the basis of the book *Leading Congress: New Styles, New Strategies,* published by Congressional Quarterly in 1990. The Center also provided support for a research conference on the U.S. Senate coordinated by John Hibbing at the University of Nebraska in 1988.

Through these activities, the need for a more extensive look into Senate leadership became apparent. In 1989, the Center commissioned nine profiles of individual senators who had helped to create and fashion the office of Senate leader. The authors, all distinguished and practiced observers of Congress, include four political scientists, three journalists, and two historians.

The third component of the project concerned dissemination. On May 17, 1990, the nine profiles were presented at a symposium cosponsored by the U.S. Senate Commission on the Bicentennial. This conference was attended by more than 150 scholars and practitioners of government and taped by C-SPAN for a national viewing audience.

This book is the result of those presentations and the discussions that followed. Perhaps Senate Majority Leader George Mitchell described it best in his introductory comments at the conference:

The two-hundredth anniversary of the Senate offers an excellent opportunity to pause and examine the institution of the Senate party leadership. While each passing Congress poses uniquely new challenges for which there are no precedents, there are many themes which can be identified as common. . . . I am pleased that the Dirksen Center has been able to assess the important contributions of these past Senate leaders.

More attention needs to be paid to the qualities and conditions of legislative leadership. *First Among Equals* is a step in that direction. We at the Dirksen Center hope it will encourage students and observers to follow its example.

> *John J. Kornacki*
> *Executive Director*
> *The Everett McKinley Dirksen*
> *Congressional Leadership Research Center*

First Among Equals

Outstanding Senate Leaders of the
Twentieth Century

Introduction

Richard A. Baker and Roger H. Davidson

T he United States Senate is rightly called a "continuing body" because only one third of its seats are subject to change in any given election year. The Senate is continuous in a larger sense as well: from 1789 to the present day, it has been an institution of remarkable structural and political continuity.

If we could somehow summon back the senators of the First Congress, who met from 1789 to 1791, they would undoubtedly recognize much of the modern Senate. They would appreciate the equality of the states in its deliberations and the ability of a single senator to forestall action through prolonged negotiation. They would share modern senators' suspicions of the House of Representatives and their zeal to serve as a check against the powers of the presidency. Those early senators would doubtless be heartened by the relative ease of communication among today's members—despite the body's growth from twenty-six to one hundred members, the centrifugal forces of modern transportation and communication that allow members to traverse the country, and the small armies of staff aides that now surround every member.

Our early senators might even be reconciled to the single great structural change in the Senate's constitutional position: the abandonment, in 1913, of state legislative selection of senators in favor of direct popular choice.

What would most likely puzzle those first senators, however, is a development that surfaced the very year the direct election amendment was ratified: the rise of party floor leadership as a distinct institution.

From the late eighteenth century through the first decade of the twentieth, baronial committee chairmen provided the chamber's necessary internal leadership. The Senate solidified this committee leadership base in 1816 by establishing permanent committees and, beginning in the 1840s, by assigning committee members according to their political party caucus. By the mid-nineteenth century, seniority was the principal in-

1

strument for allocating power, as committee chairmanships went to the Senate's most senior members regardless of their service on that committee.

Following World War I, Senate party caucuses began regularly to designate their official floor leaders. The rise of the United States to the status of a world power, and the advent of assertive chief executives such as Theodore Roosevelt and Woodrow Wilson, necessitated a coordinated Senate leadership quite beyond the capacity of individual committee chairmen. Meanwhile, the traditionally influential chairmen came to be assigned according to their seniority *within* the committee to be chaired, thus placing power in the most experienced hands. With power thus consolidated, the committee chairmen sometimes clashed with party floor leaders, whose objectives frequently differed from their own and who owed their ascendancy to factors other than seniority.

The 1912 elections split the Republican party's traditional majority, giving control of the presidency and both houses of Congress to the Democrats for the first time in twenty years. President Woodrow Wilson viewed himself as a kind of prime minister with a parliamentary majority to lead, but nonetheless he realized he had only a limited time to consolidate his party's victory. He moved quickly to ensure a strong Senate field commander for his programs by supporting Indiana's John Worth Kern as majority floor leader. A nationally prominent progressive Democrat, Kern was just two years into what would prove to be his only Senate term. He aggressively assumed the now-familiar leadership roles of scheduling legislation and seeking party unity to secure passage of a predetermined program. His resources were limited to the force of his personality, the support of his president, and the desire of his fellow Democrats to prevail over the opposition.

Eight decades have passed since Kern first exercised the nascent power of floor leadership. Since then, the posts of majority and minority leader have acquired great importance—inside the chamber, within the Washington policy-making community, and even in the national media. Successive incumbents have shaped the leadership according to their own personalities, their views of the Senate's constitutional role, and the existing political environment. This evolution can safely be judged as the most significant institutional development of the Senate's history.

The Senate is often regarded as an intensely personal and subtle institution. Casual observers and junior members find that extended study and experience are required to comprehend its legislative pulse and institutional rhythms. That subtlety extends to the work of the majority and minority leaders.

Through the years, floor leaders have routinely lamented their limited formal powers. Robert C. Byrd, when he was majority leader, once remarked that if anyone asked his occupation he would put down "slave." Bob Dole complained that a majority leader is "in some ways . . . the slave of all."[1]

Yet floor leaders possess increasingly potent resources to shape the Senate's work. Under Senate custom, the presiding officer accords them preferential recognition ahead of all other senators seeking to speak on the floor. As Byrd explained, "The power of first recognition is, by far, the most potent weapon in the majority leader's arsenal, enabling him to outflank any other senator in offering first- and second-degree amendments, substitutes, and motions to reconsider. Without it, he would be like an emperor without clothes."[2]

The majority leader, in cooperation with the minority leader, also exercises great influence in determining which matters will be brought to the floor and how much time will be devoted to them. Managing the schedule and fashioning unanimous consent agreements for allocating time and limiting debate lie at the heart of the leaders' responsibilities. These tasks require patience, diplomacy, and, above all, a sense of timing—quintessential talents for a successful legislative leader. Floor leaders work closely with the chairmen and ranking minority members of committees, as well as other influential senators, to set and pursue legislative priorities. "A good leader should not only know more about the workings of a committee and how the members arrived at the content of the bill as finally recommended," Lyndon Johnson observed in 1960, "but he must also know the problems of each individual state and the temperament of each individual senator."[3]

Leaders are judged not only by the number and quality of bills enacted at the end of a Congress but also by how fully they offer senators opportunities to express their views and by how well they keep the process moving—hardly compatible objectives. Compromise, accommodation, and extended deliberation—essential components of a leader's style—are traditionally at odds with the compelling pressures for action. Majority leaders speak for their own party and for the entire Senate as well. If the president is of their party, they must tread carefully between the potentially antagonistic roles of the Senate's emissary to the president and the president's legislative agent in the Senate.

One subtle but significant development has been the evolution of "the leadership," a collective term that embraces many of the functions now routinely performed by majority and minority leaders and their staffs. Early leaders, even when they had trusted and seasoned staff aides, relied almost exclusively on face-to-face dealings with colleagues. Today's leadership includes the two floor leaders as well as the whips, caucus chairmen and secretaries, and other senators serving on policy, campaign, or steering committees. Majority and minority staff aides routinely keep track of senators and how they are likely to vote; they also report individual senators' views on pending legislation and unanimous consent agreements. Despite its bureaucratic aspects, Senate leadership retains much of the personalized character that marked its origins.

This volume is the first major study of the Senate leadership to be cast in a biographical perspective. The essays evaluate each leader in the context of the political environment and Senate institutional setting of his era, his personal qualities, performance in office, contributions to the Senate, and place in the nation's political history.

Since the designation of John Worth Kern as majority leader in 1913, Senate Democrats and Republicans have selected twenty-four persons to lead their parties. The nine profiled here include five Democrats and four Republicans. Their collective leadership spanned two-thirds of a century, ending in 1977 with the completion of Mike Mansfield's record-setting sixteen-year tenure. In geographic representation, they encompass the nation, with a concentration in the midwestern states (Illinois, Indiana, Ohio), the southern border states (Arkansas, Kentucky), and the western states (Montana, Oregon).

Eleven other leaders have lacked either tenure or distinction and accordingly were omitted from this study. In addition, Robert C. Byrd, Howard Baker, Bob Dole, and George Mitchell served too recently to fall within the scope of a broadly historical account.

Together these essays offer a richly satisfying and broadly insightful account of a dynamic American political institution. They have also illuminated the phenomenon of leadership—so essential to the performance of legislative institutions—in the context of the individualistic Senate, where to lead is to serve as first among equals.

NOTES

1. *Congressional Record,* 96th Cong., 2d sess., 1980, S3924; ibid., 99th Cong., 2d sess., 1986, S17294.
2. U.S. Congress, Senate, *The Senate, 1789–1989,* by Robert C. Byrd, S. Doc. 100-20, 100th Cong., 1st sess., vol. 2, 1991, 190.
3. "Leadership: An Interview with Senate Leader Lyndon Johnson," *U.S. News & World Report,* June 27, 1960, 88.

CHAPTER 1

John Worth Kern
Portrait of a Floor Leader

Walter J. Oleszek

John Worth Kern, the Indiana Democrat who served in the Senate from 1911 to 1917, was something of a political anomaly. Arguably the Senate's first majority leader and a progressive Democrat, Kern had close ties to an old-line political machine in his state. A political loser for much of his electoral career, Kern finally won a coveted seat in the U.S. Senate. He was elected majority leader at an advanced age but had only two years' tenure in the Senate; no other modern floor leader of either party has been elected to this post with such limited senatorial service. Although he was the Senate's majority floor leader during one of this century's most legislatively productive periods—the "New Freedom" era of President Woodrow Wilson—Kern is seldom mentioned in analyses of congressional leadership and has received scant scholarly attention.[1]

Who was John Worth Kern? How did he get to the Senate? Why was he chosen floor leader? What did he accomplish? Are lasting precedents associated with his leadership? These are the principal questions explored in this chapter. First, however, it is worth outlining the emergence of floor leadership in the Senate and identifying Kern's place in it.

John Worth Kern, a Democrat from Indiana, is generally acknowledged as the first Senate majority leader.

Floor Leadership in the Senate

"There has never been any historical background for the mythical institution of leadership in the Senate," wrote George Rothwell Brown in *The Leadership of Congress*.[2] Unfortunately, Brown had overlooked the leadership structure already in place at the time he wrote. In fact, the Senate has always had leaders. During its first century or so, especially in the 1790s and early 1800s when there was no system of permanent committees or organized political parties, leadership in the Senate flowed from the personal talents and abilities of individual legislators. No doubt the size of the early Senate and its tradition of viewing members as "ambassadors" from sovereign states promoted an informal and personal style of senatorial leadership.

Senator Oliver Ellsworth of Connecticut, who served from 1789 to 1796, is a case in point. Of the initial twenty-six senators, Ellsworth was first among equals. Through his energy, intellect, and political sophistication, Ellsworth "exerted more practical leadership in the day-to-day activities of the upper Chamber than any other Member of that body."[3] During subsequent decades, scores of senators emerged as unofficial leaders in the Senate. Some were sectional or factional leaders; others headed important committees (by the mid to late 1840s, committees and their chairs had become centers of power); and still others (the Clays, Websters, and Calhouns) exercised wide influence because of their special political, oratorical, or intellectual gifts.

Throughout the nineteenth century, scores of prominent and influential senators were called "leaders" by scholars, commentators, and others. But no single senator exercised central management of the legislative process in the fashion of today's floor leader. As late as 1885, Woodrow Wilson could write: "No one is *the* Senator. . . . No one exercises the special trust of acknowledged leadership."[4] That "Senate parties were still without coherence, exercising only limited influence," as David Rothman writes, contributed to the dispersal of authority throughout the Senate.[5]

In a few short years, however, the political landscape changed. Party structures and leaders emerged as clearly identifiable forces in organizing and managing the Senate's proceedings. Rothman, an eminent historian of the Senate, lucidly analyzes how and why, by the turn of the twentieth century, political parties altered traditional senatorial practices. He stresses the influx of a "new breed" of senator who was a professional politician "with a deeply ingrained respect for the machinery of [party] organization," especially the party caucus. The growing role of the national government and the complexities of governance reinforced, Rothman argues, the trend toward careerist politicians who, after serving apprenticeships in state legislatures, appreciated the virtues of party discipline and unity. Finally, Rothman emphasizes that parties and leaders in the Senate assumed unprecedented authority because significant segments of the public understood the connection between party organization and the advancement of common interests.[6]

Given the importance of the party system in the late-nineteenth-century Senate, it stands to reason that those senators who chaired their respective partisan gatherings acquired levers of authority over senatorial affairs. The consensus among scholars is that the contemporary floor leader evolved from the post of caucus leader. For example, they chaired important party panels (such as the Committee on Committees), shaped the Senate's agenda of business, and mobilized party majorities behind key issues. In the late nineteenth century, writes Rothman, "party leadership for the first time dominated the chamber's business." He also notes that some of the tactics used by these late-nineteenth-century leaders, such as Republican William B. Allison of Iowa and Democrat Arthur Pue Gorman of Maryland, "were faithfully emulated by Lyndon Johnson" when he became the Senate's floor leader in the 1950s.[7] More than two decades after he wrote *Congressional Government*, Woodrow Wilson declared:

> The leader of the Senate is the chairman of the majority caucus. Each party in the Senate finds its real, its permanent, its effective organization in its caucus, and follows the leadership, in all important parliamentary battles, of the chairman of that caucus.[8]

In short, adroit caucus leaders (who worked with and through a core of political lieutenants) and a willing Senate combined to lay the groundwork for the emergence of the floor leader.

If scholars agree about the evolution of the floor leadership position, they are more tendentious about when a certain senator first functioned as the "majority leader" or "minority leader." One scholar declared that the position of Senate floor leader formally emerged "between 1870 and 1913."[9] Another analyst is more precise, writing that the post "emerged as a formal and readily identifiable party leader in the period between 1911 and 1915. . . . Before 1911 a few senators functioned as the modern-day Majority Leader functions, but they did not generally bear a formal title."[10] Finally, Senate parliamentarian emeritus Floyd M. Riddick, who had access to the conference minutes of both parties, pinpoints the exact dates when Democrats and Republicans formally and officially selected their floor leaders. For the Democrats it was January 5, 1920. "This was the first time," observes Riddick, "that the caucus minutes showed that a meeting was being called to elect a 'leader' for the party and not just a chairman of the party caucus."[11] The Republicans followed suit five years later, on March 5, 1925.[12]

Under Riddick's formulation, Democrat Oscar Underwood of Alabama was the Senate's first official floor leader, serving as minority leader from 1920 to 1923. The first majority leader was Republican Charles Curtis of Kansas, who served in that capacity from 1925 to 1929. It is evident from available records, however, that prior to 1920 several other senators unofficially functioned as the floor leader of their respective party. For Democrats, John Worth Kern of Indiana, the object of this study, fits this description and merits the title "majority leader" for the period 1913 to 1917.[13] This contention is buttressed by an extraordinary occurrence for that era. Kern was elected caucus chairman (and de facto floor leader) on March 5, 1913, after only two years' service in the Senate. Previously, seniority was a crucial factor in the selection of caucus chairs for both parties. Kern had little seniority and thus little opportunity to develop an independent power base in either the committee or party structure. In short, he became the first floor leader to derive his powers and prerogatives almost exclusively from election to this high and yet still untitled party post.

Early Political Career

John Worth Kern was born on December 20, 1849, in Alto, Indiana. He attended local schools and then entered the Normal College at Kokomo, Indiana. After graduation, Kern taught in the public schools of the area, where he demonstrated an interest and proficiency in debating. He engaged in numerous debates on public issues with various citizens of the community. To be sure, his speaking abilities proved helpful when he embarked on his political career. Kern's interest in public affairs led him, in 1867, to the University of Michigan's law school; two years later he was graduated.

Following his graduation, Kern returned to Kokomo and started a law practice. Just short of twenty when he hung out his shingle, Kern's oratorical and legal talents soon brought him many clients and established his reputation as an effective trial lawyer. He remained in Kokomo for fifteen years, married in 1870 (his wife died in 1884, and he remarried the next year), and became active in party affairs.

A Democrat from his youth, Kern was elected secretary of the Democratic County Central Committee in 1870 (Kokomo was staunchly Republican), which only a few months later nominated him for the state legislature. He lost, but the election enhanced his political visibility throughout the district. In the aftermath of the election, and to challenge GOP dominance in the area, Kern and several others established a Democratic newspaper in Kokomo. Kern wrote articles for the newspaper that won him further attention as a Democratic leader.

In 1871, the GOP-dominated Kokomo City Council (five Republicans, three Democrats) elected Kern city attorney, a post he held until 1884. His Republican backing on the council, incidentally, suggests his ability to be a fair and reasonable partisan. During this period, he was active in Democratic affairs and became prominent enough in Indiana to be named in 1876, for example, as secretary of the Democratic State Convention.

In 1884, Kern decided to run for statewide office: reporter of the Indiana Supreme Court. He won his party's nomination at the state convention and went on to achieve his first electoral victory, attracting a popular vote exceeded by only one other Democrat on the state ticket. Kern held this post four years (1885–1889). Renominated in 1888, Kern and every other Democrat running for statewide office went down to defeat in a banner year for Republicans. Kern returned to private law practice in Indianapolis, where he now resided.

In 1892, Kern was elected to the state senate, where he served two terms (1893–1897)—the first time in the majority and the second, after the 1894 election, in the minority. He was especially active on behalf of laborers (he was a strong supporter of unions), the child-labor issue, and internal legislative affairs (he sat on the Rules Committee). During the 1896 presidential campaign, he met William Jennings Bryan, the Democratic standard-bearer. Even though Kern opposed Bryan's "free silver" position, they respected one another and, as one account noted, "ever afterward remained on terms of intimacy."[14] When Kern's second term in the state senate expired, he again resumed his law practice, remaining active in Democratic politics.

In 1900 and again in 1904 Kern was the Democratic nominee for governor but lost both contests. He attracted some national attention, however, by running ahead of his party's presidential nominee (Bryan in 1900 and, in 1904, New York judge Alton Parker). He had also helped to swing Indiana's 1904 convention votes to Parker and seconded Parker's nomination at the Democratic National Convention in St. Louis. After his gubernatorial efforts, he returned once more to the practice of law and politics, traveled to Europe, and, for health reasons, spent six months (from September 1906 to March 1907) at a sanitorium in Asheville, North Carolina.

Returning to Indiana, Kern soon became embroiled in presidential politics. With the 1908 elections looming and Bryan's presidential nomination a virtual certainty, the Democratic standard-bearer and his allies searched long and hard for a vice-presidential running mate who could strengthen the ticket, satisfy labor, and appeal to party members. Unable to find an acceptable candidate in the East, Bryan and others looked to the Midwest. Indiana's Thomas Taggart, chairman of the Democratic National Convention, and others began to boom Kern for the vice presidency. Bryan agreed, and the convention chose Kern. The Democratic ticket was consistent, the *New York Times* observed, "for a man twice defeated for the Presidency was at the head of it, and a man twice defeated for governor of his state was at the tail of it."[15] In the end, the Bryan-Kern ticket went down to defeat as Republican William Howard Taft won the White House.

Election to the U.S. Senate

Despite his defeat, the 1908 election results provided a bright political opportunity for Kern. Indiana voters elected Democrat Thomas R. Marshall (soon to be vice president under President Woodrow Wilson) as governor and gave Democrats a twenty-seat majority in the Indiana House and a near majority in the senate. This meant that Democrats would elect the next U.S. senator. (Senators were still elected by a joint session of the state legislature; the Seventeenth Amendment to the U.S. Constitution, providing for the direct election of senators, was not ratified until 1913.) In reality, however, the Democratic caucus, not the state legislature, would choose a senator for Indiana.

Kern's political reputation and long party service led many Indiana voters and politicos to assume he would be the next U.S. senator. This was not to be, however. The Senate seat attracted several worthy contenders, including former House member and gubernatorial aspirant Benjamin Shiveley. The caucus sessions were raucous affairs filled with deals, duplicities, and vote-buying charges and countercharges. On the twentieth ballot, Shiveley received the required majority vote (42 of 83) and won the senatorship.[16] Shiveley's unexpected victory produced an outpouring of irate commentary. Kern even stated that the vote-buying "brewery crowd got eight [votes] away from [me]."[17]

Kern's political career appeared to be over. Now sixty years old, he once again resumed his law practice. But Kern was rewarded two years later when Indiana's other Senate seat opened. With Democrats in charge of the state legislature following the November 1910 elections, Kern was elected (90-60) to the U.S. Senate.

Kern and His Times

Kern's election to the Senate came during a period of dramatic national transformation. It was an age of change and ferment, of political and social reformation and rebellion. With the birth of the twentieth century came the close of the western frontier, the enormous growth of cities, the spread of railroads across the country, the rise of a powerful industrial economy, and major advances in the nation's material prosperity. The United States had become a world power.

But such progress was achieved at great social, political, and human cost. Railroad owners exploited farmers; young children and women labored in abysmal sweat shops; industrial accidents were endemic; cities were filled with slums, crime, and vice; great wealth was amassed by the so-called captains of industry who controlled monopolistic "trusts"; and principles of equal protection and justice were often honored more in theory than reality. Muckrakers such as Upton Sinclair (*The Jungle*, 1906), Lincoln Steffens (*The Shame of the Cities*, 1909), and David Graham Phillips (*The Treason of the Senate*, 1906) exposed the terrible plight of workers who toiled in unsafe and unsanitary conditions, the political corruption rampant in many big cities, and the links between influential U.S. senators and corporate interests that thwarted the passage of social welfare legislation.

These diverse concerns, along with so many others (Prohibition, woman's suffrage, scientific management and efficient government, taxes and tariffs, regulation of business, direct election of senators, and initiative, referendum, and recall), were nationally debated during the period from roughly 1900 to World War I, and gave rise to the so-called progressive movement. Complex in its goals and interests, the movement's fundamental objective was "progress" toward a better society. To achieve that general goal, many progressive leaders (William Jennings Bryan, Theodore Roosevelt, and Woodrow Wilson, for example) hoped to harness governmental power to promote the general welfare.

It appeared that only an activist national government could remedy the country's social and political ills, a perspective that augured fundamental changes in the roles of the legislative and executive branches, which historically had never intruded too deeply in the regulation of economic or private activities. With the emergence of new leadership in Washington, however, all this would soon change. John Worth Kern was imbued with many progressive values and objectives. Joining Benjamin Shiveley, his fellow Hoosier and an opponent of monopolistic corporate power, Kern quickly became involved in an effort to shake up his party's conservative leadership.

Prelude to Kern's Ascension to Leadership

The themes of change and reorganization that undergirded progressive thought were reflected in the November 1910 election that elevated Kern to the Senate. This election highlighted the deep divisions within the Republican ranks (which, with the exception of the Wilson years, was the dominant party from 1896 to 1932) and foreshadowed the electoral upheaval of 1912 that produced Democratic control of Congress and the White House for the first time in the twentieth century. Although Republicans retained control of the Senate in the aftermath of the 1910 election, their majority was significantly reduced (from 61-32 in the Sixty-first Congress to 51-41 in the Sixty-second). Democrats, however, captured control of the House (228-161) for the first time since 1892. Thus, for the first time in this century Congress was controlled by two different parties. It is worth noting that the November 1910 election also placed Woodrow Wilson in New Jersey's statehouse.

The 1910 election brought ten new Democrats—most of them Progressives—to the Senate. With this infusion of new blood into the party (which for years had been dominated by conservative southerners) and with President Taft's call for a special session in April 1911, the stage was set for a party struggle over the caucus chairmanship. Odds favored the election of conservative Senator Thomas S. Martin of Virginia. In an unusual move, however, William Jennings Bryan, nominal head of the Democratic party, journeyed to Washington to campaign against him. Bryan had evidently planned his campaign with senators Robert Owen,

John Worth Kern, and William J. Stone. He spent about two weeks lobbying legislative friends and urging progressive Democrats to run for the caucus chairmanship.[18]

Kern nominated his Indiana colleague, Benjamin Shiveley, but on April 7, 1911, Martin defeated the Hoosier by a 21-16 caucus vote. Senator Augustus Bacon of Georgia, a conservative Democrat, said it was the first time a roll call had occurred in sixteen years; previously, the caucus chair had always been decided by unanimous consent of the party membership.[19] The demand for a roll-call vote clearly points to the deep regional and ideological fissures within Democratic ranks.

Following Shiveley's defeat, Senator Robert Owen of Oklahoma, a Progressive, offered a resolution to revamp the Steering Committee. (By custom, the Democratic Caucus chairman appointed and chaired the Steering Committee.) Owen's resolution was designed to dilute the authority of the senior leaders and required that Democrats be divided into three groups—senior, sophomore, and freshman members—with three to be selected from each category for the Steering Committee. After Martin and other senior Democrats gave assurances that all caucus members would be treated equitably in the committee assignment process, Owen withdrew his resolution and caucus chairman Martin appointed the Steering Committee members.[20]

The efforts of the Democratic Progressives had clearly wrung concessions from Senator Martin. Shiveley was named vice chairman of the caucus and Kern and another Progressive were named to the Steering Committee.[21] Kern subsequently won appointments to the Committee on Privileges and Elections and the prestigious Finance Committee. His senior Indiana colleague had also sought the Finance post but was thwarted by "stubborn opposition" in the Steering Committee.[22] To prevent hard feelings on Shiveley's part, Kern worked diligently to safeguard their personal and professional relationship.[23] Kern's leadership role in the caucus, in sum, was recognized in important party and committee assignments that shaped much of his Senate activity during the Sixty-second Congress.

Nine days after he was sworn in, Kern introduced his first public bill (S. 944), "An act providing for publicity of contributions made for the purpose of influencing elections at which Representatives in Congress are elected." Kern was an advocate of campaign finance reform (a hardy perennial in American politics), as illustrated by the 1908 presidential election, during which the Bryan-Kern ticket pledged to publicly disclose the names of all contributors who donated $100 or more in advance (by October 15) of the November election.[24]

Kern's bill was referred to the Committee on Privileges and Elections, on which he sat. Although his bill was not reported by the committee, a comparable House measure (H.R. 2958) did receive consideration and was passed by the Senate and signed into law by the president. During floor debate, Kern spoke briefly on the legislation.[25]

During the 1911–1912 period, Kern rarely took the floor. His first lengthy stint in floor debate might even be termed his maiden speech to the Senate. It occurred on July 28, 1911, and addressed an issue that always seems contemporaneous: expenditures for committee staff aides.

Senate Resolution 118 authorized sixteen standing committees "to employ a messenger at a salary of $1,200 per annum." Kern immediately took the floor to declare that "some of us on this side of the aisle were elected last fall under a distinct pledge that we should be in favor of economy and retrenchment in the affairs of the Government."[26] Kern knew that most of the sixteen standing committees had neither convened a meeting during the session nor had any plans to do so. Why, he asked, did these panels require additional staff assistance? As a newcomer, Kern was probably unfamiliar with the ultimate purpose of the resolution, which was to provide Senate chairman with additional *personal* staff assistance. (During this period, "paper committees," headed by majority *and* minority members, were created or maintained as an indirect way of providing staff to individual senators.) Pointedly noting Kern's junior status, the chairman of the Committee to Audit and Control the Contingent Expenses of the Senate, Joseph Bristow (R-Kans.), said, "It is unfortunate that the Senate has not had the wisdom of the Senator from Indiana . . . during past years to help it transact its business."[27] Although Kern gave as good as he got, the staffing resolution was adopted. Still, he demonstrated his ability to hold his own on the floor against more senior members, his commitment to frugality in public affairs, and his willingness to challenge established senatorial practices.

Several other legislative and political matters occupied Kern during the 1911–1912 period. He was active on pension reform for Civil War veterans, workers' rights, and federal election reform. But two issues, related to his Finance and Privileges and Elections committee assignments, dominated his time: tariff revision (he favored tariff reductions) and the William Lorimer election scandal. The GOP boss of Chicago and a former House member, Lorimer had been elected to the U.S. Senate in

1909 by the Illinois General Assembly. Kern played a leading role in having the Senate invalidate Lorimer's election.

The 1912 nominating convention also dominated Kern's attention. During debate on the Lorimer case, the Senate interrupted its deliberations to permit the parties to hold their presidential nominating conventions. Democrats convened their session in Baltimore, and Kern was active in its deliberations. There were even "Kern for President" rumors during his early Senate service. But the Indianan disavowed any interest in the presidency, especially in view of Indiana governor Thomas Marshall's ambitions regarding the Democratic nomination (the governor was named Wilson's vice president shortly thereafter). As early as April 1911, Kern said he had no interest in seeking the nomination, declaring three months later in a Washington interview that "the Indiana Governor's chances were infinitely better than those of anyone else."[28] Kern was nevertheless viewed as a presidential dark horse, and Bryan even suggested his name, along with several others, for president when the Baltimore convention appeared deadlocked.

The struggle for the nomination between the leading candidates (Woodrow Wilson and House Speaker James Beauchamp "Champ" Clark) began when William Jennings Bryan objected to the convention's recommendation that Judge Alton Parker be its temporary chairman. (The temporary chairman would deliver the keynote address.) Bryan opposed the conservative Parker because he wanted Progressives to dominate convention proceedings.

On June 25, 1912, Parker's name was placed in nomination for the temporary chairmanship. Bryan then took the floor and nominated Kern for the post. Bryan argued that "a true progressive should lead the convention in the keynote address."[29] Kern then made a dramatic appeal to Parker to remove himself from the contest and suggested several compromise candidates for the post. When Parker declined to do so, "the Indiana senator withdrew from the contest and nominated Bryan himself."[30] With the convention in an uproar, the delegates elected Parker; Kern was named chairman of the platform committee and played a leading role in preparing the party platform, a progressive document that contained declarations on banking and tariff reform and on the popular election of senators.[31]

After Wilson was nominated, he summoned Kern to the "Little White House" in Sea Girt, New Jersey. "Senator Kern has had a great deal of valuable experience as a campaigner and . . . Governor [Wilson] is certain he can obtain from the senator information that will be helpful to him in conducting his candidacy," noted Senator James Martine (D-N.J.), who delivered Wilson's request to Kern.[32] The Indianan and other progressive leaders were "agreed that Mr. Wilson should not himself take the stump, but should allow others to do the speaking."[33] Although Wilson did not conduct a front-porch campaign, he asked Kern to take a leading role in speaking on his behalf, especially in New Jersey and the eastern states. New Jerseyans "regard Kern as a powerful attraction on the stump. He traversed that state thoroughly four years ago when he was a candidate for Vice President and all agree he made a hit."[34]

Kern did not campaign extensively for Wilson. First, the Senate, which did not adjourn until August 26, 1912, occupied his attention. Second, Kern was then involved in the McNamara case in Indianapolis. Labor leader James McNamara had been arrested in Indiana on the charge that he dynamited a newspaper plant in Los Angeles. Perhaps for personal financial reasons or sympathy with the cause of labor, Kern served as one of the lead attorneys in the case (involving McNamara's extradition to California), which went on during and after the campaign. Finally, Kern's generally frail health may have limited his campaign efforts: he made a little more than a dozen speeches in Indiana on behalf of Wilson and the Democratic party.[35]

On November 4, 1912, Wilson scored a dramatic victory with an over-whelming win in the Electoral College (435 to Roosevelt's 88 and Taft's 8 electoral votes), although his popular vote (6,293,019) did not match the combined total for Roosevelt (4,119,507) and Taft (3,484,956). The schism in Republican ranks undoubtedly led to the Democratic victory. Equally significant, Democrats won control of the House (290 to 127) and the Senate (51 D, 44 R, and 1 Progressive). The upheaval in political leader-ship continued into the Sixty-third Congress when Senate Democrats met to elect their floor leader.

Kern's Election as Floor Leader

Kern's record during the Sixty-second Congress demonstrated his leadership abilities. His challenge to Martin's selection as Democratic leader, his appointments to the important Steering and Finance commit-tees, his major role in the Lorimer case, and his chairmanship of the platform committee at the presidential nominating convention, in addi-tion to his national stature as a progressive leader, all pointed to his prominence. His skills at conciliation and his personal popularity clinched for Kern a post he did not actively seek: the majority leadership of the Senate.

After the November elections and in an atmosphere of momentous change, several progressive Democrats began to consider ways to ensure their control of Senate committees. Their target was the seniority system. (Recall that Senator Robert Owen had recommended a weakening of seniority to the Democratic Caucus in 1911.) The leader of the Progressives appeared to be Senator Hoke Smith of Georgia, secretary of the interior during the second Cleveland administration. As Colonel Edward House (the president's confidant) wrote to Wilson in late November 1912, Smith was "arranging with [Thomas] Gore and others to control [the Finance] Committee so that reactionaries, like [Thomas S.] Martin, will not be able to block progressive legislation."[36]

The reorganization effort was given strong impetus by the 1912 election. Eleven new progressive Democrats were elected and, together with about twenty other junior Democratic colleagues, formed a powerful bloc with no stake in the status quo. This collection of progressive senators provided the votes, ideas, and organization that infused flexibility into party and senatorial affairs.

Senator Smith's reorganization plan for Senate Democrats had several goals: to depose Martin as party leader; authorize the caucus, rather than its chairman, to select the Committee on Committees (the Steering Committee); direct that no Democrat be given a second assignment to one of the five most important committees (these were not identified) until every other Democrat had been given a chance to serve; permit each committee to elect its own chairman; and prescribe that Senate conferees be selected by the committee, rather than by the chairman, discarding the former practice of choosing the three most senior committee members as conferees.[37]

While Smith's plan was taking shape, Kern was in Indianapolis working on the McNamara trial. In fact, he first learned about the reorganization movement and his possible leadership role, according to his biographer, from a telegram. A reorganization leader wired Kern and asked that he cooperate in the group's plan to support him for party leader.[38] The Indianan wired back his favorable response but "gave no encouragement to the proposal to elect him to the leadership."[39]

Meetings of the Progressives continued throughout January and February 1913. The president-elect, who was to be inaugurated on March 5, did not endorse the Smith-proposed objectives, but it seems safe to conclude that Wilson welcomed a progressive-controlled Senate and the ouster of Martin, whom he personally disliked, as party leader. Wilson's concern, like that of many progressive senators, was not to provoke conservative Democrats into a bitter intraparty struggle that might jeopardize the president's New Freedom program.[40] If angry Old Guard members joined with Republicans, they could block administration initiatives because Democratic control of the Senate was narrow.

Kern, who had returned to Washington in January 1913, was active along with other progressive Democrats in lining up votes to elect himself floor leader. For example, although Progressives initially wanted to deny the chairmanship of the Finance Committee to conservative Senator Furnifold Simmons (D-N.C.) (some even suggested that Kern should assume the post), the Indianan won Simmons's support after ensuring that the North Carolinian would receive the chairmanship.[41] Simmons, for his part, was not to frustrate Wilson's initiatives.

When the Democratic Caucus convened on March 5, 1913, Kern's election as floor leader was a foregone conclusion. He was elected unanimously. "Knowing that they were in the minority," reported the *New York Times,* the "conservative element did not even present a candidate for the floor leadership."[42] Martin withdrew from the race at the end of February, but not before extracting several concessions from Kern and others in exchange for promoting partisan harmony. Martin was to be named to the Steering Committee and appointed chairman of Appropriations, even though Senator Benjamin Tillman (S.C.) had more seniority on that committee. One scholar notes that "senators of every kith and kin will now be looking for Martin, instead of Martin, as leader, looking for them."[43]

With Kern's election as floor leader, the caucus next authorized their new chairman to name the members of the Steering Committee. One account stated that "after a long conference with President Wilson," Kern named a nine-person committee safely packed with progressive Democrats; only two members, according to Claude Bowers (Kern's biographer and personal secretary), represented the conservative faction—Martin and James Clarke of Arkansas, who was named president pro tempore by the caucus over a more senior conservative.[44] Hoke Smith was also named to the Steering Committee.

For the next ten days the Steering Committee assigned their partisan colleagues to the various standing committees. The panel's fundamental objective was "to make the personnel of the important committees safely progressive" and to satisfy everyone's assignment requests insofar as that was practicable.[45] Although committee assignments were difficult, Kern managed to accommodate nearly everyone. Simmons was made Finance chairman, but the panel was filled with progressive Democrats; further, the caucus stripped the Finance Committee of its banking and currency jurisdiction (President Wilson established currency reform as a legislative priority) and created a new banking and currency committee, headed by progressive Senator Robert Owen of Oklahoma. (The caucus also established a new panel to handle woman's suffrage legislation.)

In the only apparent violation of the seniority rule for selecting chairmen, Martin, as noted earlier, became leader of Appropriations over Tillman (who had publicly requested that assignment) in part because of the latter's ill health.[46] Tillman, however, became chairman of the Naval Affairs Committee, on which he had served as the ranking Democrat. In general, the Steering Committee observed seniority by elevating the ranking Democrat on committees during the Sixty-second Congress to the chairmanship of those panels during the Sixty-third—always mindful, however, of another seniority custom: senators in line to chair more than one committee had to select only one to lead. The Steering Committee did reshuffle rankings on important panels to benefit progressive Democrats. Tillman, for instance, went from first to ninth on Appropriations, while Progressives, such as Luke Lea of Tennessee, were ranked ahead of Tillman, even if they had never before served on the committee.

On March 15, 1913, the caucus approved the Kern-led Steering Committee's assignment plan. The lead article the next day in the *Washington Post* declared: "SENATE IS WILSON'S, PRESIDENT'S FRIENDS IN CONTROL UNDER REORGANIZATION." As Senator Kern stated:

> We propose [by this committee reshuffling] that this great body shall be Democratic not only in name, but in practical reality, and that the charge so often made that it is controlled by a few men through committee reorganization and otherwise shall no longer have any basis in fact.[47]

Kern became chairman of the Privileges and Elections Committee and was also a member of eight other standing committees.

Following approval of committee assignments, the March 15 caucus considered several reorganization proposals, which included the earlier recommendations sponsored by Hoke Smith and other Progressives. Kern introduced these resolutions: "The first of these resolutions addressed the subject of Committee work."[48]

Resolved, That a majority of the Democratic members of any committee may call a meeting of such committee, and shall select, by a recorded vote of such members, all Democratic members of conference committees and of all sub-committees representing the committee.

Senator Kern then introduced another resolution "to regulate and govern in the future, the procedure of our party in the work of Senate organization":

Resolved, 1. That hereafter the members of the steering committee shall be elected by the conference.
2. That hereafter the majority members of committees shall elect their own chairmen.
3. That all vacancies on Committees in [the] future shall be nominated by the Steering Committee subject to approval of the Conference.

The Democratic Caucus postponed action on these resolutions until its next meeting on April 8, 1913, when it adopted the following resolution as a party rule:

Resolved, That a majority of the Democratic Members of any Committee may call a meeting of such committee, and may select, by a recorded vote of such members, all Democratic members of conference committees and of all subcommittees representing the committee.

Action on the other proposals was postponed to a later caucus session. However, so far as is known, the caucus never again considered these reorganization suggestions. Further, there is no systematic information on the extent to which the Democrats on the various standing committees observed the agreed-to party rule. In Bowers's estimation, the effect of these various changes "made difficult if not impossible the domination of the body by a small coterie of men entrenched in powerful chairmanships, and did more toward the democratization of the Senate than had been done in half a century."[49]

Senator Kern was involved in other early organizational issues. He discussed committee ratios with Republicans. For example, Senator Francis Warren (R-Wyo.) inquired, "Mr. President, as to the Committee on Woman Suffrage, let me ask the Senator from Indiana how many places he has accorded the minority there? I understand that there shall be four."[50] In fact, the ratio on this panel was set at five to four. New administrative officers were also named to key positions by the Democrats. Interestingly, President Wilson's brother was a candidate for secretary of the Senate; but the assistant Senate librarian, James Baker, who had the support of many southern senators, was selected instead.[51] Finally, to demonstrate frugality and to clean house, the Democratic leadership dismissed numerous Senate employees.

One expert masseur and two assistants who have smoothed the wrinkles from the brows of worried Senators ever since the Senate office building's baths were opened are to be dropped from the payroll under the Democratic reform era. In all sixty employees will be dismissed, making a savings of $46,000 annually.[52]

It is plain that Kern played an important role in organizing both the Senate and his party. These responsibilities, evident even in Kern's era, have been central to the success of Kern's successors. Because he was able to satisfy the interests of so many colleagues in an environment fraught with change, he kept the peace, thus promoting the unity that helped to propel Wilson's legislative initiatives through the Senate. In sum, with a new floor leader and Progressives in charge of the important standing committees, the Senate was ready to consider the program of the new administration.

Kern as Majority Leader

It is an irony of the 1913–1917 period that a rejuvenated Senate was largely and willingly led by the chief executive. For much of the period between Lincoln and Theodore Roosevelt, Congress dominated national policy making, and legislative leaders such as Speaker Joseph Cannon and Senator Nelson Aldrich rivaled the president in their influence. Under President Wilson, the White House clearly became the center of national policy-making authority. Long an advocate of party government and strong leadership, Wilson asserted control over the legislative branch as few presidents did before him. He formulated the nation's agenda, addressed the Congress in person (a practice abandoned by Jefferson), appealed to public opinion, controlled patronage to advance his legislative program, and met frequently with congressional leaders—often traveling to Capitol Hill for discussions—to mobilize support for his agenda. Wilson followed the legislative process, wrote two historians, "not sporadically and intermittently but constantly; and . . . he often intervened effectively at critical moments in the development of policy. He kept a firmer hand on legislation than any of his predecessors."[53]

Wilson's success as legislative leader was significantly influenced by the circumstances of the time: broad popular support for his national program, fractures within GOP ranks, the influx of new and inexperienced members who were willing to follow his lead, and the backing of progressive members, including Kern, who wanted Wilson to succeed. The Kern-Wilson alliance, in the judgment of one scholar, established an important leadership precedent. "Never before had the president's party in the Senate intentionally elected a floor leader for the primary purpose of implementing an executive-initiated legislative program."[54]

In this Senate–White House alliance, in which Kern regularly discussed scheduling, substantive, and vote-gathering matters with Wilson, we see the emergence of an important contemporary role for the floor leader: consult with the president (especially when he is of your own party) about administration goals and, simultaneously, convey to the White House legislative sentiment and concerns regarding those objectives. According to Bowers, Kern often went to the White House alone at night, requesting "that no publicity should ever be given to his visits to the other end of the avenue."[55]

Kern's private sessions with Wilson highlighted the majority leader's behind-the-scenes style of leadership. Little is known about these meetings with Wilson, for Kern's papers were destroyed by his second wife and the papers of President Wilson (and related scholarly studies) make few references to him. Kern's preference for solitude in analyzing and resolving political issues was recounted by his personal secretary:

> He would often lock himself up in his committee room at the capitol, but more frequently he would hide himself in his private room in the Senate Office Building, which was not connected with his public offices and inaccessible to the uninitiated by telephone. He alone carried the key and even those occupying the most confidential relations with him dared not intrude upon him there. Here he would sometimes shut himself in for hours at a time.[56]

Once his methodical analysis was concluded, Kern employed cajolery, humor, one-on-one bargaining, and personal rapport, rather than any "iron fist" approach, to implement whatever plan he had devised to resolve the matter at hand.

Majority Leader Kern worked diligently to advance Wilson's program through the Senate. Their record of achievement is truly exceptional—major tariff reform (a sharp reduction of import duties) that included the nation's first income tax as permitted by the newly ratified Sixteenth Amendment; passage of the Federal Reserve Act; enactment of antitrust laws; establishment of the Federal Trade Commission; adoption of a workmen's compensation measure for federal employees (the Kern-

McGillicuddy bill); and much more. The Senate and the White House also addressed crises associated with World War I.

The story behind these various domestic and foreign policy issues, and Kern's role in each, lies outside the scope of this work.[57] The remainder of this chapter will identify Kern's performance of several floor management roles that appear to have laid the groundwork for some of the fundamental duties of today's Senate leader. These duties include scheduling the Senate's business, promoting party unity through use of the caucus, defending the administration against partisan attacks, and sponsoring institutional innovations.

Scheduling the Senate's Business

Scheduling is a major responsibility of the majority leader. After consulting with scores of participants, the majority leader decides what, when, and in which order measures should come up for debate. The leader's scheduling prerogatives are not simply ministerial; they also mold public policy in the sense that timing the arrival of bills on the floor can determine their fate. His role in this regard is buttressed by another senatorial custom: priority of recognition.

Probably more than today's leaders, Kern took his lead from the president in scheduling the Senate's business. Not only did the administration's major New Freedom initiatives receive priority consideration, but the chief executive also offered Kern advice on scheduling. Beginning his letters with "My dear Senator," Wilson asked Kern, for example:

May I not express the earnest hope that the general development bill which has been reported out of the Public Lands Committee of the Senate may get its place on the calendar of the Senate? . . . I sincerely hope that it will be possible for this bill to be given a chance to pass this session.[58]

As another example, Wilson inquired of Kern:

Do you not think it would be very wise to pass the Rucker bill concerning corrupt practices at this session of Congress? It might help very materially to prevent any of our people from being unfairly defeated.[59]

Wilson also went to Capitol Hill to press action on his agenda. On July 18, 1916, for instance, the president made an unannounced visit to the Capitol to confer with Kern, four members of the Steering Committee, and two committee chairmen about a child-labor bill and Kern's own measure providing workmen's compensation to federal employees. A week later the Democratic Caucus voted to pass the child-labor bill before the session's end.[60] Both measures eventually passed the Senate.

As the party's floor leader, Kern had principal responsibility for devising senatorial schedules that would ensure action on priority legislation—often a difficult assignment in the face of dilatory actions by legislative opponents. Passage of the Federal Reserve Act is a case in point.

On August 14, 1913, the Democratic Caucus voted to consider banking and currency reform after enactment of the president's tariff reform measure. Unfortunately for Wilson, enough Democrats on the banking panel were opposed to the currency bill to stall its speedy consideration. Wilson was irate. Several times he called Senate Democratic leaders to the White House to discuss ways to get action on the bill. Finally, "under the threat of Senate caucus action and administration retaliation," two Democratic opponents switched sides and provided the votes to report the legislation to the Senate floor.[61]

Majority Leader Kern responded by introducing a resolution on December 2, 1913, that established a grueling schedule of daily meetings to wear out the bill's opponents. Kern's resolution (S. Res. 225), which was endorsed by the Democratic Caucus and amended on the Senate floor by Senator John Sharp Williams (D-Miss.), called for the following daily schedule:

> 10 a.m. to 6 p.m. Senate is in session.
> 6 p.m. to 8 p.m. Senate is in recess.
> 8 p.m. to 11 p.m. Senate resumes business and then adjourns unless otherwise ordered.

GOP leader Jacob Gallinger (N.H.) denounced Kern's proposal for keeping the Senate in session eleven hours per day. "The hours proposed in the resolution," he said, "are unusual, unnecessary, and oppressive."[62] Senator Williams, bluntly noting the resolution's objective, responded: "It is to begin the talking early, to continue the talking late, to continue it continuously, until men fond of talking get tired and quit, and then the Senate can vote."[63] The Senate adopted Kern's scheduling resolution on December 6. Kern kept the Senate in session until December 23 to win enactment of the banking and currency measure.

Kern's colleagues recognized his key role in scheduling. For example, Senator Reed Smoot (R-Utah), asked: "I should like to ask the Senator from Indiana whether he intends to have a night session; and if so, how soon he would desire the Senate to take a recess?" Senator Kern responded, "At 6 o'clock we will take a recess until 8 o'clock."[64] On another occasion, Kern said, "In accordance with an understanding had yesterday,

I move that the Senate proceed to the consideration of executive business."[65]

Illustrative of Kern's low profile as majority leader was Senate adoption in 1914 of its first formal rule (Rule XII) to address unanimous consent agreements. Even then, these self-imposed and flexible agreements helped to expedite action on legislation because they often functioned as a form of voluntary cloture. In Kern's time, unanimous consent agreements (which set aside formal Senate rules) limited debate on amendments and the bill as a whole, established a specific time for final action, and were employed to call up measures. Apparently, the Senate found some unanimous consent requests too vague and therefore required that each one set a specific date for a final vote, also requesting that a quorum be present before such unanimous consent agreements could be proposed. Senator Hoke Smith, on January 16, 1914, highlighted one problem that gave rise to the rules change:

During the two years I have been here I have seen the Senate embarrassed a number of times by unanimous-consent agreements that have been made and embarrassed by the doubt as to whether by unanimous consent we could do away with a unanimous-consent agreement, the older Senators all telling us that it could not be done away with and the younger Senators rather resenting the idea that it could not be done, but yielding to the experience and wisdom of the older Senators.

The Senate subsequently adopted (by a 51-8 vote) a rule that permitted a unanimous consent agreement to be revoked by another agreement on one day's notice. Kern did not participate in this debate, although he voted for the new rule, which directly affected his management of the Senate floor. In the modern Senate, the majority leader is customarily responsible for crafting virtually all unanimous consent agreements. But in Kern's time, other senators (often bill managers) negotiated and offered these agreements. A few decades would pass before everyone accepted the majority leader's prerogative to negotiate unanimous consent agreements. But the Senate's recognition of the growing significance of such agreements can be traced to the period of Kern's leadership.

In short, Kern exercised a major role in scheduling Senate business, although he was importantly influenced by President Wilson and various partisan forces. The majority leader's scheduling prerogatives, however, were still evolving. For example, the motion to adjourn the Senate is presently understood to be the prerogative of the majority leader or his designee. But in Kern's time, Minority Leader Jacob Gallinger (N.H.) successfully moved the Senate's adjournment.[66]

Promoting Party Unity Through Caucus Action

As chairman of the Democratic Caucus and floor leader, Kern regularly convened this highest of party instrumentalities to consider Wilson's initiatives and to hammer out intraparty consensus. (By contrast, deep divisions within the Republican party limited use of their equivalent forum.) Kern, like Wilson, understood that Democratic control of the national elective branches relied on these GOP fissures. To demonstrate his party's governing capacity and to set the stage for forthcoming national elections, Kern wanted Senate Democrats to stay united behind the administration's program. The Indianan recognized that it took only a few defections from his slim majority to transform his role into a "majority leader of a minority." It was therefore imperative for him to use the caucus to draft, debate, and amend bills prior to their consideration on the Senate floor so that they comported with Wilson's notions of party government.

The caucus's "binding" rule augmented Kern's ability to foster intraparty agreement on legislation. The Democrats adopted this rule in 1903 (so far as is known), when they were in the minority. Senator Joseph Blackburn of Kentucky "proposed a resolution [in the caucus] requiring unquestioned obedience to all future caucus decrees approved by two-thirds of the Democratic Senators. This was admittedly an unprecedented regulation," writes an analyst of the period.[67] On numerous occasions during the Wilson years (on tariff revision, currency reform, antitrust measures), the caucus took an official party position that obligated all Democratic senators to vote for the legislation on the Senate floor. There were several exceptions, however, to the "binding caucus": a member could not be bound "if he believed that it involved a construction of the . . . Constitution or was one on which he had made specific pledges during the election campaign" or was one that involved instructions from his state legislature.[68]

Unsurprisingly, Republican senators took the floor to taunt Democrats for their use of "secret caucuses" and to charge President Wilson with coercive interference in Senate affairs. Majority Leader Kern and other Democrats responded by pointing out that the caucuses on tariff revision were nonbinding. Kern stated, "It might be well for the Senator [Albert Cummins (R-Iowa)] to know that in all the sessions of the [Democratic] conference there was the most perfect freedom of debate," adding that "all roll calls by order of the conference" were "handed out to representatives of the press, who were always present" outside the meeting room.[69] Democrats adopted this party resolution: "Resolved, That the tariff bill agreed to by this conference, in its amended form, is declared to be a party measure, and we urge its undivided support as a duty by Democratic Senators without amendment." Only two Democrats voted against final passage of the bill.

But the Democratic Caucus was rent with divisions on the 1915 Ship Purchase bill (whereby the government would purchase a merchant marine fleet to make up for shortages). It was one of the major bills for which Kern could not deliver a majority for Wilson. He urged Treasury Secretary William McAdoo in a letter to employ his persuasive talents on certain senators: "The question was whether we would declare for the passage of the Ship Purchase Bill at this session. While a majority would have doubtless voted aye, yet those opposed and indifferent jockeyed about until at 11 o'clock the caucus adjourned . . . without action."[70] In the end, this bill provoked a bitter filibuster.

Kern kept the Senate in session long hours, even around the clock, to break the GOP-led filibuster of the bill. Talk of cloture permeated the debate (it consumed thirty-three calendar days), but nothing came of it. Finally, the Democrats gave up the struggle, revealing Wilson's slackening influence over the Senate. The Ship Purchase talkathon set the stage for the infamous 1917 filibuster that stymied President Wilson's efforts to arm U.S. merchant ships in the wake of German U-boat attacks. Castigating a "little group of willful men" who filibustered his proposal to death, Wilson called a special session of the Senate on March 5, 1917, so that senators could rewrite their rules to stop filibusters. Because Kern had lost his Senate reelection bid, Thomas S. Martin of Virginia was selected to resume the Democratic leadership. On March 8, 1917, Martin introduced a resolution establishing cloture (Rule XXII) in the Senate; it passed after brief debate by a 76-3 vote.[71]

Except on a handful of issues, the Democratic Caucus functioned effectively under Kern's leadership to promote party cohesiveness. Although Republicans often and not unexpectedly criticized "legislation by caucus," this party entity galvanized Democratic support for Wilson's program. As Banking chairman Robert Owen declared:

I think it at last comes down to the question that under our present form of government, where we are moving under party organization, there is no escape from party responsibility and the plain common-sense duty of the party to act through its organization in the management of matters for which the party feels a party responsibility."[72]

Defending the Administration (Especially Your Own)

It is not uncommon for senators to criticize administration policies and officials; this is an important and legitimate function for members of both parties and both legislative chambers. Sometimes, however, senators say things that embarrass the administration. Senate floor leaders will often respond to such charges. On July 15, 1913, for example, Republican Senator Joseph Bristow of Kansas introduced a resolution (S. Res. 132) and asked for its immediate consideration. His resolution requested President Wilson "to advise the Senate what would be a proper salary to enable the present Secretary of State [William Jennings Bryan] to live with comfort and to enable him to give his time to the discharge of his public duties for which he is now being paid the sum of $1,000 per month."[73] Secretary Bryan had publicly stated that his governmental salary was insufficient and took up lecturing at Chautauqua forums and elsewhere to supplement it. To protect Bryan and Wilson, Kern objected to the resolution's immediate consideration. Three days later, when Bristow's resolution again came before the Senate, Kern successfully moved to table it.[74]

A few days after Kern became majority leader, an incident occurred that demonstrated how little influence his title carried at that time. When he went to visit Bryan at the State Department, Eddie Savoy, the "keeper of the door" to Bryan's office and a longtime State Department messenger, informed Kern: "I'm sorry, Senator, but you can't come in; Mr. Bryan is busy!"[75] Secretary Bryan was apparently occupied with patronage matters. To soothe his ruffled feelings, Kern went to pay a call on another friend, Navy Secretary Josephus Daniels, who cordially received him. Small surprise that when Daniels was later to come under attack on the Senate floor, Senator Kern rose on a "question of personal privilege" to refute the "statements reflecting upon the official or personal character" of the secretary.[76]

Sponsoring Institutional Innovations: Creation of the Whip

"We have never had what is called a whip in the American Senate," observed Senator Justin Morrill (R-Vt.) in 1874.[77] In fact, it was not until 1913 that the Democratic Caucus named its first party whip—J. Hamilton Lewis of Illinois. Facetiously proclaimed the "biggest dude in America" by House Speaker James Beauchamp "Champ" Clark because of his fame "as the smartest dresser of the day," Lewis confirmed that "so far as I have been able to learn, I was the first Democratic whip appointed in the history of the U.S. Senate. It was during the first Wilson administration."[78] He continued the "juniority" pattern in Democratic leadership ranks, having been named whip after only two months of Senate service.

At least two explanations exist for the creation of the whip post. First, the Democrats had only a slim majority (51-45), so it was essential for party members to be ready to maintain a quorum. Absenteeism, however, was plaguing the Democrats, and the Republicans had clearly demonstrated their reluctance to help provide a quorum. The caucus therefore named Lewis as whip. His job was to assist Kern in ensuring a Democratic quorum on the Senate floor. Kern's biographer stated:

> At times when the regular Democratic attendance had dwindled to a corporal's guard [Kern's] impatience manifested itself in caucus, where on one occasion he supplemented his appeal with sarcastic protests, and a "party whip" was selected to assist him.[79]

The *New York Times* offered the other explanation: "The appointment of an assistant to Senator Kern . . . is in fact partly explained by general dissatisfaction with Mr. Kern's leadership."[80] Available evidence confirms that the first explanation for the whip's creation merits precedence over the latter.

The problem of absent senators was a constant irritant to Kern even after the whip position was established. For example, during debate on the tariff bill, Democrats narrowly won (31-28) on an amendment involving duties on bananas. Kern reportedly resented the closeness of the vote because three of his colleagues had been playing golf despite his request that they remain on the Senate floor. As the *Indianapolis Star* reported:

> This afternoon [Democratic] Senators O'Gorman, Saulsbury, and Owen were out at the Chevy Chase links playing golf when, in the opinion of Senator Kern and others, they should have been helping to fight off Republican amendments.
>
> Senator Kern . . . warned them against going away, but they jocularly replied that he had done his duty in admonishing them and went.[81]

Ironically, Lewis himself was often absent from the Senate. "In effect," wrote a scholar, "Kern had to assume Lewis' job in addition to that of Majority Leader."[82] Republicans, it is worth noting, appointed their first party whip (James Wadsworth of New York) two years after the Democratic innovation.

The leadership roles assumed by Kern are today part of any floor leader's "job description." His manner of carrying out his scheduling and other responsibilities surely differed from other floor leaders because each party leader operates in a unique political context and each brings his own style to the position. For example, Kern regularly convened the Democratic Caucus to thrash out party positions and to achieve partisan consensus on bills and amendments. Today, party caucuses (now called conferences to underscore their "conferring" rather than "binding" role) largely function as discussion forums. Kern's quiet style also contrasts with the high-profile role of his successors. Indeed, it is unlikely that if Kern held the post today he could assume a low-profile role. The majority leadership has evolved into the top post in the Senate and is recognized as such.

Kern, too, served with a president whose agenda dominated the Senate's activities. He willingly shepherded Wilson's legislative program through the Senate (and personally favored much of it). The Senate, as a result, worked nearly every day during the 1913–1914 period to enact Wilson's initiatives. "What leader did more than John Worth Kern [to] put Woodrow Wilson's massive legislative program through the Senate virtually intact?" asks a noted congressional scholar. "And what was his reward but to be retired by Indiana voters" in the November 1916 election.[83]

Ironically, Kern, a champion of direct election for senators, failed to win another Senate term from Indiana's voters. Several explanations have been offered for his defeat. One is the disunity of the Indiana Democratic party; it received neither sufficient money nor important party speakers from national campaign managers (Wilson, too, was seeking reelection in 1916). Another is Wilson's limited campaign effort for Kern in Indiana. Still another relates to the skill of GOP state leaders, who attracted the support of Progressives and ethnic voters for Republican candidates. Finally, Kern's health was a factor; he did not begin campaigning until October 3, and from then until the election, "he went from speech to sick bed, then back to the campaign, often unable to speak."[84] Senator Kern lost his reelection bid by a narrow margin (50.9 percent to 49.1 percent) to Republican Harry S. New. Wilson also failed to carry Indiana.

After Kern's defeat, William Jennings Bryan wrote newly reelected President Wilson to suggest that Kern be named to a high federal position. President Wilson responded: "There is no man in the Senate for whom I have a warmer personal feeling than Senator Kern, and you may be sure I will not overlook his claims if it is possible at any time to consider them."[85] Consideration of Kern for some federal position soon proved impossible, for he died on August 17, 1917, nine months after leaving the Senate.

The Senate has evolved from an institution with few members, few rules, and few workload burdens into an organization of procedural and administrative complexity and with enormous lawmaking, oversight, and representational responsibilities. These changes, a response to broad national and international developments, underscore the Senate's ability to adapt to internal and external challenges. Central to the Senate's evolution has been the rise of the majority leadership, which largely began with John Worth Kern.

Mirroring the overthrow of "Cannonism" in the House in 1910, the Senate undertook major changes under Kern's leadership. Seniority practices were modified, progressive senators dominated important committees, a change-oriented mood permeated the Senate, and Congress and the White House were controlled by the Democratic party for the first time in eighteen years. President Wilson's advocacy of party and legislative leadership may have enhanced Kern's role as majority leader, but the Senate itself seemed ready to augment the floor leader's responsibilities.

This transition toward an institutionalized role for the majority leader (allowing the leader to expedite floor action, for example) may be discerned in Kern's only major policy failure: the rejection of the 1915 Ship Purchase bill. Filibusters were not uncommon in the early 1900s, but they seemed to grow longer and more numerous with every passing year. The 1915 talkathon was long and bitter, and there were other, equally bitter filibusters in this period. The Senate therefore required some formal means to close off interminable and destructive debate given its expanding workload, the nation's involvement in world affairs, and public impatience with long-windedness. The result was the 1917 adoption of cloture.

The shift from no limits to some limits on debate represents the everpresent clash between two principles: the right to debate and the right to decide. The Senate has historically emphasized the former over the latter right. Lengthy debate is a cherished Senate tradition, and filibusters are difficult to stop even with cloture. No wonder that Howard Baker (R-

Tenn.), who served as majority leader from 1981 to 1985, said that leading the Senate is like "trying to push a wet noodle."[86] In short, Kern and all the party leaders who followed after him have confronted a continuing and perplexing condition: how to bridge the gulf between individual rights and collective action.

NOTES

1. Virginia Floy Haughton, "John Worth Kern and Wilson's New Freedom: A Study of a Senate Majority Leader" (Ph.D. diss., University of Kentucky, 1973).
2. George Rothwell Brown, *The Leadership of Congress* (Indianapolis: Bobbs-Merrill, 1922), 257.
3. Roy Swanstrom, *The United States Senate, 1787–1801,* Senate Document No. 64, 87th Cong., 1st sess. (Washington, D.C.: U.S. Government Printing Office, 1962), 268.
4. Woodrow Wilson, *Congressional Government* (Boston: Houghton Mifflin, 1885), 223.
5. David J. Rothman, *Politics and Power: The United States Senate, 1869–1901* (Cambridge: Harvard University Press, 1966), 39.
6. Ibid., 5–7.
7. Ibid., 72.
8. Woodrow Wilson, *Constitutional Government in the United States* (New York: Columbia University Press, 1908), 133.
9. David B. Truman, *The Congressional Party* (New York: Wiley, 1959), 98.
10. Randall B. Ripley, *Majority Party Leadership in Congress* (Boston: Little, Brown, 1969), 4.
11. Floyd M. Riddick, *Majority and Minority Leaders of the Senate,* Senate Document No. 24, 95th Cong., 1st sess. (Washington, D.C.: U.S. Government Printing Office, 1977), 4.
12. Ibid., 5.
13. Even before Kern, other Democrats might claim the informal title of floor leader. For example, in 1906 Senator Joseph S. Blackburn of Kentucky was elected Democratic caucus chair; Democrats passed a congratulatory resolution that referred to Blackburn as their "chosen official leader." See Riddick, *Majority and Minority Leaders of the Senate,* 3. Senator Thomas S. Martin of Virginia, the man Kern replaced as caucus chair, is another Democratic floor leader. He served for two years before Kern and again after Kern lost his 1916 bid for reelection to the Senate.
14. Dumas Malone, ed., *Dictionary of American Biography,* vol. 10 (New York: Scribner's, 1933), 355.
15. Cited in Paolo E. Coletta, *Political Evangelist, 1860–1908,* vol. 1 of *William Jennings Bryan* (Lincoln: University of Nebraska Press, 1964), 410.
16. Charles M. Thomas, *Thomas Riley Marshall* (Oxford, Ohio: Mississippi Valley Press, 1939), 63.
17. Ibid., 64.
18. Paolo E. Coletta, *Progressive Politician and Moral Statesman, 1909–1915,* vol. 2 of *William Jennings Bryan* (Lincoln: University of Nebraska Press, 1969), 21.
19. *Washington Post,* April 8, 1911, 4.
20. Ibid., 1. Also in 1911, nearly a dozen progressive Republicans in the Senate met separately in their own party conference and later successfully won important party and committee assignments from the regular Republicans.
21. Louis W. Koenig, *Bryan* (New York: Putnam's, 1971), 467.
22. Claude G. Bowers, *The Life of John Worth Kern* (Indianapolis: Hollendeck Press, 1918), 215.

23. "Of interest in this connection," wrote Kern's biographer, "is the fact that two years later when elected to the leadership of the Senate and the Chairmanship of the Steering Committee [Kern] voluntarily retired from the Finance committee in favor of his colleague, while permitting him to retain the equally important assignment as ranking member of the committee on Foreign Relations." See Bowers, *John Worth Kern*, 216.

24. Coletta, *Bryan*, 1:412.

25. U. S. Congress, *Congressional Record*, June 20, 1911, 2314.

26. Ibid., July 28, 1911, 3290.

27. Ibid., 3294.

28. Quoted in Thomas, *Thomas Riley Marshall*, 121.

29. Arthur S. Link, "The Baltimore Convention of 1912," *American Historical Review* 50 (July 1945): 695.

30. Ibid., 696. One scholar described Kern at the convention in this way: "He was a small man in a brown sack suit, with a long, narrow, hatchet face, small eyes deeply set close together, a long, thin nose, and a grizzled mustache and beard." See Arthur S. Link, *The Road to the White House*, vol. 1 of *Wilson* (Princeton, N.J.: Princeton University Press, 1947), 436.

31. *Official Report of the Proceedings of the Democratic National Convention* (Chicago: Peterson Linotyping, 1912), 376.

32. *Indianapolis Star*, July 6, 1912, 4.

33. Ibid.

34. Ibid., July 12, 1912, 2.

35. See Haughton, "John Worth Kern and Wilson's New Freedom," 115, 117.

36. Dewey W. Grantham, Jr., *Hoke Smith and the Politics of the New South* (Baton Rouge: Louisiana State University Press, 1958), 240.

37. Ibid.

38. Bowers, *John Worth Kern*, 286.

39. Ibid., 287.

40. *New York Times*, January 10, 1913, 6.

41. Wythe W. Holt, Jr., "The Senator From Virginia and the Democratic Floor Leadership," *Virginia Magazine* (January 1975), 15. For the suggestion that Kern should be Finance chairman, see *New York Times*, March 10, 1913, 2.

42. *New York Times*, March 6, 1913, 2.

43. Holt, "Senator From Virginia," 17.

44. See George H. Haynes, *The Senate of the United States*, vol. 1 (Boston: Houghton Mifflin, 1938), 290; and Bowers, *John Worth Kern*, 289.

45. Bowers, *John Worth Kern*, 289–290.

46. Tillman, upset at his loss of the Appropriations chair, placed his speech to the caucus on that topic in the *Congressional Record*, March 17, 1913, 30–33.

47. *Washington Post*, March 16, 1913, 6. It is difficult to determine seniority violations for chairmanships. Approximately fifteen Democrats held the top spot on several committees during the Sixty-second Congress. Except for Tillman's public statement, there is scant information about which standing committees these Democrats preferred to chair. And with seventy-three standing committees, every Democrat was assured a chairmanship; the minority Republicans also headed about twenty minor standing committees. Southerners dominated the committee system, chairing most of the panels.

48. Information in this section on the reorganization proposals is based on minutes of the Democratic Caucus, which are secret and not generally available for review. However, in 1963 Walter Kravitz of the Congressional Research Service was permitted to review the minutes for this particular period. My account is based on his unpublished report, "The Organization of the Senate in 1913," December 19, 1963, 14 pp.

49. Bowers, *John Worth Kern*, 295.

50. U. S. Congress, *Congressional Record*, March 15, 1913, 231.

51. *New York Times*, March 9, 1913, 2.

52. Ibid., March 15, 1913, 2.
53. Dexter Perkins and Glyndon G. Van Deusen, *The United States of America: A History*, vol. 2 (New York: Macmillan, 1962), 355. For an informative perspective on the leadership views of Wilson, see Arthur S. Link, *The New Freedom*, vol. 2 of *Wilson* (Princeton, N.J.: Princeton University Press, 1956), chap. 5.
54. Margaret Munk, "Origin and Development of the Party Floor Leadership in the United States Senate," *Capitol Studies* (Winter 1974), 31.
55. Bowers, *John Worth Kern*, 363.
56. Ibid., 404.
57. See, for example, the multivolume work on Wilson by Arthur S. Link and published by Princeton University Press—*The Road to the White House*, vol. 1; *The New Freedom*, vol. 2; *The Struggle for Neutrality, 1914–1915*, vol. 3; *Confusions and Crises, 1915–1916*, vol. 4; and *Campaigns for Progressivism and Peace, 1916–1917*, vol. 5—and Haughton, "John Worth Kern and Wilson's New Freedom: A Study of a Senate Majority Leader." Also see Robert C. Byrd, *The Senate, 1789–1989: Addresses on the History of the United States Senate*, vol. 1 (Washington, D.C.: U.S. Government Printing Office, 1988), chap. 22.
58. Arthur S. Link, ed., *The Papers of Woodrow Wilson*, vol. 36 (Princeton, N.J.: Princeton University Press, 1981), 464–465. Wilson also used his addresses and messages to Congress to set legislative priorities. For instance, in his December 2, 1913, address to Congress, Wilson said: "I take the leave to beg that the whole energy and attention of the Senate be concentrated upon [the banking and currency bill] till the matter is successfully disposed of." See *Congressional Record*, December 2, 1913, 44.
59. Link, ed., *Papers of Woodrow Wilson*, vol. 37, 405.
60. Ibid., vol. 37, 31.
61. Link, *Wilson: The New Freedom*, 2:234.
62. U.S. Congress, *Congressional Record*, December 3, 1913, 102.
63. Ibid., December 5, 1913, 244.
64. Ibid., December 1, 1913, 19–20.
65. Ibid., March 3, 1914, 4183. Based on a review of the *Congressional Record* when Kern was majority leader, it appears that the presiding officer accorded Kern priority recognition. This conclusion is "soft," however, because Kern spoke infrequently and rarely at length, preferring to work quietly and patiently to prod the Senate into action.
66. Ibid., September 15, 1913, 4967.
67. John R. Lambert, *Arthur Pue Gorman* (Baton Rouge: Louisiana State University Press, 1953), 303.
68. Daniel M. Berman, *In Congress Assembled* (New York: Macmillan, 1964), 226–227. Information on the number of binding caucuses is unavailable.
69. U.S. Congress, *Congressional Record*, July 19, 1913, 2556.
70. Link, ed., *Papers of Woodrow Wilson*, vol. 37, 366.
71. U.S. Congress, *Congressional Record*, March 8, 1917, 45. See Franklin L. Burdette, *Filibustering in the Senate* (Princeton, N.J.: Princeton University Press, 1940), chaps. 4 and 5.
72. U.S. Congress, *Congressional Record*, December 23, 1913, 1487. President Wilson, explaining his concept of party action, put it this way:

    In party conference personal convictions should have full play and should be most candidly and earnestly presented, but there does not seem to me to be any surrender either of personal dignity or of individual conviction in yielding to the determinations of a decisive majority of one's fellow workers in a great organization which must hold together if it is to be serviceable to the country as a governing agency. (Arthur S. Link, *Wilson: The Struggle for Neutrality, 1914–1915* [Princeton, N.J.: Princeton University Press, 1960], 3:160.)

73. U.S. Congress, *Congressional Record*, July 15, 1913, 2418.
74. Ibid., July 18, 1913, 2471.

75. *New York Times*, March 11, 1913, 3.
76. *Congressional Record*, August 9, 1913, 3215.
77. Ibid., March 26, 1874, 2488.
78. Ibid., May 12, 1936, 7045. For Speaker Clark's comment, see *Literary Digest*, April 12, 1913, 860.
79. Bowers, *John Worth Kern*, 351. Also see the *Washington Post*, May 29, 1913, 2.
80. *New York Times*, May 29, 1913, 1.
81. *Indianapolis Star*, August 17, 1913, 2.
82. Haughton, "John Worth Kern and Wilson's New Freedom," 174–175.
83. Ralph K. Huitt, "The Internal Distribution of Influence: The Senate," in David B. Truman, ed., *The Congress and America's Future*, 2d ed. (Englewood Cliffs, N.J.: Prentice-Hall, 1973), 94.
84. George C. Roberts, "Woodrow Wilson, John W. Kern and the 1916 Indiana Election: Defeat of a Senate Majority Leader," *Presidential Studies Quarterly* (Winter 1980): 67. Also see Bowers, *John Worth Kern*, chap. 18.
85. Link, ed., *Papers of Woodrow Wilson*, vol. 40, 355.
86. Diane Granat, "Senate Republicans Choose Officers: Dole Elected Majority Leader; Simpson Wins GOP Whip Job," *Congressional Quarterly Weekly Report*, December 1, 1984, 3024.

CHAPTER 2

Henry Cabot Lodge
The Astute Parliamentarian

William C. Widenor

Writing of Henry Cabot Lodge's service in the Sixty-sixth Congress, many observers have classed the Massachusetts senator as one of the great majority leaders of all time. Others, writing of the Sixty-seventh Congress, consider him to have been relatively unimportant. True, with the accession of Republican Warren G. Harding to the presidency in 1920, Lodge was showing his age. But he remained an astute parliamentarian and party manager. Most revealing, perhaps, about Lodge's tenure as Senate majority leader is that outstanding personal qualities, especially those common in great leaders, do not always guarantee legislative success. Effective leadership in the Senate is very much a product of circumstance, of the vicissitudes of politics and the country's changing legislative agenda.

Born into a prominent Boston family on May 12, 1850, Lodge attended private schools and was graduated from Harvard University in 1871. On the very day after his graduation Lodge married his college sweetheart and distant cousin, Anna Cabot Mills Davis, the daughter of the head of the

The patrician Henry Cabot Lodge of Massachusetts would later be hailed as the first floor leader of the Republican party.

Naval Observatory in Washington, D.C., Admiral Charles Henry Davis.

Lodge's early career ran on several tracks simultaneously. He was graduated from Harvard Law School in 1874 and admitted to the bar the following year. He assisted Henry Adams as editor of the *North American Review* from 1873 to 1876 and in the latter year received one of the first doctorates in history ever granted by Harvard. After lecturing in history at his alma mater for the following three years, Lodge sought a career in politics. He never lost his interest in history, however, and throughout his life continued to publish a variety of historical and literary works, some twenty-seven books in all. Although successful in his first bid for office (the Massachusetts House of Representatives in 1880), he was able to garner a congressional seat only after two failed attempts, in 1882 and 1884. He was first elected to Congress in 1886 and gained a Senate seat in 1893. He was reelected to the Senate in 1899, 1905, 1911, 1916, and 1922, serving as Republican leader from 1918 to his death in 1924.

Sixty-eight years old when he assumed the leadership post, Lodge had withstood age well. He was a tall, trim man with immaculate silvered hair and beard—allegedly as thick as when he had first arrived in Washington. Lodge spoke with an upper-class Bostonian rasp and loved to quote from the volume of Shakespeare's work, which he always carried in his pocket.

Henry Cabot Lodge: Leader of the Opposition

In 1919 Lodge was a natural choice for majority leader, but according to his wartime correspondence he had not particularly aspired to the post. Nor does it appear that he especially desired the chairmanship of the Republican Caucus (or Conference, as it was then known). Lodge had been in the Senate since 1893 and had had ample opportunity to witness party leadership on the Republican side of the aisle. He himself had counted votes during the close battle over ratification of the peace treaty with Spain (and annexation of the Philippines) in 1898, coming away much impressed by Senator Nelson Aldrich's vigor and resourcefulness in that fight.[1] It might even be said that he served a long apprenticeship as a lieutenant to the famous "Senate Four"—Nelson Aldrich of Rhode Island, William Allison of Iowa, Orville Platt of Connecticut, and John Spooner of Wisconsin—the Republicans who so dominated the Senate in the first decade of the twentieth century and who often made things difficult for Theodore Roosevelt, their own party's president.[2]

One contemporary journalist went so far as to claim that Aldrich (whom he described as "the uncrowned Republican leader") had "raised party leadership in the Senate to a position which perhaps it had never attained before," and then went on to compare Aldrich's leadership with that of Lodge during the contest over the League of Nations.[3] But the point is that until Lodge combined titular power with real power in 1919 and 1920, control on the Republican side of the aisle usually lay with powerful individuals (like Aldrich, often Finance Committee chairmen) and not with the leaders of the party conference, who performed mainly tiresome administrative duties and who prior to 1913 frequently served only for a particular Congress.[4]

From the beginning, Lodge was intent on making his mark in U.S. foreign policy, but he had had to wait. He came to the Senate when, as Senator George Moses (R-N.H.) recalled,

the rule of silence upon newcomers had more than one way of enforcing itself, when no fledgling Senator could count himself as interpares, . . . and when high committee place or a foremost seat in party conference were the concomitant of years of service not unmixed with good behavior.[5]

The new senator from Massachusetts had no difficulty accommodating himself to these conditions. His first committee assignments were inconsequential. Foreign Relations, the committee assignment he coveted most ardently, was not to be his until he had completed two sessions of service. Gratified to receive his initial appointment to the Foreign Relations Committee in 1896, Lodge aspired as early as 1900 to its chairmanship, only to be bitterly disappointed when outmaneuvered by Senator Shelby Cullom of Illinois.[6] But Cullom's real interests lay in domestic and economic matters, and consequently Lodge became de facto leader of the committee. On Cullom's death in 1914, Lodge became the ranking minority member, ready to assume the chairmanship whenever the Republicans should regain a majority.

Still, a rather unlikely combination of events conspired to bring Lodge to the powerful positions he was to hold in the Sixty-sixth Congress (1919–1921), when he chaired both the Republican Conference and the Foreign Relations Committee and came to be regarded as the GOP's first modern Senate majority leader. The principal event was Lodge's reelection in 1916. As a vocal opponent of the popular election of U.S. senators, Lodge was thought to be vulnerable in his own first direct popular election. But Massachusetts was a strongly Republican state, and Lodge won by some thirty thousand votes over John F. "Honey Fitz" Fitzgerald (John

F. Kennedy's grandfather). Lodge is said to have been disappointed in this margin of victory and attributed it to his strong stand against President Woodrow Wilson's foreign policy.[7] The second event that eased Lodge's path to Senate leadership was the death on August 17, 1918, of Senator Jacob Gallinger. The New Hampshire senator had served as chairman of the Republican Conference since 1913. Lodge, now the senior Republican in the Senate, was elected to succeed him on August 24, 1918.

The forthcoming congressional elections constituted the third crucial event in Lodge's accession to GOP leadership in the Senate. Though the Republican party was dominant in the country, the Democrats had controlled the Congress since 1913, after the conservative-progressive split in the Republican ranks catapulted Woodrow Wilson to the presidency.

The personal estrangement between Wilson and Lodge developed out of differences of opinion, particularly on issues of foreign policy. From the very start of World War I in August 1914 Lodge had been committed to doing all he could to bring about an Allied victory, an end to which Wilson was not committed until the United States entered the war in 1917. Fearful that President Wilson might still try to arrange a "peace without victory" (thereby thwarting the Allies' plans) and deeply resentful that the executive had during the war accumulated powers previously thought to have belonged to the Congress, Lodge fought the elections of 1918 in a spirit of high dudgeon. It was generally recognized, as Lodge put it, that the nation was "facing the world's greatest issues"—namely the peace settlement.[8] Lodge and Theodore Roosevelt attempted to turn the campaign into a referendum "for unconditional surrender and complete victory just as [General Ulysses S.] Grant stood."[9] Fearing that his plans for peace were being undermined, Wilson launched an appeal for the election of a Democratic Congress so that he might serve as the American people's "unembarrassed spokesman in affairs at home and abroad."[10]

It was a bitter contest and the most expensive congressional campaign to date.[11] Some scholars have attributed the Democratic loss to Wilson's mistake in issuing such a partisan electoral appeal. Lodge and Roosevelt believed that what turned the tide was their appeal for a complete Allied victory and the Allies' continued military predominance. The historian Seward Livermore has persuasively argued that the election was actually decided in the Midwest on domestic bread-and-butter issues; a significantly lower than usual voter turnout also appears to have played a role.[12]

Whatever the reasons for the Democrats' defeat, Wilson was vulnerable to charges that his personal leadership had been repudiated. For the first time in his presidency, Wilson faced a GOP-controlled Congress. The elated Lodge lost no time in impressing on his British friends the supposed magnitude of Wilson's setback, emphasizing that it was "one of the worst mid-term defeats suffered by any President and that such a defeat had never before occurred in time of war."[13]

From this point on Wilson and his ideas about a proper and just peace settlement were in trouble. Lodge, looking ahead to a Republican victory in 1920, was determined to reassert Congress's authority and to impose his version of a peace settlement. Though the president still enjoyed vast powers and great stature, the senator, as chairman of both the Foreign Relations Committee and the Republican Conference, commanded considerable advantages.

The Lodge who became Senate majority leader when the Sixty-sixth Congress convened on March 4, 1919, was not only a veteran politician but also a skillful parliamentarian. A student of the Senate's prerogatives, he had written extensively on that subject and was proud of his service in that institution and enamored of its procedures and customs. At the time of his death in 1924, he had served a longer continuous term in Congress than anyone else from Massachusetts—including such famous figures as Daniel Webster, Charles Sumner, and George Frisbie Hoar.[14] When he became majority leader, he had already served in the Senate for twenty-six years, longer than any other Senate party leader before or since. The majority leader's role was still being institutionalized, so Lodge then "commanded from the second row surrounded by his own colleagues, rather than from the front row by the center aisle where the Leaders sit today." He was also proud to be commanding from Daniel Webster's historic desk.[15]

Lodge revered the Senate as the more conservative part of the legislative branch, and his interpretation of recent American history was that the growth of executive power had

been greatly stimulated by the reform movements of the last few years, which have all been aimed at weakening if not at breaking down the legislative and judicial branches, and thus bringing the government as nearly as possible to one which consists of the executive and the voters, the simplest and most rudimentary form of human government which history can show.[16]

The Senate had a special place in the constitutional scheme of things, Lodge wrote in 1921, because it has never been, legally speaking, reorganized. It has been in continuous, and organized existence for one hundred and thirty-two years, because two-thirds of the Senate being always in office, there never has been such a thing as the Senate requiring reorganization as is the case with each newly elected House. . . . There may be no House of Representatives, but merely an unorganized body of members elect; there may be no President duly installed in office. But there is always the organized Senate of the United States.[17]

Lodge felt that the Senate's power to make treaties gave the body its special position, enabling it to halt executive aggrandizement, at least in the realm of foreign relations. Historically, chairmen of the Foreign Relations Committee are particularly protective of the Senate's prerogatives, and Lodge was no exception. "War can be declared without the assent of the Executive, and peace can be made without the assent of the House," he once pointed out, "but neither war nor peace can be made without the assent of the Senate."[18] The exemplar of the requisite approach, Lodge thought, was President James Polk's message to the Senate on June 10, 1846, seeking advice on important foreign policy measures.

In his writings, Lodge emphasized that a treaty, so-called, is "still inchoate, a mere project for a treaty until the consent of the Senate has been given to it" and that the Senate might act "at any stage of negotiation."[19] Lodge helped to reinstigate the long-standing battle between the executive and the Senate for control over the nation's foreign relations when, even before World War I had ended, he warned "that the responsibility of a Senator in dealing with any question of peace is as great in his sphere as that of the President in his."[20]

A momentous struggle was about to begin, and Lodge scarcely needed his friend, former senator Albert Beveridge, to remind him that "the future of the party is in your hands more than in those of any other man." Republican prospects would suffer greatly, wrote Beveridge, if the Democrats could claim that Wilson's League of Nations had brought about "the greatest constructive world reform in history."[21] Beveridge thought the League "a winning political issue" for the Republican party,[22] but Lodge was initially not so sure. The story of how he made it one is also an account of his brilliant floor leadership in the Sixty-sixth Congress.

If, as Lodge himself once stated, "there is no one more jealous of the prerogatives of the Senate than am I,"[23] it is also true that he valued party loyalty very highly. Many of his writings were little more than encomiums to party unity, and like his Federalist great-grandfather, Senator George Cabot, he probably feared party division and disruption above all else.[24] It may even be said, as historian W. Stull Holt once wrote, that "during the long years of his public career no member of the Republican party was more faithful in service or more ready to sacrifice ideals or anything else to party loyalty." "His politics was not personal for his own advantage or advancement," claimed one of his colleagues, "but always for his party."[25]

As he took the reins of his party in the Senate, such a reputation for party service and loyalty was a distinct asset, for the Republican majority was very thin (49-47), and the most crucial contest was likely to be one within the Republican party in the Senate—that of trying to hold the party together on certain key policies and positions. It was a formidable task. According to Ripley, individualism reigned supreme in all of the Senates between 1917 and 1933.[26] Merely to cite some of the more extreme examples, William Borah, Hiram Johnson, or Robert La Follette, is to understand what an imposing task Lodge faced.

He brought abilities of a high order to the service of the Republican party and the powers of the Senate. Although he had a well-deserved reputation for his erudition and his literary and scholarly achievements, Lodge's greatest assets as Republican leader lay in other areas. First, he knew his subject matter. One of his contemporaries, a Democrat, once said that Lodge "illustrates as well as any man I have known the maxim that 'knowledge is power', . . . his superior information was . . . the great factor in his success." He had long been a student of the country's foreign relations; he was well connected abroad and widely regarded as possessing particular expertise in the area of treaties. Secretary of State Robert Lansing, for example, thought that in the whole Senate only Lodge and Senator Philander Knox (a former secretary of state) would really understand the Versailles Treaty and appreciate what U.S. participation in the League of Nations would entail.[27] Second, he was a skillful parliamentarian, well-versed in the rules and precedents. As Holt observed:

> No one can read extensively in the *Congressional Record* . . . without being impressed by his mastery of parliamentary technique, by his adroit maneuvers to extract his party from a tight situation or to entangle his opponents, and by his knowledge of what to do under all circumstances. No one in 1919 knew better than he the various devices and methods by which a treaty could be killed, nor had anyone had more practice in the use of them.[28]

His skill in a third area, the handling of others, is less well known both because of Lodge's reputation for hauteur and because other twentieth-century aristocratic politicians have tended to leave the mechanics of politics to others. Not that Lodge was personally popular. His colleagues accepted his guidance, not out of friendship or affection,[29] but primarily out of respect for his ability. Those abilities encompassed two kinds of knowledge, as we have seen, but they also included exceptional managerial skills. High office had never been handed to Lodge; he had always had to work hard to obtain it. In the rough and tumble of 1880s Massachusetts politics, Lodge's upper-class origins and manners were a liability, not an asset. As Republican state chairman, however, he successfully managed the 1883 Massachusetts gubernatorial campaign. He then ran for Congress twice before finally being elected on his third try. He organized his own campaigns meticulously throughout his career and carried on a vast correspondence with local Republican politicians and managers across his state. When he became the senior senator from Massachusetts, he did not follow the example of his colleague Senator George Hoar and relinquish the troubles and duties of patronage to his junior colleague but, rather, "always clung with a tenacious grasp to the details of political management which he understood so well."[30]

The same attention to detail and preoccupation with control occurred during the League fight. He carried on a prodigious correspondence with prominent Republicans throughout the country and with many senators as well. Though by no means gregarious, he knew his fellow senators' political situations—whose advice they sought, who might influence or pressure them, what their respective constituencies thought, and so forth. A careful and frequent canvasser, he was seldom surprised by the outcome of any vote. Early in his career (and already an aspirant to the Foreign Relations chairmanship), he wrote to his friend Theodore Roosevelt about the hard fight over the ratification of the peace treaty concluding the Spanish-American War, the first important treaty approved by the Senate in twenty-five years. He complained vociferously about the inability of the then chairman of Foreign Relations to make a canvass and his lack of managerial talents. "He would ask me every morning how the vote stood, and I think this is about all he knew about it," Lodge told Roosevelt. "Aldrich and I, but particularly Aldrich, made the hard fighting, which does not appear on the surface. . . . We were down in the engine room and do not get flowers, but we did make the ship move."[31]

Episodes and tactics from the treaty fight reveal how Lodge used his command posts to thwart Wilson's designs. Lodge derived special advantage from being both chairman of the Foreign Relations Committee, where the Treaty of Versailles was first considered, and chairman of the Republican Conference, with its control over committee assignments.

Even before he was actually in possession of leadership posts, Lodge, in an audacious and clever move, took a long step toward finding a position on which diverse Republican senators could comfortably stand. Just before midnight on March 3, 1919 (the day before the last session of the old Sixty-fifth Congress was to end), Lodge rose to introduce a motion, soon to be known as the infamous round robin, stating that "the constitution of the league of nations in the form now proposed to the peace conference should not be accepted by the United States" and that it was the sense of the Senate that the peace treaty with Germany be concluded expeditiously and the league proposal be taken up only after the negotiation of a satisfactory peace.[32] The rules specified that such a resolution could be considered only by unanimous consent; when a Democrat objected, as anticipated, Lodge simply read into the record a statement signed by thirty-seven Republican senators and senators-elect of the next Congress indicating that they would have voted for the resolution had they had the opportunity.

Had the Democrats been on their toes and permitted a vote, the resolution would probably have been easily defeated and its impact muted. As it was, Lodge accomplished two purposes at once. He sent Wilson a strong message to the effect that, on matters of foreign policy, and especially where treaties were involved, as few as a blocking one-third of the membership of the Senate could determine policy. Even more important, Lodge had demonstrated that he was in charge and that the vast majority of Republican senators (certainly more than one third of the total membership of the Senate) were committed to a policy of united and partisan action on the treaty.

Lodge's next coup came at the outset of the new Congress and involved the composition of the Senate Foreign Relations Committee. The Republicans' narrow majority of only two seats seemed to call for only a nine-to-eight Republican-Democrat ratio on Foreign Relations, which meant that the vote of one of the continuing members, Porter McCumber (R-N.D.), might well be decisive. Lodge knew McCumber harbored pro-League sympathies and was far from subscribing to Lodge's hard-headed, pro-Allies approach to the peace settlement. Pursuant to Republican organization of the Senate, Lodge was able to persuade the Senate to authorize a Republican-Democrat ratio of ten to seven on the Foreign Relations Committee. He appears to have sounded out prospective new appointees, extracting their pledges to support him in handling the League Covenant and in pursuing a strategy of amendment and reservation.[33] In this manner he succeeded in neutralizing McCumber and greatly strengthened his own position. The four new Republican appointees were George Moses of New Hampshire and Hiram Johnson of California (both of whom became "irreconcilables," as ardent opponents of the League were called) and Warren Harding of Ohio and Harry New of Indiana, both strict party regulars. The committee already had four irreconcilable holdovers, so Lodge's appointments gave the committee an irreconcilable cast. In fact, some have speculated that Lodge appointed the additional irreconcilables as a quid pro quo for Senator William Borah's acquiescence in Republican organization of the Senate and having crucial committee chairmanships like Finance pass to such "standpatters" as Boies Penrose of Pennsylvania. But no conclusive evidence to this effect has ever surfaced,[34] although it remains a distinct possibility. But what really mattered was that Lodge and his two party loyalists (Harding and New) now occupied the decisive middle ground on the committee and were in a position to tilt its decisions as they saw fit.

Lodge had two preoccupations in the first half of 1919; one was the peace settlement and the other involved domestic politics. He wanted Germany placed under effective constraints and he also wanted to unify the Republican party so that the "Wilsonian party" might be driven from power.[35] Lodge showed great facility in merging these twin goals. There is some indication that the second goal gradually predominated. Things would have gotten really interesting if only Wilson had been able to force Lodge to choose between his twin objects. It is a tribute to Lodge's talent for political leadership that Wilson was never able to do that.

Still, most early bets would have been with Wilson. The idea of a league for peace was initially so well received that Wilson came to believe he could simply overide the opposition. Despite Lodge's early successes against the League, opinion within his own party remained deeply divided. About a dozen Republican senators vowed they would not vote for any league, while a substantial number wanted to proceed with the League experiment with only a few so-called mild reservations to the Covenant. In the middle were Lodge and a large group of party regulars who could be reconciled to American entry into the League only under the cover of "strong and effective reservations," reservations that would make the League less of a collective security organization and more of a mere world forum.[36]

Lodge was accustomed to accommodating political realities, and he determined early that the League idea was too popular to be confronted with a stark negative. He is said to have told Senator Borah that "the best we can do is to get changes that will emasculate it as much as possible."[37] Moreover, Lodge had long had an affinity for those who strove to hold "great conservative parties" together, a task that fit his own temperament perfectly.[38] To that end, he often had to be less than forthright in expressing his own views and was frequently all things to all men without bringing his own honor and veracity into question. By April 1919 he was simultaneously deemed to be a "real friend" of the League of Nations by Elihu Root, while Albert Beveridge thought he was prepared to lead an outright assault on the entire concept of a league.[39] Lodge's was indeed a difficult balancing act. As he told Root, "the situation was not an easy one for anybody who is forced as I am to be the leader and in a sense manager. Forty-nine men . . . ranging from Borah to Colt presents [sic] a variety of subjects to deal with and one not always easy to grasp."[40]

He posed, especially in his correspondence with those of a strong "irreconcilable" bent, as a man devoted primarily "to watching the votes," as one whose whole purpose was to unite Republicans on truly effective reservations.[41] The implicit warning in that pose occasionally had to be spelled out. He once bluntly told Beveridge to stop rocking the boat because there was simply no alternative to the situation he had been able to bring about: "beyond that a majority in the Senate is not to be found able to control."[42] The key word is "control." Lodge seized it early and never relinquished it. Working with Elihu Root and National Republican chairman Will Hays, Lodge made sure his party was on record as favoring "a league of nations."[43] And though he continued to support a few amendments (which would have necessitated a renegotiation of the whole treaty), he used that tack primarily to appease the irreconcilables and to force the mild reservationists back toward middle ground.

Lodge's control in the Senate hinged on his ability to work with the mild reservationists. Historian Thomas A. Bailey once asked what might have happened if Wilson and his followers had welcomed Republican mild reservationists in a timely manner.[44] In any event, Wilson's overtures were tardy—Lodge had already opened his arms to them; by the late summer of 1919 GOP mild reservationists were committed to him and to the reservations that bore his name. Interestingly, the so-called Lodge reservations grew out of a cooperative effort, more the work of Root and such mild reservationists as Senator Irvine Lenroot of Wisconsin than of Lodge himself. This collaboration explains why the mild reservationists stood so strongly behind the Lodge reservations throughout the protracted treaty fight and why even Senator Frank Kellogg of Minnesota (whom Lodge had kept off the Foreign Relations Committee) had no qualms about claiming on the Senate floor that the reservations had "not been drawn by the enemies of the treaty" but rather "by its friends, who want to save it."[45] So it was that by early September Lodge could report to Root that "our people were united on his four central points, including the all important reservation to Article X declaring that no American troops could be despatched without Congressional authorization."[46] McCumber was still not satisfied, however, with the phrasing of the reservation to Article X. But Lodge sought to accommodate even McCumber, whom he had originally sought to circumvent. He invited him to lunch, and after a lengthy discussion they were able to agree on a reservation in the form later presented to the Senate. Lodge's triumph was complete when McCumber even introduced it in his own name.

Would Wilson accept the treaty with the major Lodge reservations, or would he refuse to make the treaty at all? Lodge still expected it to be ratified with his "strong and effective" reservations, yet an alternative scenario began to develop in Lodge's mind. In this scenario, the matter of ratification was postponed and the president refused to make the treaty. Coming before the people the next year seeking a third term, Wilson (the scenario continued) would go down to a devastating defeat.[47]

But the decision about the treaty was Wilson's. Lodge was therefore not about to rely on a contingency over which he could exert so little influence. For him the only safe assumption was that the League would be ratified in some form. Therefore, the issue of his reservations remained at center stage. He was forced to continue his delicate balancing act, alternately asserting his independence from both the mild reservationists and the irreconcilables and yet keeping both groups on Republican territory. He told Root and the mild reservationists that if he himself "were to go over and vote against the treaty because the reservations were not satisfactory it would be killed."[48] To prevent the treaty's opponents from forcing his hand, he argued that he was totally dependent on how the votes in the Senate stood. He said he could do not what he wanted but only the best that circumstances would permit, and that was simply to "compel [the Democrats] to accept a ratification with reservations that will protect fully the peace, independence and sovereignty of the United States, or force them to reject it."[49] He held out that possibility to those who hoped for ratification, indicating that many Democrats were getting restive. To those who opposed ratification, he confided his feeling that the president was "immovable" and that as a consequence "ratification was sure to fail."[50] He kept his channels of communication open to the end, even to the Democrats, and willingly participated in bipartisan conferences to work on the language of the reservations.

It is possible to interpret all this as evidence that he had so internalized the role of party leader and the concomitant responsibilities of mediator that, in the end, he had no strong personal feelings on the League. This was the view of his own secretary, who believed Lodge cared little whether the treaty was ratified or not. That is true enough, but therein lay his great tactical advantage. Though he could never be sure exactly how it would end, he knew, as he confided to Theodore Roosevelt's sister Corinne, that it would end "not badly in any event for I have tried so to arrange it."[51] He had arranged it so that ratification was possible only with his strong and effective reservations, which would have made the League a much different and weaker organization.

In the last analysis President Wilson did not have the votes to divest the treaty of the Lodge reservations and to proceed to ratification. He did have enough votes, however (when joined with those of the irreconcilables), to reject ratification with the Lodge reservations. This is what ultimately happened, and it did not reflect well on either Wilson or his party. The defeat of the treaty was at least partially responsible for sending the Democratic party down to devastating losses in the elections of 1920. Other issues were certainly involved in that election, but foreign policy issues, Lodge's forte, had commanded everyone's attention. Under difficult circumstances and with a razor-thin majority, Lodge had shown what a truly effective party leader could accomplish. Some would say that his was one of *the* great examples of party leadership in the Senate. The future looked bright both for Lodge's leadership and for the restoration of senatorial power. Warren G. Harding, the landslide victor in the presidential election of 1920, was after all a senator who had proved a rather malleable party regular. Lodge would now have an opportunity to establish a Republican version of the team relationship that had existed between President Wilson and Majority Leader John W. Kern (see Chapter 1), a version in which he and the Senate would play the more powerful role. Why this did not come to pass is a story that reveals how transitory and circumstantial leadership in the Senate can be.

The Sixty-seventh Congress:
An Experiment in Party Government

Much has been written about how the 1920 Republican convention selected its standard-bearer. Lodge was certainly in the thick of the maneuvering that led to a platform straddle on the League issue and the selection of Harding. The candidate had stood with Lodge on the League issue time after time on crucial votes, first in the Foreign Relations Committee and later on the Senate floor. Lodge was also sufficiently acquainted with Harding's abilities to know that he was a mediocrity. But after eight years of executive domination, that is precisely what Lodge and his fellow senators wanted. "[Harding] will not try to be an autocrat but will do his best to carry on the Government in the old and accepted Constitutional ways," Lodge wrote to his friend Owen Wister. "For this I suppose he may be called a reactionary, but as I think that is the right way to carry on the Government it appeals to me favorably."[52]

From the point of view of electoral politics, the choice of Harding was particularly well conceived. The Republican party stood united once again and rode into office on a veritable tidal wave of votes. In the first great landslide election of the twentieth century, Harding's own popular majority surpassed seven million votes, and the Republicans added ten additional seats to their majority in the Senate. Lodge thought the result almost beyond belief. "There has never been such a change by popular majorities in the history of parliamentary government, certainly never in the United States," he opined. "We have torn up Wilsonism by the roots," he wrote, admitting he was "not slow to take my own share of vindication which I find in the majorities."[53]

The victory was in fact so overwhelming that it carried within it the seeds of future difficulties. During the campaign, Lodge had suggested the possibility of putting aside Wilson's "ill-drawn, ill-conceived League" and taking up "under the auspices of the United States a new agreement, or association, or league—whatever you call it—with all the nations of Europe under the leadership of the United States itself."[54] After the election, he wrote to the president-elect suggesting a "fresh start" involving passage of the Knox Resolution (which declared that the domination of Europe by an aggressive military power was also a menace to the safety of the United States) and an invitation to the signatories of the Versailles Treaty to send representatives to Washington to consider an agreement which would take steps to codify international law and establish a world court, to deal so far as possible with non-justiciable questions and with the proposition of a general reduction of armaments.[55]

If such a conference had come to pass, foreign affairs might have remained at the top of the nation's agenda, and Lodge might have continued to be one of the major players. In all this he was to be sorely disappointed. The election was widely interpreted as a "referendum for isolation."[56] As a result it would prove impossible to secure a majority of votes for the Knox Resolution, even on the Foreign Relations Committee. There were to be some attempts at international cooperation such as the Washington Conference of 1921–22, but that conference bore scant resemblance to Lodge's original vision. Lodge, the eastern internationalist, came to occupy a minority position within his own party. His influence waned accordingly.

A recurrent theme of the Harding presidential campaign had been the American people's longing, after the excitement of the war and the treaty fight, to return to "normalcy." It was both a successful and a prophetic slogan. As public interest in foreign policy waned, attention began to focus on domestic problems, especially on economic issues such as taxes and tariffs. Power inside the Senate began to shift back to the Finance Committee and its chairman, Boies Penrose. That, after all, was the "normal" Republican way of doing things; traditionally the leading committee chairmen had had more power than party conference leaders. Lodge did not hold a seat on the Finance Committee, and consequently, as Ripley has concluded, Majority Leader Lodge became "relatively unimportant. He was not prominent in the major domestic policy struggles of the Congress."[57]

Another analyst of Senate leadership has written that "the first Republican floor leader to have the opportunity for a team relationship like that of Wilson and Kern was Henry Cabot Lodge, when Warren G. Harding became president in 1921."[58] The pattern of the president proposing legislation to the Congress was by now so well established as to be nearly irreversible, but neither Lodge nor Harding thought to emulate the Wilson-Kern relationship. Harding had no interest in playing prime minister (a style to which Wilson had been both intellectually and politically attracted), and Lodge certainly had no intention of taking on a role subservient to the executive power. Both felt strongly that Wilson had repeatedly ignored the proper constitutional balance between the executive and the legislature. During the campaign, Harding had claimed that "government was a simple thing" and had promised to return to practices that would restore congressional power. As he expressed it, he wanted "party government, as distinguished from personal government, individual, dictatorial, autocratic, or what not."[59]

Like Lodge, Harding was also a firm believer in party unity and loyalty. When he took office on March 4, 1921, the Republican party, for the first time in ten years, was in complete control of the executive and both houses of Congress. "Party government" seemed possible, yet that concept did not define itself. Just how much power was the president willing to surrender to the Congress? Would Congress prove unwieldy and inefficient in the absence of strong presidential leadership? Might not the huge Republican majorities chafe under strong congressional leadership and split into conservative and progressive wings, as had happened under President William H. Taft?

The Republicans anticipated these problems through new institutional arrangements. In April 1921 the Republican Committee on Committees (headed by Senator Frank Brandegee of Connecticut, a close friend of Lodge) forced through a long-overdue consolidation of standing Senate committees. In one centralizing move, seventy-four committees were reduced to thirty-four; obsolete committees were abolished and Republican membership was increased on those that remained. When the Democrats complained, as expected, Brandegee retorted, "The Republicans are responsible to the country for legislation and must have control of committees. This is not tyranny; that's the . . . rule of the majority."[60]

Once again the majority party in the Senate in 1919, the Republicans resuscitated the practice of constituting a steering committee to set the party's legislative agenda and to facilitate the determination of party positions on pending legislation. This committee played only a minor role in the Sixty-sixth Congress; Lodge usurped both of its functions in his dual capacity as floor leader and chairman of the Foreign Relations Committee. Consequently, no one was surprised when McCumber, who had chaired the Steering Committee in the Sixty-sixth Congress, stepped down to take a place on the Committee on Committees. In a conscious attempt to strengthen party leadership in the Senate in the Sixty-seventh Congress, Lodge was then made chairman of the Steering Committee as well. Because he retained his other positions, this amounted to a considerable concentration of party power in Lodge's hands and led to optimism regarding effective majority party leadership.

These institutional arrangements were not the only innovations. The Republican leader in the House, Franklin Mondell of Wyoming, hoping to advance his party's legislative program and to increase cooperation between the Senate and the House, proposed joint meetings of the steering committees of the two houses. This joint panel, in consultation with the president, would set a party agenda and a party program.[61]

Though it had potential, the scheme never worked well. It did little to improve House-Senate relations or to soothe executive-congressional conflict. Harding might have used this new instrument more effectively, but conditions in the Senate probably would have thwarted him. Journalist George Brown explained the situation best when he wrote:

The Republican majority of the Senate did not function as a unit, but this was not because it lacked leadership, but because the Senators who comprised that majority were not knitted together by common ideas and purposes. Mr. Lodge had managed to hold his party together on the League of Nations because concerted party action, in some measure, was a political necessity, and every Republican Senator had a personal and selfish interest in seeing his party established in power and himself become a majority instead of a minority Member of the Senate, with enhanced prestige and prerogatives. As soon as this major necessity no longer exerted its cohesive force, the majority tended to disintegrate.[62]

Lodge further incapacitated the Steering Committee with several bizarre appointments. His motives were unclear. Some scholars have charged that Lodge viewed the committee only as a bit of nonsense:[63] he was not fond of committee meetings, was used to acting on his own, and had circumvented the Steering Committee in the previous Congress when it had been headed by McCumber. At the same time, he may only have been trying to demonstrate that the Republican party in the Senate was hopelessly divided on domestic issues and that no committee could bridge this division. In any event, the unusual appointments were those of Senator Robert La Follette of Wisconsin and Senator Joseph France of Maryland, both intensely individualistic and temperamentally incapable of representing anyone but themselves. Lodge could not have found two senators less amenable to the delicate manipulation and compromise required for the Steering Committee to be an effective agent of party government. La Follette himself drove this reality home when he opened his 1922 reelection campaign by attacking every major Republican policy.[64]

A highly individualistic Senate was not Lodge's only problem. His difficulties were further compounded by the emergence of a powerful interest group (the so-called Agricultural bloc) composed of twenty to thirty senators on both sides of the aisle who were interested primarily in one issue—farm relief.[65] Effectively organized by Republican senators William Kenyon of Iowa and Arthur Capper of Kansas (and using the tactics of insurgency reminiscent of the Silver bloc of earlier years), the Agricultural bloc quickly became a potent force. Its very emergence disclosed the paucity of Republican leadership, and before long the bloc was exercising the kind of power (both with respect to procedure and to the substance of legislation) that was supposed to have resided in the Steering Committee and the titular leadership. Power within the Republican party had been shifting to the Midwest and the West for some time. In 1922 Lodge on Foreign Relations and James Wadsworth of New York on Military Affairs were the sole easterners to chair major Senate committees. Only seventeen years earlier, in 1905, eight of the Senate's major committee chairmanships had been in eastern hands.[66] This compounded Lodge's task.

The Agricultural bloc's influence in the Senate was evident in the vast array of farm legislation that it passed, even in the face of frequent opposition from the president and the regular Republican leadership. The onslaught of special-interest legislation began when the bloc was able to dictate its terms on the agricultural commodities covered in the Emergency Tariff Act. Other legislation included a law regulating the packing industry, the provision of a billion-dollar credit for farm exports, a bill regulating grain exchanges dealing in futures, the Capper-Volstead Act to protect farm cooperatives from antitrust laws, the Curtis bill appropriating $25 million as a revolving fund for farm loan banks, and finally the Kenyon bill providing for an increased rate of interest for farm loan bank bonds without an increase in the interest rates charged to farmers.[67]

But the bloc showed its real power on a revenue issue. Both the president and the Republican party were committed to lowering the surtax on incomes. The Agricultural bloc was intent, however, on setting the surtax permanently at 50 percent. In order to prevent an open coalition between western Republican insurgents and the Democrats, first Penrose in the Finance Committee and then Lodge on the floor capitulated to the bloc. Their hope was that the House would insist on the lower rates for which they had originally voted. But to the chagrin of the president and the Senate majority leader, the bloc was able to press the House to reverse itself and to support the higher rates. The breakdown of party solidarity was at this point complete, and there was no more talk of party government.

In fact, the Republican party in the Senate was in such disarray that the majority leader was unable to control the procedure of the Senate. In early July 1921, when Washington was at its most uncomfortable, Lodge moved for a three-week summer recess, thinking he might thereby slow the progress of the bloc's many legislative proposals. But even on this he was beaten. The Senate rejected his motion 24-27, with Republicans supplying about half of the opposing votes.[68]

Lodge did not relish running in 1922 on the record of the Sixty-seventh Congress, but the dissension among Republican senators did not seem to have disturbed him greatly. Perhaps his overriding interest in foreign policy led him to minimize GOP divisions on domestic issues. But, more likely, his expectations had never been very high. Lodge continued to view the Senate as an elite preserve where individuality was prized and where principle was as important as party strategy. He was quite capable of voting against his president when he thought him wrong. Lodge, like his friend Theodore Roosevelt, valued military service highly and thought it should be rewarded. When Harding, for reasons of economy, vetoed a veterans' bonus bill, Lodge voted to override his action, causing considerable comment. But Lodge did not regard his action as at all unusual.[69]

Once again, Lodge had his most singular success in foreign affairs. The Republicans intended the Washington Conference on the Limitation of Armaments to be a proper and "truly American" substitute for Wilson's blundering in Paris. The United States was to be represented, not by the president, but by the secretary of state, Charles Evans Hughes, with the assistance of elder statesman Elihu Root, Senate Foreign Relations Committee chairman Henry Cabot Lodge, and Oscar Underwood of Alabama, that committee's ranking Democrat. The American people were to infer that the results both in Paris and in the Senate might have been totally different had Wilson shown equally good judgment. When asked to serve, Lodge was both flattered and moved. He wrote Harding in gratitude:

> I . . . have not for many years thought that there would be any political position in the world for which I would have the least desire, but as I draw towards the end I confess the work on this conference will be to me a close for my work in public life which I shall value beyond anything.[70]

The conference produced good treaties. The international situation was propitious for pacts reducing naval armaments and stabilizing the situation in the Far East and in the Pacific. The Four-Power Treaty was the most controversial as it called for consultations among the United States, Britain, France, and Japan, permitting the hard-line isolationists to raise the old hue and cry about a "secret alliance." The wisdom of appointing Lodge to the conference delegation was soon apparent. He literally escorted the treaties through the Senate. This time there were no long committee meetings to read the treaties aloud, nor did the debate drag on for months. Lodge succeeded in putting the treaties through while they were on the crest of popular support, though only after a major compromise had been reached.

In February 1922 Lodge brought the treaty before the Senate Foreign Relations Committee only to discover that sentiment on the committee favored reservations that would more clearly define the United States' obligations. After consulting with President Harding, Lodge drafted a reservation stating that the treaty was not an alliance and that it did not commit the United States to use armed force without the consent of Congress. Lodge was then able to push the treaty through. The final Senate vote was 67-27, with two abstentions. Fifty-five Republicans and twelve Democrats supported the treaty, while twenty-three Democrats and four Republicans did not. Senators France and La Follette, Lodge's unpredictable appointees to the Steering Committee, cast two of the negative votes. Lodge was not above taking credit for the outcome:

> I not only got two-thirds of the Senate, but I had thirteen to spare on the vote on the Four-Power Treaty where the fight centered, and all the other treaties passed unanimously, with single exception of one vote by France against the naval treaty. . . . I must say, speaking without regard to imputations of vanity, that it was on the whole pretty well done.[71]

Harding was also euphoric, believing his administration's name was "now secure in history." Still, it is well to remember that the Washington Conference was not originally on the administration's agenda and that its calling had been forced by an amendment to a naval appropriations bill sponsored by William Borah of Idaho. Even in the area of Lodge's special expertise, party government Republican style was not quite the success it was touted to be.[72]

In the 1922 congressional elections, the Republicans suffered a stinging rebuke, losing eight Senate seats and some seventy-five seats in the House. Lodge won a narrow victory in Massachusetts but did not increase his power in the Senate or within his party. Though he seems to have given little consideration to retiring, in truth he knew his day was passing. He was now seventy-two, and to many he seemed to belong to an earlier generation and to an earlier, more aristocratic Senate. His wife, Nannie, his good friends Theodore Roosevelt and Cecil Spring-Rice, and his son-in-law and political protégé Augustus Gardner had all long since died. Lodge gradually became less active and more withdrawn. He paid less attention to his political work and devoted more time to reading and writing. He even began to lose control of his party in Massachusetts to a faction under the control of Vice President Calvin Coolidge. In the Senate there was even a suggestion that he needed assistance as majority leader and that he be flanked by senators James Wadsworth and Irvine Lenroot, representing conservative and liberal interests respectively. Lodge squashed the idea immediately, noting emphatically that the elected leadership would continue to lead the Senate majority.[73] Though he did not put it exactly that way, it was becoming apparent that only death would separate him from his powers.

Four months before the first session of the Sixty-eighth Congress convened, President Harding died. Lodge's home-state rival, Vice President Coolidge, assumed the presidency. The Republicans enjoyed only nominal majorities in the Sixty-eighth Congress, with only fifty-one Republicans in the Senate, including such rebels as Robert La Follette, George Norris, Edwin Ladd, Smith Brookhart, and Lynn Frazier who, with the two Farmer Laborites, could easily give the opposition a 50-46 majority. These shadow majorities and the impending 1924 election figured to doom almost any legislative program emanating from the White House or the party leadership.

But Coolidge's legislative defeats were in fact usually attributable to revolts among the more regular Republicans rather than to the strategic position of those holding the balance of power in the House or the Senate. The Senate refused to consider the United States' entrance into the World Court despite urgent pleadings from the president. Lodge knew the votes were not there and made no effort to help. Coolidge opposed the Japanese exclusion clause in the Immigration Act, but Lodge voted for it, and it was enacted. The troublesome issue of a soldiers' bonus came up again and was passed by Congress only to be vetoed by Coolidge. His veto was quickly overriden, with Lodge sticking to his earlier support and voting to override.[74] Considerable pressure was directed at Lodge to change his mind. Secretary of War John Weeks, a friend from Massachusetts, wrote urging him to uphold the president on the bonus issue, arguing that it was "a question of party policy which transcends individual opinion."

But Lodge could not be moved, replying: "I simply could not change my position . . . without losing my own self respect entirely," continuing:

> If I had shifted I should have been looked upon with contempt by those whom I had deserted. . . . It has not been an easy thing to do, but on the whole in what little time may be left to me I must at least have as a companion my own self respect. That I should have sacrificed if I had changed my vote even to have obliged the President.[75]

This independence played into the hands of Lodge's foes in Massachusetts, and they seized their advantage. Although they could not prevent his being named a delegate to the 1924 Republican National Convention, they did manage to have him excluded from the convention program. Despite his long service to the party and his position as Senate majority leader, Lodge made no speeches, reaped no honors, held no convention office, and sat on no committee. Knowing what was in store for him, a group of his friends in the Senate—through George Moses of New Hampshire—offered words of comfort and advice:

> They intend to stick an elbow in your ribs at every turning in Cleveland. They will permit you to have no position in the convention except as a delegate from Massachusetts. I want to counsel you to hold this in mind . . . to remember that you are Henry Cabot Lodge, the Senior Senator from Massachusetts, the senior of all the Senators in the United States, and the leader of the majority in the Senate. Remember also that National Conventions are sucked oranges to you.[76]

Lodge did not need the advice. He took the shameful treatment afforded him by the new leaders of Massachusetts Republicanism in stride, confident of his own dignity and proud of his independence to the end. Their treatment of him might have proved a disastrous political blunder for Lodge's term in the Senate ran until 1928 and his power as majority leader remained formidable. But this was never put to the test because Lodge's time on earth was running short.

In his last years, Lodge devoted most of his time to writing and to reading old favorites from his vast personal library. He edited for publication his long correspondence with Theodore Roosevelt and wrote *The Senate and the League of Nations*, essentially an apologia for his part in the battle over the League. The latter volume was published only after Wilson's death on February 3, 1924, and Lodge's own death from a cerebral hemorrhage at Charlesgate Hospital in Cambridge on November 9, 1924. He was seventy-four years of age at the time of his death and had served in Congress continuously since 1887.

Given the issues involved in the League of Nations battle in the Senate, Lodge's role as majority leader will always be in dispute. Perhaps, on the one hand, the League might have worked in the 1920s or 1930s, with the United States as a member. On the other hand, perhaps Lodge protected the United States from obligations it was not yet prepared to assume. At any rate, Lodge demonstrated that even a fractionated, highly individualistic Senate could be led under certain conditions. Lodge's career also shows that a senator's best qualities—independence, intellectual integrity, and devotion to principle—are precisely those most inimical to the party leader's task of striving to find the "common denominator of party accord."[77]

NOTES

1. Henry Cabot Lodge, ed., *The Correspondence of Theodore Roosevelt and Henry Cabot Lodge* (New York: Scribner's, 1925), 1:391.
2. Robert C. Byrd, *The Senate, 1789–1989: Addresses on the History of the United States Senate* (Washington, D.C.: U.S. Government Printing Office, 1988), 1:372–374.
3. George Rothwell Brown, *The Leadership of Congress* (Indianapolis: Bobbs-Merrill, 1922), 112.
4. Randall B. Ripley, *Power in the Senate* (New York: St. Martin's, 1969), 28.
5. *Memorial Addresses Delivered in the Senate and House of Representatives in Memory of Henry Cabot Lodge* (Washington, D.C.: U.S. Government Printing Office, 1925), 58.
6. John A. Garraty, *Henry Cabot Lodge* (New York: Knopf, 1953), 165, 214; Lodge to Henry White, December 18, 1900, Lodge MSS, Massachusetts Historical Society.
7. Lodge to Lord Bryce, December 21, 1916, Lodge MSS.
8. *Boston Herald*, October 31, 1918.
9. *New York Times*, October 8 and 14, 1918; *Congressional Record*, 65th Cong., 2d sess., 1918, 1170–1171; *Boston Herald*, October 31, 1918; Lodge, "The Necessary Guarantees of Peace," *Scribner's Magazine* 64 (November 1918): 471–72.
10. Quoted in Garraty, *Lodge*, 342.
11. Seward W. Livermore, *Politics Is Adjourned: Woodrow Wilson and the War Congress, 1916–1918* (Middletown, Conn.: Wesleyan University Press, 1966), 113.
12. Ibid., 227.
13. Lodge to Lord Bryce, November 16, 1918, and to Arthur Balfour, November 24, 1918, Lodge MSS.
14. *Memorial Addresses*, 91.
15. Floyd M. Riddick, "Majority and Minority Leaders of the Senate," Senate Document 100–129, 100th Cong., 2d sess., 11; Richard Langham Riedel, *Halls of the Mighty: My 47 Years at the Senate* (Washington, D.C., and New York: R.B. Luce, 1969), 136.
16. Henry Cabot Lodge, *The Senate of the United States and Other Essays and Addresses Historical and Literary* (New York: Scribner's, 1921), 2, 20–21.
17. Ibid., 2.
18. Ibid., 10.
19. Henry Cabot Lodge, *A Fighting Frigate and Other Essays and Addresses* (New York: Scribner's, 1902), 223, 245, 254–255.
20. *Congressional Record*, 65th Cong., 2d sess., 1918, 1170.

21. Albert J. Beveridge to Lodge, January 28, 1919, Beveridge MSS, Library of Congress.
22. Ibid., November 14, 1918.
23. *Congressional Record*, January 31, 1924, 1719.
24. William C. Widenor, *Henry Cabot Lodge and the Search for an American Foreign Policy* (Berkeley and Los Angeles: University of California Press, 1980), 49–54.
25. W. Stull Holt, *Treaties Defeated by the Senate* (Baltimore: Johns Hopkins University Press, 1933), 258; *Memorial Addresses*, 91.
26. Ripley, *Power in the Senate*, 15.
27. *Memorial Addresses*, 125. Lansing quoted in Lindsay Rogers, *The American Senate* (New York: F. S. Crofts, 1931), 73.
28. Holt, *Treaties Defeated by the Senate*, 261–262.
29. This is not to say that Lodge had no friends in the Senate. He was close to a number of New England senators, especially Frank Brandegee of Connecticut, and was not above charming and being particularly solicitous of certain younger senators deemed to have a future. See, for example, Martin L. Fausold, *James W. Wadsworth, Jr.: The Gentleman from New York* (Syracuse, N.Y.: Syracuse University Press, 1975), 93.
30. See Widenor, *Lodge*, 49–50, and *Memorial Addresses*, 124–125.
31. Lodge, ed., *Correspondence of Roosevelt and Lodge*, 1:391–392.
32. *Congressional Record*, March 3, 1919, 4974.
33. See, for example, Lodge to Frank Kellogg, May 28, 1919, and Kellogg's reply of May 31, Lodge MSS. Kellogg, who was not sufficiently forthcoming, was not appointed.
34. Jack E. Kendrick, "The League of Nations and the Republican Senate, 1918–1921" (Ph.D. diss., University of North Carolina, 1952), 143.
35. Lodge to Charles G. Washburn, February 10, 1919, Lodge MSS.
36. Lodge to Louis A. Coolidge, August 7, 1919, Lodge MSS. The best account of the role of the "irreconcilables" is Ralph Stone's *The Irreconcilables: The Fight Against the League of Nations* (Lexington: University of Kentucky Press, 1970). The "mild reservationists" receive their due in Herbert F. Margulies, *The Mild Reservationists and the League of Nations Controversy in the Senate* (Columbia: University of Missouri Press, 1989).
37. Lodge to Albert J. Beveridge, February 18, 1919, Beveridge MSS. John McCook Roots, "The Treaty of Versailles in the U.S. Senate," 86, Widenor Library, Harvard University.
38. See, for example, Lodge to Arthur Balfour, January 28, 1906, Lodge MSS.
39. Beveridge to William Borah, April 27, 1919, Borah MSS, Library of Congress, and Root to Lodge, April 4, 1919, Lodge MSS.
40. Lodge to Elihu Root, September 3, 1919, Root MSS, Library of Congress. The unruliness of the Senate was a continuing complaint. Even after the second vote Lodge told George Harvey that "in regard to the League no one knows better than you what a narrow channel I have to navigate in with rocks on both sides" (quoted in Denna F. Fleming, *The U.S. and the League of Nations* [New York: Putnam's, 1932], 486).
41. Lodge to Louis A. Coolidge, August 7, 1919, Lodge MSS.
42. Lodge to Albert J. Beveridge, August 4, 1919, Beveridge MSS.
43. *New York Times*, June 27, 1919.
44. Thomas A. Bailey, *Woodrow Wilson and the Great Betrayal* (New York: Macmillan, 1945), 58, 171–172.
45. Kendrick, "The League of Nations and the Republican Senate," 211, 254; Herbert F. Margulies, *Senator Lenroot of Wisconsin: A Political Biography, 1900–1929* (Columbia: University of Missouri Press, 1977), 276–77.
46. *Congressional Record*, 66th Cong., 1st sess., 1919, 8778–8780.
47. Lodge to Root, September 3, 1919, Root MSS.
48. Ibid., September 29, 1919, Root MSS.
49. Ibid.

50. Lodge to Louis A. Coolidge, January 28 and February 11, 1920, Lodge MSS.
51. Lodge to Root, March 6, 1920, Lodge MSS, and Lodge to Beveridge, January 3, 1920, Beveridge MSS; Lodge to Corinne Roosevelt Robinson, February 16, 1920, Houghton Library, Harvard University.
52. Lodge to Owen Wister, June 14, 1920, Lodge MSS.
53. Lodge to Moreton Frewen, November 8 and 24, 1920, Frewen MSS, Library of Congress, and Lodge to Medill McCormick, November 13, 1920, Lodge MSS.
54. "Speech at Braves' Field, Boston, August 28, 1920," 11–12, Lodge MSS.
55. Lodge to Harding, November 10 and December 23, 1920, Lodge MSS.
56. See John Chalmers Vinson, *Referendum for Isolation* (Athens: University of Georgia Press, 1961).
57. Randall B. Ripley, *Majority Party Leadership in Congress* (Boston: Little, Brown, 1969), 92.
58. Margaret Munk, "Origin and Development of the Party Floor Leadership in the U.S. Senate," *Capitol Studies* 2 (1974): 37.
59. Harding quoted in Lindsay Rogers, "The First (Special) Session of the Sixty-seventh Congress," *American Political Science Review* 16 (February 1922): 41.
60. Quoted in Alvin M. Josephy, Jr., *On the Hill: A History of the American Congress* (New York: Simon and Schuster, 1979), 309.
61. The best accounts of these proceedings are in Brown, *Leadership of Congress* (see especially chap. 14, "The Senate in Evolution," 252–282), and in Ripley, *Majority Party Leadership,* 89–103.
62. Brown, *Leadership of Congress,* 254.
63. Ibid., 272.
64. Ibid., 262.
65. The best account of the economic distress that led to the formation of the Agricultural bloc and of its program and organization remains Arthur Capper, *The Agricultural Bloc* (New York: Harcourt, Brace, 1922).
66. Brown, *Leadership of Congress,* 278–279.
67. The bloc's accomplishments are detailed in Capper, *Agricultural Bloc,* chap. 14, and in Rogers, "First (Special) Session of the Sixty-seventh Congress," 41–52.
68. Ripley, *Majority Party Leadership,* 100.
69. Brown, *Leadership of Congress,* 277.
70. Lodge to Harding, July 21, 1921, Lodge MSS.
71. Lodge to George Harvey, April 15, 1922, Lodge MSS.
72. Harding is quoted in Francis Russell, *The Shadow of Blooming Grove: Warren G. Harding in His Times* (New York: McGraw-Hill, 1968), 485. The definitive account of the conference is Thomas H. Buckley, *The United States and the Washington Conference: 1921–1922* (Knoxville: University of Tennessee Press, 1970).
73. Fausold, *Wadsworth,* 163.
74. Lindsay Rogers, "First and Second Sessions of the Sixty-eighth Congress," *American Political Science Review* 19 (November 1925): 761–762.
75. Weeks to Lodge, May 19, 1924, and Lodge to Weeks, May 21, 1924, Lodge MSS.
76. Quoted in William Allen White, *A Puritan in Babylon* (New York: Macmillan, 1938), 297.
77. Douglas Cater, "The Trouble in Lyndon Johnson's Backyard," *Reporter,* December 1, 1955, 32.

CHAPTER 3

Joseph Taylor Robinson
The Good Soldier

Donald C. Bacon

S enate Democratic leader Joe T. Robinson of Arkansas often compared his job to that of a bouncer in a saloon. "Some of these men," he would say, "need to be taken by the scruff of the neck and the seat of the trousers and shaken into sense." Such was his style—tough, self-assured, and unforgiving. Highly disciplined and devoted to hard work, he wielded an iron authority in the Senate for fourteen years, from 1923 through the most turbulent period of the New Deal.

He spent most of his time and energy trying to make the Senate an efficient, manageable institution, and he usually kept the unruly body on a constructive track. For that, Robinson earned the gratitude of a succession of Democratic and Republican presidents from Wilson to Roosevelt. Although admired for his loyalty and dedication, he was feared by many of his colleagues. His muscular body and stern demeanor conveyed, as columnist Ray Tucker

Joseph T. "Scrappy Joe" Robinson of Arkansas used brute force and a near-perfect knowledge of parliamentary procedure to bulldoze his agenda through the Senate during his fourteen years of leadership.

described it, "the impression of brute, animal strength, and a willingness to use it."[1]

As majority leader, Robinson threatened colleagues with binding caucuses,[2] cloture, prolonged sessions, canceled holidays—whatever was necessary to complete his prescribed agenda. He thwarted filibusters through skillful orchestration of Senate rules and procedures. He intimidated committee chairmen with discharge motions and other actions if they refused to report a bill he wanted.[3] When President Franklin D. Roosevelt objected to several amendments to the Work Relief Act of 1935, Robinson had the bill stripped of the objectionable amendments and rewritten with the features FDR requested.[4] Robinson's dominance extended to conference committees, whose Senate members he carefully screened. Sometimes, to expedite debate, he would accept amendments to a bill, then have them removed by conferees. Nine amendments to the Robinson-Patman Act—the only major statute bearing his name—were accepted and then dropped in this way.[5]

Even as a freshman, Robinson dazzled colleagues with his carefully crafted speeches and mastery of the Senate's complex rules and practices. He impressed them also with his tenacious loyalty to friends and party, passion for detail, and killer's instinct in debate. Wedded to his job, he arrived early each day, stayed late, and studied legislation at home. He and his wife lived in a modest apartment a block from the Senate so he could be as near to his work as possible.

His autocratic style offended some senators. Some thought him excessively blunt and insensitive. "He was and is a domineering, browbeating boss who prefers ball bats to soft soap," writer Archibald MacLeish concluded in 1937.[6] In debate he could be terrifying. He would grow red in the face, pound his desk, gesture wildly, and stomp his feet. Raising his raspy voice to a bull-like bellow, he would pummel his opponents with scorn, ridicule, and insult. Richard L. Riedel, a Senate press gallery attendant in the 1920s and 1930s, recalled:

When [Robinson] would go into one of his rages, it took little imagination to see fire and smoke rolling out of his mouth like some fierce dragon. Even when he kidded me, he spoke in loud gasps while puffing at his cigar. Robinson could make senators and everyone in his presence quake by the burning fire in his eyes, the baring of his teeth as he ground out his words, and the clenching of his mighty fists as he beat on the desk before him.[7]

"Scrappy Joe," as the press called him, was easily riled. He nearly came to blows with Senator Robert M. La Follette, Sr., in 1917, and he had similar clashes with Republican Porter McCumber in 1922 and Democrats Thomas Heflin in 1928 and Huey Long in 1935. In or out of the Senate, he was not a man to trifle with. His response to a guard who questioned his credentials at the 1920 Democratic National Convention was a punch in the face. A prominent Washington physician who heckled him during a round of golf at the Chevy Chase Country Club was similarly rewarded.

There seemed to be two Joe Robinsons. He was a fearsome taskmaster when there was Senate business to perform. At other times, he overflowed with warmth and bonhomie so genuine that he never lacked loyal and admiring friends. Those who saw him in these off-hours invariably described him as a man of friendly, almost gentle, disposition. On a fishing trip or in the back offices of the Capitol, his colleagues often witnessed the transformation. The single-minded floor leader, intent on steamrolling the Senate into submission, would give way to a warm and genial friend. "He drew men to him," said an acquaintance.[8]

His friendships extended across party lines and tended to endure. Several intimate associates from his early years in Congress—such as Democrats Carter Glass of Virginia, Pat Harrison of Mississippi, Key Pittman of Nevada, and Henry F. Ashurst of Arizona—ultimately attained great power in the Senate. He was on equally good terms with many Republicans, including Majority Leader (and, later, vice president) Charles Curtis of Kansas, Senator David Reed of Pennsylvania, and Vice President Charles G. Dawes of Illinois. Those friendships formed an important bipartisan network of support that Robinson could tap whenever he needed political help.

Ewilda "Billie" Robinson, his wife of forty-one years, was his closest companion and confidante. A wise, shy woman, she was the one soothing influence in his life. He trusted her judgment as he did no other's and missed her profoundly when they were apart. It was to her that Robinson's doctors and colleagues reported when they worried about the effects of stress and overwork on her husband's health. Perpetually at his side, Billie was his adviser, protector, and confessor. Aside from occasional foreign travel between sessions and visits to the lavish estates and hunting lodges of wealthy friends, the childless couple lived a Spartan life in their cramped Capitol Hill apartment.

Robinson's health first became a concern around 1930, when doctors found that he suffered from heart disease. They urged him to lighten his responsibilities, avoid stress, and generally learn to relax. There is no evidence that he complied, although in his personal letters, which provide the only real clues to his private thoughts, he began to complain about his "impossible" duties and to speak freely of his yearning to be out of the political arena. He informed friends of his long-cherished desire to serve on the Supreme Court. The wish seemed less a matter of fulfilling a life-long ambition than of seeking escape from a job that was sapping his life. As for changing his work habits, his makeup simply would not allow it.

Roots of a Southern Politician

His belief in the value of hard work, his independence, his sense of duty, and his legendary tenacity he owed largely to his pioneer heritage. His father, James Robinson, was a country physician and sometime Baptist minister who in 1844 settled near Lonoke in central Arkansas and married Matilda Swaim. The couple built a two-room log cabin, cleared two hundred acres, planted an apple orchard, and raised ten children, of which Joseph, born in 1872, was the ninth.[9]

Attending rural schools that were open three months a year, Joe Robinson accumulated only forty-six months of formal education, including college. He was, however, an insatiable reader. He and his brother Edward devoured most of the several hundred books in his father's unusually large personal library. The brothers, as they plowed fields, honed their memories and speaking abilities by reciting passages from their reading.[10] At seventeen, he was certified to teach first grade in the local schools. Two years of teaching provided him enough money for his tuition at the University of Arkansas. After two years at the university, he returned to Lonoke to read for the law. In 1895 he was elected to the state assembly, becoming, at age twenty-two, the state's youngest legislator. The next year, after attending one summer session of law school at the University of Virginia, he was admitted to the Arkansas bar. That December, he married Ewilda Gertrude Miller.[11]

Arkansas was roiling with discontent and rural radicalism at the time Robinson entered politics. Some thirty years after the Civil War, divisiveness and devastation lingered. A generation of southerners who, like Robinson, came of age in that period had been marked by the bitter war and harsh Reconstruction. Its social structure shattered, its agricultural economy destroyed, the state was prostrate. Radical populism and other splinter movements rose and flourished; no state came closer to social revolt.[12] The Republican party, which ruled after the war, sank temporarily to insignificance in the post-Reconstruction era. For most voters, there remained only the Democrats. And for candidates running under the party's banner, government austerity, a balanced budget, and the concept of individual responsibility became obsessions.[13] It was in such a climate that Joe Robinson declared himself a committed Democrat.

In 1902, having gained statewide acclaim as a criminal lawyer with a flair for courtroom oratory, Robinson won election to Congress as representative of Arkansas's Sixth Congressional District. In Congress, he embraced progressive ideas first advocated by the Populists and ultimately by his own party. Those included free public education, regulation of the trusts, protection of public lands, a federal income tax, and electoral reform. "Progress is not achieved by facing backwards," he reminded voters. Still, on issues of fiscal policy and states' rights, including his state's own enforcement of racial segregation, he remained a staunch conservative.

Overall, Robinson's ten years in the House of Representatives were undistinguished. He focused largely on his state's agricultural interests, and although his popularity grew in Arkansas, Washington hardly noticed him. He bounced from one committee to another, and from one issue to another, seemingly unable to escape his anonymity as a House member. Eventually, he began to seek a forum more suited to his talents— one with more opportunities for personal expression and involvement in shaping great events. Two offices appealed to him: the U.S. Senate and the governorship. He preferred the Senate, but with popular incumbents firmly entrenched in both of the Arkansas seats, that avenue seemed closed.

Not for long. In 1912, while still in Congress, he entered the race for governor and won. The following January, Senator Jeff Davis died, creating a vacancy in the office Robinson had coveted all along. The legislature offered the job to the newly inaugurated governor. Robinson accepted eagerly, thus earning the rare distinction of having held three major titles—representative, governor, and senator-elect—all within fourteen days. He also was the last U.S. senator to be elected by a state legislature.

Robinson immediately found a home in the imperious Senate, where he was determined to excel and—this time—to be noticed. With his massive chest thrust out and shoulders thrown back—attaining the most from his five-foot, ten-inch frame—he would stride like a grand panjandrum up and down Senate corridors. Bright, stylish attire, complete with spats and a bamboo cane, set him apart from his somberly dressed colleagues. In summer, he sauntered around the Capitol in a white-linen suit.[14]

He was, upon reaching the Senate, already an accomplished speaker and debater. A master of what one journalist described as the "knock-em down and stomp-em" school of oratory, he relished the rough-and-tumble of Senate debate. He neither gave nor expected mercy. According to one observer, he presented "a maniacal visage" as he paced up and down the aisle near his desk, his voice roaring, arms flailing, fists slamming on desk tops without warning, feet stomping the floor for emphasis, accusing fingers jabbing the air or pulling at his hair. He had a comical habit of hitching up his trousers every few minutes as he spoke. His indignation mounting, "his shirt would slip up and his belt line down and—yank!—up would come the trousers," recalled a journalist of the period.[15] Like gauges registering his emotion, his voice would gradually rise to a deafening shout and his face would grow increasingly red and taut until it seemed as though his large round head would burst.

In his quest for recognition, Robinson owed much to a single speech, which in 1917 lifted him to national prominence. His remarks were directed at Senator La Follette, who for weeks had railed against American involvement in war with Germany. When La Follette unleashed a scathing attack on the government itself, Robinson no longer could contain his outrage. "You had the right to question the war if your honest judgment doubted it," he roared, pointing at the bushy-headed isolationist. "But when Congress declared war, then . . . by God, you ought to stand here and support the flag and the President." He accused La Follette of "going about the country stirring sedition, gathering the Socialists and discontented elements, and seeking to influence them against your flag, your country, and your President," concluding: "If I entertained your sentiments, I would apply to the Kaiser for a seat on the Bundesrath." La Follette, enraged by the aspersions on his patriotism, had to be restrained from assaulting Robinson, who taunted him with offers to "settle it outside."[16]

His encounter with La Follette gave Robinson the stature he craved. Discovered at last by the press, he would never again be just another senator. He was "Scrappy Joe"—the president's defender—hailed in headlines as "THE MAN WHO BRANDED LA FOLLETTE."[17] His performance, wrote journalist Mark Sullivan, "embraced that combination of convincing argument and emotional appeal which fulfills the modern definition of good oratory. . . . It might almost be called a case of making a considerable reputation with a single speech."[18]

Robinson staunchly supported Woodrow Wilson's policies even as other Democrats faltered. Cited by Wilson's biographer as one of the "young progressive group" on whom Wilson depended, he championed the Keating-Owen Child Labor Act and worked to enact bills to regulate railroads and other key industries.[19] In foreign affairs, he led the Senate fight to rearm merchant ships, voted to declare war on Germany, and was an indispensable defender of Wilson's handling of the war. After the armistice in 1918, he fought for ratification of the Versailles Treaty.[20] Wilson, in rare praise, called his steadfast ally the "moral and intellectual leader of the Senate."

Weary of war and its shortages and frightened by the looming specter of world socialism, the voters in 1918 returned the Republicans to power in both the House and Senate. For Democrats, the crushing defeat at the polls was the beginning of a long season of defensive politics as Congress's minority party.

In 1920, Robinson was named permanent chairman of the Democratic National Convention—partly to reward his courage and effectiveness in defending the Wilson administration. The convention was deadlocked through forty-four ballots, and chairing it proved particularly complex and grueling. Robinson performed flawlessly. He had clearly "won his spurs," said the New York Times, citing "the forceful manner in which he conducted the sessions during the long and tiresome grind."[21] The New York Morning Telegraph dubbed Robinson "the best parliamentarian in the United States."[22] He would preside over his party's conventions twice more, in 1928 and 1936.

When Oscar W. Underwood of Alabama stepped down as Senate Democratic leader at the end of the 1922 session, Robinson saw the event as an opportunity. It was widely assumed that Underwood's successor would be Furnifold M. Simmons of North Carolina. Simmons, at sixty-eight the oldest Senate Democrat, had long coveted the job as the capstone of his career. With promises of support from more than half of the Senate's forty-three Democrats, he expected no opposition when his party caucused to pick a new leader the following March. But he had not taken into account the soaring ambition of Arkansas's senior senator, who at fifty was just hitting his stride.

Robinson announced in December that he, too, would seek the post. For the next ten weeks, while Simmons remained at home confident of victory, Robinson and his allies conducted a sophisticated, determined campaign against long odds. Success required them to garner the support of nearly all uncommitted senators and to pry away several votes already pledged to Simmons.

Promising a break with the past, the Arkansan described his vision of leadership. He would render constructive service and not "pursue a mere policy of negation." He would mobilize a "fighting force" of Senate Democrats "that will be fully informed on every important issue arising, so that the party viewpoint on political matters may be fully and fairly set forth." He would provide Senate Democrats with more information, better party coordination, and more consultation on the formation of policy than ever before. "While it is realized that the utmost freedom of individual action should be preserved," Robinson vowed, "a constant effort will be made to foster a policy of unity and harmony among Democrats in the Senate, and to this end frequent conferences will be held." In an attempt to allay concerns about his temper, Robinson said his tenure would be one of "aggressiveness without rashness, constructively helpful and fair."[23]

Fourteen senators, well short of the twenty-two he needed, immediately promised their support. Some dozen others, including several incoming freshmen, declined commitment to either candidate. Robinson assumed that at least half of them were secretly pledged to Simmons. The remaining Democrats, including most of the southerners, informed Robinson that their support of Simmons was unshakable.

Robinson knew that his only hope would be an all-out assault on Simmons's seemingly impenetrable support base. Shortly before Christmas, he met to discuss strategy with a small group of supporters, including senators Henry F. Ashurst of Arizona, Edwin S. Broussard of Louisiana, Thaddeus H. Caraway of Arkansas, Pat Harrison of Mississippi, Key Pittman of Nevada, and Thomas J. Walsh of Montana. Several of his Republican friends, although not at the meeting, also sought ways to help him.

The group enlisted friends and patronage appointees around the country to help sway their own Democratic senators toward Robinson. They described Simmons as representing "the old conservative sentiment" and Robinson as "young, progressive, capable, and brilliant."[24] Robinson personally targeted four senators from neighboring states—Kenneth D. McKellar of Tennessee, Joseph E. Ransdell of Louisiana, Robert L. Owen of Oklahoma, and newly elected Earle B. Mayfield of Texas. All were publicly unattached to either candidate, although Robinson believed at least two—McKellar and Ransdell—were secretly pledged to Simmons.

That Mayfield had been widely denounced for his activities with the then-resurgent Ku Klux Klan did not deter Robinson. Initiating a cordial correspondence, he offered to help the Texan get off to a good start in the Senate. Whether they struck a deal is unclear. They did, in any case, have a private meeting after which Mayfield announced his support of Robinson, who later opposed efforts to bar Mayfield from the Senate.[25]

Other incoming senators received "courtesy" visits from Robinson's Senate friends. These veterans typically would offer to intercede with the next Democratic leader, whoever he might be, to help the new member obtain a valuable committee assignment, a good seat in the chamber, and a desirable suite of offices. They would not solicit votes. But Robinson's close association with the visiting senator would be mentioned, implying a link between the outcome of the leadership race and the newcomer's future well-being.

Senator-elect William C. Bruce, of Maryland, was visited by his state's senior senator, Ovington E. Weller, a Republican. Weller offered to speak to the next Democratic leader about Bruce's committee preference, which, Bruce told him, was Interstate Commerce. Bruce later described the meeting in a letter to Robinson:

While he [Weller] did not say a single word with a view to influencing my vote for the minority leadership, he nevertheless spoke of your abilities in terms which, if I had not already decided to vote for you, would have distinctly confirmed the favorable impression that I had previously formed of your claims to the position.

Bruce then tried to raise the stakes, informing Robinson that his real preference was Foreign Relations, a choice committee rarely open to junior senators. He would be grateful, he said, for any help Robinson could provide. Robinson responded, "It will afford me pleasure to look after your committee assignments." He foresaw "no difficulty" in placing Bruce on Interstate Commerce and added, "It is not impossible that we may be able to give you a place on Foreign Relations." The next day, Bruce declared his support of Robinson.[26]

Robinson induced E. H. "Boss" Crump, of Shelby County, Tennessee, to apply pressure on Senator McKellar; reluctantly, McKellar came around to Robinson. So did Senator Ransdell, upon whom descended hundreds of letters in Robinson's behalf, including an appeal from the Roman Catholic bishop of Little Rock, whose influence extended to heavily Catholic Louisiana.[27] Caravans of pro-Robinson Arkansans invaded Oklahoma to organize grass-roots pressure on Senator Owen, who soon joined Robinson's growing list of supporters.

Finally, Simmons saw the hopelessness of his candidacy. While continuing to claim the support of "more than half the members of the present Senate" as well as "other assurances" that justified his feeling "most hopeful of success," he withdrew from the race, citing poor health and a desire for party harmony.[28]

On March 4, 1923, Robinson was elevated to the position that he had fought so vehemently to gain and that he was destined to hold for the next fourteen years. Complaints about his combativeness and his failure to keep his promise of broad participation in party decision making would surface from time to time, but he would never have to face another contested race for the leadership.

Still in the minority after the 1922 elections, the Senate Democrats over which Robinson took command in 1923 were tired and dispirited. Americans, enjoying a period of peace and overall prosperity, were mostly content with their Republican-controlled government. The Wilson administration had been discredited. Congress and the presidency, it seemed, would remain under Republican rule for many years.

Senator Underwood's passive leadership had left Senate Democrats in disarray. A popular conservative whose heart belonged to the House, where he had served meritoriously before coming to the Senate, the Alabamian had not tried to mold his charges into an effective opposition force. Party discipline, as well as reward, had all but disappeared. Senior Democrats, mostly southern career politicians, held tenaciously to seats on three or more major committees. Senators of low seniority were left with less desirable assignments. Few Senate Democrats found consolation in the fact that the Republicans were equally unsettled under their leader, Henry Cabot Lodge of Massachusetts, who often could not control even the procedures of the Senate.[29]

Robinson moved quickly to bring discipline to the Democratic ranks, starting with the sensitive issue of committee assignments. In his bid for leadership, he arguably had abused the assignment process by trading choice assignments for votes. Now, he told colleagues, it was imperative to reform the whole committee-assignment procedure. The new Democratic leader knew, of course, the importance of good committee assignments. He also believed that the assignment process had been handled casually and arbitrarily in the past. He himself had waited years before getting a seat on the Committee on Foreign Relations only to be bumped from the committee after the 1918 elections, just as he was gaining stature as an internationalist. Although he later regained his committee seat, his own experiences left him bitter.[30]

Through the Democratic Steering Committee, which he controlled, Robinson made clear his intention to be scrupulously fair in parceling out committee assignments. He upset a few old bulls with his decree that no senator would have first rank on more than one important committee.[31] Assuming personal responsibility—the Steering Committee, with rare exception, merely ratifying his decisions—Robinson transformed the biennial scramble for a few committee crumbs into a ritual of fairness.[32] Senators seeking special favor were given a courteous but firm rebuff. Any attempt to bring pressure only made him bristle. He would not budge even for Bernard Baruch, his intimate friend and benefactor, who sought, as a personal favor, the appointment of New York's Robert F. Wagner to the Committee on Appropriations.[33] And when freshman Burton K. Wheeler of Montana publicly and petulantly complained about his failure to get on the committee of his choice, Robinson never forgave him.[34]

He also personally divvied up patronage, deciding not only which Democratic senators could make patronage appointments but also taking pains to see that such appointees—even pages and folding-room workers—met his standards. He once fired a teen-aged page who in his opinion was too tall for his age.

He created a tightly monitored, totally loyal leadership staff. Edwin A. Halsey, secretary to the minority, was a smart, obsequious operator with an encyclopedic knowledge of the senators. He spent hours each day drifting around the Senate floor, chatting with one senator after another, ingratiating himself while soaking up all the day's gossip, which he dutifully reported to Robinson. Later, when the Democrats returned to power and Halsey was promoted to Senate secretary, he became even more valuable to the Democratic leader. Leslie Biffle, an Arkansan, moved into Halsey's old slot as majority secretary. At his desk by the chamber door, Biffle stood in constant readiness to assist Robinson in any assignment, from running his messages to briefing him on the latest news and rumors. A nose counter of fabled accuracy, Biffle was often the first to know how senators were going to vote on a current issue.[35]

Halsey's office, just off the Senate floor, became a hangout for Robinson and his Democratic cronies in 1933. From there the leadership dispensed campaign money, liquor, food, cigars, and advice. The office not only had the "well," where senators could always get a shot of whiskey, but also the safe. The safe held the cash, collected from wealthy contributors, which the leadership doled out to Democratic senators for their campaigns. Halsey's office also was a center of communications, especially between the legislative and executive branches. When Robinson conferred with the president, Halsey's phone booth with a direct line to the White House accorded him privacy and immediate access.[36]

Although he often complained of being swamped by trivialities, Robinson refused to share his responsibilities. Perhaps a Senate leader's most demanding task is to protect the interests of his party and its individual senators. In a loosely governed body like the Senate, where anything can happen, constant vigilance is required. Robinson believed he was the sole guardian of Democratic interests on the Senate floor. His daily practice, from which he rarely varied, was to remain on the floor from the morning hour to the closing gavel. Hour after hour he would sit, watching and waiting, on the off chance a senator might try to slip a bill, resolution, or motion through the Senate in a manner that violated his party's or another senator's rights. Darrell St. Claire, former assistant secretary of the Senate, remembered Robinson sitting in the chamber "afternoon after afternoon and just by his very presence commanding people to keep still and get on with it."[37]

Relegated to defensive tactics in the 1920s, the Democratic minority under Robinson focused largely on amending Republican legislation and on exposing scandal and corruption in the Harding and Coolidge administrations. Robinson's daily revelations of corruption uncovered by a Democratic-led investigation of oil leases at the Teapot Dome storage facility helped to keep that scandal of the Harding administration alive for months.[38]

Robinson's notion of a minority party's responsibility differed from that of some of his Democratic colleagues. He rejected the idea that a minority party's duty was to oppose the majority, as he put it, "for the sake of opposition." He agreed with many Republican bills and even supported them, although this rankled those in his own party who thought he lacked partisan zeal. Similarly, his friendship with President Coolidge did not sit well with some Democrats. Once, after having tried for months to get Senate confirmation of a particular appointment, Coolidge turned to Robinson for help. The minority leader got the appointment approved in fifteen minutes, prompting Coolidge to profess: "I guess I've been dealing with the wrong leader."

Progressive Republican George Norris accused Robinson of voting "contrary to his party's policies" when he joined with the Coolidge administration to oppose government operation of the Muscle Shoals properties in 1928. Norris, sponsor of the massive regional development plan, also accused Coolidge of aiding dishonest business interests seeking to operate the project. "I don't have to take my definition of a Democrat from 'grumbling George'," Robinson fired back. Defending Coolidge, he added, "If being a Democrat means that I must give myself and feeble powers to an unjust assault upon a political adversary, then I am not a Democrat."[39]

Robinson despised senators who used the Senate as a forum for demagoguery. His dressing down of Alabama Democrat Thomas Heflin in 1928 remains one of the great confrontations in the body's history. Heflin, given to frequent diatribes against the Roman Catholic church, had accused the church and Democratic presidential hopeful Alfred E. Smith, a Catholic, of assisting in the dissemination of some forged documents linking several senators, including Heflin, to corruption. Robinson, a member of a special panel investigating the forgeries, replied that Catholics had nothing to do with the matter. He defended Smith and the principle that religious affiliation should never be a disqualification for high office. Heflin then challenged Robinson's impartiality and his right to serve as the Democratic leader. A barrage of charges and countercharges followed.

"I heard the Senator from Alabama a dozen times during the last year make what he calls his anti-Catholic speech," Robinson roared at one point. "I have heard him denounce the Catholic Church and the Pope of Rome and the cardinal and the bishop and the priest and the nun until I am sick and tired of it, as a Democrat."

Snapped Heflin: "I would like to have the senator make that speech in Arkansas."

"I will make that speech in Arkansas, and I will make it in Alabama, too," thundered Robinson.

"Yes, and if you do, they will tar and feather you," Heflin rejoined.[40]

Robinson interpreted Heflin's attack as a demand for a vote of confidence. The next day, caucusing Democrats affirmed their faith in the Arkansan, 35-1, with seven senators, including Heflin, not present. Park Trammell of Florida, who thought Robinson had made too much of the matter, was the lone dissenter.

Whether or not Robinson had inflated the issue, the press hailed him as a champion of religious tolerance and decency. "The Arkansan in that hour became a figure of more than state proportions," said the *New York Times*.[41] A natural choice to join New York governor Smith on the 1928 Democratic ticket, the southern Protestant legislator sailed to the vice-presidential nomination on a wave of national popularity. "Joe T. Robinson of Arkansaw got the nomination, with more Democrats agreeing than had ever agreed on any one thing in the history of the party," wrote humorist Will Rogers.[42] Thrown into a national campaign, Robinson held his own. For three months he toured the nation, addressing small-town audiences, mostly on the need for farm relief. His appeal for lower tariffs to help U.S. agriculture struck home in depressed farm areas.

But 1928 was destined to be another Republican year. In addition to the presidency, the GOP scored massive victories in both houses of Congress. Robinson accepted his party's defeat philosophically. He returned to the Senate still leader of a minority but personally stronger than ever. For the next two years, Senate Democrats would occupy a position entirely disproportionate to their party's crushing defeat. They not only enjoyed relative unity but also, as the nation plunged into its worst economic depression, gained crucial allies among Republican Progressives and independents.[43]

The long Republican domination of the House and Senate ended with the 1930 elections when voters, stunned by the Depression, turned out to repudiate the GOP at all government levels. The Republican majority in the House plunged from one hundred seats to a mere two. Before the new Congress began its work in December 1931, several House Republicans died and were replaced by Democrats—enough to swing the House back to Democratic control. The Senate, ruled by the Republicans in the previous Congress, 56-39, organized in 1931 with forty-eight Republicans, forty-seven Democrats, and one Farmer-Labor senator.

Eight of the Republicans, including Progressives George Norris and Robert M. La Follette, Jr., held views more attuned to the Democrats, voting with them on most issues. Although still minority leader, Robinson now headed a de facto Senate majority. President Hoover even suggested to Republican leaders that they allow the Democrats to organize the Senate. Republican leader James Watson of Indiana rejected the suggestion.[44]

The minority leader soon found that Hoover, like Coolidge, was a Republican he could work with. As with Coolidge, his frequent defense of the embattled president's policies drew angry criticism from many Democrats. The city of Washington nodded knowingly in 1930 when

Hoover appointed him as one of five delegates to the London Conference on Naval Limitation. The experience, a highlight of his life, awakened him to other opportunities for service. Apparently at this time he was first attracted to the idea of serving on the Supreme Court.

Senate Democrats, meanwhile, were chafing under Robinson's iron grip. Cloakroom grumbling increased over his autocratic style and his exclusion of fellow Democrats from policy, scheduling, and other party decision making. In seeking the leadership nearly a decade earlier, Robinson had promised them a voice in party affairs through frequent use of the Senate Democratic Conference. But in practice, as one critic complained, "he holds no conferences, trusts no lieutenants, and consults only himself."[45] Even his old running mate Al Smith condemned Robinson's practice of selective cooperation with the Republican administration, complaining: "He has given more aid to Herbert Hoover than any other Democrat."[46]

In 1931, Senate resentment finally overflowed when Robinson faltered at the height of a crucial partisan showdown over drought relief. Hoover favored limited relief in the form of loans to needy farmers. A Robinson-led coalition of Democrats, progressive Republicans, and independents had held out for a larger relief package in the form of grants. Hoover vowed to veto any bill that provided relief other than loans; the Democrats threatened to force Congress into special session unless Hoover relented.

Believing themselves right on principle and convinced that Hoover would yield in time, the Democrats were prepared for a long stalemate when their leader dropped a surprise "compromise" in their laps. Instead of the $25 million in grants he had originally endorsed, Robinson now presented a new proposal, which he and the White House had negotiated in private, to provide farmers $20 million in loans. Senators quickly saw this was no compromise; Hoover had prevailed. Nor did it go unnoticed that Hoover had brought in as his negotiator Harvey Couch, president of Arkansas Power & Light Co. and longtime fishing companion and adviser to the Arkansas senator.

Defending the new bill, Robinson condemned the original proposal as a "socialistic dole." He said he had preferred loans to outright grants all along, which was news to the Senate. The previous day he had defended the coalition proposal and urged colleagues to stand firm. Now, he argued, the choice was not between grants and loans, but between loans and no relief at all.

Outraged Democrats rose to denounce their leader. Even Carter Glass condemned him for "deserting the party." He compromised too soon, Glass charged, adding: "What I am objecting to is that those of us who followed his leadership . . . should now be reproached by the senator as having done something we should not have done."[47] Alben Barkley joined the attack. "We have witnessed within the last two or three days the most humiliating spectacle that could be brought about in an intelligent legislative body," he declared.[48] Robinson, his face "very red," the *New York Times* reported, replied that he had done "nothing whatever that justifies any such conclusion." Others noticed that he was so unnerved by the tongue lashing he was taking that he tried to light his cigar on the Senate floor, a violation of the Senate rules.[49] Still, when he threatened to filibuster until adjournment rather than accept a bill that included grants, his critics acquiesced to the compromise.

Although stunned by the vehemence of his colleagues' anger, Robinson saw no reason to alter his leadership style. His job was secure. There simply was no Democrat of comparable stature to take his place. "He has more influence than any senator of either party," claimed William J. Harris of Georgia. Only a handful of disgruntled Democrats, reinforced by the arrival of a new antagonist—Huey Long of Louisiana—continued to snipe at him. Using the Senate as a forum for his own agenda, Long upset Robinson's tightly managed world. He delighted in assailing political idols and in taunting the Senate leader. Accustomed to silencing pesky senators, Robinson could not fathom or control his irrepressible colleague.

The nation's hopes focused on Congress in 1932 as the lawmakers groped for answers to the deepening economic and social unrest. Congress, desperate for ideas, looked to the White House but got scant guidance. "I know there is great unhappiness and dissatisfaction, but I do not think any legislation can secure correction," a discouraged Robinson wrote in April.[50] "These are trying times," he said in May. "I am certainly giving the best I have."[51] Worn down by the constant pressure, he told another correspondent: "We have been keeping the Senate in session for 11 hours a day, and this added to three or four hours of committee and office work makes a long and tiresome day."[52] That summer Congress broke custom to remain in session through the Democratic National Convention. Most Senate Democrats attended the Chicago gathering anyway. The Senate minority leader stayed in Washington, explaining later that "it was necessary for me to be in the Senate practically all the time to watch the proceedings and to prevent snap judgments being taken."[53]

Robinson in this period was working harder than ever before. "I have never had quite so many things to do," he wrote. "The burdens of the people are constantly on my mind."[54] He skipped vacations, rebuffed friends who tried to entice him on weekends of fishing or hunting, avoided social gatherings, and ignored warnings that his political fences at home needed mending. "My duties here are so numerous and pressing that I am unable to give attention to political conditions in Arkansas," he told one worried supporter. "So far as I am concerned they may take whatever course the people will."[55]

A Loyal Warrior for the New Deal

Robinson found little reason to cheer even when the Democrats swept the November elections, winning the presidency for the first time in sixteen years and capturing control of Congress and statehouses across the nation. The election of twenty-one new Democrats in the Senate meant he would lead the majority for the first time. He thought about the intractable Depression and the difficulties ahead for the new Democratic president and Congress. The task before the incoming administration is "well-nigh overwhelming," he wrote.[56] The new president, Franklin Delano Roosevelt, had promised voters an array of innovative programs to solve the nation's problems. If they failed, it would be a Democratic failure. Robinson had just finished "the busiest and most difficult session of Congress" he had ever known. Ahead, he saw only more of the same— "greatly increased labor" and heavier responsibility in a thankless job he no longer relished.

Moreover, he was uncertain how he would fit into the new administration. It was widely known that many of the more liberal New Dealers viewed him with suspicion, having pegged him as just another ultraconservative southerner and a potential obstacle to their plans for an activist government. Shortly after the elections, the Arkansan was shaken by press reports of a New Deal plot to ease him out of the leadership. One account even named his replacement: first-term senator James F. Byrnes of South Carolina, an experienced Progressive seen as more attuned to the new administration.[57] Byrnes disavowed interest in his job, but Robinson continued to be dogged by rumors of insurrection.

If the rumors were meant to drive him into involuntary retirement, they failed. In fact, they seemed to stiffen his resolve not to be pushed aside, either in Arkansas or Washington. "I should be glad to take a rest from politics, but . . . my friends feel that I should continue for a time in public life, or in any event, not to permit myself to be crowded out by influences which constitute a combination of communism, socialism and anarchy," he told political associates in Little Rock.[58] He informed others, "I am giving no thought whatever to my own future and shall put in use every ounce of energy and intelligence I possess into the work of the Senate."[59]

Robinson—along with the rest of the country—had only a dim notion of what to expect from the new administration. In his broadly sweeping campaign speeches, the incoming president had promised bold ideas but had been vague on details.[60] Roosevelt's vagueness was unavoidable because the details were unknown even to him. In the weeks before his inauguration, his advisers made scant progress in refining concepts into viable legislative form. The Senate leader thus had reason to assume that the new president would welcome all the help he could get in developing a Democratic legislative program.

Shortly after the election, Robinson began to prepare his colleagues for their new responsibility. As minority members, the Democrats had played only a secondary role in Senate affairs. Now, they—many of them for the first time—would control the processes that determine the nation's laws. Showing a rare willingness to share authority, Robinson activated the Senate Democratic Conference and, through it, created informal task forces on the economy, agriculture credits, employment relief, general taxation, and agriculture markets. It was all to little avail because, as it turned out, whatever plans Senate Democrats had for thoughtful deliberation were soon trampled in the rush to legislate.

Americans expected the new administration to respond quickly to a multitude of problems. Those expectations became demands for action after a lame-duck session from December through February ended in failure.[61] Roosevelt's limp leadership in that period did little to bolster Robinson's confidence in him. "I am determined if possible to reach a definite understanding with the incoming President as to the important measures to be advanced and acted upon," Robinson told a friend. "Otherwise the greatest confusion will embarrass our efforts."[62]

But there was no such understanding between the White House and congressional Democrats when Roosevelt summoned the Seventy-third Congress into special session on March 9. The new president's plans remained as murky as ever. In his inaugural speech a few days earlier, he had promised only to recommend such "measures that a stricken nation in a stricken world may require" and had urged Congress's "speedy adoption" of these measures, "or such other measures as the Congress may build out if its experience and wisdom."

The Senate, returning in an atmosphere of great tension, organized under Democratic control. Robinson was elected majority leader without opposition. He chose—and the Senate Democratic Conference endorsed—his friend John Kendrick of Wyoming as assistant leader. (When Kendrick died a few months later, Alben Barkley, also handpicked by Robinson, succeeded to the post.) The Democrats went along only partly with the majority leader's attempt to reintroduce the binding caucus, a previously discredited device to compel party unity. They agreed to vote as one on the floor in accordance with the decision of a simple majority. But they agreed only after watering down Robinson's resolution to the point of making it virtually unenforceable.[63] As a result, Robinson never attempted to use this power, although from time to time he did call nonbinding caucuses to enlist support for administration programs.

Robinson still believed that the new president and Congress would work together to develop an anti-Depression program. The president, he soon learned, had no such notion. Like much of the nation at large, Roosevelt had little confidence in Congress. As he saw it, he had received a mandate to lead the nation; therefore, he alone would decide what laws were needed, and when. He would draft the bills, which Congress would enact with as little delay and interference as possible. He intended that the Speaker and the Senate majority leader should be his agents to see that Congress met its responsibilities. Given the country's dire condition and Congress's past failures to deal with it, few in either party were inclined to resist a leader of Roosevelt's confidence and determination.

On the day Congress convened, FDR submitted the New Deal's first bill—the Emergency Banking Relief Act—a measure designed to stabilize the banking system and to restore public confidence in financial institutions generally. With most banks closed to avoid further runs on their resources, armies of the unemployed roaming the streets, food riots breaking out, and a sense of national revolt growing stronger, the president demanded that Congress act without further delay. The House responded by passing the bill after only thirty-eight minutes of debate. Robinson drove the bill through the Senate that same afternoon—"an unheard of feat," said *Fortune* magazine. An hour later, the bill was handed to Roosevelt for his signature.

Other emergency measures followed in swift succession, including bills to slash federal spending, abolish Prohibition, provide credit to farmers, end the gold standard, assist home mortgagees, and, in a breath-taking example of experimental social planning, create a huge new authority to develop the Tennessee Valley. Many of the new laws were poorly drafted and based on questionable theory. All were enacted with feverish speed, prompting Will Rogers to quip, "Congress doesn't pass legislation any more; they just wave at the bills as they go by."[64]

Far from questioning any of these measures, Robinson was, in the New Deal's heady first weeks, inordinately proud of his work. Though short-lived, his enthusiasm and zest for battle returned. By April he was boasting of having secured "the passage of every bill sent down or recommended by the president in record-breaking time. No comparable achievement can be recalled with reference to promptness in legislative work since my service here." The president, he said, had his "whole-hearted cooperation, day and night."[65] The *Washington Post* noted "the absence of partisan rancor" in Robinson's "tactful management of administration measures" and allowed that "the administration is fortunate in having him for its champion."[66]

The Senate leader, ignoring doctors' warnings, drove himself to a near breakdown in the New Deal's frenetic first year. By June he could barely function. Quite possibly his life was saved by the adjournment gavel. His doctors prescribed extended rest, which he agreed to take only at Mrs. Robinson's insistence. "My rest is very beneficial, fifteen hours each day having been spent in bed," he wrote from Paris in September. "[I] am staging a physical come-back, but it is rather slower than I had looked for."[67] By year's end, he was feeling stronger, but he was still far from well.

The end of the New Deal's first year saw no easing of demands on the Senate leader. As soon as he would dispose of one list of "must pass" bills, Roosevelt and his advisers would send him a whole new list. The president kept expanding his program, complained Robinson, simply to win "the approval of groups specially interested in certain legislation. He seems determined to find something I cannot pass through the Senate."[68]

His value was underscored in 1934, when the Senate had to go it alone for a week while the majority leader attended an out-of-town funeral. In his absence, the Senate quickly bogged down. When Assistant Leader Barkley brought up a minor tax bill, senators loaded it with dozens of their pet provisions. Barkley had to lay it aside and turn to another bill. The Senate got so tangled in debate that he had to lay aside that bill as well. Soon the Senate had before it several bills and could dispose of none. Amused reporters noted that the Senate's most decisive action was a vote to recess so that senators could attend opening day of the baseball season. One *Washington Post* reporter wrote:

Whatever Senator Robinson's faults as a leader may be, it is now agreed on Capitol Hill that he gets things done. He is a veritable slave driver, keeping the Senate's nose to the grindstone when it is inclined to play or travel down bypaths. None of those left in charge of the New Deal program seem able to get the same results.[69]

Always the team player, Robinson rarely expressed his true feelings about the New Deal. Publicly, he continued to serve as the president's chief advocate in the Senate. Privately, he began telling friends of his growing unease over some of the new laws and the haste with which they were being enacted. He was particularly troubled by untested social welfare programs requiring huge expenditures and those granting extraordinary powers to the executive. His loyalty to presidents—particularly Democratic presidents—had always been strong. By 1935, those loyalties had begun to clash with his equally firm dedication to limited government and sound fiscal policy. "I wish that some way could be found to cast aside the leadership of the Senate," he told a relative.[70] His hunting companion Bernard Baruch was among those who sensed Robinson's unhappiness. "You do not have to tell me how impossible your work has become," the financier sympathized. "I think I can read what is in your heart."[71]

Robinson was not the only Democrat questioning the wisdom of much New Deal legislation. By 1936, many senior senators, including Glass of Virginia, Bailey of North Carolina, Byrd of Virginia, George of Georgia, and McAdoo of California, were in open revolt against the administration. Few doubted that Robinson, had he not been majority leader, would have been among them. One New Deal bill that Robinson pressed on the Senate seemed to sum up his dilemma—his "tragedy," political analyst Mark Sullivan called it. The measure, which would have denied taxpayers the right to seek refunds on a new processing tax in the event the tax should be found unconstitutional, was opposed as unfair legislation by the most able senators of both parties. Thirty-nine Democrats, including virtually all of Robinson's Senate friends and associates, voted against it. Yet, despite the bill's repugnance to a majority of his own party, Robinson led the fight for its enactment. "One wonders if Senator Robinson's fidelity to official duty is not carrying him rather far," wrote Sullivan, exposing to public debate a question that long troubled Robinson's colleagues. Continued Sullivan:

In the condition rapidly arising in the Senate, Robinson will be obliged to decide just what is his function as a Senate leader. Is he to be a representative of the president pressing unwilling Democrats to vote for legislation they do not believe in? Or is he to be a representative of the best thought, and the majority thought, of the Senate Democrats, telling the president courteously but clearly what legislation the Senate Democrats are willing to accept and enact?"[72]

Those were serious questions, which others would take up and debate in months ahead. But Robinson brushed them aside. With scant precedent to guide him, he had long since determined that a party leader must define his own role. He continued to serve the president not only as the New Deal's legislative advocate but also, by default, as FDR's chief Senate defender against a growing army of critics.

Among the most formidable of these critics was Louisiana's Huey Long, who had irritated Robinson and disrupted his orderly Senate schedule from the moment he arrived. Both men of strong egos, the pair had clashed bitterly in 1932 when Robinson criticized Long's maiden speech, labeling It a call for class conflict. Long had responded with a personal assault on Robinson, implying that he was controlled by utility and other interests through their employ of Robinson's law firm. "Now, I'm not saying that just because a man is being paid by the special interests, that would influence his activities as a U.S. senator—Oh, no," said Long mockingly. Explaining that he was averse to accepting favors from anyone he opposed, Long dramatically resigned from all the committees to which Robinson had assigned him. Robinson angrily denied Long's accusations, claiming that he no longer practiced law and shared none of his firm's income from special-interest clients.[73] Still, Long had drawn blood, and Robinson, who quietly quit his firm a few months later, longed to even the score.

The feud peaked in 1935 in a furious battle of words that began when Long launched a particularly scathing assault on Roosevelt's chief political adviser and postmaster general, James A. Farley. Earlier, Long had charged widespread corruption in Farley's Post Office Department. Long now told the Senate he had information that Farley's resignation was imminent, whereupon Robinson rushed from the chamber, called the White House, and returned to report that Long's information was wrong. What was *his* source of information, Long asked. "The President of the United States!" shouted Robinson, slamming his fist on his desk. "The source is often mistaken," Long sneered. Robinson then strode down the aisle, roaring: "It is time for the Senate to put the Louisianian in his proper place," his clenched fist inches from Long's face. "A fight might have occurred if [Vice President] Garner had not shouted an order to Huey to take his seat," wrote Long's biographer, T. Harry Williams.[74] The encounter ended with Long's repeating his oft-stated threat to campaign in Arkansas against Robinson's reelection in 1936.

Henceforth, the majority leader wrestled with his slippery opponent mostly behind the scenes. To combat Long's one-man filibuster in opposition to extension of the National Recovery Administration, Robinson invoked a seldom-used rule that a senator yielding the floor twice for quorum calls could not regain it on the same legislative day. He appointed other senators to object whenever Long made even the simplest unanimous-consent request. Finally, after he had spoken for fifteen and a half hours, with two ten-minute interruptions for quorum calls, Long was forced by a call of nature to yield the floor. It was Long's last big performance in Washington. Two months later, the colorful agitator was gunned down in Baton Rouge by a disgruntled constituent.

FDR's Reelection and the Court-packing Bill

Any doubts about Roosevelt's popularity with the voters were resolved with his resounding reelection to a second term in November 1936. With the landslide came an overwhelmingly Democratic Congress. A gain of five Democrats gave the party nearly a four-to-one majority in the Senate. Robinson, noting that the Republican opposition was moribund and that most of the New Deal agenda was already in place, looked forward to a relatively light year in 1937. "Although we have done much in helping the 'forgotten man,' " he said at midyear, "I think we have now reached the stage where some of the measures which we adopted because of necessity may be safely abandoned."[75]

He had always expressed his views frankly with the president. His frequent warnings about the danger of a runaway deficit made him an irritant to some of the president's advisers. Roosevelt would hear him out—a thin smile across his face, his huge head tilted upward—and then take whatever course he had already chosen. The senator and the president, despite FDR's early doubts, worked well together in planning legislative tactics. Typical of their informality was Roosevelt's request for his help in prying an acceptable neutrality bill out of Chairman Key Pittman's

Foreign Relations Committee. "I hope you can persuade Key to yield just as far as possible to the House bill," the president wrote. "I really believe a word from you to Key would help."[76] Roosevelt respected Robinson for his ability to deliver; he knew that sooner or later he would have to reward the majority leader. But he was not interested in Robinson's views on matters of policy.

In April 1937, Robinson had his first significant public disagreement with the White House. He balked when FDR asked Congress for "discretionary" power to cut up to 15 percent from the government's total appropriation—the step that would have given the president power usually reserved for Congress. He supported instead Senator Byrnes's alternative proposal for an across-the-board 10 percent cut in appropriations. That month he also joined Vice President John Garner in urging the president to condemn the sit-down strikes that were spreading epidemically across the nation. FDR refused. Instead he asked the majority leader to oppose an anti-sit-down-strike bill then before the Senate. Robinson dutifully went through the motions, "grinning," the press noted, as his efforts were repeatedly frustrated.[77]

Shortly thereafter came Robinson's third and most significant break with the president. It occurred over an amendment, which Roosevelt opposed and Robinson favored, that would have required states and cities to share the cost of relief programs. This time, Robinson refused to lead the opposition; Assistant Leader Barkley had to take over and beat back the measure.[78] Robinson's message was unmistakable: one way or another, his years of unswerving allegiance to the president were coming to an end. He would do the president's bidding one more time. Only this time the stakes would include something for himself.

Hanging ominously over the 1937 session was a controversy that challenged Congress and stirred its emotions as few issues ever had. This was Roosevelt's audacious attempt to "reform" the Supreme Court, which he saw as the last resistance to his crusade against economic and social injustice. By asking Congress to expand the Court, thus allowing the president to neutralize its conservative majority through his appointment of additional liberal justices, Roosevelt tampered with hallowed constitutional principles. He also demanded of his supporters a leap of faith, which they ultimately could not make. Today the Court-packing attempt is viewed as one of the great blunders in American politics, an episode that not only sullied the reputation of a highly popular president but also tragically ended one of the most forceful and effective Senate leaderships in history.

Roosevelt's problems with the Court began with its invalidation in 1935 of the National Industrial Recovery Act, viewed at the time of its passage as the cornerstone of the New Deal. The justices said that Congress in enacting the law had unconstitutionally delegated legislative powers to the executive.[79] The decision, the first of many anti–New Deal rulings over the next eighteen months, upset a balance previously existing between liberals and conservatives on the nine-member Court. Four justices usually had leaned to a liberal interpretation of the Constitution while four had taken consistently conservative positions, with Justice Owen J. Roberts often providing the swing vote.

A string of decisions followed, negating key provisions of the Agricultural Adjustment Act and Guffey Coal Conservation Act, as well as undoing programs to raise wages, reduce work hours, abolish child labor, and eliminate unfair trade practices. When New York's minimum-wage law fell, critics said it meant that no government—federal, state, or local— could act against the nation's social and economic ills.[80] Each decision took the Court further from the mainstream of public opinion and heightened public condemnation of the "nine old men"—six justices were seventy or older—who formed the nation's highest tribunal.

Roosevelt, convinced that the Court had to be liberalized, at first favored a constitutional amendment. Leading members of Congress, including Robinson and Speaker William Bankhead, sponsored such amendments in various versions. Ultimately, however, FDR concluded that the fault lay not with the Constitution but with the Court itself.[81]

In developing his concept into a viable legislative plan, Roosevelt consulted only his attorney general, Homer S. Cummings. This was to be his "delightful little secret" to be sprung on Congress when he was ready. Consultation with congressional leaders, he felt, would be counterproductive. "They would leak it to the press," he told Farley. After all, he had just won a huge mandate from the voters, which, by all rights, should have silenced his critics and virtually assured Congress's continued subservience to him. Among the many miscalculations in the historic fight to follow, Roosevelt's mischievous exclusion of Congress on this issue would prove the most costly.

Summoning congressional leaders to the White House on February 5, Roosevelt informed them that within the hour he would send to Capitol

Hill his plan to reorganize and "vitalize" the judiciary. Summarizing his forthcoming message to Congress, he declared that the federal courts were overworked. Judges were performing to capacity but still could not keep up with the flow of cases. On the High Court, part of the problem lay in the capacity of the judges themselves, raising, he said, "the question of aged or infirm judges—a subject of delicacy and yet one which requires frank discussion."[82]

Cummings explained the plan's details: whenever a justice who had served on the court at least ten years did not resign or retire after turning age seventy, the president might add a new justice to the bench. He could appoint as many as six new justices to the Supreme Court and four new judges to lower courts. The plan, breathtakingly bold in its premise, was presented not as a political effort to pack the Court with liberals but as an effort to improve legal efficiency.

Congressional leaders, who had listened in stunned silence, were dismayed. Most agreed with Vice President Garner's conclusion that "before that law comes back here for the Boss's signature, many, many moons will pass."[83] Despite his own misgivings about the plan, the insulting secrecy of its preparation, and his dread of yet another divisive fight in Congress, Robinson held his tongue. Through bitter months of controversy, he never wavered in his defense of Roosevelt's motive and method for enlarging the Court.

The Court plan, as Robinson had feared, badly split the Democrats. Bitterness became so pervasive in the House that White House strategists decided to press for the measure's passage first in the Senate. Supporters hoped that, in time, House emotions would subside. But even as Robinson pondered the problem of where he would find the votes to pass the bill, the Supreme Court on April 12 abruptly changed the nature of the fight. It capitulated to the New Deal. In a surprise decision the judges upheld the Wagner National Labor Relations Act. Most observers, noting the Court's inclination to rule that the federal government had no jurisdiction in industrial labor matters, had written off the Wagner Act as doomed. Instead the Court said the interstate commerce clause protected the act. Critics of the Court said the justices had acted to fend off self-destruction. The decision's broader meaning was clear: the conservative majority had been broken and FDR's program would go forward.[84] It was anticlimactic when the Court subsequently upheld the Social Security Act, and, on May 18, conservative justice Willis Van Devanter announced his retirement to make way for a Roosevelt replacement. Justice Roberts's swing back to the left gave the New Deal a 5-4 majority on the Court; Van Devanter's resignation would mean a 6-3 New Deal majority. The president's reasons for packing the Court were now less convincing than ever.

Yet FDR rejected the advice of Robinson and others urging him to abandon the fight or at least to lower his sights. Earlier, when Robinson reported that he could muster only about forty votes for the original bill but could probably round up a majority for a modified bill, Roosevelt said he was too pessimistic and told him to try harder. The majority leader reluctantly resumed his task. "It is my intention to work out the judgeship matter and get rid of it," he wrote.[85]

Ironically, Van Devanter's resignation thrust Robinson himself into the heart of the controversy. For years, the Democratic leader had openly discussed his wish to serve on the Court. Briefly in 1930 he thought Hoover might so honor him, although Hoover had never encouraged such notions. Roosevelt, however, had given Robinson ample reason to believe that he would be this president's choice to fill the first available Court vacancy. "Everybody connected with the administration is very strong for his appointment," Jim Farley wrote in his diary on May 20.[86] The whole Senate believed the president owed Robinson the appointment. With unusual unity, Republicans and Democrats alike warned FDR that this was one promise he had better keep if he expected future Senate coop-eration. Roosevelt, while continuing to send Robinson positive signals, refused to discuss the vacancy as long as the Court-expansion issue re-mained unresolved.

On the day Van Devanter resigned, the Senate Judiciary Committee voted to send the Court bill to the Senate floor with a recommendation that it not pass. "It is a measure which should be so emphatically rejected that its parallel will never again be presented to the free representatives of the free people of America," the committee concluded in its stinging report.[87] Meanwhile, Les Biffle's poll of Senate Democrats left no doubt that the bill, as written, was doomed. White House lobbyist Thomas Corcoran had reached the same conclusion, as had Farley and other astute vote counters in the president's camp. Yet even after Robinson, Corcoran, and Farley conspired to have James Roosevelt explain the hopelessness of the situation to his father, the president continued to insist that he could win in a showdown.[88]

Roosevelt had his reasons for standing firm. For one thing, his pride was at stake; he could not surrender without losing face. Moreover, Congress had almost always acquiesced to his requests, and he continued to believe it would do so again. The president had another reason not to abandon the fight: he had to appoint Robinson to the Court, which would mock his whole argument that the justices were too old and too conservative for the times. Robinson was sixty-five and, in the minds of most Americans, a conservative. Roosevelt felt he had to appoint a second justice—a younger liberal—to make the appointment palatable to his followers. Above all, he hated the idea of losing Robinson in the Senate.

Finally, in early June, Robinson again met with the president. He reported that the Supreme Court controversy had divided Senate Democrats and spawned dangerous ideological and regional coalitions that could threaten other bills on the administration's agenda. Again, he urged Roosevelt to modify his proposal. His arguments, at last, struck home. The president agreed that compromise was the only answer. He told Robinson to take the best deal he could get on a modified bill. Deciding to bring the matter to a head in the Senate on July 5, the majority leader wrote, "I dread the long hours and worrisome debate."[89]

Robinson picked as the administration's substitute bill a sharply diluted version of the original plan. It provided that when a justice reached seventy-five—not seventy, as originally envisioned—the president could appoint an additional justice but could make only one such appointment a year. With four justices already over seventy-five years of age, Roosevelt would have an immediate appointment and a second one in January.

With his own nomination to the Court on the line, the Senate leader began a personal crusade for the scaled-down bill. He asked senators to support the substitute not on its merits but on the strength of old friendships and political favors. His colleagues understood the bill's importance. They knew that the president might renege on his obligation to Robinson unless he could name a liberal to the Court simultaneously. On the eve of the debate, Les Biffle's final canvas showed forty senators for the measure, forty against, sixteen undeclared.

What worried proponents was not a lack of votes. Robinson was confident, and the opposition agreed, that he had a slim majority. His problem was a threatened filibuster. He knew that he could not muster the two-thirds majority necessary to cut off a filibuster. And Senator Wheeler, leader of an ad hoc coalition of liberals and southern conservatives opposed to the plan, had vowed to prevent a vote on the bill even if it meant keeping the Senate in session "until October."

The opening of the debate found Robinson in rare form. A lifetime of parliamentary and forensic experience prepared him for the event, which the press had labeled the challenge of his career. He was, for a change, feeling strong and optimistic. A stringent diet of buttermilk had cut his weight, giving him a more vigorous appearance. The fatigue and discomfort, which had bothered him intermittently, had lately subsided. Like days of old, he came to the floor well prepared and itching for a fight.

His strategy, aimed at thwarting the impending filibuster, depended on his getting favorable rulings on several points of order. Vice President Garner, disgusted with Roosevelt and the Court fight, had gone home to Texas and would be unavailable to make the necessary rulings. But the bill's supporters were in luck. In Garner's absence, the presiding officer would be Senate president pro tempore Key Pittman, one of Robinson's oldest and closest friends.

Insisting that the Senate follow its rules to the letter, Robinson stated his points of order. Pittman responded with a series of rulings: (1) the entire debate, although lasting for many calendar days, would be considered as one legislative day; (2) no senator could speak more than twice on the same subject in the same legislative day; (3) no senator could interrupt another without his consent and without addressing the chair; (4) no senator could permit interruption except for a question; and (5) no other business could be transacted without unanimous consent.[90] These restrictions, while part of the Senate's rules, were seldom enforced, and many senators objected to their being applied in this instance. The majority leader stood firm. Threatening to keep the Senate in session "long days and long nights," if necessary, Robinson warned it would be "dog eat dog" if the bill's opponents tried to prolong the debate.[91]

In defending the Court plan, Robinson worked himself into the emotional lather so familiar to his colleagues. His face reddened, his body trembled, his arms flailed as he smote the opposition. This time, one of the senators, Royal S. Copeland of New York, a physician, saw reason for concern. Approaching the railing Arkansan, he whispered, "Joe, the cause isn't worth it. You're killing yourself." Robinson paused. If it came to a test of physical endurance, he growled, he was in better shape than many of the bill's opponents. Turning to Wheeler, he added, "I think I could endure it longer than the senator from Montana."[92] Wheeler disagreed. Later, as he fielded questions with humor and characteristic sarcasm, Robinson felt a fluttering sensation in his chest. "No more questions today," he said. Looking pale and ill, he uttered a final "good-by" and left the floor.

In his crisis, Robinson had been forced to fight alone. FDR, cutting his losses, had largely washed his hands of the bill, telling his Senate advocate to take any compromise. Garner had deserted him, as had other southern colleagues. Even his wife, his closest confidante, the one person who could calm him, was absent for the most important challenge of his life. A family problem had called Ewilda Robinson to Arkansas in mid June.[93] Keenly aware of the strain on her husband and apprehensive about his heart condition, she had planned to return within a week. But in Little Rock, she injured her ankle and was confined to bed as debate began on the Court bill. Only twice before had the couple been separated during a session of Congress.

In daily letters, Robinson sought to ease his wife's worries, his upbeat description of the proceedings conflicting sharply with what she read in the newspapers. Reports of ruptures in the Democratic party "are without foundation," Robinson wrote. "The temper of everyone is good," he reported subsequently, and in another letter added, "No news here of special importance." Only rarely did he betray his true feelings. "I will be very glad to see you indeed as it is lonely around the apartment without you," he wrote on July 9.[94]

On July 12, Robinson dictated his last letter to his friend Baruch. The newspapers are "exaggerating incidents in the debate," he complained. "There is no intensity of feeling, that is, no bitterness, such as I expected." He was withstanding the pressure "very well" and "feeling unusually strong," he said. He admitted, however, that with Billie gone, "I am feeling a little lonely."[95] A few hours later, the irregular heartbeats returned. Again he had to leave the chamber. Ignoring Barkley's advice to see a doctor, he rested in a chair on the Capitol portico until the feeling subsided.

The next morning, he attended the regular daily strategy session on the Court bill and later watched the debate from the cloakroom. He did not go onto the floor. That afternoon, he informed Barkley that he was going home to rest awhile. He never returned to the Capitol. The following morning, July 14, his housekeeper found his pajama-clad body face down on the floor of his apartment. On his bed was an open volume of the *Congressional Record*. Apparently, while lying in bed preparing for the next day's debate, he had suffered a severe heart attack. He had gotten up and was in the bathroom when he collapsed and died.

"He died because he was forced into battle at a time when he should have never attempted such a fight," Senator Copeland observed, speaking for many of his colleagues. Robinson's death stunned the nation and threw the Court fight into chaos. Yet Roosevelt insisted that Barkley, the new majority leader, press on. Barkley made one last attempt to push the bill through, but the senators had had enough. They sent the measure back to the Judiciary Committee for quiet burial.

Blunt and plainspoken, Robinson was seldom given to deep thought. But once, in a reflective mood, he sought to explain why he pushed himself and others so hard:

When I see a senator of international renown fall out of the ranks, hear a murmur of regret among his colleagues, and witness their closing of the mind and go forward without ever looking backward, I am impressed profoundly with the vanity of ambition and fame. Nevertheless, one must fill his place to the end by rendering the best service of which he is capable. There is, after all, sound psychology in forgetting grief and misfortune by exhausting one's energies in constant effort."[96]

That was the strict creed by which Joe Robinson lived. He was no great innovator, no great idealist, and perhaps, in the classic sense, not even a great legislator. After four decades as a lawmaker, he had his name on only one major statute. But in the art of understanding the Senate, its role, and its eccentricities, he was unsurpassed. He did more than any predecessor to define the potential of party leadership in that body. Through sheer force of personality, he drove the Senate to a level of efficiency it has seldom equaled. Hard work, unswerving loyalty, and dedication to duty were his obsessions. As long as those qualities are valued in politics, his place in history will be secure.

NOTES

1. Anon. [Ray Tucker], *The Mirrors of 1932* (New York: Brewer, Warren and Putnam, 1931), 144.
2. Robinson persuaded the Senate Democratic Conference in 1933 to resurrect the binding caucus, a leadership tool that Majority Leader John Worth Kern used frequently in 1913 and 1914. Under Kern, the binding caucus created so much ill will that it was soon abandoned. Democrats agreed to Robinson's request after adding a provision that no Democrat would be bound to vote for a bill that proved "contrary to his conscientious judgment" or violated pledges made while a candidate for office. In such form, the binding caucus was practically meaningless. See Senator Robert C. Byrd, "The Senate Democratic Conference," U.S. Congress, *Congressional Record*, August 1, 1980, 21102–21104.
3. U.S. Congress, *Congressional Record*, March 1, 1934, 8976. Cited in Betty Jane Moore, "The Majority Leader of the United States Senate: The Leader's Effectiveness as a Major Determinant in the Leadership Model" (Ph.D. diss., University of Maryland, 1986), 327.

4. See Moore, "Majority Leader," 331–332.
5. Cecil E. Weller, Jr., "Joseph Taylor Robinson and the Robinson-Patman Act," *Arkansas Historical Quarterly* (Spring 1988): 34.
6. Unsigned article by Archibald MacLeish, "The Senator from Arkansas," *Fortune,* January 1937, 88–108.
7. Richard L. Riedel, *Halls of the Mighty: My 47 Years at the Senate* (Washington, D.C., and New York: Robert B. Luce Inc., 1969), 142.
8. T. A. Huntley, *"Times'* Scribe Depicts 'Robinson I Knew'," in *Washington Times-Herald,* July 14, 1937. Papers of Joseph T. Robinson, Special Collections Division, University of Arkansas Libraries, Fayetteville, Series 1, Subseries 2, Box 7.
9. See Nevin Emil Neal, "A Biography of Joseph T. Robinson" (Ph.D. diss., University of Oklahoma, 1958), 12.
10. Ibid., 12.
11. Ibid., 95.
12. David Y. Thomas, ed., *Arkansas and Its People,* vol. 1 (New York: American Historical Society, 1930), 113–116.
13. Ibid., 170.
14. Burton K. Wheeler, with Paul F. Healy, *Yankee from the West* (Garden City, N.Y.: Doubleday, 1962), 268.
15. Huntley, *"Times'* Scribe," *Washington Times-Herald,* July 14, 1937.
16. U.S. Congress, *Congressional Record,* October 6, 1917, 7888–7893; see also *Milwaukee Journal,* July 14, 1937.
17. Unidentified newspaper article, JTR Papers, Series 1, Subseries 2, Box 7.
18. Sullivan article, *Collier's Weekly,* [n.d.] 1917, in ibid.
19. Cecil Edward Weller, Jr., "Senate Majority Leader Joseph Taylor Robinson: His Legislative Prowess" (M.A. thesis, Texas Christian University, 1986), 11; Arthur S. Link, *Woodrow Wilson and the Progressive Era, 1910–1917* (New York: Harper and Row, 1954), 35.
20. See Weller, "Joseph Taylor Robinson," 10–11.
21. *New York Times,* July 15, 1937.
22. *New York Morning Telegraph,* March 15, 1922.
23. Typewritten statement, n.d., JTR Papers, Series 8, Subseries 1, Box 107, Folder 3.
24. E. B. Merrill, assistant commissioner of Indian Affairs, Department of the Interior, Washington, D.C., letter to the Hon. C. C. Dill, Spokane, Washington, December 18, 1922, in ibid., Folder 2.
25. See JTR letter to R. W. McFarlane, Graham, Texas, January 12, 1923, in ibid.
26. See Bruce-JTR correspondence, January 24–26, 1923. Bruce was subsequently assigned to the Interstate Commerce, not Foreign Relations, Committee.
27. See Bishop John B. Morris letter to the Hon. Joseph E. Ransdell, Lake Providence, Louisiana, December 22, 1922, in ibid.
28. See Statement of Senator Lee S. Overman in behalf of Senator Simmons, Washington, D.C., February 8, 1923, in ibid., Folder 3.
29. Randall B. Ripley, *Majority Party Leadership in Congress* (Boston: Little, Brown, 1969), 100.
30. See JTR letter to Senator Robert L. Owen, December 24, 1932. "After prolonged service on Agriculture, Interstate and Foreign Commerce, Finance, Appropriations, Military Affairs, Public Lands, Immigration and Naturalization, and several years as chairman of the Committee on Claims, I find myself without any notable seniority." JTR Papers, Series 8, Subseries 4, Box 6, Folder 1.
31. Ibid.
32. Robinson insisted on doing all the paperwork himself; his files are replete with scraps of paper on which he had worked out various combinations of assignments in an effort to please as many senators as possible.
33. Robert F. Wagner letter to JTR, March 8, 1927; Bernard M. Baruch letter to JTR, March 22, 1927; JTR letter to Baruch, March 28, 1927. JTR Supplementary Papers, Series 1, Box 4, Folders 33–34.

34. Wheeler, *Yankee from the West.* Asked why he was bucking the leadership, Wheeler responded, "Who's leading?" 209.
35. See "Biffle" notes, Papers of Joseph and Stewart Alsop, Container 37, Manuscript Division, Library of Congress.
36. See Darrell St. Claire interview with Donald A. Ritchie, December 16, 1976, Senate Oral History Collection, Senate Historical Office.
37. Ibid.
38. Robinson's role in exposing Teapot Dome kept his name before the public and helped to fan enthusiasm for him as the 1924 Democratic standard-bearer. For a brief moment it looked like he had a chance. Although refusing to seek the nomination, he allowed his name to go forward at the party's convention. Benefiting from a protracted deadlock between William G. McAdoo and John W. Davis, he emerged on the seventy-first ballot as a compromise candidate. Of all such candidates, said the *New York Times* (July 6, 1924), he was "the most acceptable to all warring factions." His fate rested on McAdoo's and Davis's willingness to withdraw in his favor. But McAdoo refused to quit, and on the 103d ballot a break in the deadlock gave Davis the nomination.
39. Unidentified newspaper article, January 9, 1928, JTR Papers, Series 8, Subseries 1, Box 108, Folder 8.
40. U.S. Congress, *Congressional Record*, January 28, 1928, 1660. Also see Cal Ledbetter, Jr., "Joe T. Robinson and the Presidential Campaign of 1928," *Arkansas Historical Quarterly* (Summer 1986): 95–125.
41. *New York Times*, July 15, 1928. Quoted in Ledbetter, "Joe T. Robinson," 103.
42. Ibid., June 30, 1928, 4. Quoted in Ledbetter, "Joe T. Robinson," 108. The Republicans picked as their vice-presidential nominee Charles Curtis of Kansas, the Senate majority leader. Both candidates were chosen partly because of their appeal to the farm vote and partly because they were both "dry" and party regulars. Their temperament and styles, however, were vastly different. Curtis was less aggressive.
43. See Associated Press article, n.d., c. 1929, JTR Papers, Series 1, Subseries 2, Box 5.
44. See Robert C. Byrd, *The Senate, 1789–1989* (Washington, D.C., U.S. Government Printing Office, 1989), 459.
45. Anon. [Ray Tucker], *Mirrors of 1932*, 146.
46. Ibid., 130.
47. *New York Times*, February 13, 1931, 2.
48. Ibid., February 15, 1931, 1.
49. See Anon. [Ray Tucker], *Mirrors of 1932*, 142–143.
50. JTR letter to Earl W. Hardin, Ft. Smith, Arkansas, April 11, 1932, JTR Papers, Series 8, Subseries 1, Box 109, Folder 5.
51. JTR letter to the Hon. H. K. Ponder, Walnut Ridge, Arkansas, May 6, 1932, ibid., Folder 1.
52. JTR letter to Mrs. Sally Scott, North Little Rock, Arkansas, May 27, 1932, JTR Supplementary Papers, Series 1, Box 8, Folder 76.
53. JTR letter to Capt. John T. Burkett, Little Rock, Arkansas, July 2, 1932, JTR Papers, Series 8, Subseries 1, Box 108, Folder 5.
54. JTR letter to H.G. Miller, Little Rock, Arkansas, December 8, 1932, JTR Supplementary Papers, Series 1, Box 8, Folder 80.
55. JTR letter to Capt. John T. Burkett, Little Rock, Arkansas, December 28, 1932, JTR Papers, Series 8, Subseries 1, Box 108, Folder 5.
56. JTR letters to Charles H. Vial, LaGrange, Illinois, December 5, 1932, and L. B. Poindexter, Batesville, Arkansas, December 8, 1932, ibid., Box 107, Folder 1.
57. See Charles P. Stewart, untitled article, Central Press Bureau, Washington, D.C., December 15, 1932, ibid.
58. JTR letter to H. B. Thorn, Speaker, Arkansas General Assembly, Little Rock, Arkansas, March 9, 1933, JTR Papers, Series 9, Subseries 1, Box 203, Folder 5.

59. JTR letter to Buck Bloom, Pine Bluff, Arkansas, December 17, 1932, ibid., Series 8, Subseries 1, Box 107, Folder 1.
60. Arthur M. Schlesinger, Jr., *The Age of Roosevelt: The Crisis of the Old Order* (Boston: Houghton Mifflin, 1957), 452–455.
61. See William E. Leuchtenburg, *Franklin D. Roosevelt and the New Deal* (New York: Harper and Row, 1963), 27–28.
62. JTR letter to William Sheppard, Little Rock, Arkansas, February 27, 1933. JTR Papers, Series 9, Subseries 1, Box 206, Folder 6.
63. See Senator Robert C. Byrd speech, "The Senate Democratic Conference," *Congressional Record,* August 1, 1980, 21102–21104; also Moore, "Majority Leader," 335.
64. See Merlo Pusey, "FDR and the Supreme Court," in *Times of Trial: Great Crises in the American Past,* ed. Allan Nevins (New York: Knopf, 1958), 235–250; also Riedel, *Halls of the Mighty,* 142.
65. JTR letter to W. C. Dawson, Lepanto, Arkansas, April 1, 1933, JTR Papers, Series 9, Subseries 1, Box 206, Folder 6.
66. *Washington Post,* April 26, 1933.
67. JTR letter to J. F. McClerkin, Washington, D.C., September 19, 1933, JTR Papers, Series 1, Subseries 10, Box 13, Folder 2.
68. JTR letter to Bernard M. Baruch, New York City, May 23, 1934, ibid., Series 9, Subseries 1, Box 206, Folder 6.
69. Franklyn Waltman, Jr., "Robinson Away, Senators Play," *Washington Post,* April 4, 1934, ibid.
70. JTR letter to H. G. Miller, Little Rock, Arkansas, January 1, 1935, JTR Papers, Series 1, Subseries 10, Box 13, Folder 3.
71. Bernard M. Baruch letter to JTR, Washington, D.C., January 17, 1934, JTR Supplementary Papers, Series 1, Box 9, Folder 87.
72. See "Mark Sullivan's Letter," unidentified newspaper clipping, July [n.d.], 1935, JTR Papers, Series 9, Subseries 1, Box 206, Folder 6.
73. Byrd, *Senate, 1789–1989,* 507.
74. T. Harry Williams, *Huey Long* (New York: Knopf, 1969), 806–807; also *Arkansas Gazette,* March 5, 1935.
75. JTR interview with S. J. Wolff, *New York Times,* July 15, 1937.
76. FDR "Confidential Memorandum" to JTR, April 20, 1937, JTR Supplementary Papers, Series 1, Box 11, Folder 104.
77. *Washington Post,* April 30, 1937; *Washington Daily News,* April 3, 1937.
78. *Washington Post,* June 22, 1937.
79. Many New Deal specialists believe that by killing the National Industrial Recovery Act, the Court actually helped FDR because it relieved him of having to suffer the consequences of an unpopular and unworkable law. See Joseph Alsop and Turner Catledge, *The 168 Days* (Garden City, N.Y.: Doubleday, Doran, 1938), 5; also Pusey, "FDR and the Supreme Court," in *Times of Trial,* 236.
80. See Alsop and Catledge, *168 Days,* 9.
81. See Leuchtenburg, *Franklin D. Roosevelt,* 232.
82. See President's Message to Congress, *Congressional Record,* February 5, 1937, 878.
83. See D. B. Hardeman and Donald C. Bacon, *Rayburn: A Biography* (Austin: Texas Monthly Press, 1987), 221–223.
84. See Alsop and Catledge, *168 Days,* 151–153.
85. JTR letter to H. G. Grady, Little Rock, Arkansas, May 8, 1937, JTR Papers, Series 1, Subseries 10, Box 13, Folder 3.
86. Papers of James A. Farley, Container 31, Manuscript Division, Library of Congress.
87. See Wheeler, *Yankee from the West,* 334.
88. See James A. Farley, *The Jim Farley Story: The Roosevelt Years* (New York: McGraw-Hill, 1948), 81–82.
89. JTR letter to Ewilda Robinson, Little Rock, Arkansas, June 28, 1937, JTR Papers, Series 1, Subseries 10, Box 13, Folder 3.
90. U.S. Congress, *Congressional Record,* July 8, 1937, 6896–6897; also Robert C. Al-

bright, "Ancient Rule Used as Curb on Opponents of Court Bill," *Washington Post,* July 9, 1937, and *New York Times,* July 11, 1937.

91. U.S. Congress, *Congressional Record,* July 6, 1937, 6796.
92. Ibid., 6976.
93. In his correspondence, Robinson referred to his wife's trip only as "the matter which took you home."
94. JTR letter to "Billie," July 9, 1937, JTR Supplementary Papers, Series 1, Box 111, Folder 117.
95. JTR letter to Bernard M. Baruch, New York, July 12, 1937, JTR Papers, Series 9, Subseries 1, Box 205, Folder 6.
96. JTR letter to George B. Gillespie, Springfield, Illinois, December 5, 1932, ibid., Series 8, Box 107, Folder 1.

CHAPTER 4

Charles L. McNary
The Quiet Man

Steve Neal

C harles Linza McNary left the talking to others, seldom making a speech in a Senate career that spanned four decades and two world wars, from 1917 to 1944. But it was said that the tall, slender man from the Pacific Northwest could accomplish more by "shooting" his starched cuffs than other senators could by speaking for hours.[1]

Though McNary was Senate minority leader, his influence extended across the aisle. Harry Truman, as a Democratic senator from Missouri, placed McNary on his short list of "good old work horses who really cause the Senate to function." McNary made a habit of gathering more information on pending legislation and the mood of his colleagues than anyone. He was also a master of parliamentary maneuvers. When his Democratic counterpart, Alben Barkley, was hospitalized for three

Republican Charles McNary of Oregon placed the national interest above partisanship as minority leader during a period that spanned two world wars.

weeks in the spring of 1941, McNary picked up much of his workload, writing: "I am familiar with the rules and procedure and, naturally, it falls on me to sort of guide the destiny of the organization these times."[2]

He did not like to waste the Senate's time and spoke with disdain of "gasbags." After enduring an all-night filibuster by Huey Long, McNary privately referred to him as a moron. "Everybody hates a man who demagogues when the doors are closed," he said of William E. Borah. But with few exceptions, McNary liked his colleagues, and they returned the affection, voting him the most popular member of the Senate from the 1920s until his death in 1944. It was no accident that he served a record tenure as minority leader.[3]

Early Life and Career

McNary was born in 1874 to an Oregon pioneer family. The third son and ninth of ten children, he was orphaned at the age of nine. He worked as a farmhand, paperboy, and an apprentice in a tree nursery, riding his horse five miles every day to the apple orchards of Adolph Wertz. There he budded, grafted, and tied the apples. McNary never lost his enthusiasm for working with trees, developing the American filbert and the imperial prune and collecting tree specimens from around the globe for his farm. In the Senate, McNary sponsored legislation that led to the expansion of national forests, the reforestation of 18 million acres, and the protection of 39 million acres of national forest land. A journalist who knew McNary well said that trees played a major role in shaping his character. "An orchardist," McNary said, "learns to respect the laws of nature."[4]

In the late 1880s, McNary got to know Herbert Clark Hoover, a quiet, studious youngster of the same age who had also been orphaned. Following his parents' death, Hoover had left his native Iowa to live with Quaker relatives in Oregon. Hoover influenced McNary's decision to attend Stanford University, where both worked to pay their expenses. As a waiter in a Stanford dining hall, McNary, it is said, could carry three platters of stew at the same time.[5]

McNary's quiet political style was greatly influenced by a lecture he heard during his first semester. When it was announced that House Speaker Thomas Brackett Reed would be lecturing on campus, McNary completed his homework ahead of time and worked an earlier shift at the dining hall so he could attend. McNary greatly admired Reed, who was renowned for his caustic wit, and kept a scrapbook of his epigrams. "He is a dull fellow," Reed told the Stanford undergraduates, "who cannot tell all he knows on a subject in thirty minutes." For more than forty years, McNary would quote Reed's advice.[6]

At the urging of his older brother, John, McNary quit Stanford after a year to return home and join him in a family law practice. Charles read for the law in his brother's office and was admitted to the Oregon bar in 1898. Handling property transactions became the younger McNary's legal specialty and he built a large clientele. McNary starred at first base for the town's baseball team and some contemporaries even suggested that he might have had a professional career if he had not gone into law practice.

McNary married Jessie Breyman, the daughter of Salem's most prominent merchant, on November 19, 1902. As a wedding gift, her parents had a home built for the McNarys on a lot adjacent to the Breyman home. With financial help from his brother-in-law, McNary also bought his grandfather's homestead, which he farmed, and where the family would spend weekends. The marriage produced no children.

In 1904, McNary managed his brother's successful campaign for Marion County district attorney and served as chief deputy. Four years later, Charles was named as the dean of the law school at Willamette University. Founded in 1842, Willamette was the first college to be established on the Pacific Coast. Until McNary's appointment, the law school was loosely attached to the university, with most courses taught in downtown law offices. McNary moved the law school to the campus, boosted enrollment, and developed a broader curriculum. Though the law school depended on tuition fees for all financial support, McNary made it his policy that no student would be denied an education for lack of funds. On numerous occasions he gave students personal checks to cover their tuition and board.

In the spring of 1913, Democratic governor Oswald West appointed McNary associate justice of the Oregon Supreme Court, where he authored opinions on workmen's compensation and the eight-hour workday that reflected his western populism. "I have labored hard to interpret the law as a progressive science, rather than a rule too old to be corrected if found inapplicable to present conditions," McNary said of his judicial philosophy.[7]

He would have been content to spend the rest of his public career on the bench, but in the statewide Republican primary of 1914, after nine weeks of recounts, he lost his bid for nomination to a full term by a single vote out of nearly seventy thousand cast. Jolted by the defeat, McNary nearly quit politics. But two years later he was elected Republican state chairman and managed Charles Evans Hughes's presidential campaign in Oregon. His political fortunes were enhanced when Oregon was the only state Hughes carried in the Far West.

McNary in the Senate

Less than six months later, in May 1917, McNary was appointed to the United States Senate, filling the vacancy left by the death of Democrat Harry Lane. After suffering a nervous breakdown, Lane died just two months after casting one of the half-dozen Senate votes against American participation in World War I. President Wilson had denounced him and the other dissenters as "a little group of willful men."

McNary became as strong a supporter of Wilson's war policies as Lane had been an opponent. Even though he retained the state Republican chairmanship during his first six months in the Senate, he studiously avoided partisanship on Capitol Hill. "I am not a standpatter. I am a progressive. Neither am I a hidebound partisan," McNary said in May of 1917. "I shall support President Wilson in all his progressive legislation. I shall stand squarely behind him in all matters relating to our war with Germany."[8]

In his bid for a full term in 1918, McNary turned back powerful challenges from Oregon house speaker Robert N. Stanfield in the primary and from former Democratic governor Oswald West in the general election. McNary strongly identified himself with Wilson's war policies, and Wilson withheld his endorsement from McNary's Democratic challenger. In keeping with his strategy as the wartime senator, McNary remained on the job in Washington, D.C., and made no campaign appearances. His political triumphs, though, were overcast by his wife's death in an automobile accident on July 3. It was the greatest blow of McNary's life; his second marriage, five years later to his former secretary, did not lessen his grief.[9]

McNary threw himself into his Senate work, forging alliances and friendships with the Old Guard and Progressives alike. During the League of Nations fight, McNary stood in the middle as one of the mild reservationists who favored Wilson's Versailles Treaty without the amendments that would have reopened the peace conference. It was during this fight that Senate Majority Leader Henry Cabot Lodge took McNary under his wing. Even though the two differed on the League, Lodge had been impressed with McNary's efforts to reach a compromise. He struck Lodge as skillful and pragmatic. The Oregon senator became Lodge's chief link with the western Progressives and was named by Lodge as the western member of the Committee on Committees. "As a member of the Committee on Committees," McNary wrote his brother in 1922, "I let no opportunity pass whereby my position could be advanced."[10]

From the beginning of his Senate career, McNary's chief interests were agriculture and forestry. He declined Lodge's invitation in 1922 for a slot on the Finance Committee. "I have no love for the mathematics of that committee," he wrote. "Such subjects as tariff and taxation are wearisome." McNary valued his ranking position on the Senate Agriculture Committee, as he wrote his brother: "I really enjoy the farm work more than anything that comes before me, and I think I shall devote the remainder of my years, be they few or many, to the advancement of rural welfare."[11]

When a depression struck the farm belt in the early 1920s, McNary fought for farm relief by sponsoring legislation that framed the decade's major domestic political debate. American farmers had prospered during World War I by sustaining the Allied war effort and saving much of Europe from starvation. But when the war ended, the foreign markets vanished and government price supports were eliminated. The average American farm income dropped by half in 1920. Thousands of farmers were bankrupted, their land and equipment sold at auctions. McNary and Secretary of Agriculture Henry C. Wallace concluded that bold measures were required.

In 1924, McNary introduced a bill designed to boost prices on farm products and stabilize the farm economy by subsidizing the sale of surplus crops abroad. The bill, cosponsored with Representative Gilbert N. Haugen of Iowa, repudiated the principles of laissez-faire and social Darwinism. Like the Populist movement of the 1890s, McNary-Haugenism was attacked as radical. The legislation was twice approved by both houses of Congress, only to be vetoed by President Coolidge, who said the bill was unconstitutional and contrary to "an economic law as well established as any law of nature." McNary responded that what Coolidge "doesn't know about such things would fill a great big library."[12]

McNary expected a more humane response from Coolidge's successor,

Hoover, whom he had known longer than anyone in the nation's capital. After going their separate ways from Stanford, McNary and Hoover had both arrived in Washington, D.C., in 1917. Already renowned as a mining engineer whose global enterprises had touched six continents, Hoover gained further acclaim for his service as Wilson's World War I food administrator and as director of European relief whose humanitarian efforts had saved millions. In 1918, Hoover provided McNary with a timely endorsement in his tough primary contest for renomination. Though Hoover had urged Coolidge to veto the McNary-Haugen bill, he won McNary's endorsement for the presidency in 1928 by pledging a more comprehensive farm relief program than Coolidge.[13]

Because of his popularity in the farm belt, McNary was asked to campaign nationally for Hoover in the 1928 general election. Following Hoover's victory, he opened his presidential transition office just down the hall from McNary's apartment at the Mayflower Hotel. Hoover offered to appoint McNary as secretary of the interior or of agriculture. McNary refused, just as he rejected similar invitations from other presidents.[14]

McNary already had the job he wanted. Indeed, he was surprised when Majority Leader Charles Curtis gave up the Senate in 1929 for the vice presidency. McNary figured prominently in the speculation about the race to succeed Curtis as Republican floor leader. Instead of aiming for the top, however, McNary brokered the battle for succession between James Watson of Indiana and Wesley Jones of Washington. "I'm trying to get the leadership fight straightened out by polls and it is rather left to me to do so," McNary wrote his sister:

Some of the members are insisting that I take it, but I simply cannot stand the additional work, with its worry and strain, added to the duties involved in my own committees, and then, there are those who feel they are entitled to it, particularly on account of seniority of service. I think I could have it if I wanted it, but I don't want to take on any more responsibilities at this session of Congress.[15]

After polling the Republican membership, McNary settled the leadership fight by crafting the compromise in which Watson became majority leader, Jones was made assistant leader, and McNary himself assumed the chairmanship of the Republican Committee on Committees.

In his new post, McNary sent letters to his Republican colleagues and asked for their committee preferences. He weighed seniority, ideology, geographical balance, and one-state interests when filling vacancies. When Senator Robert M. La Follette, Jr., applied to succeed his late father on the Finance Committee, Old Guard conservatives, alarmed at the prospect that the progressive young La Follette might eventually chair the committee, sought to block him. They nominated Guy Goff of West Virginia, who had not previously expressed an interest in the committee. McNary named La Follette to the Finance Committee.[16]

Because neither Watson nor Jones was in robust health, McNary took on additional party leadership responsibilities. The Oregon senator was urged to replace Watson as majority leader in the fall of 1929, but the death of Francis E. Warren, the eighty-five-year-old chairman of the Appropriations Committee, afforded McNary a chance to bargain for another leadership post. The ranking Republican on Appropriations, Reed Smoot, did not want to yield his chairmanship of Finance, so McNary offered Jones the Appropriations chairmanship on condition that he step down as assistant majority leader. Jones accepted, and McNary succeeded him, while retaining the chairmanships of Agriculture and the Committee on Committees.

Leader in the Majority

McNary's skill in building personal relationships was a major factor in his rise to Senate leadership. He was the only link between the GOP's eastern and western factions, and he also had a good rapport with the Democrats. As assistant majority leader, he made certain that colleagues were not embarrassed by missing key votes and would postpone floor votes to protect colleagues of both parties. If a senator wanted to be present for floor action on specific legislation, McNary arranged it. "He cares more for personal relations than he does for policies. He has more contacts than anyone else in the Senate," *Collier's* reported in 1930. "McNary is everybody's friend. They all like him," Samuel G. Blythe added in the *Saturday Evening Post*. Blythe noted that McNary "can wander over to the Democratic side and get anything he wants within reason from his opponents, and sometimes without reason."[17]

Within the Senate, McNary's two closest friends were Democratic powerhouse Pat Harrison of Mississippi and independent Republican James Couzens of Michigan. From the 1920s through the mid 1930s, the three golfed each weekend at Burning Tree Country Club. A former partner of automobile manufacturer Henry Ford, Couzens served a term as mayor of Detroit and was among the more liberal Republican senators. When McNary or Harrison had to be absent from the floor, they would arrange to be paired. "You see Pat?" McNary would tell the clerk, "he'll take care of me." Like McNary, Harrison was urbane and pragmatic. McNary described Harrison as "one of the best Senate manipulators that ever lived," wryly observing that "he always gave the country an even break when he could possibly afford to do so."[18]

Through Harrison, McNary developed a friendship with Democratic leader Joseph T. Robinson (see Chapter 3). The three men often golfed together and attended baseball games and other sporting events. McNary frequently lunched with Harrison and Robinson in the Democratic leader's Capitol hideaway, and he privately urged Robinson on many occasions not to be so blunt or public with his criticisms of Democratic senators. McNary and Robinson often went on hunting and fishing trips, and the Oregonian said they were "like brothers."[19]

McNary was disappointed with Hoover's leadership even before his friend took the presidential oath. Hoover took no stand on a farm bill McNary had introduced in December 1928 that established a federal farm board with a revolving fund to make loans and to stabilize farm prices. After his inauguration, Hoover called a special session of Congress to deal with farm relief and to enact a law to set up a farm board that would help farmers to market and store their produce, develop new by-products, and control production. But the farm board was a failure. In the wake of the stock market crash of 1929, farm prices plunged and thousands of farmers lost their land. McNary's proposal for an emergency farm-relief plan with a federal subsidy was rejected by Hoover on philosophical grounds.[20]

McNary thought that Hoover faltered badly in the face of the nation's worst depression. Believing in volunteerism and individualism, not in what he termed "government handouts," Hoover stubbornly refused to compromise. McNary supported federal relief to state and local governments. Hoover opposed it. When McNary sponsored a resolution to make government-owned surplus wheat available to the hungry, the Senate adopted it but Hoover declined to release the grain.

McNary concluded that Hoover was a well-intentioned businessman who was simply not up to the demands of the presidency. "If the engineer who was successful in Africa had more political acumen," McNary wrote his brother, "mole hills would not be viewed as mountains and tempests would take place at sea rather than in the teapot."[21]

Resentful of criticism and persistently conservative, Hoover opposed efforts by Senate Republicans to replace Watson with McNary. Hoover disdained Watson, but had come to dislike McNary even more. The *New York Times* later reported that Hoover blocked McNary's election as majority leader "because he considered him too liberal," claiming it was the only occasion on which McNary's liberalism had impeded his political career. McNary countered that he had the votes to oust Watson but had chosen not to do so. In his presidential memoirs, published eight years after McNary's death, Hoover used some of his sharpest invective for McNary's farm legislation of the 1920s.[22]

McNary supported Hoover's reelection effort in 1932 without enthusiasm or illusion. With Hoover's defeat, the stage was set for McNary's ascendancy to party leadership. Franklin D. Roosevelt's electoral landslide was such that Democrats gained control of the Senate; Watson, Jones, and Senate president pro tem George Moses (New Hampshire) were among the Republican casualties.

New Deal Minority Leader

Writing of the Democratic victory, McNary confessed,

Inasmuch as it had to be, I'm rather glad that it was overwhelming. It may cause an upturn in business. The people who felt that the country was not being run right are in charge of affairs, but sometimes a change is a good thing, and really I expect to see conditions improve soon.[23]

Republicans had been the dominant political party from the time of the Civil War to the Great Depression; only two Democratic presidents had been elected in that period. With FDR's victory, McNary became the highest-ranking Republican officeholder of the Roosevelt era. He did not lament the passing of the old order. "I believe that these terrible times have reached the ebb of their existence," he wrote his brother in March 1933, "and the good tide will soon return. Many things have been wrong for two years, especially the last, too many for mental composure."[24]

As the only surviving member of the Senate Republican leadership, McNary faced no serious competition for the minority leadership. "I expect to take charge of the Minority of the Senate, a position which I have wanted for some time and which satisfies me from the viewpoint of political power and precedent," McNary wrote his sister. His new title, he added, "will be some compensation for the loss I suffered in the change of political forces."[25]

McNary was unanimously elected in March 1933 as Senate minority leader. This was one of the few matters on which the thirty-six Republican senators could agree. Fifteen of the Old Guard stalwarts were opposed to all New Deal initiatives, but a majority wanted to give Roosevelt's programs a chance. Four Republican senators had even endorsed Roosevelt over Hoover: Bronson Cutting of New Mexico, George W. Norris of Nebraska, Hiram Johnson of California, and La Follette of Wisconsin.[26]

McNary's first leadership test was an intramural conflict. David A. Reed of Pennsylvania and Simeon Fess of Ohio launched a movement to strip the four Roosevelt Republicans of their seniority and committee assignments. "I myself have no illusions about what is going to happen to the Republican cause unless something of that kind is done," Senator Felix Hebert of Rhode Island wrote privately. "I sometimes think that we in the East take our Republicanism a little more seriously than they do in the wide open spaces."[27]

As the first Republican floor leader from the Far West, McNary was more tolerant of political independence than his predecessors. McNary had written an undergraduate essay about the Roman statesman and military leader Spurius Cassius Vecellinus that revealed much about his own political views. "He is the first one of those magnanimous patriots," McNary wrote in 1897, "who rose above his party and sowed the virtuous seeds of equal welfare."[28]

Democratic national chairman James A. Farley described McNary as "more a patriot than a partisan." Although not above playing partisan politics, McNary put the national interest first when faced with serious questions. "I agree with your philosophy that as we grow older we forget party lines even if they ever disturbed us," McNary wrote Joseph P. Tumulty, Wilson's former political adviser, in 1932. "In my personal associations there is an invisible aisle in the Senate and that invisibility extends through the whole personal existence."[29]

McNary thwarted Reed's attempt to punish the four independents, declaring: "All Republicans look alike to me." He observed that if a senator was elected as a Republican then only the voters could judge his credentials. McNary thought the four should retain their full standing as members of the caucus and were entitled to their share of committee assignments. For the Republican caucus to censure one of its own, the minority leader knew, would be counterproductive, depleting the Republican minority even further.

In the Democratic-controlled Senate, McNary had to reduce the number of Republicans on each committee to conform to the new ratio of fourteen to nine. He weighed seniority and geographical considerations in making the new assignments. If senators were transferred from more prestigious committees, McNary placed them on committees important to their constituencies.[30]

Helping Republican senators to win reelection was among McNary's priorities in allocating committee assignments. When Cutting was bumped from the Foreign Relations Committee, McNary sought to strengthen the New Mexican's home base by naming him to the Agriculture and Irrigation committees. Despite formidable opposition, Cutting narrowly won reelection in 1934. Johnson of California was given a place on the Naval Committee; Norris of Nebraska became the ranking Republican on Agriculture, moving above McNary, the former chairman.

When McNary took over the Republican floor leadership, there was little precedent for bipartisan cooperation between a GOP Senate leader and Democratic president. Indeed, as a mild reservationist in the League of Nations fight, McNary had been caught in the crossfire between Woodrow Wilson and Henry Cabot Lodge and had been critical of both for letting their bitter feud become an obsession. He thought it brought out the worst in both men and impeded national policy.[31] Roosevelt and McNary were determined not to repeat that mistake.

McNary believed Roosevelt's election had given him a popular mandate, that his programs for recovery should be given a chance, and that he should have time to carry out his New Deal unobstructed. "The Republicans will co-operate with the Democrats to promote legislation designed to improve conditions in the country," McNary declared. "We wish the new administration an abundance of success."[32]

Roosevelt soon counted McNary among his confidants and friends. After taking the oath of office, he conferred with McNary in the President's Room of the Capitol, asking the minority leader for help in approving cabinet appointments and in passing measures to deal with the Depression. McNary agreed without hesitation. "He is very affable and I think very much on the square," McNary reported to his brother, "and I am sure it will be a pleasure to work with him." Two years later, his impression of the president was even more positive: "He is a lovely fellow. I have always liked him and we get along splendidly, so much better than I did with the forgotten man, Mr. Hoover."[33]

McNary supported most of the early New Deal initiatives, voting for the Emergency Banking Relief Act; the Tennessee Valley Authority; the Civil Works Administration, which put more than four million Americans back to work; and the Civilian Conservation Corps, which produced jobs for a quarter million young people to plant trees, fight forest fires, and build dams. Consulted by Roosevelt's aides as it was drafted, McNary supported the Agricultural Adjustment Act to increase the purchasing power of farmers and to raise the ceilings for farm loans. "I shall support the President, who made a fine appearance before the Senate and House," McNary reported to his sister in 1935. His only speech during that session was an endorsement of Roosevelt's social security proposal. "McNary was more of a New Deal radical than most of the New Dealers," said Rexford G. Tugwell, the brain truster.[34]

As leader of the Republican minority, however, McNary had his disagreements with Roosevelt. An ardent protectionist who had supported the Smoot-Hawley tariff of the Hoover years, McNary led farm bloc and Republican opposition to FDR's Reciprocal Trade Agreements Act that authorized the president to cut tariffs by half with nations that made equal concessions. McNary denounced the trade agreements as harmful to American producers, but he failed to block them.

McNary also voted against the Gold Reserve Act that devalued the dollar and set the price of gold at $35 an ounce. McNary wrote to his brother:

It will go through by strictly party vote, except that Radicals and Progressives will vote with the Administration. It is a hard vote for me, but I must go with the Republicans and follow the traditional policy of the Party with respect to the monetary system.[35]

McNary and Oregon benefited greatly from the senator's friendship with the president. He obtained federal funding for bridges, schools, and hospitals in Oregon. When the state capitol was destroyed by fire, McNary secured federal funds for a new building. A WPA ski lodge was built on Mount Hood. McNary's greatest accomplishment for the Pacific Northwest was hydroelectric power development through massive government-built dams on the Columbia River. "I've got to give Charlie his dam," Roosevelt chortled as he signed the bill for construction of the Bonneville dam.[36]

Nothing frustrated McNary more than the deep divisions within his own party. The Republican insurgents who supported Roosevelt shunned the party caucus despite McNary's conciliatory gestures. From the right, McNary was criticized for accommodating Roosevelt. When Ogden L. Mills, Hoover's treasury secretary, drafted a conservative manifesto attacking the New Deal's fiscal policies, McNary refused to sign it. Senator Reed and House Republican leader Bertrand H. Snell both endorsed the Mills statement, but McNary believed that GOP criticism should be more constructive.[37]

"Everything is politics here," McNary told his brother:

The air is surcharged and I'll be d——— if I'm not getting tired of politics, especially the kind I am having to go through—leading the Minority and the so-called candidate in '36, a link between the Progressives and the Stand-patters, criticized by some for being too close to the President, by others for being too friendly toward the Conservatives and by some for being too friendly toward the Progressives. It really presents a picture no artist can paint and it's decidedly trying.[38]

"There are so many views and so much disagreement," McNary wrote more than a year later, "that I am thoroughly dissatisfied."[39]

In the 1934 midterm election, McNary and Hoover differed over Republican strategy. Declaring that Americans had a choice between regimentation and liberty, Hoover tried to frame the election as a referendum on the New Deal. McNary preferred a more forward-looking program. "It is not my intention to be active during the campaign," McNary wrote Senator Couzens.[40]

The 1934 election was yet another repudiation of Hoover. Although the White House traditionally lost congressional seats in midterm elections, the Democrats gained ten senators and nineteen congressmen. The voters ousted Old Guard senators Reed, Fess, and Hebert. McNary's call for moderation was vindicated. "The avalanche was a little more destructive than I anticipated but I am sure we each expected a harvest of Democratic gains," McNary wrote Couzens.[41]

Without mentioning Hoover by name, McNary broke his silence about the former president's role in the 1934 results, asserting:

The Republican party should quit its abstractions and alarms and get down to the level of human sympathy and human understanding. It should now be plain that a party cannot gain the attention of a people distraught by business and employment worries by extolling the nobility of the forefathers, the sanctity of the Constitution and by spreading alarms over regimentation and bureaucracy. Regimentation is a fine, mouth-filling word, but it fills no empty stomachs, and a man who is worried over where next month's rent is coming from cannot be aroused to an interest in the evils of bureaucracy.[42]

Privately, McNary ridiculed Hoover: "I wish his sentences were not so ponderous and his ideas so heavily obscured by words," he wrote Couzens. "Probably he will join the American Liberty League," he said, referring to a right-wing group that drew support from wealthy businessmen.[43]

In the winter of 1935, Roosevelt suffered several setbacks in the Senate.

His $4.8 billion relief bill was stalled, and his proposal to have the United States participate in the World Court defeated. "The President has lost considerable of his influence with his party," McNary wrote his brother.[44] In the end, Roosevelt still won approval of nearly everything he asked for, including Social Security, the Emergency Relief Appropriations Act, the Wagner Act, the Securities and Exchange Commission, and the breakup of private power monopolies. McNary supported each of these New Deal initiatives.

By the middle of Roosevelt's first term, McNary concluded that the New Deal should slow the proliferation of "alphabet agencies." "I find here the same unrest and feeling of uncertainty that I feel obtained in the East," McNary wrote a Senate colleague from Oregon:

I wish the president would make a statement concerning his program so that business could adjust itself thereto. I think he could say, "This is my program and only a great emergency will cause me to add a chapter." It would do much to restore confidence and assure more activity in private ventures.[45]

In 1935 McNary observed: "There has been tangible improvement in the country's economic structure," but conceded that "the administration would have achieved more had it conceived less. Simply it has been going in too many places."[46]

Early in his first term, Roosevelt had predicted that McNary would be his 1936 Republican opponent, and initially the Oregonian did nothing to discourage speculation. But he declined when Senator Capper invited him to discuss his possible candidacy with midwestern Republican leaders.[47] Over lunch in the Senate dining room, Couzens offered to launch McNary's presidential campaign with a $100,000 contribution. McNary wrote his response on the menu:

> The presidential bee is a deadly bug.
> I've seen it work on others.
> Oh Lord, protect me from its hug
> and let it sting my brothers.[48]

Alice Roosevelt Longworth noted that McNary's support of New Deal programs had eliminated him as a Republican standard-bearer.[49] McNary must have agreed, for he announced in 1935 that he would not seek the Republican presidential nomination. "I am not sure that it possesses any value," McNary told a Senate colleague. He viewed Roosevelt as unbeatable for a second term.[50]

McNary campaigned for reelection to the Senate in 1936 as a nonpartisan. Despite his role as Senate minority leader, he shunned the Republican National Convention and made no campaign appearances with presidential nominee Alf M. Landon. For the first time in four Senate elections, McNary did not permit the Republican State Central Committee to put its official stamp on his campaign literature. McNary, a former GOP state chairman, was no less of a Republican, but he did not want to get dragged down to defeat with the national ticket. Although nine Republican senators were defeated in the Roosevelt victory that swept forty-six states, McNary was not among them. He won a fourth term by less than 1 percent of the vote over Democrat Willis Mahoney.[51]

The Court-packing Scheme

McNary's GOP minority was reduced to sixteen, the smallest bloc of Republicans since before the Civil War. Some conservatives grumbled that McNary should be replaced with a more forceful partisan such as Vandenberg. But McNary won reelection without opposition. "I'm awaiting the opening of the Congress on Tuesday," McNary wrote his sister on January 2, 1937. "Things will then start to buzz and the days will slip by and before we know it spring will be here and you and the Colonel will be here and all will be fine."[52]

Roosevelt, however, surprised everyone on February 5, 1937, with an initiative that at last enabled McNary to mobilize an effective opposition. Angered by the Supreme Court's invalidation of a series of New Deal programs and measures, Roosevelt proposed legislation that would expand the Court from nine to fifteen members. Contending that the "nine old men" on the Court were unable to keep up with their workload, Roosevelt asked for authority to name a new justice when a member of the Court remained on the bench beyond his seventieth birthday. At the time six of the justices were over seventy years of age.

McNary's small band of Republicans was united in opposition. Johnson, who had twice endorsed Roosevelt, denounced the bill. Even Norris, a New Deal loyalist but still vigorous at seventy-five, had serious reservations, writing: "I am not in sympathy with the plan to enlarge the Supreme Court."[53]

The morning after FDR's announcement, McNary met with Republican orators Borah and Vandenberg and outlined his strategy for blocking the president's plan for the Supreme Court. He argued that if Republicans showed restraint, Democrats would be so seriously divided that Roosevelt

After the 1936 elections, Senate Republican leader Charles McNary of Oregon commanded a GOP minority of sixteen. His situation contrasted sharply with that of Senator Robinson, who was overwhelmed by the number of senators in his flock.

could not make the bill a litmus test of party loyalty. Vandenberg and Borah were persuaded to follow McNary's strategy of silence.[54] "Borah, McNary, and I had a conference in Borah's office at 11 o'clock," Vandenberg wrote in his diary: "Borah is prepared to lead this fight; but he insisted that there is no hope if it is trademarked in advance as a 'Hoover fight' or a 'Republican fight.' " McNary emphatically agreed: "As a matter of fact, this was already my attitude. . . . So the general agreement is that Republicans shall stay in the background for a week or ten days and let the revolting Democrats make their own record."[55]

McNary enlisted other prominent Republican spokesmen in his conspiracy, including House Republican Leader Bertrand H. Snell, Republican national chairman John D. M. Hamilton, and Landon, who rewrote a Lincoln Day speech he had planned as an attack on the Court bill. "Let them do the talking," McNary told Republican allies, "and we'll do the voting."[56]

Former president Hoover was the biggest threat to McNary's strategy. Hoover had promptly denounced Roosevelt's plan and was set to deliver another blast on national radio. Democratic Senator Carl Hatch told Vandenberg, "I am inclined to vote no; but you Republicans, and particularly Mr. Hoover, must not make it too hard for me." In his meeting with Borah and Vandenberg, McNary suggested that Vandenberg approach Hoover because the former president disliked Borah and McNary.

Before calling Hoover, Vandenberg got the columnist Mark Sullivan, Hoover's longtime friend, to brief the former president about the Republican scheme. With some trepidation, Vandenberg then called Hoover and asked him to join in the strategy. "Who was at that meeting?" demanded Hoover. "Who's trying to muzzle me?" When Vandenberg told him, Hoover bitterly denounced McNary and Borah. But Vandenberg persisted, arguing that McNary's plan was the best chance of thwarting Roosevelt. Reluctantly, Hoover agreed to go along.[57]

The former president's silence was short-lived. Speaking before the Union League Club of Chicago on February 20, Hoover accused Roosevelt of subverting the Constitution. "That is not judicial process," said Hoover. "That is force." In closing, Hoover declared: "Hands off the Supreme Court!" McNary swore when he learned of Hoover's speech. Borah publicly disavowed Hoover as a Republican spokesman. Former Republican national chairman Henry Fletcher, a Hoover friend, was deployed to discourage Hoover from making further speeches. Although Hoover is said to have resented the strategy, he kept silent for the rest of the debate.[58]

In the wake of his second-term landslide and the record Democratic majority in the Senate, Roosevelt expected to push through his Court-packing plan. *Time* magazine reported on February 15 that a poll of political journalists predicted "the bill would be passed without difficulty." Whatever their private reservations about the plan, the Democratic leadership, including Robinson, Harrison, Key Pittman, and James F. Byrnes, backed the president. "Nothing can beat us if you follow me on the court plan," Roosevelt told a Democratic party gathering.[59]

But there were significant Democratic defections, including Bennett "Champ" Clark of Missouri, David Walsh of Massachusetts, Tom Connally of Texas, Edward Burke of Nebraska, and both Virginia senators, Carter Glass and Harry F. Byrd. Liberal columnists Walter Lippmann and

Dorothy Thompson wrote that Roosevelt was grasping for dictatorial powers. McNary's Republicans were quiet.

Roosevelt was dealt a major blow when Burton K. Wheeler of Montana, a prominent liberal ally, joined the opposition. Wheeler, a "Son of the Wild Jackass," as western Progressives were then known, had been Robert M. La Follette's 1924 vice-presidential running mate on the Progressive ticket. He was also among Roosevelt's earliest and most important liberal allies. Though Wheeler favored a constitutional amendment to restrict the Court's authority, he now denounced Roosevelt's bill as "a sham and a fake liberal proposal." Wheeler rejected FDR's offer to let him select two or three of the new justices. Instead, he became leader of the Democratic opposition to the Court plan.[60]

Drew Pearson and Robert S. Allen reported that Wheeler and the Democratic opponents of the Court plan were relying on McNary's counsel:

McNary not once has appeared in the forefront. Yet behind the scenes he has been the mastermind of the fight against the president. The antis have never made a major move without consulting him, and Senator Wheeler, their titular generalissimo, holds on to McNary's coattails like a child to its mother's apron-string.[61]

In late March, Wheeler released a letter from Chief Justice Charles Evans Hughes that effectively refuted FDR's claim that the Court had not kept up with its workload. Later in the spring, Hughes and Justice Owen Roberts further undermined the plan by voting with the Court's liberal minority to uphold the Wagner Act, the Social Security Act, the Farm Mortgage Moratorium Act, and a minimum-wage law. The Court's approval of New Deal legislation gave other Democratic senators another reason to abandon the bill. Finally, senators Wheeler and Borah persuaded Justice Willis Van Devanter that his resignation would further weaken Roosevelt's argument for the Court bill. When Van Devanter announced his retirement, McNary called on Roosevelt to withdraw the legislation.[62]

The opposition was growing. On May 18, 1937, the Judiciary Committee recommended against the bill. Between them, Wheeler and McNary had more than enough votes on the floor to defeat the president's plan.

Down but not out, Roosevelt suggested a revised Court bill that would permit the appointment of two or three new justices. Majority Leader Joseph T. Robinson was offered Van Devanter's seat on the Court if the Senate approved Roosevelt's legislation. McNary, who knew that his friend had long wanted such an appointment, urged Robinson's immediate nomination and promised swift confirmation. Roosevelt would not formally submit Robinson's nomination, however, until the Senate voted on the Court legislation. With stubborn determination, Robinson lined up votes for a compromise bill that would allow Roosevelt to expand the Court, day and night seeking the help of his colleagues. On July 14, he died of a heart attack. McNary wrote his brother-in-law: "He died a martyr to the cause of the court plan which never should have been presented to a civilized legislative organization."[63]

Without Robinson, Roosevelt had no chance of winning the Court fight. McNary offered a motion referring the bill to the hostile Judiciary Committee. It was adopted by a 70-20 vote. McNary's strategy of silence had been golden.

Leader of the Bipartisan Opposition

In the aftermath of the Court fight, McNary noted that the Senate had three political parties: Democrats, Republicans, and New Dealers. The bipartisan coalition forged by McNary would remain a powerful force for more than a generation. Some coalition senators wanted to institutionalize their alliance against the New Deal, but McNary did not want Republicans locked into such an arrangement. When senators Vandenberg and Bailey drafted a conservative manifesto, they hoped to gain thirty signatures from colleagues. McNary thwarted them by releasing his copy to reporters. By making public the anti–New Deal document, McNary effectively discredited their effort. "Premature publicity—thanks to treachery—ended the episode," Vandenberg wrote in his diary. Bailey added that "unfortunately the statement fell into the hands of the Republican leader who thought that the utterance of it would injure the Republican cause. He thought it would steal away a Republican opportunity."[64]

McNary liked to remain firmly in control and, whenever possible, minimized formal organizational structures. He never built a statewide organization in Oregon, relying instead on his relatives and former law school students to run his campaigns. After the 1936 election and for the rest of his term as leader, McNary abandoned elections for assistant leader and whip. He informally designated his leadership team, including Warren R. Austin of Vermont, as assistant leader. McNary and Alf Landon blocked Hoover's attempt to convene a 1938 midterm Republican national convention, which McNary thought would divide the party.

McNary's relationship with new Senate Majority Leader Alben W.

As Senate minority leader, Charles McNary of Oregon, the affable western progressive, had a solid working relationship with Democratic leader Alben Barkley (left).

Barkley of Kentucky was friendly but less intimate than his bond with Robinson. Barkley had edged out Pat Harrison, McNary's best friend in the Senate, by a single vote, and McNary resented President Roosevelt's intervention in the contest on Barkley's behalf. Barkley, who described McNary as a legislative genius, valued his advice and kept him fully informed on the Democratic agenda. McNary took delight in outmaneuvering the easygoing Barkley on technical motions. Before a roll call, Senator Josh Lee of Oklahoma asked Barkley how to vote. "I don't know," snorted Barkley. "Ask Charley McNary. He's the only real leader around here."[65]

In 1939, McNary worked offstage with conservative Democratic leaders to slash $150 million from FDR's budget. All but one Republican voted for the cuts. As in the Court fight, McNary encouraged Democrats to lead the opposition and followed a similar strategy to defeat Roosevelt's attempt to reorganize the executive branch. Senator James F. Byrnes, who managed the bill for the administration, said ruefully that Hitler's storm troopers were "no more regimented" than McNary's Republican senators.[66] McNary dealt Roosevelt another embarrassment when he persuaded Key Pittman, chairman of the Senate Foreign Relations Committee, to propose the chief nullifying amendment to the extension of the Trade Agreements Act.

Clouds of War

McNary, who had never traveled beyond the shores of North America, underestimated the threat of Adolf Hitler in the months leading up to World War II. Until the Munich Pact was signed by France, Germany, Great Britain, and Italy in September 1938, in effect surrendering the Sudetenland to the Nazis, foreign affairs was rarely a topic of major discussion in the Senate. "I want to avoid all entangling alliances and agreements that might embroil us in an effort with Europe," McNary wrote in January 1939. Even after Hitler violated the accord in March 1939 by seizing the rest of Czechoslovakia by force, McNary was not greatly concerned, writing in April: "I do not think there will be a European war and I am quite certain that America will not be drawn into any such conflict as an overwhelming percentage of the Congress are opposed to it."[67]

At a White House meeting in July, Roosevelt and Secretary of State Cordell Hull asked Senate and House leaders for repeal of the arms embargo provision of the Neutrality Act. Hull was listing his reasons for believing Europe was on the brink of war when Borah interrupted and charged that the State Department had poor intelligence. The ranking Republican on the Foreign Relations Committee claimed he purchased better information than Hull obtained from diplomats; there would be no war because the British would appease Hitler. (Borah's "source" was a British political newsletter.) McNary told Joseph Alsop that he was infuriated by Borah's disrespectful treatment of Hull, yet he was not persuaded that the arms embargo should be repealed. "It is not my intention, by vote, to transfer unusual powers to the President in the matter of neutrality," he wrote after the meeting.[68]

After Hitler invaded Poland on September 1, 1939, and Great Britain and France declared war on Nazi Germany, Roosevelt called a special session of Congress to lift the arms embargo. McNary responded when Roosevelt asked him to expedite a vote on the Neutrality Act, but he still opposed repealing the arms embargo and the Neutrality Act for fear that the United States would no longer be neutral. "I fear if we send munitions to belligerents they may be followed by money and then by men," McNary wrote. "We have no business in becoming involved in the European mess that has been going on for a thousand years. Further, we got mixed up twenty years ago and the tragic results are known to all."[69]

Roosevelt eventually achieved a dramatic victory in winning the repeal of the arms embargo; McNary and all but six Republican senators had voted against lifting the embargo. As the European war escalated, Mc-Nary moved toward support of Roosevelt's foreign policy, voting against a La Follette amendment that would have limited exports to warring nations and supporting aid to Finland after the Soviet invasion that followed the Nazi-Soviet pact. McNary was the only western progressive Republican to support the nation's first peacetime draft in 1940. It was McNary who advised Roosevelt to invoke his emergency powers to conclude the destroyers-for-bases deal with Prime Minister Winston Churchill. He told Senator Claude Pepper, a Democratic ally of Roosevelt's, that although he would have difficulty supporting a formal vote to transfer destroyers he would not object if Roosevelt could justify moving ahead without legislative approval.[70]

The fight over the Supreme Court and political differences did not strain McNary's friendship with Roosevelt. McNary opposed a Senate resolution against a third presidential term in 1940 as "ill-advised" and "ill-mannered." Roosevelt confided to Interior Secretary Harold Ickes that a friend had suggested a 1940 wartime unity ticket of Roosevelt with McNary for vice president. Ickes responded that a Roosevelt-McNary combination "undoubtedly would make an unusually strong ticket." It was well known that Roosevelt would be replacing his disgruntled vice president, John Nance Garner, in 1940. Roosevelt knew, however, that McNary would not abandon the Republican party.[71]

Roosevelt's trial balloon for a bipartisan wartime ticket may have been his invitation to McNary and two other Republican leaders to attend a Democratic Jackson Day dinner. McNary declined to attend. At the dinner, Roosevelt told a story about McNary:

Once upon a time, there was a school teacher, who, after describing heaven in alluring and golden terms, asked her class of small boys how many of them wanted to go to heaven. With eyes that sparkled at the thought every small boy in the class held up his hand—except one. The teacher said, "Why Charlie, Charlie McNary, Charlie, you don't want to go to heaven? Why not?" "Teacher," he said, "sure I want to go to heaven, but"—pointing to the rest of the boys in the room—"not with that bunch."[72]

FDR's comments brought down the house, and nobody appreciated the humor more than McNary.

1940: The Vice-Presidential Race

McNary sought the Republican presidential nomination in 1940, hoping to emerge as the choice of a deadlocked national convention. His 1940 White House bid paralleled Senate Majority Leader Lyndon B. Johnson's Democratic presidential campaign of 1960. Both McNary and Johnson overestimated their political appeal beyond the nation's capital. Although favorites of Washington insiders, neither had a national political organization. McNary discovered, as Johnson would learn twenty years later, that reputation in the Senate and support from colleagues was not nearly enough to win a presidential nomination. With a deadlock at the GOP national convention, McNary was eclipsed by a fresher face, Wendell L. Willkie. On the eve of the convention, Hitler conquered France, Norway, Denmark, and Belgium. Willkie was nominated largely because he was the only contender who had alerted the nation to the threat of Nazi Germany.[73]

Reluctantly, McNary accepted Willkie's invitation to become the Republican nominee for vice president. "I just could not avoid the responsibility," McNary wrote his sister. "I am not happy about the situation at all. I either had to be disloyal to my friends in the party or be a soldier." McNary told his wife, "I am feeling all right though a little nervous from the shock and the strain. The whole thing is just too bad, but could not be avoided." Roosevelt sent McNary a warm congratulatory note on his nomination.[74]

Partly to offset McNary's strength in the farm belt, Roosevelt chose Agriculture Secretary Henry A. Wallace as his running mate. Wallace had begun his political career as a Republican supporter of McNary's farm bill in the 1920s, and McNary had taunted Wallace when he switched political parties to join the Roosevelt cabinet. "Both the Democratic nominees are warm friends of mine," McNary wrote his wife after the Democratic convention:

President Roosevelt told several people that if he could not make it, he would rather see me there than anyone, and Wallace has told the newspaper boys from time to time that Republicans should nominate me. That part is nice—to have no ill feelings against your opponents.[75]

In his acceptance speech, McNary credited the New Deal with "certain social gains which have made the lot of the average man more secure" and vowed not to relinquish "these advances" nor to question FDR's "humanitarian impulses." McNary asserted that the Republicans would govern more effectively than the New Deal. Most of McNary's campaign appearances were in the farm belt and the Far West. He traveled with a single aide who served as speechwriter, press spokesman, and advance man. On several occasions, McNary and Wallace rode on the same train and had meals together. Instead of attacking each other, McNary and Wallace exchanged praise. McNary received more attention nationally during his few months as a vice-presidential nominee than at any time in his career. He was featured on the covers of *Life* and *Newsweek*; his appearances were chronicled in weekly movie newsreels. McNary said, "I shall feel as happy as a pardoned prisoner when it is all over."[76]

McNary was neither surprised nor disappointed by the outcome of the 1940 election. He told Ralph Cake, Oregon's Republican national committeeman, that Roosevelt had clinched a third term in June when Nazi Germany's conquest of France had the effect of making FDR a wartime president. On election night, McNary thought Willkie looked petty in refusing to concede defeat. So McNary made his own concession statement before Willkie. "We are a united country. The two-party system is secure," said McNary. "We shall try to afford Mr. Roosevelt and his associates a worthy and vigilant opposition."[77]

Reports circulated that Roosevelt would name McNary as Wallace's successor as secretary of agriculture. Already Republicans Henry L. Stimson and Frank Knox had joined the cabinet because the threat of war would require bipartisan government, and McNary was among Roosevelt's closest Republican friends. McNary, however, was not interested. "Nothing to it," he wrote his executive assistant. "Of course, you know I would not take the position under these circumstances or any other so far as I know. I have no fear but that I could handle it with technique and a little skill but I would not throw my party down."[78]

Back in Washington, McNary provided Roosevelt with critical support on the 1941 Lend-Lease loan to provide emergency funds for the Allies. "I have given the matter much thought," McNary wrote his sister on February 28, "and I believe that the surest way for us to protect our country's future is by assisting in squelching Mr. Hitler now." Two-thirds of the Republican senators opposed the Lend-Lease Act when the Senate approved it on March 7. Hiram Johnson said that McNary's vote was the "severest blow" to the isolationists.[79]

McNary reported in May 1941:

The war abroad and its implications here have cast a dark shadow over Congress and everything is talk of war abroad or prospects for war here. We may get in. I have not thought so, but I am beginning to think it is probable. If we get in, I think it is because Mr. Hitler wants to fight, not because we are discreet. But I don't think he wants to fight.[80]

In November McNary joined the isolationists in fighting Roosevelt's attempt to revise the Neutrality Act so that armed American ships could carry lend-lease materials to England. The minority leader worried that revising the Neutrality Act could force an incident that would take America into the war. On November 7, the Senate narrowly approved repeal of the restrictive sections of the Neutrality Act.

Wartime Partnership

After Japan's surprise attack on Pearl Harbor on December 7, 1941, McNary was among the handful of people summoned to the White House. He stood behind Roosevelt as the president signed the declaration of war against the Axis powers. As minority leader, he pledged full support. Senate Republicans unanimously approved a resolution backing Roosevelt's war policies. Privately, McNary was highly critical of the U.S. Navy. "Indignation runs high here in connection with the disaster in Pearl Harbor," he wrote his sister. "The tragedy was wholly avoidable. The capitol battleships were sitting on the water much like decoy ducks on a calm lake."[81]

McNary was a friend and confidant of General George C. Marshall, the World War II army chief of staff, whom he had first met when Marshall was the brigadier general in command of the Vancouver Barracks. Even so, McNary protested when the Roosevelt administration sought to push through a $43 billion army-funding bill without review. McNary said that the War Department was "just pushing members of the Senate around" and called for "a little calmness and coolness." Though supportive of the Allied cause, he believed that Roosevelt was giving away the store. "The fellow that is dangerous in that line is Churchill," McNary wrote. "He has a great influence over the gentleman at the White House and he would carry off the White House if it were not difficult to put inside a plane."[82]

When Republicans gained ten senators and forty-seven representatives in the 1942 elections, McNary observed that the Democratic setbacks stemmed from dissatisfaction with the operation of the war program.[83]

Speaking on the Senate floor, Democratic Senator Tom Connally voiced his concern that Nazi Germany and Imperial Japan might misinterpret the administration's election losses. McNary jumped to his feet and berated Connally. "No issue of patriotism or unity was raised" in the campaign, McNary noted:

Many times I have felt like raising my voice in opposition to some things which I thought were major mistakes. I persuaded myself it was better for our country and our unity to withhold criticism. I intend to continue.[84]

McNary knew most of the secrets worth knowing in wartime Washington. He was among those informed about the development of the atomic bomb. McNary was untroubled about the long-term implications of such technology for he favored using modern weaponry to save American lives. He was also one of the first prominent Republicans to endorse a United Nations. "Unless the peace after this war is to be as unstable as was that after the last war," he declared in the summer of 1943, "planning must be started now."[85]

Roosevelt approached McNary in the fall of 1942 about an appointment to the Supreme Court, but McNary refused. "I would not be happy writing opinions based on what some old judge said in the threadbare past," McNary wrote his sister. "This life is too active and my position is too important to give up this time because when the war is over, the United States Senate under the Constitution will have to write the treaties of peace. For that work, I think I am fitted."[86]

McNary would not live to see the peace, dying in the winter of his seventieth year. Roosevelt and the Senate mourned his death. By placing the national interest above partisanship in the Great Depression and World War II, McNary had helped Roosevelt to achieve national unity. At the same time, he helped to revive the credibility of the Senate by shaping the strategy that blocked Roosevelt's scheme to pack the Supreme Court. For three decades, McNary was ranked as the most popular member of the Senate. "His popularity with his colleagues," said Vandenberg, "was matched only by their granite confidence in him." When asked how he maintained his relationships with other senators, McNary responded, "I always keep my word."[87]

NOTES

1. Lyle C.Wilson, "McNary's Expressive Cuffs Finally Folded," *Washington Daily News*, February 26, 1944.
2. Truman is quoted on McNary in Robert H. Ferrell, ed., *Dear Bess: The Letters from Harry to Bess Truman* (New York: Norton, 1983), 374; CLM to Mrs. W. T. Stolz, June 20, 1941, McNary MSS, Library of Congress.
3. CLM to Mrs. W. T. Stolz, November 14, 1941, McNary MSS; CLM to John H. McNary, June 14, 1935, ibid. McNary is quoted on Borah in Joseph Alsop and Stewart Alsop, *The Reporter's Trade* (New York: Reynal, 1958), 22.
4. McNary's early life is described in Steve Neal, *McNary of Oregon: A Political Biography* (Portland: Western Imprints/Oregon Historical Society, 1985), 1–13; Joseph Alsop and Robert Kintner, "Let Them Do the Talking," *Saturday Evening Post*, September 28, 1940, 18–19; and Richard L. Neuberger, "McNary of Fir Cone," *Life*, August 12, 1940, 76–78.
5. Neuberger, "McNary," *Life*, 80–84.
6. CLM to Mrs. W. T. Stolz, November 14, 1941, McNary MSS.
7. CLM to T. W. Sullivan, March 20, 1914, McNary Papers, Oregon Historical Society.
8. McNary interview, *Oregon Journal*, May 30, 1917, 2.
9. Oregon voter pamphlet, 1918 primary election, 9–12, Oregon Secretary of State's Office; Carlton Savage (McNary cousin), interview with author, March 1, 1971.
10. CLM to John H. McNary, July 24, 1922, McNary MSS.
11. CLM to John H. McNary, January 10, 1922, and August 15, 1922, ibid.
12. Neal, *McNary of Oregon*, 95–106; Donald R. McCoy, *Calvin Coolidge: The Quiet President* (New York: Macmillan, 1967), 322–328; and CLM to John H. McNary, March 21, 1928, McNary MSS.
13. McNary's relationship with Hoover is chronicled in Neal, *McNary of Oregon*, 109–117.
14. CLM to Mrs. W. T. Stolz, January 29, 1929; and Richard L. Neuberger, "Oregon's Charlie Mac," *Progressive*, March 20, 1944.
15. CLM to Mrs. W. T. Stolz, December 10, 1928, McNary MSS.
16. McNary's Senate leadership role is described in the *Philadelphia Inquirer*, November 27, 1929.
17. "Anti-Knock Charley," *Collier's*, January 25, 1930, 40; Samuel G. Blythe, "A Hunt for the Elephant," *Saturday Evening Post*, December 30, 1933, 53.
18. CLM to Mrs. W. T. Stolz, June 20, 1941, McNary MSS; McNary is quoted on Harrison in Alsop and Alsop, *Reporter's Trade*, 20.
19. Alsop and Kintner, "Let Them Do the Talking," 90.
20. CLM to Nina McNary, January 11, 1929, McNary MSS.
21. CLM to John H. McNary, December 17, 1931, ibid.
22. Hoover's opposition to McNary is recounted in "McNary Displayed Power as Leader," *New York Times*, February 26, 1944, 14. McNary claimed to have the votes in CLM to John H. McNary, November 18, 1929, McNary MSS. Herbert C. Hoover, *The Memoirs of Herbert Hoover,* vol. 3 (New York: Macmillan, 1952), 3:303–304.
23. CLM to Mrs. W. T. Stolz, November 10, 1932, McNary MSS.
24. CLM to John H. McNary, March 20, 1933, ibid.
25. CLM to Mrs. W. T. Stolz, March 6, 1933, ibid.
26. "Republicans Name McNary as Leader," *New York Times*, March 8, 1933.
27. Senator Felix Hebert to Charles D. Hilles, February 15, 1933, quoted in Roger T. Johnson, "Charles L. McNary and the Republican Party" (Ph.D. diss., University of Wisconsin, 1967), 162.
28. CLM 1897 Stanford notebook for Roman history course taught by Professor Shaw, McNary Papers, Oregon Historical Society.
29. Farley is quoted in Ray Tucker, "Leaders in Revolt," *Philadelphia Evening Ledger*, May 16, 1938; CLM to Joseph P. Tumulty, July 20, 1932, McNary MSS.
30. Herbert Plummer, "All Republicans Look Alike to McNary," Associated Press,

April 1934, McNary Scrapbook, Papers, Oregon Historical Society; and "Committee Posts Shifted," *New York Times*, March 8, 1933.

31. CLM on Lodge-Wilson feud, *New York Times*, December 29, 1922, 2.
32. *Oregonian*, March 5, 1933, 2.
33. CLM to John H. McNary, January 25, 1933, McNary MSS; CLM to John H. McNary, January 1935, McNary Papers, Special Collections, University of Oregon Library.
34. CLM to Mrs. W. T. Stolz, May 23, 1935, McNary MSS., Library of Congress; Rexford G. Tugwell, interview with author, April 12, 1974.
35. CLM to John H. McNary, January 27, 1934, McNary MSS.
36. Neuberger, "McNary of Fir Cone," 83.
37. Theodore C. Wallen, "McNary Calls Off Parley of Republicans," *New York Herald Tribune*, December 31, 1933, 1, 5.
38. CLM to John H. McNary, December 19, 1933, McNary MSS.
39. Ibid., March 5, 1935.
40. CLM to Senator James Couzens, August 14, 1934, McNary MSS.
41. Ibid., November 13, 1934.
42. "McNary Tells GOP to Quit Stalling," *Philadelphia Inquirer*, December 2, 1934.
43. CLM to Couzens, September 4, 1934, McNary MSS.
44. CLM to John H. McNary, February 26, 1935, ibid.
45. CLM to Couzens, August 14, 1934, ibid.
46. McNary statement on New Deal, July 15, 1935, ibid.
47. *Newsweek*, January 20, 1934, 19–20; *Review of Reviews*, February 1934, 31.
48. McNary's responses to Couzens told in Richard L. Neuberger's "McNary's Chances," *Life*, May 13, 1940, 14; CLM withdrawal from 1936 Republican presidential race, *Oregonian*, August 30, 1935, 1.
49. Alice Roosevelt Longworth, "Republicans Start Looking Around," *Ladies Home Journal*, July 1935, 83.
50. CLM to Couzens, November 13, 1934, McNary MSS.
51. McNary's narrow escape in the 1936 election is covered in Neal, "Squeaking Through," 153–158.
52. CLM to Mrs. W. T. Stolz, January 2, 1937, McNary MSS.
53. Norris is quoted in Joseph Alsop and Turner Catledge, *The 168 Days* (Garden City, N.Y.: Doubleday, 1938), 95.
54. Ibid., 97–100.
55. Vandenberg's notes, February 6, 1937, quoted in James T. Patterson, *Congressional Conservatism and the New Deal* (Lexington: University of Kentucky Press, 1967), 108.
56. Alsop and Kintner, "Let Them Do the Talking," 19.
57. Patterson, *Congressional Conservatism*, 108; Alsop and Catledge, *168 Days*, 98–99.
58. Richard Norton Smith, *An Uncommon Man: The Triumph of Herbert Hoover* (New York: Simon and Schuster, 1984), 242.
59. *Time*, February 15, 1937, 19; Roosevelt quoted in Alsop and Catledge, *168 Days*, 111.
60. Alva Johnston, "President Tamer," *Saturday Evening Post*, November 15, 1937, 51.
61. Drew Pearson and Robert S. Allen, "McNary Quietly Directs Opponents of Court Plan," *Philadelphia Record*, July 10, 1937.
62. Alsop and Catledge, *168 Days*, 126–127; 206–207.
63. "McNary Supports Robinson for Court," *New York Times*, July 8, 1937, 1–2; CLM to W. T. Stolz, July 14, 1937, McNary MSS.
64. "McNary Predicts Congress Coalition," *New York Times*, November 26, 1938; Vandenberg and Bailey quoted in Patterson, *Congressional Conservatism*, 209.
65. Address by Senator Barkley, *Charles Linza McNary: Memorial Addresses* (Washington, D.C.: 1944), 53–55; "Hell and Close Harmony," *Time*, August 23, 1937, 11.
66. Byrnes quoted in Alsop and Kintner, "Let Them Do the Talking," 19, 90.
67. CLM to D. D. Allen, January 18, 1939; CLM to Mrs. Hayes Beall, April 24, 1939, McNary MSS.
68. McNary's account of the White House meeting is reported in Joseph Alsop, *FDR:*

A Centenary Remembrance (New York: Viking, 1982), 200; CLM to Mrs. Harriet Gilbert, July 20, 1939, McNary MSS.

69. CLM to Scott Beeler, September 29, 1939, McNary MSS.
70. McNary's conversation with Senator Pepper is reported in Arthur M. Schlesinger, Jr., *The Imperial Presidency* (New York: Houghton Mifflin, 1973), 106–107.
71. "Ban on Third Term Opposed by McNary,' *Philadelphia Inquirer*, December 19, 1938; Harold Ickes, *The Lowering Clouds*, vol. 2 of *The Secret Diary of Harold Ickes* (New York: Simon and Schuster, 1954), 656–657.
72. *New York Times*, January 9, 1940, 14.
73. CLM to Kern Crandall, January 25, 1940, McNary MSS.
74. CLM to Mrs. W. T. Stolz, July 1, 1940, McNary MSS; CLM to Cornelia Morton McNary, July 1, 1940, McNary Papers, Oregon Historical Society; Roosevelt to McNary, July 3, 1940, President's Personal File, FDR Library.
75. CLM to Cornelia Morton McNary, July 19, 1940, Oregon Historical Society.
76. CLM, vice-presidential acceptance address, August 27, 1940, 2, Republican National Committee; CLM to Cornelia Morton McNary, September 17, 1940, McNary Papers, Oregon Historical Society.
77. Ralph H. Cake, interview with author, August 9, 1971; *New York Times*, November 6, 1940.
78. CLM to Mrs. Helen Kiefer, November 11, 1940, McNary MSS.
79. CLM to Mrs. W. T. Stolz, February 27, 1941, McNary MSS; Senator Johnson quoted in Roger Johnson, "Charles L. McNary and the Republican Party,' 348.
80. CLM to Mrs. W. T. Stolz, May 9, 1941, McNary MSS.
81. U.S. Congress, *Congressional Record*, December 11, 1941, 9650; CLM to Mrs. W. T. Stolz, December 12, 1941, McNary MSS.
82. Neuberger, "Oregon's Charlie Mac"; U.S. Congress, *Congressional Record*, June 29, 1941, 5673–5674; CLM to Mrs. W. T. Stolz, June 26, 1942, McNary MSS.
83. CLM to Mrs. W. T. Stolz, November 9, 1942, McNary MSS.
84. U.S. Congress, *Congressional Record*, November 5, 1942, 8710–8712.
85. McNary's knowledge of the Manhattan Project is described in Roland A. Young, *Congressional Politics in the Second World War* (New York: Columbia University Press, 1956); comments on postwar planning from *Oregonian*, August 5, 1943, 11.
86. CLM to Mrs. W. T. Stolz, October 12, 1942, McNary MSS.
87. Senator Vandenberg, CLM *Memorial Addresses*, 46; McNary quoted by Carlton Savage, interview with author, March 1, 1971.

CHAPTER 5

Alben W. Barkley
The President's Man

Donald A. Ritchie

T he campaign for majority leader had already gotten under way when Joe Robinson's funeral train left Washington for Little Rock, Arkansas, in July 1937. Those aboard described it as a "political convention on wheels"[1] with "a caucus in every compartment."[2] Discreetly secluded were the two contenders for the post, assistant leader Alben Barkley of Kentucky and Finance Committee chairman Pat Harrison of Mississippi. Elsewhere, clusters of senators, White House lobbyists, and reporters assessed the impact of the contest on the president's controversial plan to enlarge the Supreme Court. "The politicking was so intense," recalled one newspaper correspondent, "that the main business of the trip—burying Robinson—was all but overlooked."[3]

Described by Franklin Roosevelt as a "balance wheel" that kept things moving, Democrat Alben Barkley of Kentucky relied on his conciliatory abilities coupled with charm as majority leader.

FDR Intervenes in the Leadership Race

The real contender in the Senate leadership race was Franklin Roosevelt. The president had staked his political reputation on breaking the Supreme Court's conservative majority before it could further damage his New Deal programs, but his plan to enlarge the Court badly divided congressional Democrats, many of whom worried that a victory would make the president "absolute boss" over the Court and the Congress. Barkley's supporters called it disloyal for Democrats to oppose their president, while the dissenters saw opposition to the Court plan as a defense of the constitutional separation of powers. As a senator in Harrison's camp described the race, "It looked at that time like there was a line up in the Senate and down the Avenue on the Court question."[4]

"My dear Alben," read the president's salutation to the acting leader in a letter released to the press the day after Joe Robinson died. In it, the president decried the appearance of politics during a period of mourning but at the same time made it clear that he intended to continue his fight to reform the Supreme Court. Harrison's supporters were offended more by the letter's tone than by its contents for it implied a presidential endorsement of Barkley for majority leader. Although professing neutrality, Roosevelt wanted Barkley to win. Harrison had been one of the president's key congressional lieutenants, but FDR apparently regarded him as more conservative and less dependable than Barkley. Harrison had kept silent on Roosevelt's Court bill, and among his supporters were most of the opposition to "Court-packing." Harrison was also demonstrating increased resistance to the New Deal's tax and spending programs. Furthermore, while black voters were switching their allegiance away from the party of Lincoln, Harrison was adamantly opposed to any civil rights legislation. Finally, if Harrison became majority leader, then his chairmanship of the Finance Committee would pass to the anti–New Dealer William H. King of Utah, whom Roosevelt found "just impossible to deal with."[5]

When surveys showed Harrison in front, Roosevelt campaigned for Barkley behind the scenes. Presidential aides Tommy Corcoran and Harry Hopkins intervened with state Democratic leaders to apply political pressure on their senators. Illinois's William Dieterich, for example, buckled and withdrew his promised support of Harrison, and Missouri's Harry Truman received a call from Kansas City's political boss, Tom Pendergast, relaying the White House request to vote for Barkley. Truman had already committed himself to Harrison, who had campaigned for him in Missouri and had asked for his vote. Pendergast did not press him to renege, but Truman, always eager to stress his independence, later confessed that saying no "was one of the hardest things I ever had to do." Working hard to shed his image as Pendergast's office boy, Truman had no desire to assume the same role for the White House. He kept his word and voted for Harrison.[6]

With seventy-five senators voting at the Democratic caucus on July 21, the tally was 37-37 before the last ballot elected Barkley. For Barkley the deciding ballot looked "as big as a bedquilt." For Harrison's supporters it was an emblem of presidential deceit. The old school congressional leaders operated under the principle that a man's word was his bond. "If Sam Rayburn or Jimmy Byrnes gave me his word on something, I would have bet my life on it," said *New York Times* correspondent Turner Catledge. "That was a feeling I never had about Franklin Roosevelt or many of his New Dealers." Roosevelt's involvement in the Senate's internal affairs simply confirmed suspicions for those who saw dictatorial tendencies behind his actions, and more deeply entrenched the party's division over the Court bill. "Democratic leadership isn't in the bag," taunted Republican Arthur Vandenberg, "it's in two bags."[7]

Barkley paid dearly for Roosevelt's intervention. Leader in title rather than authority, he spoke more for the administration than for the Senate majority. The senator's detractors, and even his friends, persisted in calling him "Dear Alben," an unsubtle reminder of his indebtedness to the White House. Although Barkley dedicated himself to enacting the New Deal's legislative programs, he lacked the independence to exert leverage on the president's strategies. His success as leader would depend largely on his ability to predict and control the outcome of floor actions in the Senate, yet the Roosevelt administration often required Barkley to support legislation that had little chance of passage, thereby diminishing his standing in the eyes of his fellow senators and in the estimation of the press. For his part, Barkley accepted his role of presidential flag carrier, but it took him years to regain confidence or to command the loyalty of Democratic senators. It took him equally as long to live down his image as a hapless leader unable to command the Democratic party's disjointed forces. Journalists tagged him "Bumbling Barkley," a label that stuck, he admitted, "like tar did to Br'er Rabbit."[8]

Barkley's Leadership Credentials

In spite of impressions to the contrary, Barkley was a shrewd choice for majority leader. The Harrison-Barkley race represented a clash between the old-style, patronage-oriented senators and the issue-oriented politicians who came to office with the New Deal. However, "the new-stylers were smart enough," Catledge observed, "to pick an old-timer as their candidate."[9] Moderate, Barkley appealed to New Deal liberals as the president's choice without automatically alienating conservatives. Similarly, as a border-state man, he was acceptable to senators from both North and South. Barkley was also a party loyalist, holding the affection of professional politicians who made him a perennial keynoter and toast-master. Barkley may have lacked Joe Robinson's intimidating personality and accumulated political debts, but he compensated with his charm and his abilities as a conciliator.

Barkley even claimed the ultimate political asset, having been born in a log house on a small Kentucky tobacco farm in 1877. He spent his youth plowing fields for his father or for neighbors. Industrious and intelligent, he worked his way as a school janitor through Marvin College in Clinton, Kentucky. While a student, he read the lives of Daniel Webster, Henry Clay, and John C. Calhoun and decided that to become a United States senator was "an honor not to be excelled." He went on to study law for a year at Emory College in Oxford, Georgia, before returning to Paducah to read law. There he hung out his shingle in 1901. The next summer Barkley attended classes at the University of Virginia Law School, suggesting loftier ambitions than local law practice.[10]

As a Kentucky lawyer inclined to address a crowd of any size, Barkley claimed a certain inevitability about his entrance into politics. In 1905, he campaigned on horseback to become prosecuting attorney of his western Kentucky county. He won election to the administrative post of county judge in 1909 and was elected to the U.S. House of Representatives in 1912. Once in Washington, he remolded his political thinking from such earlier heroes as Thomas Jefferson and William Jennings Bryan into the progressive image of Woodrow Wilson. Barkley unequivocally endorsed Wilson's economic program and embraced his internationalist foreign policy. Flexibility of government and a willingness to experiment with social and economic programs became his definition of "a true Liberal."[11]

In Congress, Barkley admired House Speaker James Beauchamp "Champ" Clark, a master storyteller whose gifts as a raconteur greased the legislative process. The new representative also found "a great deal of good comradeship" among such House members as Joe Robinson, Pat Harrison, Jimmy Byrnes, and Sam Rayburn, with whom he would work for decades to come. On the House floor, Barkley polished his speaking style and revealed his skill as an orator. He delivered his first keynote address at the 1919 Kentucky Democratic convention. One biographer noted that his rhetoric was abusive of the Republican party in general, but impersonal enough to warrant a reputation as "a uniquely gentle partisan." Barkley's first keynote speech reflected a spirit of political moderation and a preference for compromise over confrontation, reminiscent of Kentucky's Henry Clay.[12]

In 1923, Barkley advanced his political career while losing a bid for the Democratic gubernatorial nomination. By supporting a severance tax on coal, embracing Prohibition, and opposing parimutuel betting, he confronted the state's powerful bipartisan combine of coal mining, whiskey distilling, and horse racing interests, led by the freewheeling Kentucky Jockey Club. His campaign theme of "Christianity, Morality, and Clean Government" appealed to western, rural counties but attracted few eastern or urban voters. Although defeated in the Democratic primary, Barkley earned statewide name recognition and the sobriquet "iron man" for his ability to give as many as sixteen speeches a day. He won further approval for his loyal support of the party's ticket that fall.[13]

Three years later, no longer a regional candidate, he ran for the Senate as the candidate of a united Democratic party and gathered influential editorial endorsements. "I do not want a Senator that I can control," Robert Worth Bingham, publisher of the Louisville *Courier-Journal*, explained when he asked Bernard Baruch to contribute to Barkley's campaign. "I want one that nobody can control."[14] Victory over an incumbent Republican promoted Alben Barkley to the Senate, where he gained some expertise and seniority as a member of the minority before the Depression revived his party's fortunes. In 1932 he delivered the keynote address at the National Democratic Convention. ("What do you mean 'note?' " asked Will Rogers. "This is no note. This was in three volumes.") Abandoning his previous stance in favor of Prohibition, Barkley threw his support behind the "wet" candidacy of Franklin D. Roosevelt. Although his shift on Prohibition risked his standing among "women and church people" back home, economic issues swept Barkley to an easy reelection that year. When the Democrats won a majority of the Senate, Robinson selected Barkley as assistant leader, which placed him on the Democratic steering and patronage committees. As one of Robinson's "chief oratorical aides," Barkley performed yeoman labor as a spokesman for the New Deal's legislative program during Roosevelt's first term and gave another rousing keynote speech at the 1936 convention—factors that earned him the president's confidence.[15]

An Unwieldy Majority

Barkley assumed leadership of the largest majority in the Senate's history. During the Seventy-fifth Congress, seventy-six Democrats faced sixteen Republicans and four independents. So lopsided was the margin that freshman Democrats had to occupy the back row on the Republican side of the chamber, known in Senate parlance as the "Cherokee Strip" for members off their reservation. President Roosevelt's landslide reelection and the popularity of his programs had contributed to the huge Democratic majority, raising expectations that senators would "have the courage of the President's convictions." But the swelled ranks of Democratic voters encompassed a multitude of competing groups, including southern rural conservatives, northern urban liberals, organized labor, farmers, blacks, and anyone else benefiting from New Deal programs. The party could not satisfy all these interests, and whatever choices it made threatened to split its conservative and liberal wings further apart. The president's Supreme Court plan was the critical element in this schism, but so were southern fears over labor union and civil rights activities, conservative opposition to federal taxing and spending programs, and the threat of presidential usurpation of congressional powers. When Barkley became majority leader, both Republican and Democratic head counters in the Senate judged that there were always twelve to fifteen "sure" votes for the administration, and some twenty to thirty votes against it. "It is the men between who must be watched," advised Democratic Secretary Leslie Biffle. On most votes the leader needed to muster a majority from this middle group.[16]

Barkley's first day as majority leader coincided with President Roosevelt's single most devastating political defeat. On the morning of July 22, 1937, Barkley met with members of the Senate Judiciary Committee. Although the administration had reluctantly agreed to recommit the Court bill to the committee, Barkley wanted to keep it on the calendar until a substitute was submitted. Democratic opponents of the Court plan angrily shouted down their new leader, and even administration supporters agreed to shelve the bill to restore party unity. Stunned and redfaced, Barkley sat silently as the Court bill collapsed. He refused to offer the motion to recommit on the floor, so that dubious honor fell to his Kentucky colleague, Marvel M. Logan. That afternoon when the Senate met, Barkley's suffering intensified. Trying to convince senators not to override the president's veto of another bill that he himself had originally sponsored, Barkley lost on a Senate vote of 71-19. Later that day, by a similar margin of 70-20, the Senate recommitted the Court bill. "The Supreme Court is out of the way?" demanded California Republican Hiram Johnson about the agreement for a new bill. "The Supreme Court is out of the way," responded Logan. "Glory be to God!" said Johnson, and the chamber erupted in applause, which Vice President John Nance Garner made no effort to suppress.[17]

After four years of unprecedented success in enacting recovery and reform legislation, and despite overwhelming Democratic majorities in both houses of Congress, New Deal initiatives sputtered to an embarrassing halt. "Important legislative programs languished," in the assessment of Tommy Corcoran, the president's legislative troubleshooter, "first because the White House's energies were devoted to salvaging whatever could be saved from the Court debacle, second because the Congress had changed its mood." Roosevelt could not understand why "Congressmen who owed their very jobs to his popularity were letting go of his coattails." Majority Leader Barkley also discovered that a "top-heavy majority worked rather badly," undermining discipline and dissipating the responsibility of individual Democratic senators. He had inherited a deeply divided party, with a significant portion no longer willing to bend to their own president.[18]

One evening in August 1937, near the end of the session, Senate Democrats held a harmony dinner at a Washington hotel. In a show of reconciliation, Harrison joined Barkley at the head table to offer a round of toasts and hear the new majority leader sing "Wagon Wheels." But harmony evaporated the next day in the Senate chamber when Senator Robert Wagner of New York unexpectedly moved the consideration of an anti-lynching bill. Barkley jumped to his feet to object that the leadership had agreed to take up other legislation first. Vice President Garner rejoined that Senator Wagner alone had sought recognition. When he was Speaker of the House, said Garner, he "could recognize a member in his seat and ask him to stand up," but not so in the Senate. Barkley countered by moving that the Senate adjourn, a parliamentary procedure designed to dissolve Wagner's motion. On a roll-call vote, liberal Democrats defected to unite with Republicans and defeat the majority leader's motion, 35-27. Republican leader Charles McNary then moved to recess the Senate, which would retain Wagner's motion as the pending business when the Senate returned. By a vote of 36-23, the Senate chose to follow its minority leader. When a Democratic senator asked how he should vote, Barkley snapped, "I don't know! Ask McNary! He's the only real leader around here. That was a hell of a harmony dinner we had last night."[19]

With southerners threatening to filibuster until Christmas, Barkley was able to persuade Senator Wagner to withdraw his bill only after agreeing to make antilynching legislation the first order of business during the next regular session. Wagner's persistence exposed a new rift in the Democratic party, one that would perplex Barkley throughout his tenure as majority leader. Through seniority, the key committee chairmanships fell to southern Democrats committed to racial segregation and white supremacy. At the same time, the Depression had swelled the congressional ranks of liberal Democrats more sympathetic to civil rights. As long as the party's agenda remained essentially economic, its diverse elements held together. When confronted with racial issues, however, the complex fabric began to unravel. (During one of Barkley's reelection campaigns, a heckler yelled: "How do you stand on FEPC [the Fair Employment Practices Commission]?" Knowing how divided his Kentucky constituency was on civil rights, the senator replied, "I'm all right on FEPC," and went on with his speech.)[20]

Like Roosevelt, the majority leader feared that antilynching legislation would alienate southern senators from other New Deal programs. But Barkley kept his word to the liberals and supported their legislation on the floor. Pat Harrison warned of dire consequences for the Democratic party if it challenged the white South on civil rights. "May I be permitted to say to all the aspiring gentlemen of this body who may entertain some hope of becoming the nominee of the Democratic Party for President of the United States," Harrison pointed at Barkley, "that you had better stop, look, and listen." Southern-led filibusters defeated all attempts to enact federal antilynching legislation.[21]

Harrison repeatedly proved himself the most powerful member of the United States Senate. In April 1938, he led the effort to repeal the undistributed profits tax, while Barkley stood among only four senators who supported the administration's position to retain it; journalists called the vote "a public humiliation for Senator Barkley." Harrison's stature rose as more senators became disenchanted with the New Deal, while Barkley was accused of consulting the White House even before salting his soup. Reporters especially loved Harrison because he "knew everything that was going on" and was glad to tell them what he knew. In March 1939, *Life* magazine polled Washington correspondents to identify the ten most able senators. Pat Harrison was fifth, while Barkley did not even make the list. In terms of "influence," Harrison ranked first. Newsmen cited him as "the best wrangler in the Senate," "a natural leader," "shrewd, smart as the devil," and "the conservative balance wheel," although "downright lazy." They labeled Democratic whip Jimmy Byrnes, fourth in the poll, as the "best legislator on Capitol Hill" with "tremendous influence behind the scenes," but "not overly strong on principle." Joseph Alsop and Robert Kintner singled out Byrnes as "the real leader of the Senate majority," to whom Barkley had yielded "all but the shadow of his power." However true these appraisals, the competition did not last long. In 1941 Harrison died and Byrnes resigned to take a seat on the Supreme Court, leaving the leadership field to Barkley alone.[22]

The Majority Leader and the President

The majority leader's public image ebbed and flowed with presidential popularity. In November 1937, President Roosevelt called Congress back into extraordinary session to complete a legislative program that included executive reorganization and minimum wage and maximum hours protection for workers. But a hostile Congress adjourned after five weeks without passing a single major bill. The fortunes of the president and majority leader began to improve in 1938. The victory of Senator Claude Pepper in the Florida Democratic primary in May 1938 provided evidence that southern voters supported the proposed Fair Labor Standards Act and led to its enactment. Still, the president suffered major defeats on taxes and administrative reorganization. Majority Leader Barkley took the blame from New Deal liberals for not passing the president's program, and from conservative Democrats for following the president so faithfully. "When the President's control of Congress is strong and real," wrote *New York Times* columnist Arthur Krock (a fellow Kentuckian), the leadership could carry through its measures. "When the President's control is absent, they fail to carry them through. This is the present plight of Senator Barkley."[23]

Barkley's identification with the president was fused even more firmly during the 1938 Kentucky primary. Fresh from rejecting the president's Court-packing plan, and seeking to gain control of the party machinery before the 1940 presidential convention, Democratic conservatives aimed to defeat Roosevelt's handpicked majority leader. They threw their support behind Kentucky's youthful governor Albert B. "Happy" Chandler, who challenged "Old Alben" for the senatorial nomination—and who boasted openly of his presidential ambitions. President Roosevelt ranked the Populist-sounding, conservative-leaning Chandler as a "Huey Long type, but with less ability." Not wanting to lose his majority leader and intending to purge Democratic conservatives from Congress, the president took a direct hand in Barkley's campaign. Roosevelt personally telephoned John L. Lewis (the price Lewis demanded) to raise campaign funds for Barkley from the United Mine Workers. In July, the president made a series of whistle-stop speeches in Kentucky on Barkley's behalf. As they disembarked from the campaign train in Covington, the wily Chandler managed to leap into the presidential limousine and plant himself between Roosevelt and Barkley. Otherwise the presidential visit benefited Barkley, who easily defeated Chandler in the primary and went on to win a landslide reelection.[24]

The press also revealed that the New Deal had used its patronage resources to reelect the majority leader. Newspaper correspondent Thomas L. Stokes uncovered evidence that the Works Progress Administration (WPA) in Kentucky was supporting Barkley. After touring the state and interviewing relief agency officials, Stokes published a Pulitzer prize–winning series of articles charging that WPA workers had kicked back a percentage of their salaries as political donations. Earlier, when Senator Carl Hatch first advocated legislation barring WPA workers from political activity, Barkley opposed the bill on the grounds that state candidates had state machines that they would similarly employ. Indeed, Stokes accused Governor Chandler of tapping various state workers to finance his challenge to Barkley. Both candidates were guilty of perpetrating "a grand political racket in which the taxpayer is the victim." Although Barkley and WPA administrator Harry Hopkins denied most of his charges, Stokes's reporting hit the mark squarely. As Hopkins's friend Robert Sherwood commented, "I can say with assurance that there were not many members of Congress at that time who had never used W.P.A. in one way or another to shore up their own political fortunes." The Kentucky exposé helped to spur enactment of the Hatch Act to shield federal employees from political coercion.[25]

Beyond presidential popularity, other institutional factors shaped Barkley's Senate leadership. During the 1930s, the enormous growth and complexity of issues facing Congress made the structure of the Senate, its rules, committee system, and staff support, increasingly inadequate. As leader, Senator Barkley described the rules of the Senate as "the most archaic conglomeratory decisions that ever prevailed in any parliamentary or legislative body" and advocated modernization. Lacking a professional staff, the legislature depended on the executive branch to draft almost all major legislation, even to write speeches for the bills' floor managers. "With occasional exceptions," Floyd Riddick wrote at the time, "Congress did little more than look into, slightly amend, or block the bills upon which it was called to act." Tommy Corcoran pointed out that Congress lacked the "technical equipment to draft a big, modern statute." Outside of the executive branch, New Dealers argued, the only other legislative technicians came from the large corporate law firms. And Corcoran asked: "Why is it any worse to have us hand a member of Congress a copy of a bill than it is to have [corporate lawyer] John W. Davis do it?"[26]

Because Congress did not modernize its structure until the Legislative Reorganization Act of 1946, Barkley was the last Senate majority leader to operate under the old system. Although he had the services of the "efficient firm of Biffle, Biffle, Biffle and Biffle" (as he described the ubiquitous Leslie Biffle, secretary of the Senate Democrats), limited staff resources meant Barkley often had to depend on administration-drafted legislation and ghostwritten speeches. "I would take a little old memorandum up there to Mr. Barkley," Ed Prichard recalled of his days on the White House staff. "He'd read it, and talk to me about five or ten minutes. And he would go in there and make a speech on the floor and have a dialogue with other senators that would convince you that he'd been up all the night before working on the matter." He had, Prichard reiterated, "a nimble, nimble mind—and I certainly don't say that in derogation."[27]

Barkley's ability to absorb information and repeat it authoritatively made it difficult to judge his depth of understanding and involvement. "Whether he understood legislation or not," a *Chicago Tribune* correspondent recorded, "Alben gave the impression of being completely informed." Darrell St. Claire, secretary of the Senate Democratic Patronage Committee, found Barkley "fairly nimble in his views and his expressions, and discussions, and debate." Although a remarkably good extemporaneous speaker, the majority leader rarely studied any issue thoroughly. "I don't think he ever really went into depth on anything," said St. Claire, noting that whenever Barkley called for a lectern at his desk, it indicated that he needed to read a text prepared by someone else. "As he got more and more polish, and became the master of the reflective story, or the attributive joke, he had an amazing amount of relative pieces of humor that he could throw into his speeches." St. Claire concluded, "I think he became something of a show horse on the Senate floor."[28]

Nevertheless, by 1940 Barkley had won credit for getting the Senate's legislative program "streamlined for speed." Barkley viewed his role primarily as one of promoting the administration's legislation. "There must be one man in the Senate upon whom responsibility is fixed for guiding the legislative program through the Senate, seeing that bills come along in their proper order," he explained. "He must have some judgment about which bill ought to be taken up ahead of other bills depending upon their importance and their immediate necessity." As majority leader, Barkley daily sat on the edge of his seat, as he said, "watching legislation, watching amendments, and outlining the program for the next two weeks, trying to satisfy senators who have bills they want taken up ahead of others, which is really a difficult problem sometimes to work out."[29]

Senate leadership in Barkley's time was no easy business. Writing in 1940, Joseph Alsop and Robert Kintner detailed how the Senate's institutional components—"the committee system, the parliamentary procedure, the debate, the roll call"— each presented traps for a leader:

> As the unhappy Barkley has too often learned, the slightest misstep will allow a committee to make the wrong report, or tangled parliamentary procedure to bring the wrong business before the Senate, or a debate to go the wrong way, or an important roll call vote to be lost.[30]

Although they dismissed most floor proceedings as "a grandiose performance" that hid the real transactions in the cloakrooms and lobbies, the reporters considered floor management a critical legislative art. "Each day the situation changes, for senators come and go, waverers jump from side to side, and the line-up shifts on every amendment." A leader must know the voting profile of every senator, in the minority as well as the majority, to project how each vote might go, what timing should be employed, and what inducements might be needed. To keep abreast of shifting attitudes, the leadership conducted informal polls—as many as twenty for a major legislative fight. "The temper of a legislative body is surprisingly uncertain," Alsop and Kintner concluded; "there are times when you can walk away with the Treasury by unanimous consent, and times when you would be hard put to get a majority vote for the Ten Commandments."[31]

Like his predecessors, Barkley retained his committee assignments. He believed a majority leader needed to be familiar with every bill that came before the Senate, to "lead in its advocacy," or to block its passage depending on the position of the administration and the majority party. From his experience, senators learned more about a bill during the closed-door, executive session meetings of the committee considering it than at any other stage. While majority leader, Barkley served on the Finance, Foreign Relations, Banking and Currency, and Interstate Commerce committees, chaired the Library Committee, and was appointed to several special and select committees. Later, when the Legislative Reorganization Act of 1946 limited him to two committees, he chose Finance and Foreign Relations. This assortment of committee assignments and the conflicting demands of floor leadership kept Barkley from becoming a legislative specialist. Rather than master details, he played the generalist who knew something about everything and who used his gifts as a speaker to carry his argument.[32]

"Rather than the heavy-handed iron rule of a Robinson, Barkley's method was one of easygoing rapport with a warm undercurrent of laughter," wrote Richard Riedel, who watched the scene as a staff member in the Senate press gallery. "He would sit down by a colleague, ease him into a benevolent mood with a bit of droll humor, and while they were chuckling together, Barkley would solidly close in with his reasoning on the issue at hand." Whether in committee or on the Senate floor, the majority leader deftly played the "master broker," searching for areas of agreement between opposing sides, defusing tensions, and coaxing the discussions along with appropriate anecdotes. He could call up a story to apply to any situation and speak on seemingly any subject for as long as necessary, and then some.[33]

Barkley's habitual storytelling sometimes worked to his disadvantage. He simply liked to talk too much, having, as Jim Farley chided, "no terminal facilities." Harold Ickes recorded in his diary how President Roosevelt dismissed the notion of Barkley as a presidential candidate by citing his excessively lengthy speeches, which suggested that the senator lacked all sense of proportion. Roosevelt also vetoed Barkley as keynote speaker for the 1940 convention because his speeches were "too long and tiresome." As it developed, the chosen keynoter made such indifferent references to Roosevelt in his address, that it took Barkley's speech as permanent chairman to reinvigorate the convention and to whip up enthusiasm for the president's third-term nomination. Ickes admired how Barkley appealed to the pent-up emotions of the crowd and "very cleverly turned it into a Roosevelt demonstration by one or two adroit and well-phrased remarks." Despite such achievements, Barkley's storytelling habits and long-winded speeches too often made him appear lacking in substance.[34]

The majority leader's daily efforts to reach legislative compromises further painted an image of a cautious politician, inclined to go with the tide. "All legislation is a matter of compromise," Barkley defined it, although he preferred the word "adjustment," by which he meant that no senator could enact a bill "just as he introduced it." Other senators, he knew would undoubtedly have an opinion about it, "and they may find mistakes or deficiencies in it which can be corrected by amendment." Legislation rarely got through the Senate, wrote Barkley, "without either a committee or the Senate itself on the floor changing it in any way that it sees fit to make the bill better." Journalist William S. White used "accommodation" to describe Barkley's knack for compromise. Assessing Barkley's leadership, he concluded that he was "a *good* leader *because* he was convivial, garrulous, cheerfully ready to take his lumps from day to day." White found Barkley "untypical in this matter of accommodation; it was his habit to press on without compromise to the end."[35]

Those who underestimated Barkley as majority leader overlooked the doggedness with which he would "press on without compromise" to enact legislation that the Roosevelt administration considered essential. Although some reporters admired James Byrnes's de facto Senate leadership and compared his adroit backstage maneuvering favorably to Barkley's lumbering, straightforward style, Byrnes was often too quick to compromise. In fact, his willingness to weaken Roosevelt's executive reorganization bill was largely responsible for its defeat. Similarly, Byrnes was ready to back down on Lend-Lease legislation of 1941. Assistant Secretary of War John J. McCloy, who followed Lend-Lease closely through the Senate, told Harold Ickes that he had gained new respect for Barkley. According to McCloy, as Ickes noted in his diary, "Barkley stubbornly refused to yield on proposed amendments that even Jimmy Byrnes was willing to accept. Apparently thanks are due to Barkley for the fact that the bill came out in as good a shape as it did."[36]

Barkley's Wartime Leadership

As the Lend-Lease bill demonstrated, Barkley's record as a floor leader improved when the national focus shifted from domestic to international issues following the outbreak of war in Europe. The stance of southern Democrats as Wilsonian internationalists, and their willingness to follow the administration's lead on foreign policy (although they continued to bolt on domestic issues), helped greatly in reforging party unity. Throughout the 1930s, Senate isolationists had enjoyed broad public support, which translated into passage of neutrality legislation. In July 1939, President Roosevelt invited congressional leaders to an evening meeting at the White House to discuss repeal of the Embargo Act. Turning to the majority leader, the president asked: "Have you got the votes in the Senate to repeal the embargo law?" Barkley replied: "We do not have them— they are not there." Accepting the majority leader's assessment, the president conceded that Congress might as well adjourn in August. On September 1, German troops invaded Poland, and Roosevelt called Congress back into session. Working on the administration's behalf, Barkley and the chairman of the Foreign Relations Committee led the effort to repeal the arms embargo and permit belligerent nations to purchase American arms on a "cash and carry" basis. Barkley endorsed the president's "destroyers for bases" swap with Great Britain and fought hard to enact the nation's first peacetime military draft.[37]

The attack on Pearl Harbor further improved his standing. "It was much easier for the majority leader during the war than it had been before and much easier than it has been since because everybody was in favor of winning the war," Barkley later wrote. "Everybody favored all the appropriations necessary to win the war. We were all going in the same direction then." The war gave the administration more control over Congress than it had held since the Supreme Court fight. Largely abandoning the New Deal and concentrating on winning the war, Roosevelt's legislative record improved markedly, with many bills rushed to enactment after little or no debate. A tally of the Senate's schedule during 1942 reveals that only thirty-four measures that year were debated for more than half an hour.[38]

Yet as Roosevelt reestablished his dominance over Congress, the mood on Capitol Hill grew testy. Acknowledging that war was primarily an administrative responsibility, Congress unhappily accepted a subordinate role. Then, as wartime agencies imposed emergency restrictions on the public, members of Congress took the blame from their constituents for permitting bureaucratic inconveniences. The congressional image slid lower when the press accused elected officials of seeking special privileges while average citizens were required to make sacrifices for the war. One nasty flap involved the issuance of gasoline ration "x-cards," which permitted their holders to purchase unlimited quantities of gasoline. After the newspaper stories revealed that some two hundred members of Congress had requested x-cards, Sheridan Downey (D-Calif.) moved that they waive their rights and voluntarily restrict their use of gasoline—a motion the Senate rejected 2-68. Senator Barkley, wrote columnist Raymond Clapper, flew into a rage over Downey's proposal and complained that press criticisms were undermining the dignity of Congress. Barkley saw no need for the Senate "to pass a resolution binding the membership to be honorable men." Clapper advised the majority leader to "let down his blood pressure and think it over," pointing out that Congress's deteriorating image was the failure, not of the press or the executive branch, but of Congress itself to provide leadership during a national crisis.[39]

Democrats bore the brunt of public displeasure, the majorities diminishing with each election. From their high of seventy-six in 1937, Senate Democrats shrank to sixty-nine in the election of 1938, to sixty-six in the 1940 election, and to fifty-eight after November 1942. Meanwhile, prosperity returned with wartime employment, which, combined with necessary increases in military spending, gave Republicans and conservative Democrats justification for dismantling New Deal agencies. The expanded conservative coalition killed the Works Progress Administration, Civilian Conservation Corps, National Youth Administration, and National Resources Planning Board. It slashed funds for the Office of Price Administration and Office of War Information and stalled the administration's postwar public works program. Finding it difficult to attack the nation's commander in chief during wartime, antiadministration senators directed their fire at Roosevelt's appointees, including First Lady Eleanor Roosevelt, who resigned as assistant director of the Office of Civilian Defense.[40]

Displeasure over the Senate's backseat role during the war manifested itself in such poor attendance that the majority leader frequently found it difficult to maintain a quorum. Clerks called the roll repeatedly without enough senators answering to keep the proceedings going, delaying business for hours. On a few occasions, Senator Barkley dispatched the sergeant-at-arms to bring senators back for a quorum, a tactic that riled tempers all the more. One day in 1942, during a filibuster against legislation to abolish poll taxes, Barkley made a motion to have absent members arrested and brought to the chamber. "Do you mean Senator McKellar, too?" asked the deputy sergeant-at-arms. "I mean *everyone!*" Barkley snapped. The dyspeptic senator from Tennessee was therefore roused from his hotel room and driven to Capitol Hill before he realized he was being used to break a southern filibuster. Kenneth McKellar did not speak to Barkley for over a year, even though they sat beside each other in the chamber. When the Senate Democratic Conference met in

January 1943, McKellar's candidate for conference secretary defeated Barkley's choice. McKellar also moved to strip the majority leader of his authority to fill vacancies on the Democratic Steering Committee, which made committee assignments. Only Barkley's threat to resign as leader stopped McKellar's motion by a secret-ballot vote of 33-20—reflecting the continued split within the party over Barkley's leadership.[41]

When Allen Drury began covering the Senate as a United Press reporter in 1943, his first impression of Alben Barkley was that of "a man who is working awfully hard and awfully earnestly at a job he doesn't particularly like." Drury judged the majority leader reasonably capable, "a good man if not a great leader." In short order, however, Barkley rose in his esteem for making "a great deal of sense" in committee hearings. "He is a good politician and a good-natured, easygoing man," Drury noted in his diary. "I suspect he deserves his *E* for Effort." That assessment was not universally shared, particularly within the executive branch. Although Barkley was one of the "Big Four" leaders (along with Vice President Henry Wallace, Speaker Sam Rayburn, and House Majority leader John McCormack) who gathered in President Roosevelt's bedroom on Monday mornings for strategy sessions, and although he carried the ball faithfully for the president on every issue, his loyalty was often taken for granted. Roosevelt valued the majority leader's judgment on how the Senate might vote but placed less reliance in Barkley's opinions on issues. The president's assistants made Barkley a convenient scapegoat for the administration's legislative losses. Asking Barkley to offer amendments with little chance of passage, the White House staff would complain that had he employed some other tactic or showed better sense of timing, the defeated measure might have survived.[42]

By contrast, Barkley earned begrudging respect from his Senate colleagues. For years senators belittled his title as a "White House gift" and grumbled that the majority leader represented the executive branch more than his own. "But when they see him, day after day, evening after evening, battling alone for the President's program, they feel drawn to him personally," wrote Arthur Krock:

> Mr. Barkley is a likable man, always ready to put down bitterness with a laugh and candid enough in the cloakroom about his own troubles. He may therefore have the curious experience of gaining respect and loyalty in the Senate in the very degrees he loses them in the political control room of the New Deal.[43]

Surrounded by reporters, Majority Leader Alben Barkley (left) and House Speaker Sam Rayburn emerge from a weekly congressional leadership meeting at the White House in 1944.

The Majority Leader Resigns in Protest

Krock's prediction came true in 1944, when Barkley unexpectedly resigned as majority leader, an incident that exposed the stress and strain between Congress and the White House during the war. Concentrating on global issues, President Roosevelt had grown more impatient with congressional parochialism and paid less attention to its concerns and complaints. Members of Congress found the president more aloof and patronizing than ever and resented being made the target of his attacks. That January, Roosevelt's State of the Union message assailed "bickering, self-seeking partisanship," and "the whining demands of selfish pressure groups who seek to feather their nests while young Americans are dying." Reflecting the unanimous opinion of his economic advisers that taxes should finance a much larger share of the cost of the war as a brake against inflation, Roosevelt asked for "a realistic tax law—which will tax all unreasonable profits, both individual and corporate, and reduce the ultimate cost of the war to our sons and daughters." Having broadened the number of taxpayers tenfold and instituted the first withholding taxes, Congress had little appetite for so steep a rise in taxes during an election year. Legislators cut the president's requested $10.5 billion in additional revenue to $2.2 billion.[44]

When Roosevelt returned from his meeting with Winston Churchill and Joseph Stalin at Teheran, he determined to veto the truncated tax bill as a lesson to the special interests represented on Capitol Hill. On February 19, the "Big Four" leaders gathered in the president's bedroom. Roosevelt held these weekly meetings to demonstrate his desire to work through, rather than around, his party's leadership in Congress. But as Wallace noted, their visits were often little more than social calls, with the president exchanging gossip and tipping his legislative hand only indirectly. Privately, both Barkley and Rayburn expressed regret that Roosevelt so rarely took them into his confidence.

On this day in February, however, the president railed against the tax bill, especially provisions that allowed the timber industry to count its profits from cutting down trees as capital gains rather than as annual income. Wallace wondered if by focusing on trees the president was not obliquely warning Rayburn about oil. But, more clearly than his vice president, Roosevelt recognized the lumber lobby's powerful influence in Congress. Senator Barkley took sharp exception and debated with the president for almost an hour. Although he had supported Roosevelt's original tax proposals in the Finance Committee and on the floor, Barkley had signed the conference report and felt certain that the bill as passed was the best the administration could expect that year. He worried that, should Congress fail to override the president's veto, there would be no new revenue at all. At a second meeting, Barkley recommended that the president sign the bill with a protest. But it became clear that Roosevelt had gotten his Dutch up and would not compromise. "What's the use?" Barkley sighed, as he drove back to the Capitol with Henry Wallace. "I can't get the votes in the Senate under the methods that are being followed."[45]

Even so forewarned, Barkley was stunned when he read the president's veto message. "It has been suggested by some," wrote Roosevelt in a sentence that deeply offended the Senate majority leader, "that I should give my approval to this bill on the ground that having asked the

Congress for a loaf of bread to take care of this war for the sake of this and succeeding generations, I should be content with a small piece of crust." The first president ever to veto a revenue bill, Roosevelt had drawn the line between himself and Capitol Hill. He assailed every legislator who had voted for the measure by declaring it "not a tax bill but a tax relief bill providing relief not for the needy but for the greedy." The tone of the veto message astonished the press gallery, with one journalist comparing it to "a mad dog snarling at a postman."[46]

Suppressing an urge to respond immediately, but making little effort to disguise his fury, the majority leader told reporters he would make a speech the next day "without regard for the political consequences." Barkley spent a sleepless night pacing the floor. This would not be the first time he had opposed the president. In 1939, he had made headlines by voting against the president's request for full funding of the WPA, after his headcounts had shown diminishing support in the Senate, and he decided to work for more realistic funding levels. Now the issue was a matter not of political tactics but of personal integrity and good faith. He supported the New Deal out of a commitment to liberalism. "I was not just a yes-man, a me-too man," he fumed. "I believed in . . . the program, because I was a liberal and a progressive long before I ever heard of Franklin D. Roosevelt." Now Barkley felt bound by his conviction that the majority leader must support the administration. Because his disagreement with the president had become irreconcilable, Barkley decided it was his duty to resign from the leadership. As the conservative critic James Burnham reasoned, "If he had thought of himself as the representative of his party colleagues, there would have been nothing unusual in his differing with the President—whether of his own or another party—and no occasion whatever for talk about resigning."[47]

Word had spread before Barkley rose to speak on February 23. Senators took their seats, members of the House filled the back of the chamber, and correspondents packed the press gallery. In contrast, seats in the public galleries remained mostly empty, the few visitors treated to an unexpected spectacle. The majority leader began to speak with only a few typewritten pages in hand; his secretary was still transcribing the remarks he had dictated that morning. Putting aside his grudge against Barkley, Senator McKellar "ran copy," hand carrying additional pages of the speech as they arrived in the cloakroom. From Henry Wallace's vantage in the presiding officer's chair, senators afforded the speech the kind of rapt attention that fans give to a prize fight, except that one of the contenders was missing from the ring. For forty-five minutes the majority leader addressed Roosevelt's veto message, item by item, rebutting its "calculated and deliberate assault upon the legislative integrity of every Member of Congress." If Congress had "any self-respect yet left" it would pass the bill over the president's veto. As for himself, after carrying the flag for the president for seven years, he would tender his resignation when the Democratic Conference met the next morning. When Barkley took his seat, senators rose in a sustained standing ovation and lined up at his desk to offer congratulations and support. Reporters stampeded from the gallery to file their stories, and Vice President Wallace hurriedly left his chair to telephone the president at Hyde Park.[48]

"Alben must be suffering from shell shock," Roosevelt commented when he heard the news. "It doesn't make sense." Another phone call came from James Byrnes, the director of war mobilization, potential vice-presidential candidate, and the so-called assistant president, who was widely suspected of having prepared the veto message. In his own defense, Byrnes pinned the authorship on two Kentuckians, Director of Economic Stabilization Fred Vinson and his assistant Ed Prichard, and claimed that Roosevelt himself had coined the phrase "not for the needy but for the greedy." Years later, Prichard admitted that he and Benjamin Cohen (Byrnes's general counsel) had written the veto message, but they never divulged their role to the indignant majority leader. For his part, Barkley blamed Byrnes and Vinson, men "more clever than honest," for having misadvised Roosevelt. Anticipating that the Democratic Conference would overwhelmingly reelect Barkley, Byrnes urged the president to make peace and drafted a conciliatory telegram for his signature. "You and I may differ, and have differed on important measures, but that does not mean we question one another's good faith," Roosevelt telegraphed Barkley. "I did not realize how very strongly you felt about that basic decision. . . . Certainly, your differing with me does not affect my confidence in your leadership nor in any degree lessen my respect and affection for you personally."[49]

As reporters and photographers clustered outside the door, members of the Democratic Conference accepted Barkley's resignation and then unanimously reelected him. "Make way for liberty!" shouted the burly senator from Texas, Tom Connally, when a delegation of senators pushed their way out to notify Barkley in his office. Barkley then appeared before the cheering conference. "By his one-vote margin in the 1937 contest when he was first elected leader, the impression was given, and it has

Although he had been majority leader since 1937, Alben Barkley was depicted as the strong "new" leader of the Senate after his dramatic break with President Roosevelt in 1944.

been the impression ever since, that he spoke to us for the President," said Utah's Elbert Thomas. "Now that he has been unanimously elected, he speaks for us to the President." Echoing that sentiment, the press hailed "Barkley's Declaration of Independence."[50]

Politicos and the press speculated over Barkley's ultimate motive. Had he resigned to protect himself back in Kentucky (where in dramatic upsets just months earlier Republicans had elected a governor and filled a vacancy in the House of Representatives), or to promote his national political ambitions? Or had he acted out of indignation? "I think he just exploded," said Prichard, who guessed that Barkley had snapped under the burden of wartime leadership. "Becoming angry was something of a habit with him," recalled Senator Claude Pepper. Senate liberals like Pepper resented Barkley's defection at a time when conservatives were whittling down and abolishing New Deal programs, and when the president was engaged in a world war and intense international diplomacy. The staunch New Dealer from Florida believed the president's veto message had enraged Barkley but that the roots of his rage went much deeper. "The president did not regard Barkley as strong or fully trustworthy," Pepper observed. "Barkley had never put together an effective leadership organization; the aides he hired were barely competent. He seldom anticipated the future or avoided a crisis through skillful and timely action." Pepper interpreted Barkley's threat to resign as a ploy to release himself from his obligations to the president and to return to a "sanitized" leadership post. Senator Pepper's views were distinctly in the minority. He was the only senator to speak in favor of Roosevelt's veto, and one of only fourteen who voted to sustain it. Barkley led thirty-nine Democrats, thirty-two Republicans, and a Progressive in voting to override.[51]

Restored to leadership with far greater personal prestige, respect, and authority, Barkley never altered his philosophy of the job. He continued to promote the president's program and served as liaison between the White House and the Senate. He continued to attend "Big Four" meetings to give the president his assessment of forthcoming legislation, suggesting that the president call particular senators to the White House to explain his position and to reduce the chances of controversy, at least within his own party, before bills reached the Senate floor. Yet his act of independence had demonstrated that a senator could repudiate the president without political recrimination. "Little was said publicly," Floyd Riddick observed, "but it was mentioned in unofficial conversations continuously for a long time." At the White House, the president treated him without rancor, but their relationship suffered from Barkley's rebellion. Privately, the president remarked that Barkley could show his real spirit by taking more initiative and by asking to come to the White House, rather than by waiting to be summoned. To his budget director, Roosevelt added that "he had made up his mind that it is impossible to get along with the present Congress; and that he is losing no sleep over the matter."[52]

As the Seventy-eighth Congress prepared to recess for the political conventions in the summer of 1944, reporter Allen Drury questioned the majority leader about the schedule:

"By God, I'm getting fed up with this," snapped Barkley, his face flushed. "These Republicans come across the aisle here, wearing out my carpet all the time asking for a recess and then they issue a statement saying there shouldn't be one because we've got too much work to do. I imagine we'll go right on through the conventions."[53]

But, as always, he softened his stand, asked not to be quoted, and suggested they would "work it out." Chances were good, the correspondent concluded, that

> old Alben, who lets himself be imposed upon by Republicans as well as Democrats, and, along with Biffle, carries nine-tenths of the detail of the Senate on his back, will probably "work it out" when the time comes, and the Republicans will get their recess.[54]

Not until Barkley reached the Democratic convention in Chicago that summer did he realize the full extent of his estrangement from Roosevelt, which cost him not only the vice presidency but his succession to the presidency as well. In their few meetings since Barkley's rebellion, the president had showed "a certain intangible reserve" toward him yet had agreed to have the majority leader place his name in nomination as a sign that they had buried their differences. Sensing the mood of the convention crowd, Secretary of Labor Frances Perkins thought Barkley represented the "people's choice" among the delegates for the vice-presidential nomination, but President Roosevelt emphatically dismissed his name from a list of potential running mates. "It makes you awfully depressed when you know a fellow will do things like that," Barkley confided to Henry Wallace. After first displaying "a great show of high temper," Barkley swallowed his disappointment, went on as promised to deliver his nominating speech, and campaigned for Roosevelt's reelection that fall. In November, Roosevelt won his fourth term as president and Barkley his fourth as senator, and their relationship warmed once again. One of their last meetings took place in a White House bathroom, while the president shaved as he recounted his trip to Yalta and questioned Barkley on the latest legislative picture. As majority leader, Barkley fought his last major battle for the Roosevelt administration, getting former vice president Wallace confirmed as secretary of commerce. He accomplished this by taking federal lending agencies out of the Commerce Department's jurisdiction, thus mollifying Wallace's conservative opposition.[55]

The death of Franklin D. Roosevelt on April 12, 1945, ended a unique partnership. Forgetting his reservations, Barkley recalled his great respect for Roosevelt as a leader, his devotion to New Deal reforms, and his "beautiful memory" of their years of association. In the fall of 1945, Barkley performed a final duty for his departed chief by chairing a joint committee to investigate the circumstances of the attack on Pearl Harbor. Congressional Republicans had made an issue of Roosevelt's handling of Pearl Harbor, which they pictured at best as a bungled defense, and at worst as a devious ploy to get the nation into the war. Barkley defused their charges by proposing a congressional investigation of the incident and then serving himself as its chairman. Barkley's strategy was to give dissident Republicans full opportunity to make their charges, while presenting sufficient testimony to rebut them. The tactic took longer than anticipated, however, causing the majority leader to devote excessive amounts of time and attention to the committee from September 1945 to July 1946, and prompting liberal Democrats to complain of a "leadership vacuum" in the Senate. His judicious approach to the investigation paid off, however, when enough Republican committee members signed the majority report to avoid a party-line vote for Roosevelt's exoneration. Barkley had won "the political battle of Pearl Harbor," but the victory did little to help congressional Democrats. Voters had "had enough." That November, Democrats lost their majorities in the House and Senate for the first time since the Depression.[56]

A New President—and a New Majority

Senator Barkley accepted his new status as minority leader with an equanimity that bolstered his standing among senators in both parties. By contrast, his friend and protégé, Lister Hill of Alabama, used the loss of the majority as the occasion to resign as Senate Democratic whip. A chronically cautious southern liberal, Hill believed civil rights issues would increasingly estrange the Truman administration from southern Democrats. Unwilling to risk his seat, Hill retreated from the leadership to distance himself as much as possible from the coming political strife.[57]

No quitter himself, Barkley felt a continued obligation to the Democratic president. He and Harry Truman had been friends for ten years in the Senate and had worked together harmoniously during Truman's brief vice presidency. Their views on domestic and international affairs were virtually identical, easing the majority leader's shift in allegiance to the new president. But Truman was no Roosevelt. The new president continued the weekly congressional leadership meetings, conducting them more expeditiously and going into even less detail than his predecessor. Because he treated the White House as his home rather than his workplace, Truman shifted the meeting place from the presidential bedroom to the executive offices in the West Wing, sacrificing the former sense of intimacy. Still, the majority leader continued to play the loyal president's man. On one occasion, he broke his traditional support for organized labor to vote in favor of the president's plan to draft striking railroad workers into the military. "If one vote is going to destroy my whole record of 20 years in the Senate," said Barkley, "then so be it." The Barkley-Truman relationship was not without tension, however. President Truman complained that the majority leader sometimes treated him coldly, and the majority leader protested the lack of communication from the White House. No one had consulted with him, for example, over the tax proposals in the president's State of the Union Message, prompting Barkley to instruct a Truman aide: "I'm supposed to be the catcher and I should give the signals." Truman made amends by incorporating suggestions from Barkley and House Democratic leader Sam Rayburn into his tax bill veto message.[58]

Barkley grew restive during the Eightieth Congress. He considered the Republican majority "pretty rotten" on domestic issues, "except that I do appreciate their cooperation in our foreign policy." He worked hard to cement a bipartisan approach to foreign policy during the early Cold War era. Previously, Barkley had deferred to the foreign policy leadership of Tom Connally (D-Tex.), chairman of the Foreign Relations Committee. In the Eightieth Congress he similarly bowed to Republican chairman Arthur Vandenberg, who had embraced Truman's international program. Carrying his concept of the majority leadership one step further, Barkley argued that although it was the duty of the majority leader to represent the majority, "by and large, no matter what party is in power—no matter who is President—the majority leader of the Senate is expected to be the legislative spokesman of the administration." Separation of powers was an important constitutional principle, Barkley noted, but carried too far it could harm the public good. A successful government, he said, depended on "an intimate relationship between the President and Congress," which meant submerging personalities and political rivalries.[59]

Barkley's encouragement of the Republican majority to cooperate with the Democratic president meant taking a back seat not so much to the quiet, colorless Republican majority leader, Wallace White, but to the real Republican leaders of the Eightieth Congress, Arthur Vandenberg and Robert Taft. Holding only a truncated majority and desiring to create a legislative record that would advance their party's bid for the presidency in 1948, Republican leaders welcomed Barkley's cooperative efforts. During these two years in the minority, Barkley behaved more like an institutional man than a partisan. Grover Ensley, staff director of the Joint Economic Committee, offered one example of this when he recalled how Barkley had so elaborately praised a speech delivered by the new Republican senator from Vermont, Ralph Flanders, that Flanders bowed in response. Later, when the opportunity arose, Barkley walked across the chamber to chide the Vermonter for his flippancy. "Now, Flanders took this very seriously," said Ensley. "He respected and was grateful for Barkley's counsel. Here was somebody from a different party coming over to explain to a freshman senator the etiquette of the Senate."[60]

The minority leader's standing with the press rose as well. "For a long time it was the fashion to regard Mr. Barkley as a wheel horse, but rather dull," one radio broadcaster commented. "Yet over the years he has grown steadily to the position of high respect in which he is now held." In May 1948, *Collier's* magazine presented Barkley its award for distinguished congressional service. A decade after a similar poll of journalists had left Barkley off its list of the ten most effective members, now more than two hundred newspaper editors ranked him first. "Under conditions that would have caused a less determined man to walk out and rest, he continued to work for his country through his party," commented one judge. "As his position came down he seemed to grow in stature," said another. "By his wisdom, humor, and moderation, plus his devotion to the system, he has strengthened the concept of party responsibility," another concluded. Commending Barkley on the award, Senator Carl Hatch added, "No matter what the circumstances, good or bad, the Senator from Kentucky has grown steadily in stature and strength."[61]

Family tragedy muted the personal triumphs. Barkley's wife, Dorothy, died of heart disease in 1947. Mrs. Barkley, who had been an invalid for many years, required medical care that amounted to more than her husband's annual salary of $10,000 (he had given up his law practice when he entered Congress). Barkley supplemented his income with a "night job"—a heavy schedule of speaking engagements around the country. After a day's session in the Senate, he would travel to another city, make an address, collect his fee, and head back to Washington to take his front-row seat in the chamber the next day. William S. White of the *New York Times* marveled that Barkley could still deliver an impressive impromptu speech in the Senate "after flying in at three o'clock in the morning redeyed from some dreary lecture."[62]

These widely scattered speaking engagements, combined with his quadrennial convention addresses and a dozen years of service as Senate floor leader, earned Barkley special recognition within the Democratic party. When in 1948 he once more rallied his party's now dispirited forces with a passionate keynote speech, which received a half-hour spontaneous demonstration, he could no longer be denied the vice-presidential nomination, although he was still not the president's first choice. With Truman far behind in the public opinion polls, the running-mate nomination seemed more of a consolation prize, but Barkley accepted it proudly. Still the "iron man" at seventy-one, he set out on a six-week campaign tour, speaking in thirty-six states. The Democratic ticket's surprise victory in November converted Barkley from floor leader to presiding officer of the United States Senate.[63]

From Vice President to Freshman Senator

"Barkley, as Vice-President, was in a class by himself," wrote Harry Truman. "He had the complete confidence of both the President and the Senate." President Truman invited Barkley to attend meetings of the cabinet and the National Security Council, and sent him across the nation making speeches, laying cornerstones, and performing other ceremonial duties. Yet Barkley also spent from half to three-quarters of his time presiding in the chamber, serving as the last vice president to carry out that constitutional role on a routine basis. As president of the Senate, Barkley lost the right to speak in the chamber without the Senate's consent, or to vote except to break ties, and he worried that he might forget himself one day and enter into the debate. Parliamentarian Charles Watkins observed that the former majority leader, though well acquainted with the rules, would occasionally mix them up and become obstinate about their interpretation. When he ignored the parliamentarian's advice, the Senate reversed his rulings. These reversals, however, dealt with Barkley's effort to make it easier for the Senate to achieve cloture against filibusters, consistent with his position as majority leader. His rulings were struck down by the conservative coalition that continued to employ every parliamentary means available to defeat civil rights initiatives. Nationally, Barkley enjoyed great affection as "Veep," which increased when the septuagenarian courted and wed an attractive young widow, Jane Rucker Hadley, in 1949.[64]

After Truman declined to run again in 1952, Barkley made his last try for the Democratic nomination for president. By now, however, he had become more of a beloved character actor than a leading man in national politics. Organized labor blocked his candidacy on the grounds that he was too old to run. "He wants to be President more than he wants anything else in the world!" President Truman commented in a private memo. "He can't see, he shows his age." The presidency would kill his old friend within three months, Truman predicted. Barkley felt like walking out of the convention but, instead, accepted an invitation to deliver a farewell message to the delegates. He used the occasion to once more defend the party's record under Roosevelt and Truman, which had "given the American people a greater share in the enjoyment of the fruit of their labor than any other administration in the history of the United States."

Alben Barkley retired to Paducah, where he prepared his anecdotal memoir, *That Reminds Me*, and hosted a short-lived television show, "Meet the Veep." Restless in private life after so many decades in public office, he ran again for the Senate in 1954. At age seventy-six he waged a vigorous campaign that unseated Republican Senator John Sherman Cooper.[65]

Barkley's defeat of a Republican incumbent contributed to the single-vote Democratic margin that elevated Lyndon B. Johnson to majority leader. The former majority leader was "not much of a power in Johnson's Senate," as one of Johnson's staff noted, but as a veteran and genial "spinner of yarns," he was welcomed back into the club. Senator Barkley accepted prestigious assignments on the Finance and Foreign Relations committees but refused to take a front-row seat with senior members. Instead, he joined other freshmen in the back row.[66]

He employed that "back row" theme in his last public address. Invited to give the keynote speech to a mock convention at Washington and Lee University on April 30, 1956, Barkley delivered an old-fashioned partisan speech that blamed all problems of society on the Republicans, claimed all solutions for the Democrats, and defined their difference as that between stagnation and progress. He had served his country for half a century and now had returned as a junior senator. "I'm glad to sit on the back row," he said. "For I would rather be a servant in the House of the Lord than to sit in the seats of the mighty." Appearing to bow to accept the applause of the crowd, Barkley collapsed on the stage and died of a massive heart attack.[67]

In his eulogy, Senator Earle Clements of Kentucky called Barkley "a Senator's Senator," a designation that other senators seconded in tributes that reflected qualities in Barkley they attributed to themselves. To the liberal economist Paul Douglas, Barkley "believed firmly in the diffusion of economic and political power." Walter George, a conservative target of Roosevelt's ill-fated party "purge," honored Barkley for making "no pretense of agreeing to things in which he did not believe." Hubert Humphrey declared him "one of the great political orators of all time," while Majority Leader Lyndon Johnson credited him with "a genuine and unaffected interest in the problems of others." As a result, said Johnson, "people rejoiced with him when he was happy, mourned with him when he was sad. And at all times they reposed in him the trust and confidence that are accorded only to very close and very dear friends."[68]

Assessing Alben Barkley

Alben Barkley served ten years as majority leader and two as minority leader, always with presidents of his own party. His leadership spanned the waning of the New Deal, the United States' entry into World War II, the beginning of the Cold War, and postwar economic reconversion. In assessing Barkley's leadership, Roosevelt had called him "the sort of balance wheel that has kept things moving forward all these years." Parliamentarian Floyd Riddick noted that Barkley may not have wielded control over the Senate as forcefully as had some earlier majority leaders but that he exerted much influence and did "a good job of directing the legislative program toward granting the requests of the Administration." Barkley's genius was not his legislative draftsmanship, commented political scientist Stephen K. Bailey, but his "almost uncanny sense of the possible in the legislative process." Recalling how Barkley could assemble and put forward facts "in sincerity and sound judgment," House Speaker Sam Rayburn believed Barkley's "weapon was his argument." *New York Times* correspondent Russell Baker commended Barkley's "mission of leavening the pompous business of politics." Another observer, Dean Acheson, recalled Barkley as a giant of the Senate, a popular, expansive man who made himself the center of whatever circle he joined. Never unduly generous in his evaluations of Congress, Acheson doubted that Barkley had contributed much to American political thought and leadership, but "he did contribute to the means by which that thought and leadership were translated into successful action."[69]

Although comparisons with his predecessors find Barkley's leadership lacking, assessments are kinder when he is judged against his immediate successors. Neither Scott Lucas of Illinois nor Ernest McFarland of Arizona performed impressively as floor leaders, and both failed to achieve Barkley's level of prestige. More legislative mechanics than leaders, they made the post "misery without splendor." Writing in 1949, William S. White charged that Majority Leader Lucas could not "even control from one hour to the next the order of business on his own floor." The amiable McFarland offered an even less active and aggressive leadership. Unimpressed home-state voters defeated Lucas in 1950 and McFarland in 1952, each after only two years as majority leader.[70]

During the 1950s, Lyndon Johnson eclipsed them all with his virtuoso performance as Democratic leader. Johnson could rant and threaten as effectively as Joe Robinson and humor and conciliate as smoothly as Alben Barkley. He also operated with less presidential constraint, for (unlike Barkley, Lucas, and McFarland) his entire term as Democratic leader took place with a Republican in the White House. After Johnson, Senate majority leaders reverted to Barkley's style—more tolerant of individual senators, more open in the operation of party machinery, and more generous with power and responsibility. Although majority leaders since Barkley's time have worked closely with the president, often serving as presidential spokesmen on Capitol Hill, they have not embraced Barkley's sweeping concept of the leader as president's man. Presidents still aim to lead Congress, but the Roosevelt-Barkley model of partnership remains decidedly unique for Senate majority leaders.[71]

NOTES

The author wishes to thank Richard Baker, Terry Birdwhistell, Bill Cooper, James Klotter, Floyd Riddick, and Martha Swain for many helpful suggestions regarding this essay.

1. Turner Catledge, *My Life and The Times* (New York: Harper and Row, 1971), 96.
2. Statement by Senator Prentiss M. Brown on the Supreme Court Bill, July 22, 1937, Joseph Alsop Papers, Library of Congress.
3. Catledge, *My Life*, 97.
4. Joseph Alsop and Turner Catledge, *The 168 Days* (Garden City, N.Y.: Doubleday Doran, 1938), 239–240; John H. Bankhead to Alben Barkley, July 20, 1937, Alben Barkley Papers, University of Kentucky.
5. Alsop and Catledge, *168 Days*, 268–272; Martha Swain, *Pat Harrison: The New Deal Years* (Jackson: University Press of Mississippi, 1978), 148–154; James A. Farley, *Jim Farley's Story* (New York: Whittlesey House, 1948), 89; James F. Byrnes, *All in One Lifetime* (New York: Harper, 1958), 98–100; Harold L. Ickes, *The Lowering Clouds 1939–1941*, vol. 3 of *The Secret Diary of Harold L. Ickes* (New York: Simon and Schuster, 1954), 3: 164–166. A voting analysis of the ninety-seven Democratic senators who served two or more terms between 1933 and 1945 located Barkley at thirty-fifth, Harrison at seventy-second, and King at ninety-first in their support of New Deal

legislation. James W. Hilty, "The Dimensions of the New Deal Policy Agenda: Senate Voting, 1933–1945" (Paper delivered at the Social Science History Association Meeting, Philadelphia, October 29–31, 1976).

6. "James A. Farley Oral History," University of Kentucky Library, 3–5, Farley; *Jim Farley's Story*, 92–93, 181–182; William P. Helm, *Harry Truman, A Political Biography* (New York: Duell, Sloan and Pearce, 1947), 49–53; Robert H. Ferrell, ed., *The Autobiography of Harry S. Truman* (Boulder: Colorado Associated University Press, 1980), 83; Turner Catledge, interview with Martha Swain, Catledge Papers, Mississippi State University, 4–5. Barkley asserted in his memoirs that Truman asked to be relieved of his promise to vote for him because of political pressure; Barkley also insisted that the White House "kept hands off in the race." Alben W. Barkley, *That Reminds Me* (Garden City, N.Y.: Doubleday, 1954), 155–156.

7. Barkley, *That Reminds Me*; Byrnes, *All in One Lifetime*, 99–100; Catledge, *My Life*, 67; Swain, *Pat Harrison*, 161, 286; Catledge, interview with Martha Swain, 18–19; Philip A. Grant, "Editorial Reaction to the Harrison-Barkley Senate Leadership Contest, 1937," *Journal of Mississippi History* 36 (May 1974): 127–141.

8. Barkley, *That Reminds Me*, 155. Barkley complained that Alsop and Kintner were leading a "scurrilous and contemptible" campaign to belittle him as majority leader, *New York Times*, October 17, 1940.

9. Catledge, interview with Martha Swain, 2–3.

10. Barkley, *That Reminds Me*, 24–105; James K. Libbey, *Dear Alben: Mr. Barkley of Kentucky* (Lexington: University Press of Kentucky, 1976), 1–10; U.S. Congress, *Congressional Record*, 79th Cong., 2d sess., 6571, 82d Cong., 1st sess., 1710.

11. Libbey, *Dear Alben*, 98; Barkley to Mrs. J. A. Blomgren, April 3, 1939, Barkley Papers; J. B. Shannon, "Alben W. Barkley, 'Reservoir of Energy,'" in *Public Men In and Out of Office*, ed. J. T. Salter (Chapel Hill: University of North Carolina Press, 1946), 245–246.

12. Gerald S. Grinde, "The Emergence of the 'Gentle Partisan': Alben W. Barkley and Kentucky Politics, 1919," *Register of the Kentucky Historical Society* 78 (Summer 1980): 256–258.

13. "Typescript (uncorrected) of Interviews Between Alben Barkley and Sidney Shalett," reel 17, side 1:9, Barkley Papers; George W. Robinson, "The Making of a Kentucky Senator: Alben W. Barkley and the Gubernatorial Primary of 1923," *Filson Club History Quarterly* 40 (April 1966): 123–135; Robert F. Sexton, "Crusade Against Parimutuel Gambling," in *Kentucky: Its History and Heritage*, ed. Fred J. Hood (St. Louis: Forum, 1978), 195–206; John Ed Pearce, *Divide and Dissent: Kentucky Politics, 1930–1963* (Lexington: University Press of Kentucky, 1987), 26–27.

14. Robert W. Bingham to Bernard M. Baruch, March 10, October 20, 1926, Robert Worth Bingham Papers, Library of Congress.

15. Barkley to Edwin A. Halsey, October 25, 1932, Halsey Papers, Library of Congress; Barkley, *That Reminds Me*, 141; Joseph Alsop and Turner Catledge, "Joe Robinson, The New Deal's Old Reliable," *Saturday Evening Post*, September 26, 1936, 66. Barkley won his Senate elections with 51.8 percent of the vote in 1926, 59.2 percent in 1932, 62 percent in 1938, 54.8 percent in 1944, and 54.5 percent in 1954. *Guide to U.S. Elections*, 2d ed. (Washington, D.C.: Congressional Quarterly, 1985), 617–618.

16. O. R. Altman, "First Session of the Seventy-fifth Congress, January 5, 1937, to August 21, 1937," *American Political Science Review* 31 (December 1937): 1071; interviews with Charles McNary and Leslie Biffle, 1938, Alsop Papers; see also Otis L. Graham, Jr., "The Democratic Party, 1932–1945," in *From Square Deal to New Deal*, vol. 3 of *History of U.S. Political Parties*, ed. Arthur M. Schlesinger, Jr. (New York: Chelsea House, 1973), 3: 1939–1964.

17. Alsop and Catledge, *168 Days*, 288–289; Swain, *Pat Harrison*, 163; U.S. Congress, *Congressional Record*, 75th Cong., 1st sess., 7363, 7374, 7381.

18. Thomas G. Corcoran, "Rendezvous with Destiny," C29–30, Thomas G. Corcoran Papers, Library of Congress; "Typescript (uncorrected) of Interviews Between Alben Barkley and Sidney Shalett," reel 16, side 1:4, Barkley Papers.

19. "Dinner Tendered to Senator Alben W. Barkley, Hotel Raleigh, August 10, 1937,"
Barkley Papers; U.S. Congress, *Congressional Record*, 75th Cong., 1st sess., 8694–
8697; Polly Davis, *Alben Barkley: Senate Majority Leader and Vice President* (New York:
Garland, 1979), 41–45; on the filibuster against the antilynching bill see also
Franklin L. Burdette, *Filibustering in the Senate* (Princeton, N.J.: Princeton University Press, 1940), 191–199.
20. Nancy J. Weiss, *Farewell to the Party of Lincoln: Black Politics in the Age of FDR* (Princeton, N.J.: Princeton University Press, 1983), 96–119, 241–249; J. Joseph Huthmacher, *Senator Robert F. Wagner and the Rise of Urban Liberalism* (New York: Atheneum, 1971), 238–243; Harry McPherson, *A Political Education* (Boston: Little,
Brown, 1972), 66.
21. U.S. Congress, *Congressional Record*, 75th Cong., 3d sess., 253–257; Swain, *Pat
Harrison*, 200–206; Catledge, interview with Martha Swain, 8–10.
22. Swain, *Pat Harrison*, 179, 193; Catledge, interview with James Shoalmire, Catledge
Papers, Mississippi State University, 69, 76; "Washington Correspondents Name
Ablest Congressmen in *Life* Poll," *Life*, March 20, 1939, 13–18; Joseph Alsop and
Robert Kintner, "Sly and Able: The Real Leader of the Senate, Jimmy Byrnes,"
Saturday Evening Post, July 20, 1940, 18–19; Altman, "First Session of the Seventy-
fifth Congress," 1093. A typescript of the results of the *Life* poll, in the Joseph
Alsop papers, shows Barkley placing seventeenth on the longer list.
23. O. R. Altman, "Second and Third Sessions of the Seventy-fifth Congress, 1937–
38," *American Political Science Review* 32 (December 1938): 1099–1123; Alsop and
Kintner, "Sly and Able," 41; *New York Times*, August 1, 1939. See also Richard
Polenberg, *Reorganizing Roosevelt's Government, 1936–1939: The Controversy Over Executive Reorganization* (Cambridge: Harvard University Press, 1966).
24. "Reminiscences of Lee Pressman," Oral History Research Office, Columbia University, 119–121,; Terry L. Birdwhistell, "A. B. 'Happy' Chandler," in *Kentucky*, 209–
220; Walter L. Hixson, "The 1938 Kentucky Senate Election: Alben W. Barkley,
'Happy' Chandler, and The New Deal," *Register of the Kentucky Historical Society* 80
(Summer 1982): 309–329; William E. Leuchtenburg, *Franklin D. Roosevelt and the
New Deal, 1932–1940* (New York: Harper and Row, 1963), 266–270; Harold L. Ickes,
The Inside Struggle, 1936–1939, vol. 2 of *The Secret Diary of Harold L. Ickes* (New York:
Simon and Schuster, 1954), 2:342; Davis, *Alben Barkley*, 66–67; Pearce, *Divide and
Dissent*, 39–45.
25. "The WPA is giving 100% cooperation" to Senator Barkley's campaign in Estill
County, wrote District Director Ernest Rowe to WPA state administrator George
H. Goodman, June 16, 1938, Barkley Papers. John Henry Hatcher, "Alben Barkley,
Politics in Relief and the Hatch Act," *Filson Club History Quarterly* 40 (July 1966):
249–264; Thomas L. Stokes, *Chip Off My Shoulder* (Princeton, N.J.: Princeton University Press, 1940), 534–536; George McJimsey, *Harry Hopkins: Ally of the Poor and
Defender of Democracy* (Cambridge: Harvard University Press, 1987), 122; Robert E.
Sherwood, *Roosevelt and Hopkins: An Intimate History* (New York: Harper, 1948), 98;
David L. Porter, *Congress and the Waning of the New Deal* (Port Washington, N.Y.:
Kennikat, 1980), 109–135.
26. Floyd M. Riddick, "Third Session of the Seventy-sixth Congress, January 3, 1940,
to January 3, 1941," *American Political Science Review* 35 (April 1941): 302; Thomas
G. Corcoran, interview with Joseph Alsop, July 27, 1938, Alsop Papers.
27. Barkley to Robert M. La Follette, Jr., June 8, 1943, Barkley Papers; "Kentucky's
New Dealer: Ed Prichard Remembers," videotaped interviews, Division of Special
Collections and Archives, University of Kentucky Library.
28. Walter Trohan, *Political Animals: Memoirs of a Sentimental Cynic* (Garden City, N.Y.:
Doubleday, 1975), 53; "Darrell St. Claire: Assistant Secretary of the Senate," oral
history interviews, Senate Historical Office, 85–86.
29. Riddick, "Third Session of the Seventy-sixth Congress," 286; Alben W. Barkley,
"The Majority Leader in the Legislative Process," in *The Process of Government*, ed.
Simeon S. Willis et al. (Lexington, Ky.: Bureau of Government Research, 1949),
42–47.

30. Alsop and Kintner, "Sly and Able," 18–19.

31. Ibid., 38, 41.

32. Russell Long used Barkley as his model when selecting his own committees. "I thought that inasmuch as Alben Barkley had been majority leader longer than any other Senator, he would make a wise decision as to committees he asked for." Accordingly, Long, too, chose Finance and Foreign Relations, later resigning from the latter, explaining: "Having been on both committees, I do not think it is a very good assortment of committees." U.S. Congress, *Congressional Record*, daily ed., 99th Cong., 1st sess., S6378. Barkley, "Majority Leader," 39, 46.

33. Richard Langham Riedel, *Halls of the Mighty: My 47 Years at the Senate* (Washington, D.C.: R. B. Luce, 1969), 145; Stephen Kemp Bailey, *Congress Makes Law: The Story Behind the Employment Act of 1946* (New York: Columbia University Press, 1950), 227.

34. "James A. Farley Oral History," 2; Ickes, *Secret Diary*, 2:395; 3:173, 250, 264; for a vivid description of Barkley's speaking style, see Shannon, "Alben W. Barkley," 248–249.

35. Donald Young, ed., *Adventures in Politics: The Memoirs of Philip La Follette* (New York: Holt, Rinehart and Winston, 1970), 251; Barkley, "Majority Leader," 47; William S. White, *Citadel, The Story of the U.S. Senate* (New York: Harper, 1957), 105–106.

36. Alsop and Kintner, "Sly and Able," 18–19; Ickes, *Secret Diary*, 3:456.

37. Barkley, "Majority Leader," 44–45; Davis, *Alben Barkley*, 85–104. See also Wayne S. Cole, *Roosevelt and the Isolationists, 1932–45* (Lincoln: University of Nebraska Press, 1983); and Alfred O. Hero, *The Southerner and World Affairs* (Baton Rouge: Louisiana State University Press, 1965).

38. Barkley, "Majority Leader," 45; Floyd M. Riddick, "The Second Session of the Seventy-seventh Congress (January 6–December 16, 1942)," *American Political Science Review* 37 (April 1943): 290–305.

39. Riddick, ibid., 302; Roland A. Young, *Congressional Politics in the Second World War* (New York: Columbia University Press, 1956), 20–21; Raymond Clapper, *Watching the World* (New York: Whittlesley House, 1944), 199–200.

40. Richard Polenberg, *War and Society: The United States, 1941–1945* (Philadelphia: Lippincott, 1972), 73–98, 184–197; Richard L. Strout, *TRB, Views and Perspectives on the Presidency* (New York: Macmillan, 1979), 8–10, 13–14; Donald A. Ritchie, *James M. Landis, Dean of the Regulators* (Cambridge: Harvard University Press, 1980), 103–108.

41. U.S. Congress, *Congressional Record*, 77th Cong., 2d sess., 8905–8916; Floyd M. Riddick, "First Session of the Seventy-seventh Congress, January 3, 1941, to January 2, 1942," *American Political Science Review* 36 (April 1942): 293–294; Riedel, *Halls of the Mighty*, 89–90; Robert C. Byrd, *The Senate, 1789–1989: Addresses on the History of the United States Senate* (Washington, D.C.: U.S. Government Printing Office, 1989), 520–522.

42. Allen Drury, *A Senate Journal, 1943–1945* (New York: McGraw-Hill, 1963), 11, 16, 20; Ickes, *Secret Diary*, 2:395, 3:173; *New York Times*, August 1, 1939; see also Ernest W. McFarland, *Mac: The Autobiography of Ernest W. McFarland* (privately printed, 1979), 120.

43. *New York Times*, August 1, 1939.

44. James MacGregor Burns, *Roosevelt: The Soldier of Freedom* (New York: Harcourt Brace Jovanovich, 1970), 424–426, 437; Polenberg, *War and Society*, 197–198; "Kentucky's New Dealer: Ed Prichard Remembers." A study of New Deal revenue bills concludes that Roosevelt viewed taxation less as an economic issue than as "a matter of morality and fair play," Walter Kraft Lambert, "New Deal Revenue Acts: The Politics of Taxation" (Ph.D. diss., University of Texas at Austin, 1970), 502–503.

45. "Reminiscences of Henry Agard Wallace," 1320, 1711, 3086, 3105, Oral History Research Office, Columbia University; Davis, *Alben Barkley*, 139; Barkley, *That Reminds Me*, 170–172. On Roosevelt's weekly meetings with congressional leaders, see D. B. Hardeman and Donald C. Bacon, *Rayburn: A Biography* (Austin: Texas

Monthly, 1987), 227; and David B. Truman, *The Congressional Party: A Case Study* (New York: Wiley, 1959), 296–297.

46. Barkley, *That Reminds Me*, 172–173; Samuel I. Rosenman, ed., *The Public Papers and Addresses of Franklin D. Roosevelt, 1944–45* (New York: Harper, 1950), 80–83; Drury, *Senate Journal*, 85–86; "The Revolt of Congress," *U.S. News and World Report*, March 3, 1944, 29; George W. Robinson, "Alben Barkley and the 1944 Tax Veto," *Register of the Kentucky Historical Society* 67 (July 1969): 197–210.

47. Drury, *Senate Journal*, 86; Barkley, *That Reminds Me*, 173; "Typescript (uncorrected) of Taped Interviews Between Alben Barkley and Sidney Shalett," reel 4, side 1:5–6, Barkley Papers; James Burnham, *Congress and the American Tradition* (Chicago: H. Regnery, 1965), 155. For Barkley's previous threats to resign, see *New York Times*, March 8, 1940, and January 7, 1943.

48. Barkley, *That Reminds Me*, 174–175; Drury, *Senate Journal*, 89–90; Strout, *TRB*, 15–17; U.S. Congress, *Congressional Record*, 78th Cong., 2d sess., 1964–1966.

49. William D. Hassett, *Off the Record with F.D.R., 1942–1945* (New Brunswick, N.J.: Rutgers University Press, 1958), 325–326; Byrnes, *All in One Lifetime*, 210–211; Edward F. Prichard, oral history, University of Kentucky, 32–34; "Reminiscences of Henry Wallace," 3103–3104; Rosenman, ed., *Public Papers and Addresses of Franklin D. Roosevelt*, 85–86. For tax policy maneuvering inside the Roosevelt administration, see John Morton Blum, *Years of War, 1941–1945*, vol. 3 of *From the Morgenthau Diaries* (Boston: Houghton Mifflin, 1967), 3:64–78.

50. Drury, *Senate Journal*, 91–93; U.S. Congress, *Congressional Record*, 78th Cong., 2d sess., A 1430

51. Prichard, oral history, 34–35; Claude Denson Pepper, *Pepper, Eyewitness to a Century* (New York: Harcourt Brace Jovanovich, 1987), 125; U.S. Congress, *Congressional Record*, 78th Cong., 2d sess., 2049–2050. Led by the state's largest lumber dealer, Florida's business community turned against Pepper after his support of the tax veto. Robert Sherrill, *Gothic Politics in the Deep South: Stars of the New Confederacy* (New York: Grossmann, 1968), 138–147.

52. Barkley, "Majority Leader," 46; Floyd M. Riddick, "The Second Session of the Seventy-eighth Congress," *American Political Science Review* 39 (April 1945): 334–335; "Reminiscences of Henry Wallace," 3201; Hassett, *Off the Record with F.D.R.*, 237; Polenberg, *War and Society*, 199.

53. Drury, *Senate Journal*, 180.

54. Ibid.

55. "Reminiscences of Frances Perkins," 525, 530, "Reminiscences of Henry Wallace," 3370–3371, 3424, 3895, and "Reminiscences of Arthur Krock," 92, Oral History Research Office, Columbia University; Barkley, *That Reminds Me*, 169–170, 190–194; Davis, *Alben Barkley*, 156–174; Barkley draft letter to Franklin Roosevelt, January 1945, Barkley Papers. See also Barkley's election-year endorsement of FDR in Alben W. Barkley, "The Record of the New Deal," in *The New Deal: A People's Capitalism*, ed. J. George Frederick (New York: n.p., 1944), 75–89, in Barkley Papers.

56. Wayne Thompson, "The Pearl Harbor Inquiry, 1945," in *Congress Investigates: A Documented History, 1792–1974*, ed. Arthur M. Schlesinger, Jr., and Roger Bruns (New York: Chelsea House, 1975), 5: 3265–3294; Pepper, *Pepper*, 150.

57. Virginia Van Der Veer Hamilton, *Lister Hill: Statesman from the South* (Chapel Hill: University of North Carolina Press, 1987), 150; U.S. Congress, *Congressional Record*, 80th Cong., 2d sess., A3040. Barkley had contemplated not running for reelection as a senator in 1944, perhaps because of his wife's serious illness, his own uncertain health, and signs of a Republican tide in Kentucky. See Barkley's handwritten draft of an announcement of his retirement, c. 1943, Barkley Papers.

58. Harry S. Truman to Barkley, August 9, 1945, Barkley Papers; Alben W. Barkley, "President *and*—Not *vs.*—Congress," *New York Times Magazine*, June 20, 1948, 26; U.S. Congress, *Congressional Record*, 79th Cong., 2d sess., 10237; Susan M. Hartmann, *Truman and the 80th Congress* (Columbia: University of Missouri Press, 1971), 133–137; "Reminiscences of Henry Wallace," 4810.

59. Barkley to David Barkley, January 23, 1947, and to Wahwee [Laura Louise Barkley] MacArthur, July 8, 1947, Barkley Papers; Hartmann, *Truman and the 80th Congress,* 103; Malcolm E. Jewell, *Senatorial Politics and Foreign Policy* (Lexington: University Press of Kentucky, 1962), 57; Barkley, "Majority Leader," 46; Barkley, "President and—Not vs.—Congress," 14, 24–26.

60. Randall B. Ripley, *Majority Party Leadership in Congress* (Boston: Little, Brown, 1969), 147–155; "Grover W. Ensley: Executive Director, Joint Economic Committee, United States Congress, 1949–1957," oral history interviews, Senate Historical Office, 88–89; note also Wallace White's comments on Barkley's courtesies to the minority, U.S. Congress, *Congressional Record,* 79th Cong., 1st sess., 8191, and 79th Cong., 2d sess., 10235; and Arthur Capper to Barkley, November 9, 1944, Barkley Papers.

61. U.S. Congress, *Congressional Record,* 80th Cong., 1st sess., 10237, and 2d sess., 5481–5482, A3040–A3041.

62. U.S. Congress, *Congressional Record,* 80th Cong., 1st sess., 1809–1810; Barkley, *That Reminds Me,* 71; Jane R. Barkley, *I Married the Veep* (New York: Vanguard, 1958), 58–59; William S. White, *The Making of a Journalist* (Lexington: University of Kentucky Press, 1986), 170. According to Neal R. Pierce, *The Border South States* (New York: Norton, 1975), 229, Barkley did not scrupulously report his lecture fees, and the Internal Revenue Service claimed most of his estate for tax deficiencies and penalties.

63. H. Lew Wallace, "Alben Barkley and the Democratic Convention of 1948" *Filson Club History Quarterly* 50 (July 1981): 231–252; Barkley, *That Reminds Me,* 203.

64. Harry S. Truman, *Year of Decisions,* vol. 1 of *Memoirs* (New York: Doubleday, 1955), 1:57; *New York Times,* September 4, 1949; "Floyd M. Riddick: Senate Parliamentarian," oral history interviews, Senate Historical Office, 66–67, 127–128.

65. Robert H. Ferrell, ed., *Off the Record: The Private Papers of Harry S. Truman* (New York: Harper and Row, 1980), 261; Barkley, *That Reminds Me,* 223–232.

66. McPherson, *Political Education,* 28; Riedel, *Halls of the Mighty,* 147–148; Barkley was among only three of twenty-four freshman Democratic senators to be appointed to first-rank committees between 1953 and 1958. See Barbara Sinclair, *The Transformation of the U.S. Senate* (Baltimore: Johns Hopkins University Press, 1989), 13.

67. U.S. Congress, Joint Committee on Printing, *Memorial Services Held in the Senate and House of Representatives of the United States, Together with Remarks Presented in Eulogy of Alben William Barkley, Late a Senator from Kentucky,* 84th Cong., 2d sess. (Washington, D.C.: U.S. Government Printing Office, 1956), 101–106.

68. Ibid., 30, 39, 50, 89, 97, 109, 137.

69. Franklin D. Roosevelt to Barkley, January 8, 1943, Barkley Papers; Riddick, "Third Session of the Seventy-sixth Congress," 286; Bailey, *Congress Makes a Law,* 208; Joint Committee on Printing, *Memorial Services,* 134–135; Bernard K. Duffy and Halford R. Ryan, eds., *American Orators of the Twentieth Century: Critical Studies and Sources* (Westport, Conn.: Greenwood, 1987), 123; Dean Acheson, *Sketches From Life of Men I Have Known* (New York: Harper, 1961), 140–141. In 1957, when Senator John F. Kennedy's committee to commemorate the five most historically significant senators polled American historians and political scientists, Barkley tied for eleventh place. See U.S. Senate, Special Committee on the Senate Reception Room, *Senate Reception Room,* 85th Cong., 1st sess., Committee Print no. 3 (Washington, D.C.: U.S. Government Printing Office, 1957).

70. *New York Times,* March 20, and July 3, 1949; Edward L. Schnapsmeier and Frederick H. Schnapsmeier, "Scott W. Lucas of Havana: His Rise and Fall as Majority Leader in the United States Senate," *Journal of the Illinois State Historical Society* 70 (November 1977): 302–320; Truman, *Congressional Party,* 104–117, 289–308.

71. Rowland Evans and Robert Novak, *Lyndon B. Johnson: The Exercise of Power* (New York: New American Library, 1966), 39–41. See also Donald S. Matthews, *U.S. Senators and Their World* (New York: Vintage, 1960), 118–146; and remarks of Senator Robert C. Byrd, U.S. Congress, *Congressional Record,* 96th Cong., 2d sess., 8348–8353, 9757–9763.

CHAPTER 6

Robert A. Taft
A Study in the Accumulation of Legislative Power

Robert W. Merry

O n the walls of the Senate Reception Room, just east of
the Senate chamber, are
frescoes depicting five senators ad-
judged by the Senate to be the five
greatest legislative politicians produced by that venerable institution.
There is Henry Clay of Kentucky,
of course, and Daniel Webster of
Massachusetts and South Carolina's
John C. Calhoun. From the twentieth century, there is Wisconsin's
Robert LaFollette. The fifth man,
placed in this honored circle just four
years after his death, is Robert A.
Taft of Ohio, who served from 1939
to 1953.

An intensely partisan Republican with strong conservative convictions, Taft emerged in the midst of
the New Deal era as a stubborn and

*Robert A. Taft's mastery of issues and
parliamentary rules gave him immense power throughout his fifteen
years in the Senate.*

somewhat self-righteous politician standing athwart history yelling "Stop!" Although a relentless opponent of the political *Zeitgeist*, he nevertheless had a remarkable impact on his time. A naysayer, to be sure (and a brilliant one), Taft was also a legislator of rare talent. Using his considerable bargaining skills, he accumulated power in the Senate by mastering more details about more subjects than any of his peers and by maneuvering brilliantly between political conviction—for which he was famous—and his equally intense desire to move legislation.

Taft did not become a Senate leader because of personality traits normally associated with great legislative power. In fact, he had few of what we now call "interpersonal skills"—the back-slapping, arm-twisting ability to manipulate colleagues seen in contemporary leaders such as Lyndon Johnson. He could be brusque to the point of rudeness and never disguised his lack of respect for mediocre colleagues. But he was utterly devoid of pettiness, possessed an innate fair-mindedness, worked harder than anyone else around him, and was always totally prepared for any meeting, debate, negotiation, or confrontation.

His mastery of legislative details was such that one frequent adversary, Leverett Saltonstall (R-Mass.), once remarked that when he and Taft were on the same side of an issue, he "had a great feeling of satisfaction" and felt more confident of his position. When in opposition, however, Saltonstall said he "pondered greatly" to make certain he was right from his point of view and could withstand a forensic assault from Taft.[1]

Though he hungered for the White House and sought three times to secure his party's presidential nomination, Taft was first and foremost a man of the Senate, a legislator's legislator. Always vigilant in protecting the prerogatives of the legislative branch against encroachments of executive power, he also never tired of forcing the Senate into thorough, time-consuming deliberations in the interest of legislative precision. He once shouted at an impatient colleague on the Senate floor:

Time after time we pass things up here only to have the agencies downtown find meanings in them which we never intended. I don't say this is the fault of the Executive, either. It is principally the fault of Congress for not taking time enough to legislate thoroughly.[2]

Taft's immense power did not come primarily through formal titles and position, for he eschewed, until the very end of his career, the actual title of Senate Republican leader. He always managed, however, to be the man at the crucial place at the crucial time—whether by leading the Republican Policy Committee, by serving on various committees, or simply by being on the Senate floor, where his mastery of both the issue at hand and the parliamentary rules of the chamber could come into full play. "It might almost be said," wrote journalist and Taft biographer William S. White, "that the institution of the United States Senate had been created for Robert A. Taft, or men like him, and he for it."[3]

The Taft Tradition

Like most politicians, Robert Taft was a product of his family, his region, and his early political experiences. But his strong personal qualities intensified these early influences, calcifying them into a set of bedrock principles that guided him throughout his political life.

Dominating the Taft family during Robert's childhood years was the immense figure of his father. In addition to his large physical stature, William Howard Taft was a man of force in his personal as well as professional life. Despite his image as a jovial and sociable man, Will Taft was in fact a shrewd analyst of personality and political opportunity who harbored large ambitions for himself and his family. Like his own father, Alphonso Taft, Will went to Yale University. He graduated second in his class, and again like Alphonso, he became a lawyer and served on the bench as a young man. He also, like his father, sought to instill in his children the virtues of hard work, diligence, and national service, in addition to the importance of striving for excellence and advancement. "Mediocrity will not do for Will," Alphonso complained when his son was ranked fifth in a large class.[4]

Indeed, mediocrity would not do. William Howard Taft served as governor of the Philippines when Robert was a child, ascended to the White House while Bob was at Yale, and became chief justice of the United States during his son's early adulthood. The elder Taft emphasized effort and dedication, expressed the view that the "soft life" undermined character in children, and constantly admonished his son to fight hard to overcome the obstacles of a harsh world.[5] Young Bob Taft responded to his father's admonitions, meeting his standards at every step along the way. But given his earnestness and drive, he also felt compelled to shun any benefits brought by his famous name. Hence, even as he sought to please his much-revered father, he also sought distance from the most influential man in his life.

There can be no doubt that mediocrity would also not do for Bob Taft. In 1906, he graduated first in his class at the Taft School, a private school

established by his uncle Horace in Watertown, Connecticut. He was val-
edictorian both at Yale in 1910 and at Harvard Law School in 1913.[6] He
was not as successful, however, in separating himself from his famous
father, once writing: "I had a deathly fear that I would be accepted because of my father and not for myself."[7]

The result was that Taft developed a reluctance to project himself in
groups of people. He was manifestly self-conscious, once noting that a
close friend called this trait a "quiet reserve." In a letter to Martha Bowers
(later to become his wife), he wondered if perhaps for others this "reserve" didn't go by a harsher name.[8]

Years later in the Senate these twin traits of excellence and reserve
were much in evidence. On the one hand, there was drive, an uncommon
dedication to work and study, and the zest for competition. On the other
was reticence, self-consciousness, and the lack of camaraderie. Journalist
William S. White tells of a casual dinner he shared with Taft during which
the writer lightly recounted certain drinking feats he had seen performed
by Winston Churchill. Appearing taken aback, as if the remarks were
intended as criticism of himself, Taft responded: "Do you think I would
be a better politician if I drank more?" The "oddly touching" incident,
as White called it, echoes Taft's early letter to Martha Bowers.[9]

Taft was also influenced by the midwestern values of Cincinnati. He
grew up in a Republican, intensely nationalistic, and self-reliant region
whose journalistic voice was that of Colonel Robert McCormick's conservative *Chicago Tribune*. The guiding political spirit was Abraham Lincoln, who had saved the Union, freed the slaves, and founded a political
party that dominated the country's electoral landscape for the better part
of six decades. In pre–New Deal America, when the GOP held sway over
the nation, the Midwest often held sway over the GOP. Of the seven
Republican presidents between Grover Cleveland and Franklin Roosevelt,
five were born in the Midwest, and four maintained strong ties to the
region throughout their lives. Thrift, hard work, resourcefulness, and
self-reliance formed the bedrock political values and translated themselves into fiscal frugality, isolationism, and a fierce protection of individual freedoms.

When Taft was practicing law in Cincinnati and coming of age politically in the 1920s, there was no reason for him to fear any serious
threat to the hegemony enjoyed by his party and political outlook. During his second term in the Ohio House, from 1925 to 1926, when Taft
served as majority leader, his party dominated the chamber with 110

seats; the Democrats had only 20. The margin in the state senate was 33 to 2.[10]

By the time Taft was elected to the state senate in 1930, the Great Depression had struck and the party's fortunes had been devastated. He was the only Republican to survive the voters' ire and become part of Hamilton County's three-person legislative delegation. The GOP clung to the Ohio legislature by the relatively slim margins of 70 to 58 seats in the House and 18 to 14 in the Senate. Two years later came the electoral earthquake: Franklin Roosevelt swept Hamilton County by 4,500 votes, and the Republicans, including Taft, were tossed out. Democrats took over the Ohio House by a margin of 84 to 51 and captured a 16-to-16 tie in the Senate.[11]

Taft was to spend the rest of his life fighting this new political force, liberalism. As he saw it, the East was the spawning ground for Roosevelt's despised New Deal. It also nurtured the even more despised liberal wing of his own party, later epitomized by his archrival, Thomas E. Dewey. Some close observers of the senator perceived in him a protracted inner conflict between East and Midwest.[12] Taft, after all, had been educated in the East and served on the Yale Corporation with no less a symbol of the eastern establishment than Dean Acheson, secretary of state under Harry Truman. And yet he appeared to be uncomfortable with the political culture of the East. Indeed, members of the Taft family had a habit of using the term "easterner" as a kind of epithet, and the senator himself often interchanged the terms "easterner" and "New Dealer."[13] He chafed at what he considered the easterners' intellectual and political arrogance, and his natural allies in the Senate always seemed to be westerners or midwesterners such as Eugene D. Millikin of Colorado and Arthur H. Vandenberg of Michigan. For many Americans, he came to personify the values and heritage of the American hinterland.[14]

Ultimately, Taft came to view the East as the bastion of a brand of politics that threatened all he held dear—thrift and self-reliance, protection from foreign adventurism, constitutional liberty. "If Roosevelt is not a Communist today, he is about to become one," he said in 1936, stirring a chorus of boos as he ran for his state's favorite-son designation at that year's Republican National Convention.[15] This was campaign hyperbole, of course, but it also reflected the extent to which he believed the nation was locked in an epic political struggle, a view manifest in Taft's political behavior and rhetoric throughout his Senate career.

Among Taft's early political experiences, probably none posed a more difficult choice than the Cincinnati reform movement in the 1920s. His response to the movement offers telling insights into his political temperament. The reformers had targeted the Cincinnati Republican machine and its boss, Rudolph K. Hynicka, charging that they were hidebound and incapable of delivering the services needed by an expanding city. Politically vulnerable, the machine was largely swept out of office.

Taft was presented with a dilemma. Many of his friends in Cincinnati society were prominent reformers; yet the machine had fostered his early political career. In the end, without much evidence of agony, Taft stuck with the machine. Taft biographer James T. Patterson suggests a number of motivations, the most pronounced of them being loyalty to his machine supporters; ambition for future advancement, which a lack of political steadfastness could handicap; and an instinctive fealty to the status quo, a foundation of Taft's conservatism. Of these, the latter was the most decisive, says Patterson, and reflected the partisanship that characterized his entire career. "Bob Taft's instinctive regularity and his unrelenting partisanship were entirely in keeping with his temperament and upbringing," writes Patterson. "He was practicing what he believed."[16]

Early Senate Years

Taft was forty-nine years old when he arrived at the U.S. Senate following his impressive victory over a Democratic incumbent. He encountered both adversity and opportunity in the Senate of 1939. The adversity came in the form of a deeply entrenched New Deal led by a still formidable Franklin Roosevelt. The president had lost some prestige with his hotly contested plan to expand the Supreme Court and appeared stymied each time he tried to expand the New Deal, but he nevertheless dominated the national debate. In the Seventy-sixth Congress, Democrats held the Senate by a margin of 69 seats to 23 for the Republicans and dominated the House 260 seats to 169.[17]

Opportunity presented itself to Taft in two guises. One was the emergence of the so-called conservative coalition (an alliance of opposition Republicans and southern Democrats disenchanted with the New Deal). The other was the GOP's leadership void. No Republican of legislative brilliance had emerged to present a bold and consistent critique of the New Deal, to seize the opportunity provided by shifting coalitions, or to offer imaginative and forceful leadership for the opposition to the New Deal.

Although Taft took care in those early months to avoid defining a role for himself, he gained seats on three highly desirable committees—Appropriations; Banking and Currency; and Education and Labor. He attacked his committee work with all the zeal and attention to detail for which he subsequently became famous. He cultivated a reputation for careful preparation, for presenting his arguments forcefully (if a bit hyperbolically), for conducting himself with rectitude and fairness (as well as characteristic brusqueness), and for not wasting his own or anyone else's time. As Taft emerged as a contender for the Republican presidential nomination in 1940, Walter Lippmann wrote:

> While [Taft's] views are conventional and often narrow and frequently lacking in insight and experience, he has the saving grace of intellectual humility. He will examine patiently the evidence, and he will listen carefully to reason. . . . He is not intoxicated with his own rhetoric or in love with himself as a public personage.[18]

The *New York Times*'s Turner Catledge observed: "He was not a warm or genial man—he was cold, and could be extremely hard and righteous—but there was a tremendous honesty about him that commanded respect, and beneath his frigid exterior he was a shy, pleasant sort of man."[19]

Catledge also recounted a Kansas-to-Washington train trip he and the senator shared in 1940; Taft was battling for the GOP nomination at the time. Kansas political leaders had warned him that public sentiment was turning against Nazi Germany and that he would have to mute his isolationism if he wanted the nomination. When Catledge visited him in his compartment, he was mulling the issue, his voice distant, his glasses slipping off his face. "I'm just not going to do it," he muttered repeatedly. As Catledge wrote later, "He couldn't shift his views for political expedience."[20]

Taft's colleagues soon realized he was no ordinary politician. After they got past the often harsh rhetoric and the fierce partisanship, they found a man of rare conviction who eschewed political gamesmanship, spoke straight from the shoulder, and delivered on his political promises. A senior aide recounted that during passage of the Taft-Hartley Act he advised the senator that labor leaders were right in making a particular argument. Taft suggested they simply concede the point. Fine, said the aide, but first they should get something in return. Taft's stare made it plain to the aide that this was one senator who did not make tactical trades on substantive matters.[21] As Harry Lundeberg, head of the Seafarers International Union, put it, Taft "doesn't give you a lot of sweet con like the others."[22] Another perennial political foe, Dean Acheson, described a Taft speech thus: "Typical—bitterly partisan and ungracious, but basically honest."[23]

Another Taft trait, his willingness to compromise, enhanced his effectiveness as a senator. After all the partisanship and rhetoric, after he had mapped out his position and enunciated the principles, he was then almost always prepared to sit down and find the compromise that would move legislation forward. Those who bargained with him found him much more flexible and willing to compromise than his rhetoric led them to expect. Francis O. Wilcox, chief of staff of the Senate Foreign Relations Committee from 1947 to 1955, noted that although Taft was strongly isolationist, he was more reasonable than Wilcox had anticipated when Taft joined the committee in 1953. "After he was on the committee for a period of time," said Wilcox, "I thought, by golly, here was a real senator who did his homework and did his best to understand the issues involved."[24]

This zest for understanding the intricacies of issues and for negotiating became evident early in Taft's Senate career. When in early 1941 Roosevelt opted for price controls to curb inflation and named an economist to head a new price control agency, Taft attacked, calling the move "the most outrageous power grab which this country has ever seen." But while he vehemently opposed the administration's unilateral moves toward controls, he did not oppose them in principle and eventually voted for legislation that permitted the administration, under strict congressional guidelines, to impose them. Indeed, he even voted to extend controls to certain farm products that were exempted under the legislation, though this effort proved unsuccessful.[25]

Compromise was out of the question, however, when it meant violating Taft's basic beliefs. On one such "core issue," that of American involvement in World War II, he was unyielding. When Henry L. Stimson, a Republican nominated by Roosevelt for secretary of war, came before the Senate Military Affairs Committee for confirmation hearings, Taft badgered him with hypothetical questions designed to force Stimson to acknowledge that he favored U.S. intervention. Stimson protested, calling the line of questioning "unfair" and adding, "You have got to refrain from asking dogmatic questions, and I have to refrain from answering such questions." But Taft accomplished his purpose, which was to force the nominee into an evasive posture. In the process, he also reinforced his reputation as a harsh and insensitive political pugilist.[26]

When Roosevelt proposed the leasing of old military equipment to Britain under the Lend-Lease Program, Taft attacked. Roosevelt had likened his proposal to the act of lending a garden hose to a neighbor to help him put out a fire. Taft retorted that "lending war equipment is like lending chewing gum. We certainly do not want the same gum back."[27] But the forces of history would eventually outweigh Taft's isolationism, as the Lend-Lease bill demonstrated. On a 38-51 vote, the Senate killed a Taft amendment to curb presidential powers to deploy troops abroad, then passed the measure 60-31.[28]

Along the way, though, Taft was gaining a reputation as a highly effective legislative tactician; his reputation grew measurably following the 1942 elections. Republicans did very well that year, coming within ten votes of controlling the House and gaining nine seats in the Senate (bringing them up to thirty-seven seats against fifty-eight for the Democrats).[29] These gains drastically altered the political arithmetic in the Senate, and the fabled conservative coalition vaulted to prominence, holding the balance of power on domestic matters in that chamber for years to come. At the center of this powerful coalition was Robert Taft.

Allen Drury quickly discovered Taft's importance when he was assigned to cover the Senate for United Press in 1943. Writing in a journal subsequently published in book form, he said:

> Taft continues to impress me as one of the strongest and ablest men here. He is quick in debate and quick in humor. . . . Taft, perhaps more than any other, is the leader of the powerful coalition of Republicans and Southern Democrats which has things pretty much its own way right now. This makes him, in terms of actual strength on the floor, one of the three or four most powerful men in the U.S. Senate at the present time.[30]

After 1942, the Senate not only had more Republicans, but it also had more anti–New Dealers of both parties. Taft developed close political associations with Eugene E. Millikin of Colorado, a member (and later chairman) of the Finance Committee, and the irrepressible Kenneth Wherry of Nebraska (dubbed by *Time* as "the ex-undertaker who wants to bury the New Deal"),[31] as well as such solid conservatives as Ralph O. Brewster of Maine, C. Wayland "Curly" Brooks of Illinois, and Homer Ferguson of Michigan. And he pursued political alliances with some of the more powerful southern conservatives, including Walter George of Georgia, the powerful and knowledgeable Finance Committee chairman, Harry Byrd of Virginia, and, most notably, Georgia's Richard Russell, arguably the only senator this century to rival Taft's accumulation of informal legislative power.[32]

Taft lavished time and effort on forging alliances with the southern oligarchs, who normally had little to do with Republicans. But the Ohioan's earnestness impressed these men, and they came to see that they shared many of his fundamental views on domestic matters, including his opposition to federal power, his fiscal conservatism, and his preference for limited government.[33] White noted that these southerners were not simply Democratic rebels lying in wait for a chance to attack the national party. They disliked the direction set in the White House and genuinely worried about the political implications of those policies back home. White also perceived that there were other, less tangible, reasons for the southerners' interest in Taft. Like them, he was a skilled parliamentarian; he was a traditionalist; he was well born (and his father had been pro-South); and his word was utterly reliable. Even Harry Truman once remarked that there is nothing devious about Bob Taft.[34]

Taft first courted George and Byrd, eventually developing, through them, a working association with Russell. He also took care over the years, as his relationship with the southerners deepened, to avoid clashing with them over their essential internationalism. "He tried . . . to leave that subject pretty well alone," wrote White.[35] Though the initial payoff from this association with southern Democrats was insignificant, it was to grow in importance over time.

Yet even in 1944 he joined southern Democrats and some other conservative Republicans to thwart FDR's plan to create a federal ballot for U.S. soldiers away at war. The stated idea was to ease the way for soldiers to vote by giving them ballots listing the offices of president, vice president, senator, and representative. Bypassing state ballot procedures, these ballots would be available to all soldiers who asked for them. Opponents of the plan assumed that the soldiers were likely to vote for Roosevelt, their commander in chief, and hence any action that increased soldier voting would favor the incumbent president and his party. It was a highly partisan affair, and some Republicans feared getting tarred with the brush of partisanship if they resisted a move to foster democracy at the front. That did not deter Taft. He argued that the plan unconstitutionally deprived states of the right to regulate elections and would thwart soldier voting in state elections. He favored an approach confining the distribution of federal ballots to those soldiers who applied for them. When the administration bill came to the Senate floor, where Roosevelt forces were sure they had the votes, Taft took command of the opposition forces. Drury wrote:

> It was the most partisan exhibition I have seen so far in the Senate, and on an issue which is sheer dynamite. This did not deter the gentleman from Ohio one little bit. He was at his most vigorous, jumping up and challenging the opposition right and left, heckling Barkley, shouting at Lucas, using every possible parliamentary procedure to keep the soldier-vote bill from coming to the floor. It was an amazing performance.[36]

Though Taft's amendment did not pass, his arguments had some impact. The Senate modified the administration's approach before passing the bill. But in the House, the arguments of Taft and his allies prevailed, and the state ballot plan won. The House then prevailed in conference, and the final bill was so watered down that Roosevelt simply let it become law without his signature.[37]

This was merely one instance of Taft exploiting the political circumstances of the Seventy-eighth Congress. He also helped to tweak Roosevelt on a consumer subsidy program under the auspices of the Commodity Credit Corporation (CCC). Under the program, the government bought commodities with CCC monies and then sold them to consumers at lower prices. Farmers of course deplored the program, which held down farm prices, and conservatives opposed the use of federal money to assist consumers already faring quite well under the war economy.

Characteristically, Taft sought a middle ground, opposing the large subsidies proposed by the Roosevelt administration but supporting modest amounts to foster production of certain commodities. He also supported continuation of the CCC, highly popular in the farm belt but at the vortex of the subsidy issue. As a result, Taft was attacked by farmers for supporting even modest subsidies and by liberals for wanting to limit them. Initially, subsidy opponents prevailed, largely because Walter George, who, as Drury witnessed,

> rose and with his magnificent voice, which rolls down into the depths below the sea and then rises into majestic crescendo while the lightning streaks and the thunder blares, proceeded to call down the wrath of God on the whole subsidy program.[38]

The CCC bill that reached the White House banned the subsidy program, but Roosevelt vetoed it, and lawmakers, fearful over the threat to the popular CCC, restored authority for the subsidies. The episode nevertheless showed how the president's political standing with Congress had deteriorated. Taft applauded. Congress, he wrote, "has finally regained its independence for the first time in ten years."[39]

Though Taft held no leadership posts, his stature in the Senate continued to grow. Then came a real opportunity to mold both policy and strategy for Senate Republicans—the death of Senate Republican leader Charles McNary of Oregon. A western Progressive and leading conservationist, first elected in 1916, McNary had become a fixture in the Senate, a well-loved parliamentarian who presided over the Republican minority during its darkest days in the political wilderness (see Chapter 4). But by 1935 many had come to view McNary as too mild-mannered to lead any attack on the New Deal. "Halfway between the extremes is usually the point of wisdom," McNary had once declared, and halfway was generally where he could be found.[40] Many Republicans, tired of the powerlessness dictated, first, by their numbers and, later, by the imperatives of war, wanted more forceful leadership. As it became clear that McNary likely would not return to the Senate after his brain surgery in 1943, Nebraska's Wherry told Drury that the party's "young bloods" wanted (as Drury put it) "somebody who will get in there and fight, show a little opposition, organize the Republicans into a really strong unit capable of Action. The nature of the action is apparently not specified, just so it's action."[41]

This sentiment among Republicans had already thrust Taft into a position of informal leadership. As his son, Robert Taft, Jr., noted, Taft "always wanted to win, he didn't mind getting into a fight." Thus, continued Robert, in the early days of Taft's Senate career—when Republicans were so much in the minority and so accustomed to "being beaten about the ears, taking the crumbs left over from the Democrats"—his father's impatience with that situation and attacks against it made him a leader largely by default. He added that his father would "take on any subject that came up," and that, as the press came to rely on his pronouncements, he became a de facto party spokesman.[42]

Though Taft was mentioned as a possible successor to McNary, he did not seek the post. The new GOP leader became Wallace White of Maine, described as "a kindly, honorable, upright man . . . the first to agree that he is Senate Republican leader in name only."[43] His ascension had been predicted by one Senate wit "if the law of inertia applies," wrote Drury, who discovered him to be a colorless fellow who responded to questions by zeroing in on details and showing little expansiveness. He concluded, "Friendly, colloquial, and as New England as they come, the little man from Maine is a nice fellow."[44] As minority leader, he fit the political purposes of Robert Taft, who had no desire to monitor the often dreary floor debate. It soon became clear that White continually deferred to Taft, looking back to him at crucial moments on the floor for all the important signals.[45]

Hoping to establish a different leadership post, Taft created a Republican policy committee, called the GOP Steering Committee, and soon found himself heading it. As the de facto intellectual and political head of the GOP, Taft now had the responsibility consistent with his already large, and growing, power.[46] He quickly became national spokesman for the Republican party and just about anyone else who opposed the New Deal.

With the death of Roosevelt and the ascension of Harry S. Truman in 1945, this process accelerated. Truman appeared hapless as the nation found itself in the painful transition from war to peace, a transition that brought economic dislocations and political demands aimed at the governing Democrats. Consumers demanded more meat, more gasoline—more consumer goods in general. Workers demanded wage boosts to stay abreast of the cost of living. Business leaders demanded an end to production and price controls. Returning veterans demanded jobs. Everybody demanded an end to the era of sacrifice.[47]

These economic and political circumstances opened up a number of battlefronts between the Truman administration and opposition Republicans. For Taft, the most notable of these related to price controls and labor relations. On the former, Taft assumed leadership of the congressional opposition and became a relentless critic of the Office of Price Administration (OPA), which he regarded as too rigid and too preoccupied with curbing business profits as opposed to prices. Business, especially small business, he argued, was getting caught between demands for higher wages and governmental curbs on prices. The result, as *Time* magazine suggested, was a squeeze on production:

> In agriculture, every new price ceiling has caused a new dislocation; the U.S. has alternated dizzily between meat shortages and grain shortages, between a shortage of ice cream and a shortage of butter. In industry, the problem is vastly more complicated.[48]

With strong Republican backing and scattered support from conservative Democrats, Taft charged at the administration, attacking Chester Bowles, the director of economic stabilization, when he testified before the Banking and Currency Committee in April 1946. In characteristic fashion, Taft interrupted testimony and pressed Bowles with leading questions that displayed his mastery of figures and details. Bowles, a hulking, jut-jawed social planner who thrived on controversy, shot back, "Before you attack my point of view, why don't you listen to it? I think that's the courteous way." But Taft pressed on.[49]

He clearly had political sentiment on his side as the dislocations born of controls began to affect consumers. Led by Taft and Wherry, the Senate passed two amendments to restrict OPA actions. Though the House passed a more moderate bill, the conference produced a measure close to the restrictive Senate version. The administration was livid. Attacking Taft by name, Truman said his handiwork was the "mainspring" of "an impossible bill" that "provides a sure formula for inflation."[50] Bowles promptly resigned, and Truman vetoed the bill, leaving the OPA dead. The result was a surge in prices and a hurried scramble to produce another bill, which was eventually signed by Truman, although it closely resembled the measure he had vetoed a month earlier. Columnists Stewart Alsop and Joseph Alsop wrote:

> It was a fascinating performance, demonstrating at once the success of [Taft's] legislative methods, the nature of his economic opinions, and the cold-turkey boldness which led Taft . . . to go far out on the limb of a highly controversial issue.[51]

If Taft proved to be Truman's nemesis on the price-control issue, then he utterly obliterated the president's labor initiative, altering his own image in the process: Taft was emerging as the president's leading congressional opponent. In May 1946, with the country's railroad workers on strike, Truman asked for congressional authority to draft the strikers and thus command them to return to work. With the nation fed up with economic dislocations stemming from labor stoppages, the House granted this authority within two hours on a vote of 306-13.[52] Equally quick action was anticipated in the Senate.

But Taft rose to stop the antilabor juggernaut and to bring some measure of balance to the debate:

> I am not willing to vote for a measure which provides that the President may be a dictator. It offends not only the Constitution, but every basic principle for which the American Republic was established. Strikes cannot be prohibited without interfering with the basic freedom essential to our form of Government.[53]

In this effort, Taft was joined by what ordinarily would have been an unlikely ally, Florida's very liberal Claude Pepper. But Taft was clearly the leader. Three days after Truman's request, when embarrassed Senate Democrats sought to delay a vote, Taft pressed ahead, demanding a roll call. The Truman proposal was killed, 13-70.[54]

By this time, as William S. White flatly stated, Taft was "the most powerful figure in the Senate."[55] He began to attract more attention—and more respectful attention—from the press. In the summer of 1946, he was the subject of cover stories in *Newsweek* and *U.S. News & World Report*. Even the column-writing Alsop brothers, who despised Taft's isolationism and had written critically of him, began to treat him more respectfully. They later recalled that one of them was so charmed by Taft that he had to undergo a "de-brain-washing" by the other before he sat down to write.[56] *Newsweek* proclaimed that although he was merely halfway through his second term, "in the influence he wielded in his party's councils, Taft reigned supreme—the undisputed and dominant Republican figure not only in Congress but the nation as well." The magazine explained that the Ohio senator "had no glamour, no engaging hobbies, few close friends, and little of the personal magnetism that draws a popular following. . . . Taft's success stemmed rather from his amazing legislative know-how."[57]

With the 1946 elections came Taft's first opportunity to take total command of the Senate. The GOP gained control of both chambers, with fifty-one seats in the Senate against forty-five for the Democrats.[58] Although Wallace White remained Senate Republican leader, Taft assumed pivotal positions throughout the chamber, becoming chairman of both the GOP Steering Committee (now renamed the Policy Committee) and the high-profile Labor and Public Welfare Committee. He was also ranking Republican (behind his ally Millikin) on Finance and leading senator of the group that allocated GOP committee assignments. "No other senator had so many major jobs," wrote *Time* in an effusive cover story that described Taft as "the biggest political figure in Washington, boss of probably the most efficiently organized GOP Senate the nation has ever seen." The magazine noted that Michigan's Arthur Vandenberg would hold considerable sway over foreign affairs, but added:

The dominant figure, most of the time, will be Taft—working overtime in his quiet office, slouching in his seat on the Senate floor, jumping to his feet to argue in his flat voice, grinning like a Cheshire cat even when he is wrathful, disgorging facts, facts and more facts from his fat briefcase.[59]

In an attempt to strengthen party unity, Republican leader and isolationist Robert Taft of Ohio (left) *deferred to the internationalist, bipartisan foreign policy of fellow Republican Arthur Vandenberg, chairman of the Foreign Relations Committee.*

The Taft Style

Taft's legislative style and political persona had propelled him to the minority leadership in the 1940s. They would now enliven and bolster his leadership of the majority in the Eightieth Congress. Up to this point his accumulation of power had been largely informal, based on the force of his personality and intellect, his ability to grab his colleagues' attention, and his political courage. He was not always well liked and in fact often infuriated certain colleagues on particular issues. But other senators listened to him. He was the one who stirred his colleagues to consider issues seriously. He was the one who could direct political behavior in the Senate based on his ability to frame issues and articulate his positions. In addition, he was always on hand for the tough job, the time-consuming challenge, the research task on deadline. Nobody worked harder or put in longer hours, and nobody could master so many details related to so many issues in so short a time. In fact, the "Taft style" played such a central role in his accumulation of power that it bears a closer look.

First, of course, there was the intellect. He possessed a mathematical mind—the kind that allows a person to sit down to play bridge for the first time in years and excel as if he had been playing regularly. Taft was also quick and highly organized. During his law practice in Cincinnati, he became famous among colleagues for his method of writing briefs: he would spread out dozens of law books on a huge conference table and then, pinpointing the passages he wanted, dictate a brief that was virtually letter-perfect.[60]

Second, Taft had a voracious appetite for hard work and long hours. In a cover story, *Time* recounted a typical day: Up at 7 A.M.; the usual breakfast of one egg; then, large briefcase in custody, the drive to his Senate office. After dictating letters, he received callers, including a committee from a dental association, the president of a college, the representatives of a radio station, a delegation from an Ohio rural electrification cooperative, and a newspaper reporter to talk about foreign policy. At noon, a luncheon. At 2 P.M., a meeting of the Policy Committee. At 4 P.M., more visitors. At 7 P.M., he packed his briefcase again:

> In went: the draft of an article he had promised to write for the *Encyclopedia Britannica*, a report on RFC consolidation, a report on the monetary committee of the International Chamber of Commerce, an article on the Nuremberg trials, the Economic Report of the President.[61]

He spent long hours reading scholarly articles, presidential speeches, and statistical abstracts, thoroughly preparing for any issue he wanted to tackle. When a study assignment emerged in the Policy Committee, a common phrase was, "Let Bob do it." And he frequently accepted. Although many Republican senators were experts in their primary fields, nobody came close to Taft in mastering so many major subjects.[62] One official of the National Education Association said his group had considered Taft an adversary until he joined forces with it on a particular issue; he "crammed his mind with more facts and figures than any man I've ever seen. Before it was all over, he was giving *us* the answers."[63] *Time* confirms this picture, observing: "His easy digestion of facts sometimes annoys colleagues whose mental digestion is not so good."[64]

Third, there was "his deep political courage."[65] Everyone agreed that Taft operated on the basis of deep conviction. He would never trim or fudge on an issue if his principles were at stake. And he would stand up on a matter of conviction even when such actions were not necessary and posed serious political risk. Probably nothing illustrates this more crisply than his 1946 speech at Ohio's Kenyon College attacking the war crimes tribunals of that period in Germany and Japan. "They violate the fundamental principle of American law that a man cannot be tried under an ex post facto statute," he said. "About this whole judgment there is the spirit of vengeance, and vengeance is seldom justice."

The Kenyon speech was widely reported, and Taft was quickly pilloried in the press and in political circles. As John F. Kennedy noted in *Profiles in Courage*, Senate Majority Leader Alben Barkley suggested Taft "never experienced a crescendo of heart about the soup kitchens of 1932, but his heart bled anguishedly for the criminals at Nuremberg." Newspapers in his home state joined the attack. The *Toledo Blade* said the speech demonstrated that Taft had "a wonderful mind that knows practically everything and understands practically nothing." Far from seeking to defend Nazi criminals, whom he called "despicable," Taft sought to posit his strict views of constitutional justice. Though his point was totally lost in the flurry of criticism that ensued, his action later won him acclaim. Kennedy wrote, "What is noteworthy . . . is Taft's unhesitating courage in standing against the flow of public opinion for a cause he believed to be right."[66]

Although blunt and combative, Taft would never engage in personal attacks. Similarly, he seldom responded to attacks on himself and kept his own political rhetoric fastened to facts. Senator Everett Dirksen of Illinois once noted that Taft "never permitted the element of personality to enter into his considerations when conviction and principle were involved."[67] Robert Taft, Jr., noted that his father "had strong opinions about people, but he didn't express them much. People weren't the important thing; issues were."[68] And the Alsop brothers confirm this, writing: "Arguments are largely wasted on him, for the simple reason that he is not much of a respecter of the opinions of others. Facts are what he respects."[69]

His ferocity about facts could be politically intimidating, as when he would badger witnesses in committee hearings or argue with colleagues over how to frame a debate. Drury recounted a floor encounter between Taft and Maryland Democrat Millard Tydings. Although "a thoroughly capable and logical man," Tydings was "driven temporarily off base by Taft's attack" and lost any ability to hold his own. "Taft demolished his arguments without any trouble, and Tydings accepted with relief Taft's suggestion that it go over to Monday for further clarification."[70] Democrat

Ernest McFarland of Arizona did not fare so well during a debate on the school lunch program. "McFarland, slow, amiable and obviously frustrated by a vocal and parliamentary attack too swift and sure-footed for him to counter, defended the school-lunch provision heatedly for a little while" before offering a significant compromise.[71]

Taft's preoccupation with issues and procedures was so complete that it was virtually impossible to draw him into a personal feud. An incident in the Education and Labor Committee in April 1946 is illustrative. Chairman James E. Murray of Montana was unveiling his national health insurance bill; Taft dismissed the bill as "socialistic" and suggested the committee was being used "as a propaganda machine." Murray shot back: "That's a slander and a falsehood. You're just reflecting your general conduct on the Senate floor."

When Taft, ignoring the insult, mildly asked permission to submit an opposition bill, Murray cut him off. "I demand you subside. You've been impertinent and insulting."

Taft: I intend to offer a complete bill.
Murray: You can shut your mouth up and get out. You're so self-opinionated and so self-important.

Taft suggested the committee adjourn pending the chairman's ability to regain his composure.

Murray: No, I won't adjourn.
Taft [*to the committee reporter*]: I hope you're getting all this, because I intend to take it to the floor.
Murray [*yelling*]: Don't take it down.
Taft: You mean the chairman refuses to take down the statements I make?,
Murray [*screaming*]: I'm chairman of this committee, and I want you to subside. If you don't shut up, I'll get these officers in here and have you thrown out.

At that point, Taft quietly and calmly left the hearing room.[72]

Finally, Taft was utterly honorable in his dealings with colleagues. William S. White wrote: "There is no instance known to me in all his days in the Senate where Taft let down an associate in any agreed enterprise, no matter how sticky the going might have become."[73] He harbored a reputation for rigid intellectual honesty, as when he stood up to thwart legislation to gut enforcement of a conservative nemesis, the OPA. "I don't like price control," he told his colleagues, "but it is a necessity for the war effort, and so long as we have it, it must be enforced."[74] And he met his own high standards of political fairness. In 1947, when Taft began his big effort to get the Taft-Hartley labor bill through his Labor Committee, he extended himself to have New York's liberal Irving Ives sit on the committee. Ives, a freshman Republican with close ties to Taft's archrival, Thomas Dewey, had an impressive background in labor law, and Taft felt, as he put it to White, "that the Dewey side had a right to a seat there." The result was added political difficulty for Taft on the highly divided committee, but he was willing to pay that price.[75]

To be sure, Taft carried some political and personal liabilities as well. He could be rude, and he sometimes displayed a kind of intellectual haughtiness, occasionally coming "dangerously close to the line that separates the man of argument from the man of arrogance."[76] That description was penned more than twenty years after an acquaintance in Cincinnati noted that he displayed a "rectitude which succeeds in stopping just short of self-righteousness."[77] Taft's bluntness was legendary. A colleague on the Yale Corporation, James Lee Loomis, in Washington to check on a railroad bill, went to the Senate lobby and called Taft off the floor. When Taft appeared, Loomis asked if the bill would reach the floor that day. "Over my dead body," replied the senator, and he turned abruptly around and stomped back into the chamber. One important Wisconsin Republican, encountering Taft at a Washington reception, thanked him for a recent telegram of appreciation he had received from the senator. Taft replied absently that he never saw the thing; he added that his staff chief sent such telegrams out by the dozen.[78]

In his public pronouncements, these flights of candor and bluntness could be disastrous. During a national tour in 1947, he said rising food prices stemmed from excess demand. Asked if that meant people should eat less, he replied, "Yes, eat less meat, and eat less extravagantly." The quote dogged him throughout the rest of his life.[79]

His preoccupation with detail was schoolmarmish at times. Too often he sought to amend a bill even when his colleagues clearly did not want to amend it but to move it along. Drury recalled an incident when Taft was simply shouted down on the Senate floor for seeking to amend a surplus-property measure. To laughter in the press gallery, he pressed for what he insisted was "the best possible compromise" when, in Drury's words, "there wasn't any need for compromise." One reporter quipped that the *A* in Taft's name must stand for "amendment." Drury recounted that "he got swamped in a roar of nos, and that was that."[80]

And although Taft had a mind for detail, it was less adept with subtle concepts. Dean Acheson observed that Taft's "otherwise excellent mind" suffered from a defect "which Justice Holmes found also in that of Justice John Marshall Harlan the elder: 'Harlan's mind,' he said, 'was like a vice, the jaws of which did not meet. It only held the larger objects.' "[81] The result was that Taft's political judgments sometimes lacked sharpness. White noted that, following the 1946 elections, Taft could conclude only that the public was opting to dismantle the New Deal, writing: "He never could grasp to what extent men reacted far more trivially or emotionally than perhaps ideally they should."[82]

On balance, of course, Taft's political and personal assets far outweighed his liabilities at the beginning of 1947, as he assumed the role of the most powerful man in the United States Senate. These were tough days for Taft's rival in the White House. By the end of 1946, Harry Truman was coming to terms with the fact that he had reached for large goals and had barely accomplished small ones. His beloved Congress had turned against him. Although he fancied himself a man of the people, he lacked the people's support. As Truman biographer Cabell Phillips put it,

> They had been tired of war when he came in, and now they were tired of Democrats. . . . It was strikes and high prices and black markets and rent gougers and "government by crony" and a score of other annoyances, large and small, real and imagined, that set the public mood of disaffection in those first Truman years.[83]

In October 1946, *Time* wrote that "few U.S. Presidents have been jeered at the way Harry Truman was jeered at last week." The magazine noted that New Dealer columnist Samuel Grafton mocked: "Poor Mr. Truman . . . an object for pity." The president's approval rating in the polls had plummeted from a high of 87 percent shortly after he assumed the office to a mere 32 percent.[84]

Into the vacuum stepped Bob Taft. With Wallace White acting as nominal leader, Taft set the policy, the agenda, and the strategy. The *New Republic* reported that White quietly told reporters: "Taft is the man you want to see,"[85] while Taft himself complained to a friend that he could not express an opinion without reporters interpreting his words as Republican policy.[86] His power rested on four basic factors: first, the Democrats were in a panic; second, his long effort to foster good relations with southern Democrats had paid off in the form of a close working relationship with these potential ad hoc allies; third, he maintained almost total control over the Republican party in the Senate; and fourth, he ran a remarkably efficient operation that anticipated issues, incorporated the opinions of the Senate GOP rank and file, and brought to the fore the facts and information needed for political decisions. "Congress," said the *New Republic* in the spring, "now consists of the House, the Senate and Bob Taft."[87]

Taft-Hartley

All of Taft's leadership abilities emerged in the 1947 fight to push the Taft-Hartley labor bill through Congress. He immersed himself in the subject for weeks, often working well past midnight, as action on the measure heated up in his Labor and Public Welfare Committee. He reassured opponents by ensuring Senator Ives a seat on his committee. And he signaled early that he sought a balanced bill and would himself be willing to compromise in order to get it.[88]

The country was ready for legislation aimed at clipping labor's clout. The rash of postwar strikes, the demagoguery of labor kingpins such as the United Mine Workers' John L. Lewis, the reports of communist penetration of some unions, the scourge of rising prices—all contributed to the public mood. Fully seventeen labor bills designed to trim labor's power were introduced on the opening day of the Eightieth Congress. By spring more than a hundred bills had been thrown into the hopper on both sides of the Capitol building.[89]

But Taft's analytical acumen suggested to him that pitfalls lay ahead. He assumed that Truman would veto any labor bill, so it had to be moderate enough to ensure an override. The House, more rigidly conservative, was likely to produce a bill that would not pass the override test. Hence the Senate version had to leave Taft well positioned for the House-Senate conference committee. Meanwhile, in his own committee he was anticipating the likely defections of his three GOP members—Ives, George Aiken of Vermont, and Wayne Morse of Oregon—over antilabor provisions.[90]

Although organized labor attacked him as an advocate of a "slave labor bill," Taft's views were actually quite moderate. He accepted the right of workers to bargain collectively with their employers and to strike. He opposed the anticommunist oaths for labor leaders that some lawmakers favored. And he disliked most government intervention in the labor-management relationship. Yet he felt the 1935 Wagner Act had gone too far in giving labor leaders power over their workers and labor unions power over employers. He therefore opposed the closed shop, secondary boycotts, and jurisdictional strikes.[91]

In committee he frequently found himself on the losing side as GOP mavericks joined forces with the Democratic phalanx against the labor measure. *Time* said Taft's initial proposal had been "flattened into a pancake by his own committee." But he accepted these defeats in good grace with the idea of reversing them, if possible, on the Senate floor. Taft managed to get all three liberal Republicans on the committee to support the final version, and all but two Democrats approved the measure as well.[92]

But he had lost on several major provisions, and committee liberals, including some GOP colleagues, were seeking to break the measure up into several components for floor consideration. This was a major threat to Taft, who needed to take an omnibus measure to conference in order to deal on equal terms with the House, which had approved an omnibus measure. In addition, he knew that if his bill were split up, Truman would be able to respond selectively to its various provisions and "sit squarely on the fence," as *Time* put it. "Truman could then court labor's support by killing the harshest proposals, try to win public support by approving the mildest."[93]

Taft met the challenge directly. He went back to committee and secured a 7-6 vote in favor of the omnibus approach. The swing vote on this procedural matter: Irving Ives. The liberal New Yorker did not like the omnibus approach because it meant a tougher bill, but he felt he could not oppose his chairman, who had placed him on the committee, on this nonsubstantive matter. With that committee vote in hand, Taft easily dealt with the matter on the floor.[94]

He managed to reverse his committee defeats on several other matters. But, ever mindful that the endgame was a veto override, he engineered a major compromise on one provision and accepted defeat on another. The compromise came on the means of controlling secondary boycotts and jurisdictional strikes. Taft had wanted both employers and employees to have access to the courts in order to stop such actions, but labor's opposition was so intense that he proposed a plan allowing only employers direct access to the courts. When more conservative Republicans fought for the original amendment, Taft departed from them and voted against it. The result was a provision that most senators could live with and further evidence of Taft's reasonableness.

But on the matter of whether to allow industrywide collective bargaining, Taft took the matter to a vote—and lost. Although five of his supporters were not on the floor for the roll call, Taft decided against any move for a subsequent vote. Instead, he walked across the floor for a congratulatory handshake with Ives, who had led the opposition. Notwithstanding that defeat, Taft had dominated the floor during the labor bill consideration. "The 68-to-24 vote by which the Senate passed the labor bill last week," wrote *Time*, "was a testimonial to Taft's conduct of that debate." The magazine predicted that the final conference-committee bill "would be pretty much Taft's."[95]

Time was right. Taft's well-chosen tactics had placed him in a good position for the conference negotiations. Although in many respects he preferred the tougher House bill, he defended the Senate version down the line, his aim to get a final bill that could attract the support of both liberals and conservatives in an override vote. Accordingly, he managed to convince his House counterpart, Fred Hartley of New Jersey, that the Senate version offered a greater chance of eventual success. In the end, the House voted 331-83 to override Truman's veto; the Senate vote was 68-25. The measure represented a big accomplishment: the first major alteration of New Deal legislation, it also was a rare feat in that it had cleared Congress over the categorical opposition of the executive branch. Said *Time*, "The nation had a new labor law, by majority rule."[96]

Taft-Hartley capped a Congress characterized by Taft's leadership of the Republican party and dominance over the president. He led Congress to a tax-reduction bill, also cleared over Truman's veto. And he helped to thwart Truman's calls for a minimum-wage increase and for civil rights legislation (the latter helping to cement the conservative coalition so crucial to Taft's congressional power). In broad political terms, he was striking heavy blows at the despised New Deal and helping to define a Republican alternative. In the process, he was becoming more and more famous. *Time* wrote that Taft's presidential campaign train would soon begin to roll, and the engineer clearly was the Ohio senator:

> He had put it together in the yards of the 80th Congress, where virtually every piece of major legislation had been given his boost or his boot. Frankly, loudly, obstinately and often, he had declared his stand. Nobody, friend or foe, would accuse him of not speaking his mind.[97]

Naturally, he picked up criticism along the way. Some conservative Republicans disliked what they saw as his proclivity for compromise—some of the GOP's "young bloods" began calling him "compromising Nelly."[98] Others felt he had arrogated too many prerogatives to himself. "I don't mind one man calling the signals, taking the ball, throwing the forward pass, running around and catching it, making the touchdown

Although Robert A. Taft of Ohio was not named Republican leader until 1953, this 1948 cartoon depicts his power and influence over the GOP.

and then marking up the score," one senator complained, albeit anonymously. "But I'm *goddamed* if I like it when he rushes over after that and leads the cheer."[99]

The Sad, Worst Period

With the end of the 1948 congressional session came two crushing disappointments in Bob Taft's political life. First, the Republican National Committee rejected his candidacy for the party's presidential nomination in favor of his longtime political adversary, Thomas Dewey. Then the voters rejected Dewey in favor of another term for Harry Truman and tossed out the Republican majorities in the House and Senate. Thus began what White has called Taft's "sad, worst period. . . . He took up, over a long time and in many ways, an attitude of a sour and embittered political frustration that was, in simple fact, unworthy of his personal tradition and beneath all that he had been."[100]

He became more intensely partisan and even flirted with Mc-Carthyism, suggesting at one point that the Wisconsin senator should "keep talking and if one case doesn't work out he should proceed with another." He developed an offhandedness that some colleagues and members of the press found disturbing. Taft opposed the nomination of former army general George Marshall as defense secretary. Asked if his opposition stemmed from his objection to having a former military man as civilian head of the military, he replied, "Oh, I suppose that's as good a reason as any."[101]

But Taft did play a major role in congressional passage of two landmark bills, which provided federal funding for housing and for primary and secondary education. His contribution to these measures reflects his independence of mind and his intense desire to compete in the legislative arena, hence his willingness to compromise. It also reflects his philosophical breadth. Far from being the rigid ideologue portrayed by his critics, Taft was obsessed by the public policy problems of his day and dedicated to the government's need to address them. On both issues, he formed close alliances with liberal Democrats and proved instrumental in forging the compromises that made passage possible. And he did not shrink from battle with Republican colleagues normally allied with him on the big issues of the day. Grover W. Ensley, executive director of the Joint Economic Committee from 1949 to 1957, recalls a memorable exchange between Taft and House Majority Leader Charles Halleck of Indiana as Congress struggled to adjourn in 1948:

> I thought Halleck was going to explode. He was disturbed about the public housing provision in the Senate [housing] bill. Finally Taft just threw up his hands and walked out, and the bill didn't go through until a year later when Congress was Democratic controlled."[102]

As early as 1946, Taft had championed major housing and education initiatives, leading the way for Senate passage of housing legislation that year, and of both housing and education initiatives in 1948. After the 1948 education measure passed the Senate, *Newsweek* said Taft had "almost single handedly pushed [the bill] through the Senate."[103] But the House was not ready for either initiative until 1949.

As we have already observed, throughout the 1940s, Taft's accumulation of power and influence in the Senate was largely informal. He did head the Republican Policy Committee, and in the Eightieth Congress was chairman of the Labor and Public Welfare Committee. But his actual power far exceeded that suggested by his formal titles and positions. Beginning in 1944, when he spearheaded the creation of the Steering Committee (later the Policy Committee) and became its head, he was the actual Republican leader in the Senate. From this relatively modest position he exerted more influence over his party than most party leaders who actually enjoy the formal titles. What is more, because of his close ties to key southern Democrats and his knack for breaking legislative deadlocks, Taft was frequently the Senate's single most powerful member.

Eisenhower and Taft

After 1952, however, Taft was Senate majority leader during a Republican administration. Along with Dwight Eisenhower's victory, the GOP had gained a minuscule edge of forty-eight to forty-seven in the Senate.[104] Taft's approach to the majority leadership quickly made him indispensable to the new president and easily made him the second most important politician in the land. But Taft's tenure as Senate leader was tragically brief—by April 1953 he was showing signs of the cancer that would take his life only three months later, on July 31. He was nevertheless able to demonstrate anew the talents and dedication he brought to lawmaking. He also showed the largeness of spirit that characterized much of his Senate career.

Taft had hoped to move beyond the Senate by the time the Eighty-third Congress convened, setting his sights once again on the White House. He almost got the nomination at the 1952 Chicago convention. But his party nominated Eisenhower instead. Many political observers wondered if General Eisenhower, a staunch internationalist and national hero with no ideological bent, and Taft, the GOP's leading ideologue and isolationist, could possibly get along. Events during the general election intensified these questions. Finding it hard to conceal his bitterness, Taft extracted a series of promises from Eisenhower in exchange for his dedicated support. Finally, during the last six weeks of the campaign, he campaigned vigorously for Ike throughout the West and Midwest and did all he could to rally his supporters behind the candidate.[105]

The relationship between these two powerful politicians got off to a rough start. One of Taft's stipulations at the pre-election "summit" with

Eisenhower had been that the victor not discriminate against Taft men in filling administration jobs. Taft and his allies soon concluded, however, that Eisenhower's team was putting what William S. White called "a remarkably legalistic interpretation" on the agreement. Not one of the original Taft recommendations for cabinet posts was accepted, and in two instances the Eisenhower forces seemed particularly insensitive to the Senate leader.[106]

The first was Eisenhower's designation of industrialist George M. Humphrey of Ohio as treasury secretary. Though Taft did not object to the nomination per se, he was chagrined that he was not consulted, regarding it as a violation of long-standing political courtesies governing presidential appointments of persons from a senator's home state. This slight paled, however, next to the president-elect's nomination of Martin Durkin of the plumbers' union to be secretary of labor. Not only had Durkin been a lifelong Democrat and supporter of that party's 1952 presidential nominee, Adlai Stevenson, but he had also been a relentless critic of the senator's cherished Taft-Hartley Act. Unable to maintain his public silence on this move, Taft quickly pronounced the choice to be "incredible."[107]

But, as annoying as the nominations were, Taft would not allow them to undermine his relationship with the fledgling Republican administration. As he had demonstrated over so many years, his interest was in the large aspects of governing, not in personalities or ego. He would never contribute to any action that would rupture the party. Besides, as Robert Taft, Jr., has noted, he felt a great responsibility to those who had supported the Eisenhower ticket based on his recommendation.[108] He therefore blamed the early slights on former Dewey advisers who had joined the Eisenhower administration and absolved the new president himself of any complicity. A typical Taftian gesture, it also preserved the possibility for a deepening relationship between the two men. To signal his conciliatory attitude, Taft publicly set as his goal the Senate confirmation of the entire Eisenhower cabinet by inauguration day. Although he did not succeed, his good-faith efforts were important in the early days of the new Republican era.[109]

Taft's basic approach was two-pronged. First, he signaled his willingness to work with the administration, to support it enthusiastically, and to help make it succeed at every opportunity. But if the Eisenhower forces wanted that support, they had to come to him. Second, he moved to clip the power of the Dewey forces in the Senate so that it would be clear that the administration's only avenue of success was through Taft. White records that senators such as Pennsylvania's James Duff and Massachusetts's Leverett Saltonstall

were smoothly thrust by Taft into far-back seats. It became commonplace in Washington to suggest, with some truth, that the surest way to Eisenhower's favor in Congress was to have been a pro-Taft and an anti-Eisenhower man before the 1952 convention.[110]

Slowly, the trust between Eisenhower and the majority leader deepened. The president established weekly meetings with congressional leaders and invited Taft to come by at any time, even without an appointment. He made an appearance at a reception at Taft's Georgetown home and nominated Taft's son, an Irish scholar, as ambassador to Ireland.[111] Eisenhower soon wrote, "Senator Taft has been the model of cheerful and effective cooperation."[112] For his part, Taft also was warming up to the president. "He is, I think, a man of good will," the senator told a friend early in 1953. A few weeks later, he observed, "He is grasping things pretty well."[113]

With this groundwork in place, the two men became a powerful policy team. One important key was Eisenhower's commitment to involve congressional leaders, notably Taft, in policy discussions before presidential decisions were made. Another was Taft's perception that he must make this administration succeed as the first Republican presidency in a generation; the alternative was another long duration in the political wilderness.[114]

Two issues that exploded in 1953 illustrate the developing relationship between the two men and Taft's contribution to the new administration's early success. One was Eisenhower's nomination of career diplomat Charles E. Bohlen as ambassador to Moscow. The other concerned the president's innocent but politically unwise decision to seek a congressional resolution on secret agreements between the United States and the Soviet Union at the 1945 Yalta Conference.

Though Bohlen was a Republican, his nomination troubled Taft and a good many other Republicans. He had accompanied Roosevelt to Yalta, a conference that for many had developed the odor of a sellout to the Soviets. To Republicans, Yalta exemplified the inadequacy of New Deal foreign policy in the face of the communist threat. Bohlen had played a relatively minor role at the conference, and he probably could have defused the Yalta issue at his confirmation hearings before the Senate Foreign Relations Committee had he accepted the Republicans' anti-Yalta line. But he defended the summit outcome as being in the country's interest at the time. The Foreign Relations Committee cleared the nomination by a unanimous vote, but difficulties immediately emerged on the Senate floor.[115]

A group of senators led by Wisconsin's Joseph McCarthy initiated an attack on Bohlen that threatened to subvert the new president's prerogatives before he even had a chance to establish his foreign policy. Pat McCarran, a Nevada Democrat, accused the new secretary of state, John Foster Dulles, of concealing FBI evidence against Bohlen, and McCarthy demanded that Bohlen submit to a lie detector test. McCarthy also suggested that Dulles be required to testify under oath on the matter. Accompanying all these demands was a whisper campaign suggesting Bohlen's FBI file contained a vague reference to homosexuality.[116]

Taft was livid over the smear campaign and what he considered a stupid effort to split the Republican party at such a crucial juncture. He attacked McCarthy for questioning the honor of the secretary of state and dismissed the call for the use of lie detector tests as a violation of the country's constitutional civil liberties:

> The suggestion has been made that Mr. Dulles be called before the Committee on Foreign Relations and be placed under oath. I think this is a ridiculous suggestion. Mr. Dulles' statement *not* under oath is just as good as Mr. Dulles' statement under oath, as far as I am concerned.[117]

But when the attack persisted, he proposed a compromise that allowed a senator from each party to inspect summaries of the FBI file. This was readily accepted (though it was roundly attacked by the *New Republic*), and Taft and Alabama's John Sparkman undertook the inspection task. When they returned after three hours of study to say categorically that there was nothing in the files to disqualify Bohlen, the battle was over. Bohlen was confirmed, 74-13.[118] The *New Republic* crowed, "Thus it came to pass that the confirmation was hailed as a victory for Eisenhower over the Republicans, a victory aided and abetted by almost solid Democratic support."[119]

The Bohlen incident carried immense importance. A defeat on that issue, particularly one engineered by a rump group of Republicans, would have been disastrous to the new administration, which clearly needed to establish its authority in matters of foreign policy. No one doubted that it was Taft's prestige, coupled with his unquestioned credentials as an anticommunist, that made the difference. But, having saved the administration from a major embarrassment, he immediately set about to ensure that no more such actions came out of the White House. He passed word to the president's men: "No more Bohlens!" In the process he served notice that the president would be foolhardy to move on such a nomination again without first consulting the man who would have to sell the decision in the Senate.[120]

Taft had made it clear, further, that he was willing to lead the opposition when White House policy proposals violated his fundamental principles. This had happened in February during a furor over a Yalta resolution. Eisenhower sent to Congress language for a resolution condemning secret agreements that had been subverted by the Soviets to enslave the peoples of Eastern Europe. Taft and his wing of the party considered the text wholly inadequate because the Republican position, as stated in the 1952 party platform, had been a complete repudiation of the secret agreements themselves.

Dulles and others in the administration argued that any U.S. repudiation would provoke the Soviets to abandon them also. But a more pressing consideration was Eisenhower's need to foster a bipartisan foreign policy, especially given the isolationist strains that remained in his own party. And congressional Democrats made it clear they would not be a party to any resolution that attacked Roosevelt's legacy. Meanwhile, congressional Republicans argued that after railing against Yalta for so many years they hardly could acquiesce to such namby-pamby language.[121]

Taft shared this view, and he carefully conveyed to the administration that he could not support the president's language. Additionally, in the Foreign Relations Committee he led a move to strengthen the language, a move that both upset the administration and united Senate Democrats in righteous wrath. Once this impasse materialized, however, Taft merely stepped back and allowed the issue to wither away. Thus, he established his fealty to principle, avoided a direct confrontation with the president, and scored what has been called a "curiously subtle and negative little victory."[122]

These were the days of Taft's greatest glory. The country was entering a post–New Deal era, and, although more of the New Deal was preserved than Taft himself would have wished, he was at the vanguard of national policy making in every sphere of American life. He was dealing with a president he respected and who seemed genuinely interested in his views and recommendations. His political dominance of the Senate was well established and unchallenged. As the country's quintessential lawmaker, he had reached a position of legislative power seldom matched before or after. It was not to last. He began suffering from a pain in his hip in April

1953, and it was soon diagnosed as a symptom of cancer. Doctors never did determine where the cancer was located, but it spread quickly through his body and soon he was forced to relinquish the leadership to his chosen successor, California's William Knowland. By July 4, he was admitted to New York Hospital for the last time. He died twenty-seven days later.

The immediate political consequence was that Taft's Republican party lost its one-vote margin in the Senate when Ohio's Democratic governor Frank Lausche named Democrat Thomas A. Burke to replace Taft. (Since independent Wayne Morse agreed to vote with the Republicans on organizational matters and Vice President Richard Nixon stood by with a tie-breaking vote in favor of Taft's party, nominal Republican control of the Senate was assured for the remainder of the Eighty-third Congress.) More important, Eisenhower lost the one man who could galvanize the coalitions needed in the Senate for his various initiatives. In his absence, the balance of influence shifted to Lyndon Johnson and his party. Although cautious about confronting the popular Eisenhower, Johnson was deft at keeping the administration off balance on important issues.[123] Thus, with Taft's death, Eisenhower's range of options, both in policy and tactics, narrowed.

Taft is often seen as the forerunner of the brand of conservatism that eventually captured first the party with Barry Goldwater in 1964 and then the country with Ronald Reagan in 1980. This view does not withstand thorough analysis, however. Taft's Republicanism was rooted in the era predating the New Deal, primarily as seen in his cherished Midwest. The conservatism that emerged triumphant after his death was a decidedly post–New Deal brand of politics rooted primarily in the emerging American West and South.

Taft, for example, always pressed his isolationist views as far as the political circumstances of the day would allow. He came close to being a pacifist. This is a far cry from the conservative Republicanism of Goldwater and Reagan, both internationalists who gloried in postwar America's global role and fought for a strong military to back it up.

What is more, later conservatives became tireless defenders of executive power and the prerogatives of the presidency. For them, the legislative branch represents a powerful threat to the constitutional standing of the presidency, as well as to the freedom of the American citizenry. This would have struck Robert Taft as alien. Like most American conservatives until recent years, he considered the legislative branch to be the country's greatest bulwark against arbitrary executive power.

Nor did the Goldwater-Reagan conservatism incorporate anything like Taft's interest in federal housing, education, and health programs. Though clearly a fiscal conservative who believed the federal government should be kept small and in check, he also believed this outlook needed to be leavened by governmental compassion.

Robert Taft was in many ways the defender of a brand of politics that was fading from the scene. He was truly a traditionalist, harking back to simpler days before the Great Depression, the New Deal, World War II, and the era of nuclear confrontation. When he died, this particular brand of politics died with him. And yet throughout his Senate career, he thrust himself into the vortex of politics, becoming an imposing figure in nearly all the major debates of his time, molding events with a force rare even in politicians totally in tune with their times. That is testimony to his intellect, his personality, his devotion to work, and to a rare parliamentary brilliance. His colleagues recognized this, which is why one can still get a glimpse of him on the frescoed walls of the Senate Reception Room.

NOTES

1. U.S. Congress Senate, *Robert Alphonso Taft, Late a Senator from Ohio: Memorial Addresses Delivered in Congress* (Washington, D.C.: U.S. Government Printing Office, 1954).
2. Allen Drury, *A Senate Journal, 1943–1944* (New York: McGraw-Hill, 1963), 155.
3. William S. White, *The Taft Story* (New York: Harper, 1954), 195.
4. Henry F. Pringle, *The Life and Times of William Howard Taft*, vol. 1 (New York: Farrar and Rinehart, 1939), 22.
5. James T. Patterson, *Mr. Republican: A Biography of Robert A. Taft* (Boston: Houghton Mifflin, 1972), 14.
6. Data sheet, Taft file, Senate Historical Office, Washington, D.C.
7. Patterson, *Mr. Republican*, 54.
8. Robert Taft to Martha Bowers, May 25, 1913, Robert Taft Papers, Library of Congress, Washington, D.C.
9. William S. White, *The Making of a Journalist* (Lexington: University Press of Kentucky, 1986), 159.
10. Ohio Historical Society Archives, Columbus, Ohio.
11. Ibid.
12. White, *Taft Story*, 37.
13. Ibid.
14. Carl Solberg, *Riding High: America in the Cold War* (New York: Mason and Lipscomb, 1973), 30.
15. *New York Times*, July 5, 1936.
16. Patterson, *Mr. Republican*, 126.

17. *Congressional Quarterly's Guide to Congress*, 2d ed. (Washington, D.C.:Congressional Quarterly, 1976), 182-A.
18. *New York Herald Tribune*, February 13, 1940.
19. Turner Catledge, *My Life and The Times* (New York: Harper and Row, 1971), 118.
20 Ibid., 118–119.
21 Victor Gold, "Taft's Last Stand," *Washingtonian*, October 1989, 103.
22. *Life*, September 23, 1947, 40.
23. Dean Acheson, *Present at the Creation* (New York: Norton, 1969), 410.
24. Francis O. Wilcox, oral history interviews, February 1–June 13, 1984, Senate Historical Office, Washington, D.C., 137.
25. Patterson, *Mr. Republican*, 236–237.
26. Ibid., 238–240.
27. U.S. Congress, *Congressional Record*, February 22, 1941, 1277.
28. *Editorial Research Reports*, vol. 2 (Washington, D.C.: Editorial Research Reports, 1941), 415.
29. *Congressional Quarterly's Guide to Congress*, 182-A.
30. Drury, *Senate Journal*, 10. Drury began keeping his journal in 1943, the year he began to cover the Senate for United Press.
31. *Time*, February 24, 1947, 23.
32. Patterson, *Mr. Republican*, 252.
33. Ibid., 260
34. White, *Taft Story,* 58–59; Patterson, *Mr. Republican,* 440.
35. White, *Taft Story*, 60.
36. Drury, *Senate Journal*, 57.
37. Patterson, *Mr. Republican*, 264.
38. Drury, *Senate Journal*, 74–75.
39. Robert Taft to Aunt Fannie, July 22, 1943, Robert Taft Papers.
40. Steve Neal, *McNary of Oregon* (Portland, Ore.: Western Imprints, 1985), xii.
41. Drury, *Senate Journal*, 40.
42. Robert Taft, Jr., interview with author, January 9, 1990, Washington, D.C.
43. Joseph Alsop and Stewart Alsop, "Taft and Vandenberg," *Life*, October 7, 1946, 102.
44. Drury, *Senate Journal*, 103.
45. White, *Taft Story*, 58.
46. Ibid., 57.
47. Cabell Phillips, *The Truman Presidency* (New York: Macmillan, 1966), 101.
48. *Time*, March 4, 1946, 20.
49. Patterson, *Mr. Republican*, 309.
50. *Time*, July 8, 1946, 19.
51. Alsop and Alsop, "Taft and Vandenberg," 104.
52. *Congressional Quarterly Almanac, 1946*, vol. 2 (Washington, D.C.: Congressional Quarterly, 1948), 298.
53. White, *Taft Story*, 45.
54. *Congressional Quarterly Almanac, 1946*, vol. 2, 304.
55. White, *Taft Story*, 45.
56. Joseph Alsop and Stewart Alsop, *The Reporter's Trade* (New York: Reynal, 1958), 136.
57. *Newsweek*, July 15, 1946, 28.
58. *Congressional Quarterly's Guide to Congress*, 182-A.
59. *Time*, January 20, 1947, 23.
60. Robert Taft, Jr., interview with author.
61. *Time*, January 20, 1947, 23.
62. Floyd M. Riddick, former Senate parliamentarian, oral history interviews, 1978–1979, Senate Historical Office, Washington, D.C., 234–239.
63. Quoted in Alsop and Alsop, "Taft and Vandenberg," 103.
64. *Time*, January 20, 1947, 24.
65. Ibid., 25.

66. John F. Kennedy, *Profiles in Courage* (New York: Harper, 1956), 241–244.
67. U.S. Congress, Senate, *Robert Alphonso Taft*.
68. Robert Taft, Jr., interview with author.
69. Alsop and Alsop, "Taft and Vandenberg," 103.
70. Drury, *Senate Journal*, 19.
71. Ibid., 155.
72. *Time*, April 15, 1946, 20.
73. White, *Taft Story*, 59.
74. Drury, *Senate Journal*, 190.
75. White, *Taft Story*, 68.
76. Drury, *Senate Journal*, 19.
77. Patterson, *Mr. Republican*, 108.
78. Ibid., 343.
79. *Life*, September 23, 1947, 40.
80. Drury, *Senate Journal*, 254.
81. Acheson, *Present at the Creation*, 484.
82. White, *Taft Story*, 56.
83. Phillips, *Truman Presidency*, 126.
84. *Time*, October 7, 1946, 21; October 21, 1946, 23.
85. "Old Guard Supreme," *New Republic*, January 13, 1947.
86. White, *Taft Story*, 61.
87. TRB, *New Republic*, May 3, 1947, 11.
88. Patterson, *Mr. Republican*, 355–356.
89. Robert J. Donovan, *Conflict and Crisis: The Presidency of Harry S Truman, 1945–1948* (New York: Norton, 1977), 299.
90. *Time*, March 3, 1947, 21–22.
91. U.S. Congress, *Congressional Record*, 80th Cong., 1st sess., 3834–3840.
92. *Time*, April 28, 1947, 20.
93. *Time*, May 12, 1947, 21.
94. Patterson, *Mr. Republican*, 357–361.
95. *Time*, May 26, 1947, 24.
96. *Time*, June 30, 1947, 16.
97. *Time*, August 4, 1947, 9.
98. Drury, *Senate Journal*, 40.
99. *Time*, January 20, 1947, 24.
100. White, *Taft Story*, 80.
101. Ibid., 89–90.
102. Grover W. Ensley, oral history interviews, October 20–November 1, 1985, Senate Historical Office, Washington, D.C., 44–46.
103. *Newsweek*, April 12, 1948, 17.
104. *Congressional Quarterly's Guide to Congress*, 182-A.
105. Patterson, *Mr. Republican*, 578.
106. White, *Taft Story*, 207.
107. *Congress and the Nation, 1945–1964* (Washington, D.C.: Congressional Quarterly, 1965), 20.
108. Robert Taft, Jr., interview with author.
109. Patterson, *Mr. Republican*, 589.
110. White, *Taft Story*, 225.
111. Patterson, *Mr. Republican*, 592.
112. Dwight D. Eisenhower, *Mandate for Change, 1953–1956* (New York: Doubleday, 1963), 194–195.
113. White, *Taft Story*, 218.
114. Ibid., 227.
115. *Congress and the Nation, 1945–1964*, 106a–107a.
116. Piers Brendon, *Ike: His Life and Times* (New York: Harper and Row, 1986), 248.
117. White, *Taft Story*, 235–236.
118. *Congress and the Nation, 1945–1964*, 106a–107a.

119. *New Republic,* April 6, 1953, 5.
120. White, *Taft Story,* 237–238.
121. *Congress and the Nation, 1945–1964,* 109.
122. White, *Taft Story,* 248.
123. Robert W. Merry, "The Prism of History: Johnson Was King Among 20th-Century Senate Leaders," *Congressional Quarterly Weekly Report,* April 16, 1988, 982–983.

CHAPTER 7

Lyndon B. Johnson
The Senate's Powerful Persuader

Howard E. Shuman

I f Lyndon Baines Johnson were a character in a novel, readers would find him hard to believe. One of the most extraordinary men of our times, he was a bundle of contradictions. Notoriously impatient, he could nevertheless bide his time and keep his own counsel so that on political issues, his timing was superb. While he used McCarthy-like tactics to bring down Leland Olds (President Harry Truman's nominee for a third term on the Federal Power Commission), he fashioned the downfall of McCarthy. As Senate leader, he destroyed the substance of three civil rights bills; as president, he resurrected and expanded them. A populist who cared for and helped poor people, he also steered massive government largess to those with wealth and power. He could be a Uriah Heep one moment and a bully the next. He was the Senate ringmaster who dominated the

Democrat Lyndon B. Johnson's prowess as majority leader in the Senate is legendary.

199

members, yet he needlessly harbored an intense inferiority complex toward Ivy League graduates and the eastern establishment.

Although a man of massive intelligence with an I.Q. at the high end of the scale, he was "foxy" bright and probably never harbored a philosophical idea. He was a genius at process but was uninterested in its theory, concerned only with results. He had an immense ego. His shirts were embroidered with the "LBJ" monogram. His wife was called Lady Bird, which matched his initials. The names of his daughters, Lynda Bird and Luci Baines; his ranch; and his dog, Little Beagle Johnson, conformed as well. He hung his own life-sized portrait above the mantle in his Senate office, dubbed the Taj Mahal because of its mass and decor.

Lyndon Johnson was a master of intrigue. A man of enormous vitality, nervous intensity, and what Sam Rayburn called "vaulting ambition,"[1] he could seduce, dominate, or mesmerize friend and foe alike. Except that he never took any vows of poverty, he was a whirling dervish in the Senate bazaar. He was both magician and sorcerer. Some thought he could tether a broomstick. He often seemed a figure from mythology, a half-human siren with mystical powers derived from some hidden cave or shadowy valley in the Hill Country of Texas.

When he appeared in the Senate dressed in a loud suit, sprawled in the majority leader's chair with his legs stretched across the aisle, he seemed the essence of a riverboat gambler or a snake-oil salesman at the county fair. Some thought him a political Elmer Gantry.

Both charming and boorish, delightful and foul-mouthed, he craved praise, hated criticism, and was almost paranoid about even temporary foes. He would exaggerate and lie. At times he enveloped himself with self-pity. He hated funerals and had a mercurial temper. He could proffer friendship and heap praise on a colleague at one moment, and threaten, ridicule, and scorn him the next. He abused his staff, but none was more loyal and hardworking than his; some staff members even named their children for him. He was king of the Senate before Robert Kerr (D-Okla.) was ever called that.

Sports analogies leap to mind. He was a genius at the political hidden ball trick, concealing his intentions from his most intimate colleagues. He was the master of the one-on-one, routinely dominating the most determined opponent. He could stall with the best four-corner ball-control experts. He once delayed a roll call vote in progress for more than an hour until Hubert Humphrey (D-Minn.) and his needed vote could be extracted from the dense clouds above Washington's National Airport.

The suspense he engendered as he won critical roll calls by switching a single vote at the penultimate moment was as exciting as any ninety-yard two-minute drill of a professional football team in the final moments of a play-off game.

He would have made a great military strategist—but was a Montgomery, not a risk-taking Patton. In the Senate he knew where he was going, how to get there, and how the inner recesses of his adversary's mind worked. A set-piece man, Johnson was slow to move and obsessed with tedious preparation, taking action only when he knew success was certain.

Clark Clifford, Johnson's counselor for three decades, said the single phrase to describe him was "raw power."[2] Paul H. Douglas (D-Ill.) compared the Senate under him to a Greek tragedy: "All the action takes place offstage, before the play begins. Nothing is left to open and spontaneous debate, nothing is left for the participants but the enactment of their prescribed roles."[3]

Johnson was the master of an intelligence system that has yet to be rivaled by MI5 or the CIA. No detail of a senator's life or needs went unattended. He knew the crooks, the drunks, and the womanizers; who wanted what suite of offices and what committee assignments; and what pork-barrel project was essential to each senator's state or political survival. He was so powerful and omniscient that some applied to him Sir Winston Churchill's description of Sir Stafford Cripps, "There but for the grace of God, goes God."

Gaining Power—The Senator from Texas

The Senate Class of 1948

When Johnson came to the Senate on January 3, 1949, few would have predicted either his meteoric rise to power or his ultimate mastery over that body. He had spent over ten years in the House of Representatives, where he was known as the stereotypical swashbuckling Texas congressman. He made a close and unsuccessful try for the Senate in 1941, and a closer and successful bid in 1948 when he won the Democratic primary by only eighty-seven votes in a disputed race. Majority Leader Scott Lucas (D-Ill.) dubbed him "Landslide Lyndon" at the opening caucus of the Senate Democrats in 1949,[4] a nickname he came to hate. His accomplishments were little known, except perhaps for his work on the House Armed Services Committee and its predecessor, the Naval Affairs Committee, and his extraordinary success in gaining funds to finish a Colorado River dam in his district and in securing contracts for his Texas benefactors, George and Herman Brown. He also had some prominence as a protégé of Franklin D. Roosevelt.

Few of his new colleagues were aware of his energetic, sometimes ruthless, climbs to power in lesser posts, his "long line of political daddies,"[5] and his mastery of the methods and procedures to seize power. Johnson determined to play the role of the traditional freshman senator— seen but not heard, subdued and deferential to his elders, and servile to Senate folkways. This was a 180-degree turn from his behavior in the House and stood in particular contrast to his recently concluded Senate campaign. Abandoning his brashness, he set out to curry favor and power by traditional Senate methods. Lucas described him during 1949 and 1950 as "a gentleman of the old school." His "activities were negligible, his warm personality and genial conduct made a favorable impression upon all Senators irrespective of their political affiliations."[6]

Johnson also abandoned the New Deal and what was for Texas, but not the country, a liberal image. Before he was sworn in, he told Robert C. "Bobby" Baker, "I am a Texan and I've got a Southern constituency and so I'm going to be more conservative than you would like me to be or than President Truman would like me to be."[7]

Johnson's base of support in Texas and his reelection were obvious concerns, perhaps obsessions, during his first term. "I got elected by just eighty-seven votes and I ran against a caveman," he told Baker.[8] On the issues, therefore, he was for the Taft-Hartley Labor Act, the Kerr bill to deregulate the price of natural gas, and the return of offshore oil to the states, and he opposed liberalizing the filibuster rule and Truman's Fair Employment Practices Commission.

Although he had not been the handmaiden of oil and gas interests as a member of the House (they were not major factors in his congressional district), Johnson committed himself in the Senate to support "nearly anything the big oil boys want because they hold the whip hand and I represent 'em."[9] During World War II, he had voted against removing price controls on oil and had earned the suspicions if not enmity of the big oil producers as a result.

In December 1948, from his office in the Cannon House Office Building, Lyndon Johnson phoned Bobby Baker, at twenty years of age, a six-year veteran of the Senate floor staff. Energetic, crafty, and persuasive, Baker knew as many Senate secrets and personalities as LBJ would ultimately possess. Later called "Little Lyndon," Baker was treated like an adopted son by his patron. "Mr. Baker," Johnson said, "I understand you know where the bodies are buried in the Senate. I'd appreciate it if you'd come to my office and talk with me."[10]

Talk they did. Johnson told him, "I want to know who's the power over there, how you get things done, the best committees, the works." According to Baker, Johnson

peppered me with keen questions for a solid two hours. . . . No senator ever had approached me with such a display of determination to learn, to achieve, to attain, to belong, to get ahead. He was coming into the Senate with his neck bowed, running full tilt, impatient to reach some distant goal I then could not even imagine. . . . Politics simply consumed the man.[11]

Committee Assignments

Among Johnson's first acts was the cultivation of Senator Richard Russell (D-Ga.). Through him and his power with the Democratic Steering Committee, Johnson sought and gained a position on both the Armed Services and the Interstate and Foreign Commerce committees. In 1949, those two bodies were among the six most powerful of the fifteen Senate standing committees. No Democratic freshman got a place on the other four—Appropriations, Foreign Relations, Finance, or Judiciary.[12]

Johnson sought the Armed Services Committee because of his previous service on its House counterpart and because he wanted access to Richard Russell.[13] Johnson courted the bachelor Russell as he had wooed bachelor House Speaker Sam Rayburn (D-Tex.). Married to the Senate, Russell arrived early and stayed late. "I made sure that there was always one companion, one Senator, who worked as hard, and as long as he, and that was me, Lyndon Johnson."[14]

The Interstate and Foreign Commerce Committee was important in Johnson's effort to court his state's powerful oil and gas interests. It had jurisdiction over both the price of natural gas and the members and activities of the Federal Power Commission. The committee also oversaw the Federal Communications Commission with the power to issue and regulate radio and television licenses, not an unimportant family interest.[15] His committee positions both added to and detracted from his personal reputation. As a freshman, Johnson chaired the special Commerce subcommittee that handled Truman's renomination of Leland Olds to the Federal Power Commission. Olds was a strong supporter of regulating natural gas.

In a letter to the editor of the *Denver Post*, replying to a critical editorial, Johnson charged that Truman appointed Olds because of a deal made with radical New York congressman Vito Marcantonio and his American Labor party to "keep [Henry] Wallace out of the [New York state] race."[16] In his speech on the Senate floor to oppose Olds, Johnson said, "I do not charge that Mr. Olds is a Communist, although I recognize the line that he followed, the phrases he used, the causes he espoused, resemble the party line today."[17] Johnson's performance—aimed chiefly at his constituents—alienated him from the dominant liberal wing of the Democratic party for many years to come.

From the day Johnson entered the Senate, with only occasional early lapses, he was extraordinarily careful to position himself as something more than a Deep South, oil-and-gas-state senator. Yet he regularly and routinely nurtured relations with both forces. "Johnson's balancing act was infinitely delicate," wrote journalists Rowland Evans and Robert Novak. "While rejecting *formal* membership in the southern caucus, he accepted an *informal* membership."[18] Johnson's first major speech in the Senate was to oppose the reform of the filibuster rule, the Fair Employment Practices Commission, Truman's civil rights program in general, and to favor state, not federal, jurisdiction over poll taxes and lynching laws.[19] His refusal to become a member of the caucus, which momentarily ruffled Russell's feathers, his later insistence that he was a "westerner" and not a southerner, his failure to cosponsor the Kerr gas bill (although he voted for it and was a strong behind-the-scenes supporter), and his refusal to sign the Southern Manifesto and its call for massive resistance to the 1954 Supreme Court's *Brown v. Board of Education* school desegregation decision all signaled his ambitions for higher office. When the band members who accompanied him in the 1948 campaign were told they had lost their radio station jobs, Johnson told them not to worry: "Someday you'll sing on the steps of the White House."[20]

When the Korean War broke out in the summer of 1950, Johnson saw an opportunity to emulate the watchdog Truman Committee of World War II. He successfully urged Russell and the Armed Services Committee to establish a preparedness subcommittee at a time when it had no other subcommittee, and to make himself chairman. It was established by the end of July as a bipartisan group with Johnson and two other freshman members on the Democratic side joined by the three senior Republicans.[21] Johnson garnered a professional staff that was larger than that of the full committee. It was the first significant example of Johnson's skill in building a Senate empire. His chairmanships of the ad hoc Commerce and the Armed Services subcommittees during his first two years were extraordinary coups in the oligarchical Eighty-first Senate and brought Johnson a favorable cover story in *Newsweek* and a major piece in the *New York Times Magazine.*

Johnson's thrust for power may also be discerned from the location of his seat in the Senate from early 1949 until he became Democratic leader in 1953. Johnson and Robert Kerr were the only freshmen to sit in the front row, albeit the ninth and tenth seats from the center toward which power flowed. But power also moved from back to front, as well as from left to right (from the seated senators' view) on the Democratic side. No freshman was closer to the center than Johnson. In the ninth seat in the row behind him was Harley Kilgore, the West Virginia senator eight years Johnson's senior and ranked twenty-second out of fifty-four Democrats. In the third row's ninth seat was Warren Magnuson of Washington, four years Johnson's senior and twenty-seventh among Democrats. To his immediate right was J. William Fulbright of Arkansas, four years Johnson's senior and ranked twenty-ninth among Democrats. Johnson and Kerr ranked fiftieth and fifty-second respectively.[22]

Fortuitous Events

A series of unprecedented vacancies in the Senate Democratic party structure helped to propel Lyndon Johnson to the leadership of the Senate. The sequence began in 1947, two years before he arrived, when Lister Hill resigned as Democratic whip. Lucas of Illinois succeeded him. In January 1949, Majority Leader Alben Barkley (D-Ky.) resigned to become vice president under Truman. Scott Lucas then succeeded Barkley, and Francis Myers, a first-term member from Pennsylvania, filled Lucas's whip post. Both men were figureheads: the de facto leader was Russell.

For the twenty-five years before 1949, there had been only two Democratic majority leaders. In 1950, however, both Lucas and Myers were defeated and the Democrats' control of the Senate narrowed to two votes. Russell declined White House entreaties to take the job of majority leader and picked Ernest McFarland of Arizona, another figurehead, to replace Lucas.[23] After Clinton Anderson (N.M.) turned down the whip position, Robert Kerr persuaded a somewhat reluctant Russell that Johnson was the man for the job. Russell thought Johnson and McFarland came from states that were too close regionally, and he still remembered that Johnson had refused to join the southern caucus.[24]

Russell was eventually persuaded to make Johnson the party whip, although the post was then so meaningless that neither the *Newsweek* cover story nor the *New York Times Magazine*'s piece on Johnson mentioned that he held it. Unlike present-day whips, who sit next to their party leaders on the front row, Johnson remained in his old spot, eight seats away, his only perquisite a small hideaway room in the Senate wing of the Capitol. Johnson's priorities during his two years as whip were chairing the Preparedness Subcommittee and improving his relationships with other senators. But the job was an institutional steppingstone to power.

Johnson's fortuitous rise to power continued when Republican Barry Goldwater defeated Majority Leader Ernest McFarland in Dwight D. Eisenhower's landslide victory in 1952. The Republicans organized the Senate by a margin of forty-eight to forty-seven as maverick Wayne Morse left the GOP to establish himself as what he called an Independent party of one. Johnson jumped at the chance to become leader. He first called Russell to propose that Russell take the job, promising that he would take on the drudgery that it entailed. But Russell turned down the post and asked Johnson to take it, which he did with alacrity. Johnson insisted, however, that Russell occupy the aisle seat directly behind the leader's chair. Russell's support for Johnson was not a nomination but an anointment. By the time the Senate Democrats met in January to elect their leader, Johnson had the job sewn up and received only token opposition from the liberals who proposed the superannuated James E. Murray of Montana.

The Senate Milieu

When Lyndon B. Johnson became his party's Senate leader in 1953, the Senate had three fundamental attributes: it was the small state's Mecca; it gave the South "unending revenge upon the North for Gettysburg;"[25] and it was guided by a coalition of Dixiecrats, conservative Republicans, and senators from mountain states rather than by party political considerations. Contrary to present-day myths about the "good old days," there was very little party discipline.

The Senate, under the U.S. Constitution, is not only the creature of the states, but—as we have noted—of the small states in particular. The thirty-four senators from the seventeen smallest states, with one-third-plus-one votes in the Senate, represent only 7 percent of the people.[26] It was said during the Johnson era that these states had lots of senators but very few people. The thirty-four senators from the seventeen largest states, with one-third-plus-one votes in the Senate, represent 70 percent of the people, or a ratio to the small states of ten to one. This ratio has remained constant for more than forty years.

Majority votes in the Senate have thus been enormously difficult to fashion when there is a determined minority, even on an issue with wide public support. And it is almost impossible to carve out a winning margin when the Constitution requires a two-thirds vote—for example, to override a veto, to advise and consent to a treaty, to convict for impeachment, to pass a constitutional amendment, or to expel a member. In addition, throughout the Johnson years, Senate rules required a two-thirds vote to stop a filibuster.[27] The Senate, the only constitutionally malapportioned legislative body in the country, was the graveyard and the filibuster was the gravedigger for civil rights legislation for almost a century following the Civil War. From the late 1930s, southern Democrats, most of whom shared the views of conservative Republicans on domestic issues, forged an alliance with them, and with senators from the mountain states and a handful of small-state fiefdoms. This coalition dominated the Senate for twenty years until the Democratic congressional landslide of 1958, and it continued in a less formidable form for at least another decade.

In 1949, the year Johnson arrived in the Senate, seventeen of the twenty most senior Democrats were from below the Mason-Dixon line, the Southwest (largely an extension of the cotton culture), or the small mountain states.[28] Kenneth McKellar of Tennessee, who came to the Senate on March 4, 1917, was the president pro tempore and presided in the absence of the vice president. Seven southern senators and four each from the Rocky Mountain and southwestern states chaired the fifteen standing committees. No Democratic senator from the East, the Midwest, or Pacific coast chaired any standing committee.

The power of the southern caucus came from their unity, their dogged determination to protect segregation, and Russell's leadership. They were also backed by, and accurately reflected, an equally determined public opinion in their states. Their success exemplifies the power of a resolute minority to conquer an irresolute and diffused majority. They had many weapons, including the rules of the Senate, which favored talk over action; control of the Democratic Policy Committee, which determined what bills the Senate would consider; and control of the Steering Committee, which made committee assignments.

Russell was the guardian and the master of the Senate's rules. There were four key provisions. First, Rule XXII required a two-thirds vote of the entire Senate to limit debate, or impose cloture, on the motion to proceed to the consideration of a bill, necessary to take a bill from the calendar and to place it before the Senate. Second, Rule XXII provided no limit on debate on the motion to proceed to the consideration of a change in the rules. Third, if a civil rights bill did get before the Senate, or was added to another bill as an amendment or a rider, Rule XXII also required a two-thirds vote of the *entire* Senate to limit debate. Finally, there was the rule of germaneness, which prevented the passage of a civil rights bill or amendment in two conflicting ways. First, there was *no* rule of germaneness on a legislative bill. Thus, senators could talk a civil rights bill to death by reading recipes from cookbooks or other extraneous literature. But second, in a carefully calculated procedure, there *was* a rule of germaneness when an appropriations bill was before the Senate. Appropriations bills are needed to keep the government running. To protect against a civil rights rider, which a simple majority of those present and voting could add to a money bill, germaneness was required.[29]

In return for supporting the South on the filibuster and procedural issues affecting civil rights, the southwestern and Rocky Mountain states, who had very few black citizens, got southern support for an array of vital interests, especially subsidies for irrigation and reclamation projects.[30] The guarantor, the enforcing instrument of the deal, was that members of the coalition held the strategic positions on key committees, especially on the Appropriations Committee.[31]

The Appropriations Committee was the most powerful committee in the Senate. Its twelve Democratic senators averaged fifteen years of seniority; seven of them were also chairmen of seven of the Senate's fifteen standing committees. The top six of them ranked from first to eighth in continuous service in the Senate and had been there from fifteen to thirty-two years. Six of the twelve were from the Deep South and five from the West or Southwest. Five of the eight Republicans were very conservative.[32] Although the Appropriations Committee was fiscally conservative, it seldom failed to be generous to the programs and projects of the ruling coalition. At the same time, it cut deeply into programs for the populous urban states. It took a quarter of a century until death, defeat, and retirement—tinged by revenge—broke up the coalition. Although there was a deep sense of frustration on the part of moderate and liberal senators from the North or Far West, few were either independent or suicidal enough to speak out against the Appropriations Committee's chokehold on the Senate.[33]

Seating arrangements in the Senate further bonded the alliance together. Semicircular seating patterns, like those in the Senate chamber, help destroy party discipline. Winston Churchill opposed the semicircular and favored the oblong chamber, noting that although "it is easy for an individual to move through those insensible gradations from Left to Right, . . . the act of crossing the Floor is one which requires serious consideration."[34] This difficulty was particularly apparent in the Senate of 1949 with the conservative coalition of Dixiecrats, Republicans, and westerners. The Dixiecrats and their allies dominated the center seats. They did not have to cross the floor or change their party affiliation to vote with their soul brothers on the Republican side. They expressed their comradeship by slight movements of their chairs, through body language, and other subtle signs as they moved through "various shades" or "insensible gradations" to provide mutual support. Although the Democrats had fifty-four members who in January 1949 voted to organize the Senate, at any other time the southern caucus could produce fifty-five to sixty votes to defeat their Democratic colleagues, whose votes guaranteed their chairmanships, on any important matter.

Senate Staff

In 1949 Senate personal and administrative staffs were small. Allowances for personal staffs were only marginally based on the size of a state. The largest states got about one-third more funds for staff than the smallest states. Thus with their greater population, mail, and casework, they were relatively overworked and underpaid.

Committee staffs were also small. Except for the Appropriations Committee, there were few subcommittees. On the whole, staff members were beholden to the chairman and the ranking minority member. The Agriculture Committee had four professional staff members to serve its thirteen members. The Armed Services Committee had five professional staff for its thirteen members, and the Finance Committee had no professional staff for its major jurisdictions of taxes and Social Security. Staff work for taxes was done by the Joint Committee on Internal Revenue Taxation, whose members included only the top three majority and top two minority members of the Finance Committee. Junior members had no official staff and the work was performed by their personal staff. Great reliance was also put on Treasury Department staff, whose members actually attended the mark-up sessions of the committee and offered advice and counsel, while both the personal staffs of junior senators and the public were excluded. The Treasury Department was not known to invite staff from the legislative branch to its sessions on tax proposals.

When Social Security matters were before the Finance Committee, the Social Security Administration and outside experts provided the staff. The system of centralizing staff and avoiding subcommittees was designed to keep power in the hands of the chairman and the ranking member. As Warren G. Magnuson, a Senate insider, mused approvingly after his retirement in 1980, "In my day, a fellow didn't introduce a bill of major importance without the committee chairman's approval."[35]

As most of the committee chairmen were either southerners or their allies, during filibusters the staffs of their committees were put to work writing lengthy speeches. The officers of the Senate and their staffs, with rare exceptions, were either sons of the South or beholden to the southern hierarchy. They wore gray uniforms. Speaking about the Senate establishment, Senator Joseph S. Clark (D-Pa.), called it "the antithesis of democracy. It is what might be called a self-perpetuating oligarchy with only mild overtones of plutocracy."[36]

Exercising Power

Divide and Conquer

Having gained power in this setting, how did Johnson consolidate and exercise it? His first act as leader was to select Earle C. Clements (D-Ky.), Barkley's successor, as Democratic whip. In picking Clements, Johnson established a pattern he repeated throughout his leadership career, namely to divide and conquer. Clements was an insider and an old pro with a respectable liberal voting record. Although the big-state liberals wanted one of their own, they could not oppose Clements. Similar tactics are evident when Johnson later tapped Mike Mansfield of sparsely populated Montana as whip. Other examples abound. Johnson had J. William Fulbright and A. S. Mike Monroney (D-Okla.), both liked and respected by their colleagues, serve as principal sponsors of the 1956 Natural Gas bill. Robert Kerr (D-Okla.), who had made a fortune in oil, was kept offstage: his sponsorship of the gas bill during Truman's presidency had been a disaster, and Truman successfully vetoed it.

When Johnson wanted to split the liberal vote and knock out all the Fourteenth Amendment enforcement provisions of the 1957 Civil Rights bill, he chose Clinton Anderson, who led the biennial crusade to change the filibuster rule,[37] and the Republican progressive George Aiken of Vermont, rather than James Eastland (D-Miss.), Harry Byrd (D-Va.), or South Carolina's Strom Thurmond (then a Democrat), to sponsor the amendment. Johnson got the old New Deal antitrust crusader Joseph O'Mahoney of Wyoming and the young and liberal Democrat Frank Church of Idaho to sponsor the weakening jury-trial amendment to the same bill. All these acts either split or neutralized the Northeast and Far West liberal faction of the Democratic party. All four men chosen by Johnson were from sparsely populated states with few black citizens.

Johnson used the same tactics in bringing down the radical right-wing demagogue Joseph McCarthy, Republican of Wisconsin. Assured of the liberal vote, he arranged the appointment of a bipartisan group of conservative Senate insiders to the select committee to investigate McCarthy. The Senate, on the basis of the committee's report, voted to "condemn" McCarthy 67 to 22. No Democrat voted for McCarthy.

Risks and Dangers

One may speculate on the initiative and good luck that propelled Johnson into the leader's chair, but the position entailed great risks to his career. After the electoral defeats of Lucas, Myers, and McFarland, who would want the job? The party leader is associated with the programs, policies, and proposals of his own party's president or platform, however out of step they may be with the economic interests and political views of his state. He is in danger of being seen as the president's lackey not only by his constituents but also by his colleagues who, after all, function under a constitution that has rightly been termed "an invitation to struggle" between the president and Congress. For one who had been elected by eighty-seven disputed votes, the majority leadership was a high-stakes gamble.

Johnson avoided most of these pitfalls by both luck and design. During his two years as whip, from 1951 to 1953, his activities were invisible and uncontroversial. His eight years as Democratic leader were served under a Republican president. Until the last two years, he never commanded a majority of more than two, and in the first two years he led a minority of one. William Knowland (R-Calif.), who succeeded Robert A. Taft as the Republican leader, complained in 1953 that he was the majority leader but led a minority. His 48-47 majority vanished on some issues when the independent Wayne Morse voted with the Democrats. Johnson replied, "If anyone has more problems than a majority leader with a minority, it is a minority leader with a majority."[38] Johnson used the narrow margins as an excuse to avoid promoting policies that President Eisenhower threatened to veto or that commanded strong support by the Democratic party but were not popular with the Senate alliance or his Texas constituents.

His Texas background was also an asset. Democratic majority leaders tend to come from border states like Kentucky, West Virginia, Arizona, Montana, Arkansas, or Texas. The leader had to bridge the ideological gap between Democrats from the northern urban states and the then-ultraconservative southerners.

The Interests of Texas

To the dismay of a large and important section of his party, Lyndon Johnson made the interests of Texas those of the Democratic party in the Senate. On civil rights, the filibuster, and gas and oil, Johnson led a bipartisan coalition that took stands opposed by at least half of the non-Dixiecrats in the Senate and by an even greater percentage of the national Democratic party. He provided a large audience of senators for his fellow Texan Price Daniel when the latter delivered the opening speech in favor of the natural gas bill, and for Senator Joseph O'Mahoney when he introduced the jury-trial amendment to the 1957 Civil Rights bill. But he would clear the Senate for a speech by a party colleague advocating the majority views of Democratic senators. The latter complained that they were elected to office by supporting Democratic party positions only to find them defeated by their own leader and their own party's powerful committee chairmen. In addition, some of them were punished for their determination to promote orthodox national party views. By making the Texas position the official party position in the Senate, Johnson could remain both majority leader and a senator from Texas.

"The Johnson Rule"

In 1953 Johnson devised what he called the "Johnson rule" concerning committee appointments. In theory it provided that no Democratic senator could serve on any two of the five most desired committees—Appro-

priations, Finance, Armed Services, Foreign Relations, and Judiciary—
before a more junior member could exercise his right to serve on one. In
practice the rule was less than perfect, and its administration left plenty
of room for maneuver, for rewards to friends, and for punishment of
serious transgressors against the ruling coalition.

Seen as a major reform, the Johnson rule had its genesis in an obscure
report issued in January 1953 by Republican Senator William E. Jenner
of Indiana, chairman of the Rules Committee when the Republicans organized the Senate. The Eighty-second Congress had forty-nine Democrats and forty-seven Republicans, and the Eighty-third Congress had
forty-eight Republicans, forty-seven Democrats, and Independent Wayne
Morse.

Jenner, with the backing of the new majority leader, Robert A. Taft (R-
Ohio), proposed that the Republicans, with only forty-eight of ninety-
six votes, control each of the fifteen standing committees by one vote; that
nine of the ten most desirable standing committees be increased by two
members each (one majority and one minority) to fifteen members (this
would expand the majority-minority ratios to 8:7, rather than 7:6); that
the Appropriations Committee be expanded from twenty-one to twenty-
three members, changing its majority-minority party ratio from 12:9 to
12:11; and that the five least desirable committees be reduced from thirteen to eleven members.[39] With minor modifications, these proposals
were accepted, enabling Johnson to institute his rule.

The effect of the Jenner report was to create twenty additional spots
on the ten most desirable committees. It preserved the existing Democratic seats on the nine most attractive committees and made it possible
for Johnson and the Democratic Steering Committee to place two freshman Democrats, Mike Mansfield of Montana and Stuart Symington of
Missouri, on the Foreign Relations and Armed Services committees respectively.

The chairmanship of the Steering Committee and the institution of
the Johnson rule made it possible for Johnson to build credits among
those favored by the new assignments, an example of what biographer
Doris Kearns describes as:

a most visible benevolence which reminded recipients at every turn of how much
he had done for them. . . . The cost to the recipient of the goods Johnson delivered
seemed fair enough to him—gratitude, affection, a trust manifested by the willingness to let him decide what was best for them.[40]

The Jenner report permitted Johnson to offer choice assignments without

A master in the art of persuasion, Democratic leader Lyndon B. Johnson applies the celebrated ''Johnson Treatment'' to Senator Theodore Francis Green (D-R.I.), chairman of the Foreign Relations Committee.

offending the ruling barons whose committee positions had been grand-fathered.

The Treatment

As a college debater Johnson has mastered forensic speaking, the law-yer's private pleading in the judge's chamber—and it was in one-on-one situations, rather than before a large audience, that he was his most persuasive. When he read from a script, he was wooden and seldom eloquent. Speaking off-the-cuff, however, Johnson was extraordinarily effective at rallies, making stump speeches, or campaigning from the back of a train. He was also a master mimic. But Johnson's forte was what came to be called "The Treatment."

What was The Treatment? Some thought it the "dominant ingredient" of Johnson's Senate success.[41] George Tames's photographs of Johnson in action are incomparable, and Rowland Evans and Robert Novak have written the definitive description:

> The Treatment could last ten minutes or four hours. It came, enveloping its target, at the LBJ Ranch swimming pool, in one of LBJ's offices, in the Senate cloakroom, on the floor of the Senate itself—wherever Johnson might find a fellow Senator within his reach. Its tone could be supplication, accusation, cajolery, ex-uberance, scorn, tears, complaint, the hint of threat. . . . Its velocity was breath-taking. . . . Interjections from the target were rare. Johnson anticipated them be-fore they could be spoken. He moved in close, his face a scant millimeter from his target, his eyes widening and narrowing, his eyebrows rising and falling. From his pockets poured clippings, memos, statistics. Mimicry, humor, and the genius of analogy made The Treatment an almost hypnotic experience and rendered the target stunned and helpless.[42]

One victim of The Treatment is said to have described the ordeal this way: "I came out of that session covered with blood, sweat, tears, spit, and . . . SPERM."

When Hubert Humphrey, the most articulate and persuasive of the Senate liberals, was sent as their agent to negotiate with Johnson, he would leave the caucus of his allies fired up to do battle with Johnson. Another victim of The Treatment, he would return having lost virtually every point including, his friends felt, his trousers. They described the negotiations with Johnson with the phrase: "We gave him an orchard and he gave us an apple."

The Democratic Policy Committee

During Johnson's leadership, the Democratic Policy Committee, which determined party policy and the bills to come to the floor, was extraordinarily stable. Although ostensibly representative of the party in the Senate, it was in fact controlled by Johnson and the ruling coalition. Its membership in 1953, which the majority leader had the sole right to appoint, consisted of Johnson, party whip Earle Clements, and conference secretary Thomas Hennings (Missouri). Its other six members were Theodore Green (Rhode Island), Lister Hill (Alabama), Richard Russell, Robert Kerr, James Murray (Montana), and Edwin Johnson (Colorado). Between 1953 and 1961 there were only two changes. In 1955 Carl Hayden was added after Edwin Johnson left the Senate, and Mike Mansfield was added in 1957 when he replaced Clements as whip. Johnson, Russell, and Kerr ruled the committee despite a facade of ideological and geographical representation.

Liberal senators who initiated legislation in committee were frustrated by the lack of leadership support to get it to the floor and dismayed by lackadaisical efforts to get it passed. They were continuously accused by Bobby Baker, who often bragged "I have ten senators' votes in the palm of my hand,"[43] of not knowing how to count. They could count, but of course the ten votes that Baker and Johnson controlled were rarely available to them on critical votes.

The Steering Committee

By Senate Democratic party tradition, Johnson, as floor leader, chaired not only the Policy Committee but also the Steering Committee and had the right to appoint its members. He announced on January 7, 1953, that Clements and Hennings would serve on both committees. The holdover members of the Steering Committee—the committee on committees— were Walter George of Georgia, Carl Hayden of Arizona, Dennis Chavez of New Mexico, Allen Ellender of Louisiana, Spessard Holland of Florida, and J. Allen Frear of Delaware. The first five were members of the "inner club," and Frear was known as "one of Lyndon Johnson's most dependable satellites."[44] Johnson's additional appointments that year were three more southerners, Burnet Maybank of South Carolina, John McClellan of Arkansas, and A. Willis Robertson of Virginia. The others were Matthew Neely of West Virginia, John Pastore of Rhode Island, and one liberal from the Midwest, Hubert Humphrey.[45] The population of the ten largest states contained more than half the people of the country and was the key to the election of a Democratic president. But in the Senate, only a single senator from one of those states filled any of the twenty-four slots on the two key Democratic party committees during Johnson's eight years as leader. That big state was Texas and its representative, of course, was Lyndon Johnson.

Russell and Johnson controlled the Steering Committee, even though Russell was not a member, and they had twelve certain votes. The committee was a fortress of southern and Dixiecrat control and determined the careers and destinies of other senators. The stories are legion of visits by newly elected Democrats to the Senate shortly after their election. They asked Bobby Baker about committee assignments. He suggested they consult with Russell and Johnson, who then asked them how they stood on the filibuster rule. It was the touchstone for committee assignments.

Assignments were not made until after the vote on that issue. In 1959, eight of the fourteen freshman Democrats voted with the South and the small states to table or kill the motion to change Rule XXII, the filibuster rule. Six of the eight got seats as freshmen on the five most desirable committees, three of them on Appropriations, a virtually unprecedented event.

Those who offended or seemed to offend Johnson in any major way were punished. Frank Church, for example, was shunned for months.[46] Edmund Muskie (D-Maine) fared badly in his freshman committee assignments when he failed to vote with Johnson on Rule XXII.[47] It took Paul Douglas, who opposed the depletion allowance, seven years to get a seat on Finance, during which time he was passed over in favor of seven Democratic senators of equal or lesser seniority.

Kerr and Frear, who like Douglas were members of the 1949 class, joined the Finance Committee in 1951. Russell Long, their contemporary, was added in 1953. Smathers, two years Douglas's junior, was selected in 1955. Johnson put himself on in 1955 and also added Barkley (who returned to the Senate in that year and who had been on the committee before). When another opening occurred, Clinton Anderson, equal in seniority with Douglas, was given the spot on grounds that his name began with the letter *a* and Douglas with *d*. Douglas was finally selected a year later, but he ranked eighth and sat at the bottom end of the table while Kerr sat next to the top. Johnson left the committee in 1957. Like the pigs in George Orwell's *Animal Farm*, some senators were more equal than others.

Personal Favors

Johnson exercised power by commanding the battlements or by placing his trusted lieutenants in key positions. The Senate was an institution he could manage.[48] The House of Representatives was too large and unwieldy for his kind of personal control. In the Senate, Johnson dealt with individuals like Russell, Taft, Kerr, Dirksen, and Anderson, who brought their own political power base to the bargaining table. There, Johnson was the superb broker of power. In the White House, however, he dealt with subordinates who fawned on him, not daring to deviate from his whims or policies. He therefore got better advice as Senate leader from his colleagues than he did as president.

Other Senate institutions that he dominated during his leadership provided additional tools of power. Johnson, Kerr, and Bobby Baker ran the Democratic Senatorial Campaign Committee. Ostensibly favoring no one, the triumvirate nevertheless gave more campaign funds to their favorites. For example, in 1960, Delaware's Frear got five times as much money as another incumbent senator from a very large state. Nonincumbent candidates were at the mercy of the committee. In 1958, some were asked to pledge support for the filibuster rule or the depletion allowance before funds or additional funds were forthcoming. Late in the 1958 campaign it appeared that many dark-horse Democratic candidates had a chance to win. Consequently, Johnson and the committee pushed money into their campaigns in part to secure their allegiance in the event they were elected. In general, a small-state candidate was more apt to benefit than a big-state candidate; money went further in Wyoming than in Ohio.

The leader was also in a position to do favors across party lines. Margaret Chase Smith (R-Maine) was among the most independent members of the Senate. She then held the record for answering the most consecutive roll-call votes in the history of the Senate—almost three thousand. Johnson protected her record, both in the timing of votes and in making certain no roll-call vote was concluded before she answered to her name. It was widely believed that her critical vote against Lewis Strauss in 1959, when the Senate rejected his nomination as secretary of commerce under Eisenhower, was at least in part the result of Johnson's past favors and blandishments.

Often Johnson gathered IOUs from fellow senators, even when he did them no favor. Some part of Johnson's Houdini-like victories was merely show. He knew where every vote was before the roll call began and always had several in reserve. But he extracted a price even for letting a senator off the hook for a vote he did not need, insisting on a future favor or commitment in return. To this panoply of power, which could influence or control what happened to a senator's bills, committee assignments, campaign funds, and floor votes, Johnson could add other favors as well. Trips abroad for the senator and his wife, choice office space, the assignment of a committee staff member to serve the senator, or providing a crowd for a speech—almost nothing was too mundane for Johnson's attention.[49]

The Press

Johnson got superb coverage by the national press. It was an important element in the exercise of power, due in part to the milieu and the times and in part to a series of special relations Johnson developed with the kingpins of the news. Only occasionally, as when he lost his temper under sharp questioning by veteran Associated Press reporter John Chadwick a few hours before his 1955 heart attack, were the overall relations poor. Most members of the press, however, were not as charmed by Johnson as were many of his Senate colleagues. He was unable to dazzle reporters at press conferences as he could his colleagues in one-on-one situations.

Even though most journalists kept a fairly vigorous independence of mind, the period of Johnson's Senate leadership occurred before the heyday of investigative journalism. Rarely did anyone report on senators' personal lives or peccadilloes. Those who covered the Senate saw themselves as part of the institution. I heard one senior wire service reporter shouting to his colleagues in the Senate press gallery at the end of a long Senate session, "*We've* adjourned. *We're* coming in at 10 A.M. tomorrow."

Astonishingly, a review of the *Washington Post*'s coverage of the Senate at the time of Bobby Baker's firing for offenses that later sent him to jail reveals only one story on Baker—filed by James McCartney for the *Chicago Daily News*'s wire service, to which the *Post* subscribed.[50]

But Johnson carefully cultivated the Washington bureau chief of the *New York Times*, Arthur Krock, and its Senate reporter, fellow Texan William S. White. White was Johnson's Boswell. His book, *Citadel*, canonized Senate institutions that most people criticized—the filibuster, seniority, the "inner club," and the coalition of Dixiecrats and conservative Republicans—and then denigrated the Senate's critics. It was White who said approvingly: "The Senate might be described . . . as the South's unending revenge upon the North for Gettysburg."[51] White's front-page stories on the Senate, often with a favorable Johnson spin, were read and copied by editors throughout the country. His reports paid little attention to the substance of issues behind electoral contests, focusing instead on who was going to win or lose. In his columns he was more personal, excoriating Johnson's opponents with his own private language, including epithets like "red hots," "kamikazes," "knee-jerk liberals," and "limousine liberals."

Johnson also befriended *Washington Post* publisher Philip Graham, although this affected *Post* coverage far less than his relationship with White affected the news columns of the *New York Times*—no reporter wrote blander columns than Robert Albright, the *Post*'s Senate correspondent. But the relationship did affect editorial policy. On the eve of a Senate vote on the filibuster rule or a civil rights amendment, the *Post* would not change its long-standing policy in favor of limiting the filibuster and supporting civil rights legislation, but it would intone that "now is not the time" to take action.

Legislative Record

The Eighty-fourth Congress, 1955–1956

When the Eighty-fourth Congress convened in January 1955, the Democrats controlled the Senate by a margin of forty-nine to forty-seven. Lyndon Johnson was not only the Democratic leader but also the majority leader. Dwight Eisenhower was in the White House; Richard Nixon presided over the Senate; Walter George was president pro tempore; Robert Taft had died of cancer; and the honest, lumbering, and bull-like William Knowland of California was the minority leader. Johnson was quicker and more clever than Knowland and regularly outmaneuvered him.

At the end of the year the *Congressional Quarterly Almanac* declared that "the session was not noted for partisan clashes. . . . Few milestones were erected, . . . showdowns [were] deferred" and "Congress concentrated on routine legislation."[52] The Senate met on 105 days, held 87 roll-call votes, and adjourned for the year on August 2. The era of the yearlong Congresses with more than five hundred Senate roll-call votes lay ahead. Among the measures passed were a three-year extension of the Reciprocal Trade Act, legislation to raise the hourly minimum wage, the Formosa

Resolution, the Upper Colorado River Project, and an omnibus housing bill, the latter a major Johnson coup.

The housing bill was one instance when he provided the ten senators that he and Bobby Baker claimed to control. In addition, he brought in six Republican and four southern Democratic votes to support an authorization for 800,000 new public-housing units. In a private celebration afterwards, his erstwhile antagonist Paul Douglas praised Johnson's skill. "I didn't think you could do it, and I will never know *how* you did it, but you did it, and I'm grateful."[53]

In the 1956 session, the Senate met for 119 days but adjourned on July 27 when it refused to consider the House-passed civil rights bill in an election year. More legislation was enacted in 1956 than during any of the three previous Eisenhower-era sessions. There were 638 new public laws, many of them due to the enterprise of Johnson, who drove the Senate to new numerical, if not substantive, legislative records. He would pile up more than a hundred bills on the legislative calendar and pass them in a single day. Support under Social Security for the disabled was a landmark measure because of the conversion of Walter George, the conservative former chairman of the Senate Finance Committee.

The Eighty-fifth Congress, 1957–1958

President Eisenhower defeated Adlai Stevenson in 1956 by a victory margin barely surpassed by Roosevelt's 1936 landslide. Yet the Senate remained in Democratic hands by the previous margin of forty-nine to forty-seven. The 1957 session was memorable for passage of the first civil rights bill since 1875, although some listed its weakening as a failure of the session.[54] The Middle East Resolution, giving Eisenhower advance authority to use troops to protect free nations in that region from "overt armed aggression," was passed in the Senate by a 72-19 vote. A Mansfield amendment calling for continued support of the United Nations Emergency Force was passed on an almost straight party-line vote of 48-43 when only two Republicans joined with all forty-six voting Democrats to approve it. The economy, inflation, and the budget were major issues. The Senate adjourned on August 30, 1957, after it met for 133 days, took 107 roll-call votes, and saw 316 bills enacted into law.[55]

The 1958 session was dominated by two events, *Sputnik* and the recession. The launching of *Sputnik* by the Soviet Union on October 4, 1957, after Congress had adjourned, provided the stimulus for Congress to establish the National Aeronautical and Space Administration (NASA) and to pass a defense education bill with emphasis on math and science. The Senate responded to the 1958 recession (which the Eisenhower administration insisted on calling a "rolling readjustment") with a program that emphasized highways, public works, airports, rivers and harbors, and reclamation projects. In the face of administration opposition, only modest measures were approved. An attempt to cut taxes to stimulate the economy was rejected by the administration and by Johnson and Rayburn.

Eisenhower got action on 47 percent of his requests from the relatively cooperative and nonconfrontational Congress. Many looked on the Rayburn-Johnson congressional leadership as the model of bipartisanship. The 1958 *Congressional Quarterly Almanac* reported that the second session of the Eighty-fifth Congress was "as remarkable for what it didn't do as for what it did do."[56] What it did was to lay the groundwork for a smashing Democratic victory. Democrats in the Senate increased to sixty-five against thirty-five Republicans—the largest transfer of seats between parties in Senate history. The Eisenhower administration's lack of action on the 1958 recession was the biggest factor in the Democratic victory. But the massive majority was to diminish the power of both the Senate leader and the southern caucus and its coalition on whose behalf Johnson acted. Ironically, it also provided the foundation on which Lyndon Johnson, as president, would build his Great Society.

Lyndon Johnson and Civil Rights

Johnson got more credit for passing the first civil rights bill since 1875 than for any other act as leader. Johnson critics Evans and Novak called it "the miracle of 1957" and a "legislative *tour de force*" (although they also called it "tame and toothless" and "without . . . much real impact on the reality of the civil rights struggle"). Johnson partisan William S. White termed it "the most skillful single legislative job of leadership I ever saw."[57] The lavish praise (much of it solicited by Johnson) heaped upon him was unsurpassed in his Senate career. Yet at almost every stage of the proceedings on civil rights measures—from the aborted 1956 bill, through the fight to change the filibuster rule, until final passage of the 1957 bill and the 1960 proposals—the effect of the motions he made, the proceedings he arranged, and the votes he cast was to weaken or strike the substance of civil rights measures and to make it more difficult to pass a meaningful bill. Johnson was a genius at, in the old Texas phrase, making a silk purse out of a sow's ear. He could oppose, fight, delete, and water down a measure or an amendment, or table or kill a procedure important to the substance or passage of a bill, and then take credit for a major legislative victory when it passed.

The Aborted 1956 Bill

On July 23, 1956, the House of Representatives passed a civil rights bill by more than the two-thirds' margin necessary to override a presidential veto. Its substance was almost identical to that of the bill that would pass the House in 1957.

Senators Paul Douglas and Herbert Lehman (D-N.Y.), failing in their efforts to keep it from being referred to the hostile Judiciary Committee, tried to file a petition to discharge the committee from its further consideration. Under the rules, however, the petition had to be filed in the "morning hour" unless by unanimous consent. Majority Leader Johnson blocked the filing by a motion to "recess" overnight, which took precedence over other business.

At the beginning of the Senate's proceedings the next day, in what would ordinarily have been the morning hour, president pro tempore Walter George ruled the discharge petition could not be filed except by unanimous consent. As the Senate had recessed instead of having adjourned, there was no new "legislative day" and hence no morning hour in which discharge petitions could be filed. Johnson had recessed, rather than adjourned, the Senate each day since Friday, July 13, to prevent any action on the civil rights bill. The Senate continued to recess until July 26, the night before it adjourned for the year.

After his attempt to file the discharge petition was ruled out of order, Douglas moved to adjourn the Senate for five minutes to bring a new legislative day and a morning hour. Johnson moved to table the motion and crushed Douglas by a 76-6 vote. In 1956, Senate elevators were manned by student operators. Senators notified the operators they were waiting by giving three rings on the call button. After his humiliating defeat, Douglas turned to his legislative assistant and said, "Punch that button three times. Let's pretend we're senators."

Johnson finally adjourned the Senate on the night before the final day of the session. In the morning hour the next day Douglas was allowed to file his discharge petition, too late for any action.

The 1957 Fight Over the Cloture Rule

That 1956 debate strengthened the determination of the losers to make a major effort to change Rule XXII (see p. 208 for the key provisions of the rule). Because there was no way to shut off a filibuster on the motion to proceed to change the rules, the only way to change the filibuster rule was to move at the beginning of a Congress to proceed to the consideration of the rules under the provisions of Article I, section 5 of the Constitution. It provides that "each House may determine the rules of its proceedings." Proponents argued that a rules change could then be made by a simple majority vote of the Senate. In January 1953, Vice President Barkley said he would rule favorably on such a motion, but before he could do so, Majority Leader Taft, with the support of Minority Leader Johnson, moved to table, and thus kill, the motion. The vote to table was 70-21.

In 1957, those who opposed Clinton Anderson's efforts to liberalize the cloture rule argued that the Senate was a continuing body and that the rules automatically carried over from Senate to Senate. Supporters of civil rights claimed it was circuitous to argue that the rules carry over because the Senate is a continuing body and that the Senate is a continuing body because the rules carry over. They argued that all bills and resolutions are introduced anew, the Senate is newly organized and new committees are appointed, and the newly elected one-third of the Senate could alter the party alignment—as happened in both 1953 and 1955—to provide a new majority and a new mandate, which the Senate had the right to carry out. In short, the continuing-body argument was irrelevant: whether the Senate was or was not a continuing body, a majority had the right to adopt the rules.

Opponents of civil rights argued that the Senate would be in a parliamentary jungle if it tried to adopt a new filibuster rule. Senator Russell combined that argument with a threat to rewrite each of the forty rules and thus provide a self-fulfilling prophecy. But civil rights supporters countered that the House of Representatives, which adopted new rules at the beginning of every Congress, entered and left the parliamentary "jungle" in a matter of minutes.

The profilibuster, anti–civil rights alliance prevailed and, with the critical support of Senator Johnson, the Senate voted to table Anderson's motion 55-38. There were three absentee senators, all of whom favored Anderson's motion, which meant forty-one senators supported the move.

A shift of only seven votes and a favorable ruling from Vice President Nixon could have brought success.

The unexpected size of the vote and its near success shocked the southern alliance. They knew that any actual and organized use of the filibuster would ultimately bring an end to Rule XXII. Yet they also knew that if they did not use the filibuster the Senate would pass a civil rights bill.

Johnson played a decisive role in preventing a change in the rule. Anderson combined a request for a ruling by the chair with his motion to proceed to adopt new rules under Article I, section 5 of the Constitution. This was vital to success. Vice President Nixon was prepared to rule that a majority of the Senate had the right to change the rules at the beginning of a new Congress. Whether the vote came on a motion to table or on an appeal from the ruling of the chair was critically important. If a Republican vice president ruled favorably after the Republican president had proposed the legislation, he would no doubt be supported by more than a majority of his own party—which, combined with the Democratic support, could provide the winning margin. However the vice president ruled, the proponents knew they would make gains over 1953. But a favorable ruling from Nixon meant an opportunity for spectacular gains. Johnson and his southern allies wanted a vote *before* the vice president ruled.

The Senate follows an unwritten rule that the chair will recognize the majority or minority leader over any other senator, even if he is not first on his feet to ask for recognition. Accordingly, before Nixon could rule favorably on the Anderson motion, and while Anderson was on his feet requesting a ruling of the chair, Johnson asked to be recognized and moved to table the Anderson motion. This prevented a vote on supporting a ruling of the chair.

Twenty-seven Democrats and twenty-eight Republicans supported Johnson. It was the strongest position for the southerners and their pro-filibuster, anti–civil rights allies, and it was engineered by Lyndon Johnson. (Six of the nine members of the Democratic Policy Committee voted to kill Anderson's motion.)[58]

Thus Johnson's exercise of the unwritten rule of recognition and the use of the tabling motion (which is a negative form of majority cloture for it stops debate by killing a motion, amendment, or bill) were the decisive moves in this Senate battle. It was ironic. Acting in the cause of unlimited debate, Johnson shut off the debate on changing the rule on unlimited debate. Although the fight was lost, it strengthened the proponents of changing Rule XXII. The rules struggle gave a political urgency to civil rights legislation and improved chances for a meaningful bill.

The Judiciary Committee Graveyard

On June 18, 1957, when the House-passed civil rights bill arrived in the Senate, its companion bill and fifteen other civil rights bills lay lifeless in the Senate Judiciary Committee. This was not unprecedented. Eight bills had died there in the preceding two Congresses. The Judiciary Committee deserved its reputation as the graveyard for civil rights bills. The chairman was Senator James O. Eastland of Mississippi. The Steering Committee and its Republican counterpart ensured that a majority of the committee members belonged to the southern, small-state, conservative Republican alliance headed by Senator Russell.

Hearings on civil rights legislation had been held in the Constitutional Rights Subcommittee and were finished by early March 1957. On March 19 a bill was reported, with majority and minority views, to the full committee, and a bill identical to the House bill was introduced on March 21. The chairman and a majority of the committee, members of the coalition of southern Democrats and conservative Republicans, prevented action. On regular Monday meetings that were held between April 1 and June 17, opponents failed to provide a quorum and filibustered until the Senate convened at noon so that points of order could be made against any action, and Chairman Eastland refused to recognize the subcommittee chairman so he could move to adopt the bill.

If a civil rights bill were to be passed in 1957, the House bill could not be referred to the Senate Judiciary Committee. Rule XIV allowed a House-passed bill, after a first and second reading, to be placed on the Senate calendar by the action of a single senator. The rule had often been used in the preceding ten years to get a bill before the Senate, especially at the end of a congressional session when Senate committees had not finished work on a companion bill. After the abortive effort to get the 1956 bill out of the Judiciary Committee, and considering that committee's tactics in 1957 and preceding years, it would have been suicidal to send the House bill to the Judiciary Committee.

After the second reading of the House bill, therefore, Senators Knowland and Douglas objected to further proceedings on the bill so they could place it on the Senate calendar. Senator Russell raised a point of order and claimed that Rule XXV, which specified the jurisdiction of committees, took precedence over Rule XIV. He argued that sending the bill to the calendar would "throw out the window the laws, the rules, and the Constitution to get at 'these infernal southerners' in a hurry." Russell's point of order was defeated 39-45 in a precedent-shattering vote. Johnson supported Russell and had convinced thirty-four Democrats and six Republicans to follow him. But eleven Democrats and thirty-four Republicans voted to keep the bill out of the Judiciary Committee.[59]

It was a momentous event. First, it was probably the only way a civil rights bill could at that time be placed before the Senate. Second, it was the first important occasion that the coalition of southern Democrats and conservative Republicans was shattered on the civil rights issue. Since the advent of the modern cloture rule in 1917, no civil rights bill had reached a vote in the Senate. In only four of twenty-two attempts had cloture prevailed, and never on a civil rights bill. Third, for the first time in many years, the Senate asserted a disciplinary action over one of its committees, voting that the Judiciary Committee was a servant of the Senate as a whole. The rebuke was unique and was critical in helping to get the civil rights bill passed. Yet Johnson, who fought it, got the credit for the result.

Senate Floor Action

The Senate bill as it came from the House provided for the establishment of a civil rights commission and a civil rights division in the Department of Justice, the enforcement of the right to vote by court-ordered injunctive relief under the provisions of the Fifteenth Amendment, and the enforcement of the Fourteenth Amendment provision that no state shall deny to any person "the equal protection of the laws." This latter provision permitted the attorney general to seek injunctive remedies where citizens were denied the right to equal schooling and access to public parks, restaurants, hotels, motels, lunch counters, and other public institutions or public businesses.

After the bill was placed on the calendar, word circulated that Johnson was determined to eliminate all Fourteenth Amendment protections and to add a jury-trial amendment to the voting-rights procedures. At the time, all-white juries were universal in most southern states. The effect of these two moves was to make the bill as passed by the Senate largely a victory for the forces of segregation.

In 1964 Johnson, as president, sent to the Congress essentially the same Part III provisions enforcing the Fourteenth Amendment rights that he stripped from the Civil Rights Bill of 1957. In his autobiography *The*

Vantage Point, Johnson tells how degrading it was to his black family employees when, on trips to Texas, they could not eat in all-white restaurants or sleep in Holiday Inn motels. But in 1957 their humiliations were not in the forefront of his mind.[60]

Johnson convinced a majority of the Senate that deleting Part III of the 1957 bill and adding a jury-trial amendment to the voting rights section was necessary to get legislation passed, and that if it weren't watered down the southerners would filibuster. In fact, because of the close vote on changing the filibuster rule and the overwhelming determination of the Senate to pass a bill, Russell and his brethren had no intention of filibustering. According to Senator Russell:

Our group held numerous meetings and the wisdom of launching a filibuster was often discussed. All members of the group were living with the problem from day to day, defending the things dearest to our heart while under heavy fire. *At no time did any member of our group declare in any of our meetings that it was his belief that a filibuster was advisable, much less that one could be successfully waged. The contrary view was expressed on innumerable occasions* (emphasis added).[61]

The southerners did not dare use the filibuster out of fear that a much stronger bill would result. They were sufficiently convinced that a filibuster would so outrage the country and the Senate that they had more to lose than to gain by its use. Their condemnation of Senator Thurmond after his record-breaking twenty-four-hour "talkathon" is proof of this. They were afraid, as Russell said, "that a filibuster was certain to make a bad bill infinitely worse."[62] They were also aware that two-thirds of the Senate's members appeared willing to vote to break a filibuster if the southerners exercised it. The key test was the 71-18 vote by which the Senate moved to take up the bill.

In addition to eliminating the Fourteenth Amendment protections entirely and adding the jury-trial amendment, Johnson stopped further action on the bill. As a substitute for the Fourteenth Amendment protections, the Knowland-Douglas axis prepared an amendment that would have helped to enforce the Supreme Court school desegregation decision. Before Douglas could offer the amendment and while there was general turmoil and confusion on the floor, Johnson moved by unanimous consent, although his motion could not be heard, that no further amendments be introduced. It was a part of the comity of the Senate that before the majority leader calls for a third reading of a bill or cuts off further amendments, all senators are canvassed to determine if anyone has an amendment to offer—but Johnson went against precedent. As Russell recounted:

I happened to learn that a determined effort would be made to revive some of the provisions of Part III that had been stricken from the bill. The new amendment appeared harmless on its face, but if it had been adopted it would have placed the stamp of congressional approval on the erroneous, if not infamous, decision of the Supreme Court requiring the mixing of the children in the public schools without regard to the wishes of the parents of either race. We, therefore, quickly closed the bill to amendments in order to assure that none of the victories that we had gained would be snatched from us.[63]

The Congress passed and the president signed the 1957 Civil Rights Act. The Civil Rights Commission and the Justice Department's Civil Rights Division were established, although the latter had almost nothing to enforce. No schools, public parks, hotels, motels, restaurants, or lunch counters were desegregated as a result of that act. Few blacks were registered to vote or voted because of its provisions. In fact, in some parishes of Louisiana and counties of Alabama and Mississippi fewer blacks were registered to vote in 1962 than in 1956.[64] The Senate bill resembled the soup that Abraham Lincoln described as being made from the shadow of a pigeon that had starved to death. As a result, Russell claimed the result was "the sweetest victory of my 25 years as a Senator from the State of Georgia."[65] Only by elevating symbol over substance can the bill be called the "miracle" of 1957.

The Civil Rights Act of 1960

The 1960 act was a modest attempt to add substance to the 1957 law. Almost no cases had been brought because the latter law applied largely to individuals rather than to a group or class. In addition, the aggrieved parties were poor and politically powerless. The 1960 act sought to remedy this by authorizing federal judges to appoint "referees" to assist blacks to register and vote. The plan was described by Roy Wilkins, head of the National Association for the Advancement of Colored People (NAACP), as a "fraud." "The Negro has to pass more check points and more officials," Wilkins charged, "than he would if he were trying to get the United States' gold reserves at Fort Knox."[66]

An amendment to send federal registrars into the Deep South proposed by Douglas and Javits was killed 53-24 by a tabling motion sponsored by Senate leaders Dirksen and Johnson. Five years to the day later, on March 18, 1965, President Johnson sent that identical provision to the Senate, where it was introduced by Senate leaders Dirksen and Mansfield and became the voting-rights law.

In 1960, Johnson played a more moderate prosouthern role on parliamentary issues than in 1957. But on the *Congressional Quarterly Almanac's* list of the nineteen most controversial substantive amendments, Johnson voted with the eighteen-member southern bloc 68 percent of the time. He supported them more often than did seventy-four other senators.[67]

On the parliamentary side, he launched around-the-clock sessions of the Senate to try to break the southern filibuster. One session lasted nine days—157 hours and 26 minutes—broken only by two recesses. The longest unbroken session was 82 hours and 2 minutes. He was supported on several procedural motions by lopsided votes, 67-10, 55-6, and 65-7, with the southerners and most of their allies deliberately absent from the floor. From February 15 until March 8, Johnson recessed the Senate, instead of adjourning, in order to help break the filibuster.

Yet the filibusterers prevailed. By breaking down into teams of two, with one senator speaking and the other relieving his colleague with occasional questions, six or eight southern senators could hold the floor for a twenty-four-hour period, and only three or four of them had to speak extensively. Quorum calls were demanded during and after each perform-ance, and often more than an hour was required for a quorum to appear. During that period, the two filibusterers could rest. The effect was to wear out the small majority of dedicated supporters of civil rights, who had to provide fifty-one bodies at any hour of the day or night for proceedings to continue.

This filibustering technique was honed in 1960. In the end, the prob-lems of a majority of the Senate trying to break a filibuster were far more burdensome than the efforts of the eighteen or so filibusterers who spoke at most for a few hours every third or fourth day. Passage of the bill did little to promote black voting in the South and nothing to enforce the Fourteenth Amendment. Senator Joseph Clark (D-Pa.) described the bat-tle as one in which "the roles of Grant and Lee at Appomattox have been reversed."[68]

The Ebbing of Power—The Eighty-sixth Senate

The New Senate

The election of 1958 brought spectacular Democratic gains in the House and the Senate. After the admission of Hawaii, Johnson com-manded a majority of 65-35, in sharp contrast to his 49-47 margin in the Eighty-fifth Senate. Liberal Democrats were jubilant over the gains, but the ruling barons were downcast, preferring instead just enough Democratic votes to ensure Democratic organization of the Senate and their committee chairmanships, but not enough to pass progressive legislation. They redoubled their efforts.

The Republicans elected Everett Dirksen as minority leader. He and Johnson were far more compatible than Johnson had been with the highly intelligent but humorless and rigid Taft, and the less intelligent but equally humorless and rigid Knowland. In cunning, subtlety, and parliamentary skills, Dirksen was the first Republican leader who was Johnson's equal.

The 1959 session opened with a rules fight in which Johnson again demonstrated his parliamentary skills. He tabled the Anderson motion to change the filibuster rule with a 60-36 vote—a disappointment for those hoping to change the rules, for even with fourteen new Democratic votes from areas outside the South, they had lost eight votes from the previous effort. Notably, six of the eight new Democratic senators who voted with the South on the filibuster rule were rewarded with choice seats on the expanded committees.

A small, dark cloud appeared on Johnson's horizon when on Washington's birthday newly reelected William Proxmire rose on the Senate floor to complain of Johnson's arbitrary leadership. Johnson sent liberal Senator Richard Neuberger of Oregon to the floor to defend his leadership. Neuberger complained that Proxmire was biting the hand that was feeding him and should be grateful for whatever largess flowed from Johnson's beneficence. Just before Proxmire's speech, a senator read Washington's Farewell Address, as was customary on the anniversary of the first president's birth. The wags put it that in taking on Johnson on his home turf, Proxmire was giving his own farewell address.

The infusion of Democrats in both the House and the Senate weakened the command of both Johnson and Rayburn and placed them on the defensive, although the coalition of southern Democrats and northern Republicans "demonstrated its continued potency."[69] But a standoff between President Dwight Eisenhower and the Congress helped engender more partisanship and fewer accomplishments. The president toughened his stand, especially on spending issues, and wielded his veto pen to accomplish his ends.

Moreover, all the announced Democratic candidates for the presidency and the single Republican candidate adorned the Senate chamber—a fact that did not make for a constructive Congress. The two-month fight over the voting-rights bill, with its twenty-four-hour sessions, also did not help matters. On that issue, Johnson and the Senate attacked the filibuster problem procedurally but weakened the House bill substantively. With a much larger majority, Democratic accomplishments decreased, and except for statehood for Hawaii and a tough labor bill, there was little significant legislation.

Johnson's plan to return to the Senate after the national convention (where he hoped he would be the party's presidential nominee) to enact critical legislation was unsuccessful. A minimum-wage bill, Medicare, and a $1.1 billion school construction bill all languished in the postconvention session. Democrats and Republicans alike were delighted to adjourn on September 1, 1960, leaving these and other differences to be fought out in the campaign and by a new president and a new Congress.

The Ebbing of Johnson's Power

After the initial procedural roll-call victories at the beginning of the civil rights battle, Johnson's legendary legislative power began to ebb. Because of Eisenhower's newfound obstinacy, the reformation of the conservative coalition, and the greater expectations of his own enlarged majority, life was much more difficult for the majority leader. Some of the old magic, especially during the postconvention session, had vanished. By January 3, 1961, Johnson's mastery over the Senate was gone. An incident on that day symbolized that fact. In 1960, Johnson had not only been elected vice president under John F. Kennedy, but he had also been reelected as senator from Texas. Sworn in as senator at noon on January 3, he immediately resigned from that office. But in the morning, as Johnson presided over his last party caucus as majority leader, there was a contretemps.

Mike Mansfield was elected as the new majority leader. He then proposed that Johnson, as vice president, should continue to preside over that and future Democratic caucuses. But Mansfield, a self-effacing man, had misjudged the tenor of the caucus. Personal animosity and institutional pride compelled a group of senators to revolt against having the vice president, a member of the executive branch, exercise power over them as it would violate the separation-of-powers doctrine. Among the most influential objectors were Albert Gore, Sr., of Tennessee and Clinton Anderson, the consummate insider and Johnson ally. Although Mansfield's motion carried, Johnson was stunned by the forcefulness of the opposition. He subsequently turned the post over to Mansfield.[70]

The irony is that Johnson's Democratic opponents in the Senate became the strongest supporters of his legislative program as president. His Great Society legislation and the Civil Rights acts of 1964 and 1965, whose provisions he had killed in 1957 and 1960, could not have been passed without their support. As Paul Douglas wrote in his memoirs:

Had I been told in 1956 that ten years later I would be one of Lyndon Johnson's strongest supporters, I would have thought the seer was out of his mind, for I was then locked in mortal combat with him as I tried to pass civil-rights legislation, abolish the filibuster, plug tax loopholes, and prevent the oil and gas industry from getting special favors. Our differences seemed irreconcilable.[71]

Senator Robert C. Byrd, himself a majority leader of the Senate, had the following perspective on the Johnson leadership: "His prowess as majority leader is legendary. But Lyndon Johnson could not lead this Senate today as he led the Senate in his day. I do not say that with any measure of disrespect for him, but it is a different Senate today."[72]

NOTES

1. D. B. Hardeman and Donald C. Bacon, *Rayburn: A Biography* (Austin: Texas Monthly, 1987), 389.
2. Clark Clifford on Bill Moyers's "Second Look," Public Broadcasting Service, May 28, 1989.
3. Doris Kearns, interview with author, January 26, 1972; Doris Kearns, *Lyndon Johnson and the American Dream* (New York: Harper and Row, 1976), 136.
4. Rowland Evans and Robert Novak, *Lyndon B. Johnson: The Exercise of Power* (London: George Allen and Unwin, 1967), 30.
5. Robert A. Caro, *The Path to Power* (New York: Knopf, 1983); Hardeman and Bacon, *Rayburn: A Biography*; Alfred Steinberg, *Sam Johnson's Boy* (New York: Macmillan, 1968).
6. Evans and Novak, *Lyndon B. Johnson*, 33.
7. Bobby Baker with Larry L. King, *Wheeling and Dealing: Confessions of a Capitol Hill Operator* (New York: Norton, 1978), 40.
8. Ibid.
9. Ibid., 41.
10. Ibid., 34.
11. Ibid., 40.
12. U.S. Congress, *Congressional Directory, 1949* (Washington, D.C.: U.S. Government Printing Office, 1949), XLII, XLVI.
13. Kearns, *Lyndon Johnson*, 103.
14. Merle Miller, *Lyndon* (New York: Putnam's, 1980), 142; Kearns, *Lyndon Johnson*, 105.
15. Robert A. Caro, "Annals of Politics," *New Yorker*, December 18, 1989, 43–82.
16. *Denver Post* editorial, October 11, 1949; letter to the editor, Lyndon Johnson [Palmer Hoyt], October 15, 1949. Senate Collection, Appointments file, Container 336, LBJ Library.
17. Miller, *Lyndon*, 146.

18. Evans and Novak, *Lyndon B. Johnson*, 32.
19. U.S. Congress, *Congressional Record*, March 9, 1949, 2047.
20. Caro, *New Yorker*, January 22, 1990, 102.
21. U.S. Congress, *Congressional Directory, 1949*, XLIII.
22. Ibid., 292–293.
23. Evans and Novak, *Lyndon B. Johnson*, 41–43.
24. Ibid., 43.
25. William S. White, *Citadel* (New York: Harper, 1957), 68.
26. U. S., Bureau of the Census, *Statistical Abstract of the United States: 1979* (Washington, D.C.: U.S. Government Printing Office, 1979), 12.
27. This is a complex matter. Until 1949 the Senate required a two-thirds vote of those present and voting to apply cloture to a bill. No cloture could be applied at all to the motion to proceed to the consideration of a bill, that is, to get it off the calendar and before the Senate. In March 1949, a compromise was struck. The rule was changed to require a two-thirds vote of the entire Senate to apply cloture both to the motion to proceed and to a bill itself. This did not apply, however, to a motion to proceed to the consideration of a change in the rules. Since then, the rule has been modified several times and presently requires the affirmative vote of sixty senators to invoke cloture except for a rules change, which requires two thirds of those present and voting, a quorum being present.
28. U.S. Congress, *Congressional Directory, 1949*, 172.
29. U.S. Congress, *Senate Manual Containing the Standing Rules, Orders, Laws and Resolutions Affecting the Business of the United States Senate* (Washington, D.C.: U.S. Government Printing Office, 1979), Rule XVI, 15.
30. Howard E. Shuman, "Senate Rules and the Civil Rights Bill: A Case Study," *American Political Science Review* 51 (December 1957): 969.
31. U.S. Congress, *Congressional Directory, 1949*, XLI, XLV, XLVI.
32. Ibid., 172–174, XLI-XLIX.
33. See Richard F. Fenno, Jr., *The Power of the Purse* (Boston: Little, Brown, 1966), 515; and U.S. Congress, *Congressional Record*, March 14, 1961, 3638, 3640, for examples of those who did.
34. Winston S. Churchill, *Closing the Ring*, vol. 5 of *The Second World War* (London: Cassell, 1952), 150.
35. *Washington Post*, May 21, 1989, D6.
36. Ibid., January 16, 1990, B6.
37. Anderson's passion to change the filibuster rule came not from his views on civil rights but from a major fight he had with Senator Elmer Thomas of Oklahoma, who used the filibuster against Anderson's agricultural policies when he was Truman's secretary of agriculture.
38. U.S. Congress, *Congressional Record*, February 24, 1954, 2218.
39. Ibid., January 7, 1953, 232–233 (daily edition).
40. Kearns, *Lyndon Johnson*, 114.
41. Evans and Novak, *Lyndon B. Johnson*, 104.
42. Ibid.
43. Author's interview with James McCartney, then of the *Chicago Daily News*, now with the Knight-Ridder chain, who quoted Baker, January 26, 1990.
44. Evans and Novak, *Lyndon B. Johnson*, 28.
45. Press release, January 7, 1953, Senator Lyndon B. Johnson. Steering Committee members were not published in the *Congressional Directory* and the membership in the early Johnson years was very hard to find. I am indebted to Claudia W. Anderson and the Lyndon Baines Johnson Library for the information.
46. Author's interview with Thomas Dine of Church's staff.
47. Evans and Novak, *Lyndon B. Johnson*, 200–202.
48. Kearns, *Lyndon Johnson*, 129.
49. See Evans and Novak for additional examples of the "Johnson Network," 99.
50. Author's interview with McCartney.
51. White, *Citadel*, 68.

52. *Congressional Quarterly Almanac, 1955,* vol. 11 (Washington, D.C.: Congressional Quarterly, 1956), 44.
53. Evans and Novak, *Lyndon B. Johnson,* 51.
54. *Congressional Quarterly Almanac, 1957,* vol. 13, 79.
55. Ibid., 78.
56. Ibid., 58.
57. Evans and Novak, *Lyndon B. Johnson,* 120, 140; quoted in Robert C. Byrd, *The Senate, 1789–1989,* vol. 1 (Washington, D.C.: U. S. Government Printing Office, 1988), 615.
58. *Congressional Quarterly Almanac, 1957,* 284.
59. Ibid., 302.
60. Johnson, *Vantage Point* (New York: Holt, Rinehart and Winston, 1971), 154–155.
61. U.S. Congress, *Congressional Record,* August 30, 1957, 15171–15172.
62. Ibid., 15171.
63. Ibid.
64. *Report of the United States Commission on Civil Rights '63* (Washington, D.C.: U.S. Government Printing Office, 1963), table A, 32–35.
65. U.S. Congress, *Congressional Record,* August 30, 1957, 15172.
66. *Congressional Quarterly Almanac, 1960,* 185.
67. Ibid., 204.
68. Ibid., 185.
69. Ibid., 117.
70. Byrd, *The Senate,* 624.
71. Paul H. Douglas, *In the Fullness of Time* (New York: Harcourt Brace Jovanovich, 1972), 233.
72. U.S. Congress, *Congressional Record,* April 18, 1980, S3922, and March 3, 1986, S1913 (daily editions).

CHAPTER 8

Everett McKinley Dirksen
The Consummate Minority Leader

Burdett Loomis

This man of the minority earned the respect and affection of the majority, and by the special way he gave leadership to legislation, he added grace, elegance, and courtliness to the word "politician." That is how he became the leader of the minority, one of the leaders of our nation. That is why, when the Senate worked its way, Everett Dirksen so often worked his way. That is why, while he never became President, his impact and influence on the nation was greater than most Presidents in our history.

—Richard M. Nixon, in his eulogy for Everett M. Dirksen

More than twenty years after Richard Nixon's eulogy,[1] Everett McKinley Dirksen remains a fixture in our collective political memory. Part of Dirksen's stature derives from his memorable physical appearance—he was a "massive, silo-shaped man with an unruly shock of silvery hair."[2] Indeed, as Dirksen moved from the House to the Senate, and then to the Senate leadership, his hair became progressively wayward, apparently taking on a life of its own. But Dirksen's physical presence, coupled with his shuffling gait and ever-present cigarette, merely

Everett M. Dirksen played a central role in the Senate's evolution from the "inner club" days of the 1950s to the individualism that began in the late 1960s.

framed the centerpiece of his style—*the voice*. The voice could transfix almost any audience, from a ladies' literary society to a circle of hard-nosed reporters to his Senate peers. A 1962 *Time* cover story celebrated Dirksen with affection and awe:

He speaks, and the words emerge in a soft, sepulchral baritone. They undulate in measured phrases, expire in breathless wisps. He fills his lungs and blows word-rings like smoke. The sentences curl upward. . . . Now he conjures moods of mirth, now of sorrow. He rolls his bright blue eyes heavenward. In funereal tones, he paraphrases the Bible and church bells peal. "Motherhood," he whispers, and grown men weep. "The flag," he bugles, and everybody salutes.[3]

Viewed from afar, Dirksen stands as a key transitional figure in the development of the modern Senate. He understood, better than his contemporaries, the significance of using the media as a tool in shaping the agenda of the nation and the Washington establishment. He knew that expertise, hard work, and legislative skills were essential in a Congress that increasingly rewarded the efforts of its individual members. Dirksen also understood, even early in his minority leadership, that the essence of his position was to serve his Senate colleagues:

In sum, the Minority Leader is supposed and tries to keep himself informed on all matters within the domain of the Senate relating to legislation and governmental matters and to keep the members of his party informed likewise. In other words, he is a man of all work.[4]

Dirksen's "man of all work" is akin to Senator Howard Baker's perhaps more prosaic observation that the "principal duty of the leadership is janitorial."[5] Dirksen was a strong and assertive leader in the mold of Lyndon Johnson and Robert Taft. Yet he also established procedures for communication, committee assignments, and consultation with the majority that subsequent Republican leaders have maintained and refined. A flexible, pragmatic legislator whose career spanned almost four decades, Dirksen was perfectly suited for the task of easing the Senate's transition from its "inner club" era to its modern individualism, all the while resisting the lure of too much change and too little respect for tradition. As a man of the minority, he could give himself a little extra leeway in defining his role within the policy process. He could be responsible to himself, unlike a president with an agenda or a legislative majority with its own priorities.

The Senate in the Early 1950s

The U.S. Senate was a tradition-laden body in 1951 when Everett Dirksen entered as a freshman senator from Illinois. Its profound conservatism derived both from ideology and institutional imperatives. Historically, the Senate has celebrated the rights of the individual, and, by extension, the minority. William S. White observed that the Senate of the early 1950s embodied John Calhoun's doctrine of concurrent majority. White observed:

It was not, *and is not*, a tenable act to press upon any minority, sectional or otherwise, policies or laws that are quite literally intolerable, though of course care must be taken not to equate the truly intolerable with the merely repugnant.[6]

The doctrine of concurrent majorities required, however, the observance of norms and practices that served to concentrate power in a handful of senators. Regardless of ideology, these key legislators protected the Senate as an institution. At midcentury, this institutional conservatism virtually precluded the adoption of liberal policy initiatives. As political scientist Donald R. Matthews notes in his important 1960 study of the Senate: "The folkways of the Senate . . . buttress the *status quo* within the chamber, and the distribution of power within the chamber results in moderate to conservative policies."[7]

Junior senators, with rare exceptions, served demeaning apprenticeships on insignificant committees, while an inner core of senior members made the central policy and procedural choices. Specialization meant that most key decisions were made in committees where southern Democrats, given their seniority, served disproportionately as chairmen or as ranking members in 1953–1954. In addition, "the ideological spread of the Senate was relatively narrow by later standards," notes Barbara Sinclair. "The membership was predominantly conservative and moderate. . . . [Thus,] the policy decisions of the committees tended to be broadly acceptable to the Senate membership."[8]

Senators had few resources in the 1950s. Consequently, the force of personality, not the strength of one's staff, was the key ingredient of influence. Indeed, the average senator employed only a "dozen or so" staff members in the 1950s.[9]

In sum, the Senate of the early 1950s was a decentralized, committee-dominated institution in which the parties' floor leaders did not regularly play a major role in determining legislative outcomes. Individual senators did not exercise much influence unless they had moved into the "inner club" of the chamber's elders. There were, of course, exceptions—Hubert Humphrey's inclusion in the inner circle, for example. In any event, no one foresaw the monumental changes in store for the Senate. In fact, by the late 1960s, political scientist Randall Ripley would write:

The shape of the contemporary Senate is now clear. The distribution of power based on personal skills and institutional positions is predominantly individual-istic. . . . Committee chairmen have more power than many nonchairmen. But they are not strong enough to threaten the basic independence or substantive power of individual members.[10]

The Evolving Senate

What happened to change the Senate of White's *Citadel* to the highly individualistic chamber described by Ripley and others? There were at least three major agents of change: (1) Lyndon Johnson's service as majority leader from 1955 to 1960, (2) the 1958 election, and (3) the stirrings of interest-group representation in Washington beginning in the 1960s.

It is true that Robert Taft brought great prestige to the majority leadership during his brief tenure in 1953. But Lyndon Johnson is the man who most defined the post's possibilities and importance.[11] At the same time, Johnson may be the only modern leader to head a centralized Senate, given its increasing individualism. Indeed, Johnson himself hastened the fragmentation by breaking down the Senate oligarchy of the early 1950s.[12] Ralph Huitt has argued that Johnson's leadership

suggests that the successful senatorial leader . . . (1) can and does help individual senators to maximize their effectiveness in playing personal roles in the Senate, and (2) structures roles and alternatives so that a maximum number of senators can join in support of the proffered solution of an issue.[13]

Johnson, and later Dirksen, represented perhaps the two most powerful, effective leaders of the postwar era. Personality may explain part of this seeming incongruity, but both leaders found ways to take advantage of their specific situations—Johnson with razor-thin party margins in the Senate and a Republican in the White House, Dirksen with two-to-one Democratic majorities and a Democratic president. Johnson's centralized leadership style generated considerable acceptance for Dirksen's similar, if less harsh, mode of operation. All in all, Johnson demonstrated to all senators, Democrats and Republicans alike, the possibility, if not the virtue, of strong leadership. As minority leader, Dirksen took full advantage of the extensive groundwork that his Democratic counterpart had laid.

The so-called Johnson rule was also instrumental in changing the Senate. It guaranteed that all senators, including freshmen, would be assigned to one major committee. Dirksen roughly followed suit for Republicans, maneuvering around the seniority system to provide all his troops with adequate assignments. Operating without a formal rule, Dirksen could collect at least as much individual credit as could Johnson, and later Mansfield, who relied on an across-the-board policy.

The 1958 election also wrought major changes in the Senate. Dirksen's accession to the minority leadership coincided with the worst electoral drubbing for the Republicans since the Depression. In the Eighty-fifth Congress (1957–1958), Democrats outnumbered Republicans in the Senate by a bare 49–47 margin. After the 1958 off-year election, the Democrats' advantage stood at an apparently commanding count of 64-34.[14] Not only was the party balance drastically altered (and committee ratios and floor voting transformed), but the 1958 class was also liberal and talented, including a host of able House veterans. For the next decade, Senate Democrats retained majorities ranging from twenty-eight to thirty-six seats. Only in his last few months as minority leader did Dirksen enjoy the presence of more than forty senators on his side of the aisle.

In the ten years following the 1958 election, liberal northern Democrats retained their numbers and advanced in seniority. As power became increasingly decentralized, they stood to gain the most. For example, there were 86 subcommittee chairmanships in the Senate in the Eighty-fifth Congress, and southerners held almost half of them (39, or 45 percent). By 1968, the number of chairmanships had risen to 103, but only 32 (or 31 percent) remained in southern hands.[15] Still, liberals were frequently frustrated in their attempts to exercise power, especially inside the committee system.[16] More and more, they turned to the floor to press their policy initiatives.[17] This allowed the Republican leadership an opportunity to affect legislation, to the extent that it could provide substantial votes on one or another amendment.

As more issues came to the floor of the House and Senate, starting in the 1960s, interest groups could more easily seek to influence outcomes, in that floor actions were much more public than those taken in committees. The growth of government in the 1960s, both through new or expanded programs and regulation, generated increasing numbers of Washington-based interests. Most of this growth took place in the 1970s and 1980s, but the trend had begun in the wake of the Great Society's policy initiatives.[18]

As the Senate shifted from a committee-centered chamber of the early 1950s to a more centralized structure under Johnson, culminating in an increasingly individualistic body of the late 1960s, Dirksen was ideally positioned to take advantage of the evolution—the perfect leader for a rapidly changing institution. Throughout his political career, Dirksen had been more than willing to review and alter his own policy and procedural positions. Most important, he could act tactically on the key issue of restricting debate (cloture), because he was unburdened by strong philosophical beliefs that would mandate a certain course of action.

His florid oratorical style and carefully disheveled appearance obscured his skills as a legislative tactician, at least beyond Capitol Hill. But Senate Republicans had chosen their leader wisely. Dirksen would be an effective, hardworking legislative craftsman who could change with the times while operating with a corporal's guard of fellow partisans.

Dirksen's Path to Senate Leadership

In January 1959, almost to the day of his sixty-third birthday, Dirksen became minority leader of the U.S. Senate. Few expected great things of him. After all, only five years before he had been excoriated as one of Senator Joseph R. McCarthy's strongest defenders. Moreover, Dirksen appeared to be a throwback. At the time, younger and more liberal politicians were pushing their way toward center stage in the Senate. Within two years, however, both his colleagues and the press were praising him. By 1962 *Time* called him the "most effective G.O.P. floor leader" in forty years. Dirksen's salutary performance might have surprised some, but even a cursory review of his early political career reveals a man of tremendous ability.

Prologue to Senate Leadership

Dirksen's political career can be characterized by four major attributes: (1) great ambition, (2) careful creation of a public persona, (3) legislative professionalism that emphasized expertise and hard work, and (4) flexibility that often shaded into opportunism.

Ambition. In 1943, midway through his sixth House term, Dirksen organized a campaign among his GOP colleagues to push his name as a possible presidential nominee. He had no realistic hopes for the presidency but thought that the vice-presidential nomination might well be within his grasp.[19] Thirty-six House Republicans, all but four from the Middle West, signed the petition.[20] During the spring of 1944, Dirksen pressed his campaign in twenty-seven states. This was no modest trial balloon, and its eventual failure (when party nominee Thomas E. Dewey selected Ohio governor John Bricker as his running mate) was in no way a major setback for a forty-seven-year-old House member who had never so much as chaired a subcommittee. Dirksen had enhanced his overall political stature, which would redound to his benefit either inside the Congress or out. Indeed, two years later, when the Republicans gained a majority in the House, Dirksen made an abortive run for the floor leadership. As with the vice presidency, he withdrew his name before a vote was taken but continued to keep his eye on higher office.

Dirksen's ambition was a constant in his career, from his first run for the House to his last campaign for the Senate, when he won reelection at age seventy-three despite failing health. At two critical junctures Dirksen ran against strong incumbents. He challenged a sitting Republican House member in 1930 and lost by only fifteen hundred votes. Continuing to campaign for the next two years, he finally captured the nomination with a sixteen-hundred-vote margin (and won the general election handily in spite of the Roosevelt landslide). Having retired from the House in 1948 because of failing eyesight, Dirksen resumed his political career as soon as his condition improved, taking on the formidable task of unseating Senate Majority Leader Scott Lucas. By April 1949, he was planning for the 1950 Senate race.

In the 1950s, Dirksen retained hopes for a spot on the national ticket. His 1952 Republican convention speech, however, attacking Dewey's party leadership, may have disqualified him from future considerations for higher office. With his 1956 reelection, Dirksen could turn his ambitions toward the chamber itself, where he became minority whip in 1957 and floor leader two years later. From that time on, he focused on his legislative duties. Still, as with many senators, the fires of presidential ambition were slow to die down. Former senator Howard Baker reports that "the first time I heard him say that 'that boat had pulled away from the dock' was in 1968, after Nixon's election."[21]

The Thespian as Legislator. Dirksen first faced the public as an actor. He was a mainstay of the Pekin Players during the post–World War I years. Between 1919 and 1926 he wrote more than one hundred works (plays, poems, short stories, and five full novels), including one melodrama set in China, which he sold to a Chicago publisher for $300.[22] His theatrical passions were so intense, his mother extracted a deathbed promise from him in 1923 to forswear drama as a career. She did not mention politics.

Dirksen's thespian background shone through his political performances from his initial campaign through his final days as minority leader. Beyond his relish for the limelight, Dirksen's training and experience as an actor brought specific political benefits. First, his speaking abilities ranked him among the Senate greats. He could bring senators to the floor and hold them there, in part because he was unpredictable, in part because he was substantively sound, but in the main because he was entertaining. True to his dramatic training, Dirksen's *appearance* of spontaneity was often just that, an appearance. His papers are filled with speech outlines that he had carefully constructed and then memorized. Louella Dirksen noted that her husband "never carried the written outline to the platform . . . and rarely used notes."[23] Although he might improvise from his basic speech, the senator was clear about what his orations were designed to do and how they would serve his goals. Underlying the apparent spontaneity was a script, and Dirksen was a good enough actor to carry off this kind of difficult performance.

Second, and more generally, Dirksen understood the value of drama in politics. On occasion his flair for the dramatic led him astray, as with his televised attack on Dewey at the 1952 Republican convention. For the most part, however, his theatrics in the Senate were helpful in framing important policies and political issues. In many ways, Dirksen came to view the Senate as a stage on which he performed both as director and leading man.

Hard Work and Expertise. Dirksen worked extremely hard on his legislative tasks without regard to his health. Coupled with his native political skills, this capacity for work made Dirksen a most effective legislator and an especially strong leader. Even in his first, unsuccessful, campaign for the House, Dirksen won plaudits for his abilities. The *Peoria Star*, which opposed his candidacy, editorialized:

The district has never experienced anything like him. Without newspaper support, with the business interests of the district arrayed against him, he waged one of the most astonishing campaigns this district has ever witnessed. That he came so close to victory is a tribute to his ability as an orator, his good nature, and his unbounded energy. He has arrived.[24]

Eighteen years later, as he retired from the House, Dirksen received similar accolades from legislators on both sides of the aisle. The *Washington Post* and the *Washington Evening Star* sang his praises, as did Speaker Sam Rayburn. And in 1946, when *Pageant* magazine surveyed members of Congress to name their most effective colleagues, Dirksen finished second among House members, one slot higher than the legendary Rayburn.[25]

Dirksen's reputation from his House service, along with his appetite for long hours and his ability to understand complex legislation, served him well in the Senate from the start. In an era that placed high value on apprenticeship, Dirksen was admitted almost immediately into the counsel of the top leaders. During his first term, he was appointed chairman of the Republican Senate Campaign Committee. Much of his early success can be attributed to his "born-again" conservatism, which was most welcome to the Republican leaders, but Dirksen's political skills and willingness to work tirelessly allowed him to make the most of his opportunities.

Flexibility. Along with his rhetorical abilities, Dirksen displayed infinite capacity for change. His flexibility, in fact, was central to his political style, making him an effective legislative leader. He could communicate with colleagues of all political stripes, and he could often make tactical moves to affect legislation when the Republicans' minority status might have appeared to render the Senate party powerless. Although Dirksen was frequently ridiculed, both within the legislature and on the campaign trail, for his "flip-flops," these charges had little impact on his legislative or electoral performances. [26]

Dirksen's legendary changes in position were heartfelt on many occasions, as when he renounced his isolationism in September 1941.[27] At the same time, it is true that his variability frequently incorporated raw political opportunism, often fed by his ambition. The most notable example of this behavior, for which Dirksen paid a heavy price, came between 1950 and 1955. Turning his back on a seven-year (1941–1948) record of internationalism and moderation in the House, Dirksen campaigned for the Senate in 1950 as a rabid anti-Communist who mocked the Marshall Plan and returned to his former isolationism. In an even more profound change, Dirksen made peace with his longtime Republican adversary, *Chicago Tribune* publisher Colonel Robert McCormick. Political scientist Jean Torcom Cronin concludes:

What had been his admirable flexibility was now base political opportunism. His willingness to change his mind when he came up against a better argument, or new facts, was now a total lack of principles. These changes were to stay with him and color his image for the rest of his life. . . . His ambition, his overriding desire to be part of the "big show," . . . won out over any doubts he may have had in deserting his previous and so strongly held convictions.[28]

For his first several years in the Senate, Dirksen was strongly associated with the McCarthy wing of the Republican party. Although he maintained better relations with President Eisenhower than many of his colleagues, there was no question where Dirksen stood. Ultimately, this worked to his great disadvantage. His biographer, Neil MacNeil, convincingly argued that in 1954 Dirksen's political career was at its nadir:

> More than ever before he was [at age fifty-eight] clearly isolated as a member of a minority and now discredited faction of his own Republican party. The Senate did more than censure Senator McCarthy; it repudiated those who stood with him, none more than Dirksen.[29]

Yet little more than two years later, in 1957, Dirksen was chosen minority whip; by 1959 he was floor leader and well on his way to becoming a great power in the Senate. How was this possible?

Dirksen's Entrance to the Leadership

Dirksen wasted no time in redirecting his political career in 1955–1956. His actions of this period were those of an ambitious, skilled politician who systematically moved out of the conservative Republican camp without alienating the senior party leaders who could affect his future. Dirksen's most important ally was President Eisenhower, who increasingly turned to him for guidance that floor leader William Knowland and others were unable or unwilling to provide. As early as 1953, in the wake of Taft's death and Knowland's ascent to the majority leadership, Eisenhower placed his reliance on Dirksen. The president wrote to Dirksen, asking him to be " 'verbal leader' of the middle-of-the-road philosophy . . . in the Senate."[30] Eisenhower cultivated Dirksen's friendship throughout his presidency, and Dirksen reciprocated by refraining from mounting any serious attacks on the president.[31]

Dirksen's vocal support for Eisenhower sprang in part from his desire to run for reelection in 1956 with the immensely popular president at the head of the ticket. As 1956 proceeded, Dirksen emerged as the chief Senate advocate for administration policies—especially on foreign policy, where he had once again moved toward an internationalist position. As he opted for greater, more visible support for Eisenhower, Dirksen retained the allegiance of the old-line Senate conservatives, who saw in his actions the legitimate positioning of a senator seeking reelection.

The 1956 elections found Eisenhower and Dirksen handily returned to office, but a spot in the Senate Republican hierarchy opened up as Senator Eugene Millikin (R-Colo.), the chair of the Senate GOP Conference, lost his seat. Coupled with this vacancy was floor leader Knowland's growing desire to run for governor of California in 1958. Thus, replacing Millikin "expanded into a question of the dynastic succession of the Senate."[32] The party's whip would become the leading candidate to replace Knowland, and the moderate incumbent, Leverett Saltonstall (R-Mass.), was unacceptable to such senior conservative powers as Knowland and Styles Bridges (R-N.H.). Without mentioning Knowland's possible departure, Saltonstall was offered the caucus (conference) chairmanship, which was presented to him as a promotion. He accepted, and Dirksen, Bridges's candidate, was installed as whip without any real contest.[33]

Knowland's gubernatorial candidacy was a great opportunity for Dirksen, who made the most of it. He increasingly served as Eisenhower's key link to the Senate, all the while maintaining his strong ties to his conservative supporters within the chamber. In the aftermath of the disastrous (for the Republicans) 1958 elections, Dirksen was the obvious, if not altogether enthusiastic, choice to lead the Senate minority. Opposed by Senator John Sherman Cooper (R-Ky.), Dirksen won a 20-14 victory among the much-reduced ranks of Republican senators. One key component of Dirksen's victory was his announced intention to push for the election of a liberal as whip, which was accomplished through some strategic vote-switching by him and five colleagues to elect Senator Thomas Kuchel (R-Calif.) as the second-ranking leader.

Between 1955 and 1958, Dirksen focused all his skills and energies on gaining the Senate party leadership. His rhetorical talents would also serve him well as he led the shrunken Republican minority into battle over the next decade. Although he had not yet completely won over the Republican moderates, he had risen to the floor leadership without alienating them and had managed to retain the strong support of his conservative allies. Equally important, he was a popular president's most prominent and steadfast supporter. Much as Lyndon Johnson stood ready and able to recast the role of the majority leader in 1955, Dirksen was poised to revamp the minority leadership in 1959.

The Minority Leader, 1959–1969

In assuming the Republican floor leadership, Dirksen could now boast of various assets, none more valuable than the simple fact that he was not his predecessor. Knowland had been neither personable nor communicative in the Senate, and he frequently failed to support his president's policy initiatives. He alienated the moderates and enjoyed neither the skill nor the desire to deal effectively with the press. The reduced Republican minority could ill afford such a dour leader. Dirksen quickly moved to consolidate his strength by establishing a more positive and popular leadership style that sustained him for the next decade.

True to his thespian roots, Dirksen's first two years as floor leader represented a "tryout" of his style, which he polished throughout the 1960s. He encouraged participation among all Republican senators and maintained congenial working relationships with the executive branch and the chamber's Democrats—especially President Eisenhower and Majority Leader Lyndon Johnson. In addition, he communicated effectively with the press (taking this responsibility seriously) and was rewarded with accolades from both the media and his colleagues. The *New York Times* observed, for example, that Dirksen was "probably the most effective leader the Republicans had in the Senate in years."[34] More important was the praise he received from those who had most distrusted his rise to leadership—the Senate Republican moderates. Senator Margaret Chase Smith (R-Maine), who had voted against Dirksen for floor leader, stated that:

As I have watched him perform the duties of minority leader I have increasingly come to conclude that his election to that position was a very wise action by the Senate Republicans. . . . He has shown a capacity for understanding . . . by which one can disagree agreeably—by which one can differ with another without rancor.[35]

The Dirksen Leadership in Full Bloom

The task before the minority leader was clear when Dirksen took the reins in 1959; there were, as Cronin concludes, only "fragments of power" for him to rearrange and consolidate.[36] By the early 1960s, Dirksen had in fact pulled together the fragments to provide him with tenuous, but real, power within the Democrat-controlled Senate. He had (1) revamped the formal, decentralized structure of the Republican leadership; (2) become a recognizable voice both in the Senate minority and in the Republican party in general; (3) taken advantage of strong relations with the Senate majority leader and two successive Democratic presidents; and (4) developed an effective, noncoercive style that emphasized participation and communication for all minority senators.

Revamping the Minority Leadership. In contrast to the centralized Senate Democrats, who had concentrated power in the floor leader's hands, the chamber's Republicans traditionally operated with several leaders.[37] After Dirksen's selection as minority leader, however, Republicans became much more centralized in practice, if not on paper.

In the early 1960s, the formal structure of the Senate leadership remained intact; aside from Dirksen, Senator Kuchel served as minority whip, Senator Saltonstall as conference chairman, and Senator Bridges as chair of the Policy Committee. In addition, from the start of the Eighty-seventh Congress in 1961 through the remainder of the 1960s, Republicans organized a joint leadership structure that met weekly and embraced both House and Senate leaders, plus the national chairman.[38]

The nominal leadership meant little on a day-to-day basis. One Republican leader concluded that "the formal party leadership, like Topsy, 'just grow'd' " and that there was no formal whip organization.[39] Rather, Kuchel's job was "more nearly described as Assistant Minority Leader than Whip."[40] Likewise, the conference rarely met, and the Policy Committee staff often felt isolated from Dirksen. The one important formal element of the Republican leadership was the weekly luncheon meeting, which allowed for the minority to exchange views on a regular basis. In many ways, this meeting was a functional equivalent to the conference, although Dirksen, not the conference chair, ran the proceedings.

In addition, Dirksen was aggressive in the Committee on Committees, where he had only a modest formal role. The Republicans appointed members on the basis of seniority, but Dirksen used his own seniority to provide leverage in obtaining the assignments he desired. The signal instance came in 1959. Senator Gordon Allott (R-Colo.) bid for an Appropriations Committee seat, and several senators stood ahead of him on the seniority list. At the head of the list was Senator Dirksen, who, as one senator recounted, "said he would take Appropriations unless the rest of the guys waived it for Allott. By that kind of maneuver Gordon got on Appropriations. . . . Everybody might have waived anyway, but they had to waive."[41]

Such maneuvering had a salutary effect on committee assignments in general. Because of the example set by Dirksen and other leaders, senior

Republicans felt themselves under considerable pressure to give up a choice committee assignment on behalf of junior members. As Dirksen gained the confidence of all GOP factions in the Senate, he could centralize the party leadership with little fear of being undercut by one clique or another. Crucial to this process was Dirksen's ability to communicate effectively—if not continually—with his colleagues. Although some senators voiced modest complaints on this score, Dirksen was, above all else, a communicator. Most important, his network ranged far beyond his Republican peers; as with his leadership style, no formal structure could easily contain him.

Voice of the Minority. The election of 1958 had placed the Republicans at a severe numerical disadvantage on Capitol Hill. Matters worsened for them in the 1960 presidential election, which returned the White House to the Democrats. Suddenly, the GOP lost its voice. Richard Nixon pulled up stakes to run for governor of California, and no one outside the legislative party leadership could lay claim to speak for the minority. This was the context in which Dirksen moved front and center in American politics. He accomplished this by meeting with the press each Thursday during the legislative session, in the wake of the weekly joint leadership meeting, accompanied by his House counterpart, first Charles Halleck (R-Ind.) and later Gerald Ford (R-Mich.). Quickly dubbed the "Ev and Charlie Show," the performances attracted a lot of attention—not all of it positive. Although Dirksen was enough of a character to attract attention in any setting, this weekly "show" meant highly coveted, regular appearances before the American people. Ironically, the initial impetus for such a Republican performance came from President Eisenhower, who understood the value of well-focused press attention and urged Dirksen to get it.[42]

Some Republican members of Congress thought that two older, midwestern conservatives did not adequately represent their party; some were surely jealous. And some in the press, most notably the widely syndicated *Washington Post* cartoonist Herblock, painted Dirksen and Halleck as buffoons. Apparently, Dirksen did not object to the characterization:

He enjoyed the notoriety, and he was delighted with the attention he was getting. The publicity was bad, but it was publicity. . . . Dirksen . . . knew that the public attention that they were getting simply could not be bought, and that he could turn it to his own advantage. . . . In time, he sensed, the criticism would wane, and he would be better off for the national notoriety he was now receiving.[43]

"The Ev and Charlie Show Goes High Hat," by cartoonist James Berryman, July 15, 1961.

Republican leader Everett Dirksen's weekly press conferences with his House counterpart, Charles Halleck, made Dirksen a national celebrity, although the spotlight was not always flattering.

Halleck was never completely comfortable in his role as national spokesman. But, of course, Dirksen was immediately at home. To showcase its leaders, the Republican National Committee budgeted $30,000 annually to produce the weekly news conference. For its initial two years, the "Ev and Charlie Show" remained at risk; in January 1963, it received some modest restructuring in large part to rein in the irrepressible Dirksen. But one journalist thought these efforts to remake Dirksen as a "conventional, solemn, hard-hitting spokesman for the party," were, as he put it:

Preposterous. He is not a solemn man; he is a conscious humorist. He is not a hard hitter; he hits with pillows and bags of water and old cornstalks. His methods are unquestionably more entertaining, and probably more effective, than whole Congressional Records full of conventional bombast.[44]

In a Democratic era, Dirksen reminded the public that there was a Republican party and that there were other perspectives beyond the president's. Perhaps the rambling act of a veteran thespian was not what many Republicans might have preferred. But they had no real alternatives to the man who played so shamelessly, and effectively, to the media. Throughout the 1960s, as measured by the number of "press mentions," no senator received more consistent attention than did Dirksen, with that coverage reaching a peak in 1965–1966, when he appeared in more Associated Press stories than any of his colleagues.[45] Compared to other modern-era minority leaders, Dirksen attracted considerably more media coverage than such party leaders as Lyndon Johnson (in 1953–1954), Hugh Scott, or Robert C. Byrd.[46]

Obtaining press attention can become an end in itself; and, although Dirksen did exhibit such tendencies, he ordinarily had a purpose behind his publicity mongering. Senator James Pearson (R-Kans.) reflected that, given the Democratic congressional majorities, it was important for "Dirksen [to have] a good relationship with the press. Plus, he'd give them tidbits of information."[47] Many of these scraps came from the weekly Republican leadership meetings, of course, but more important to the media, to say nothing of his colleagues, was Dirksen's role as a conduit for information from the majority leadership and, frequently, the president.

Dirksen, Democrats, and Presidents. In resurrecting his political career after the early 1950s, Dirksen relied heavily on his relationship with President Eisenhower. For the rest of his congressional tenure, excepting his final nine months with Richard Nixon as president, Dirksen was to maintain excellent relations with the chief executive. Indeed, his close ties to Kennedy and Johnson permitted him privileges, information, access, and political favors that made him an important asset.

Dirksen's basic attitude, which mirrored that of Johnson in his two-year stint as minority leader, was that it was not the duty of the opposition to oppose.[48] Of course, he did oppose many Kennedy and Johnson administration proposals, especially on domestic matters. On international and defense policies, however, Dirksen usually saw things from the president's point of view, regardless of who controlled the office. Much like his relations with the press, Dirksen's connection with the White House served both sides in the bargain. Dirksen could wield private information and easy access as weapons in his leadership arsenal, while Kennedy and Johnson could cultivate his pride and "fascination with power" to help them gain bipartisan support for their foreign policies.[49]

Although Dirksen had reasonably close ties to Kennedy, with whom he had served since 1946 in both the House and Senate, his relationship with Johnson was especially strong and complex. The two men served together in the House for a decade, and they entered the Senate within two years of each other. As floor leaders of their respective Senate parties, they forged extremely close ties that remained strong after Johnson became president. One close observer noted that "Johnson would call . . . and say, 'Ev, I'm coming up.' And he'd show up in Dirksen's back room and sit down and have a drink, with that big, ugly dog that he had, and the Secret Service people."[50] Johnson knew he could rely on Dirksen's support on most international issues; he also knew the Republican leader would listen on a wide range of other, national interest, legislation such as civil rights.

His regular conversations with the president gave Dirksen great leverage with his fellow senators and, to an extent, the press. He often appeared to know more than Majority Leader Mansfield largely because he was more willing to express himself. MacNeil contends that Dirksen was not only more willing to detail information gleaned from the president but he also knew more about Johnson's real views than Mansfield and the other Democrats did.[51]

However strong his personal and stylistic ties to Johnson, Dirksen's support of the office of the president, especially in time of war, came to represent the core of their relationship after 1966. In fact, Dirksen's very closeness to the White House ultimately diminished his authority among his own partisans, most notably the younger Republican senators.

Inside the Senate, Dirksen cultivated cordial working relations with the majority Democrats, both through the formal party leaders and the conservative southerners. Coming on the heels of the distant and authoritarian leadership style of Knowland, Dirksen's tendencies toward consultation and compromise were greatly welcomed, first by Johnson and then Mansfield. The personal bonds between Dirksen and Mansfield are especially noteworthy, as Senator Pearson observed:

He and Mansfield were enormously close. It's difficult to find adequate adjectives to describe the closeness. Mansfield and Dirksen were close personal friends. With Johnson it was different. They were close, but it was more an honor among crooks. They understood—they knew what was going on in each other's mind.[52]

Senate floor leaders Everett Dirksen (left) *and Mike Mansfield* (right) *meet with President Lyndon B. Johnson at the White House.*

Although the Dirksen-Mansfield relationship developed in the context of huge Democratic majorities, various senators have contended that their friendship would not have changed had the partisan balance been otherwise. The gregarious Dirksen and the stolid Mansfield cooperated to make the Senate work. One senior Republican senator concluded that their "combination would operate this way no matter what was the [party] proportion."[53] Even when Mansfield was sliding a proposal past his fellow partisans, he would consult with Dirksen.[54]

While maintaining his cordial relations with Johnson and Mansfield, Dirksen always kept open the natural Republican channels of communication with southern Democrats. Their affinity on a wide range of domestic issues allowed Dirksen a great deal of flexibility in formulating a minority strategy. Especially when cloture was considered necessary to stop a real or threatened filibuster, the Democratic leadership had to negotiate seriously with Dirksen, whose opposition to cutting off debate would almost certainly doom the motion to failure.

A Noncoercive Style: The "Gentle Oilcan Art." In her work on the contemporary House leadership, Barbara Sinclair emphasizes the extent to which "keeping peace in the family," along with building winning coalitions, is central to the effectiveness of the top party leaders.[55] His rhetorical skills and relations with presidents aside, the cornerstone of Dirksen's leadership style was his communicative, trusting, noncoercive approach toward his Republican colleagues. Despite occasional grumbling among fellow senators, Dirksen maintained "peace in the family" for more than a decade, which allowed him and the Republicans inordinate power within an institution dominated by Democrats.

One Republican senator observed in the late 1960s that

Dirksen has done a superb job of really trying to hold his troops together. Seldom have I seen a fellow with as much tact and patience as he has with all kinds of fundamentally strong people and fundamentally difficult people—they must be, or they probably wouldn't be where they are.[56]

Another senator agreed:

There were no twisted arms. . . . One time [Dirksen] wandered over to my desk, [and] he said, "I could sure use your vote on this." And I said, "No, Everett, I can't do it." He said, "Okay," and walked away. That was it. He didn't twist arms.[57]

Much like House Ways and Means Committee chair Wilbur Mills (D-Ark.), Dirksen eschewed outright coercion.[58] Yet a toughness remained about his style, especially when it became a matter of political exchange. He campaigned for his colleagues, raised funds for them, and expected a return on this investment. Dirksen "was a very good book-keeper," said one senator, "your credits and debits were always taken into account."[59]

Senators have regularly contrasted Dirksen's leadership style with that of Lyndon Johnson. One recalled that Dirksen "was never pushing anyone around. He'd try to reach agreement. I never heard him threaten or talk tough, like LBJ. He was a gentleman."[60] Dirksen would often cajole his colleagues, both privately and publicly. Most did not relish opposing him in debate on the Senate floor, fearing that he might make them appear foolish. In addition, he was persistent in seeking support, but without Johnson's relentlessness or intolerance.

Undergirding much of the Dirksen leadership was the genuine affection his fellow Republican senators felt toward him; this was also true of Mansfield and some Democrats. This goodwill complemented Dirksen's hard work on legislation and on running the Senate's business. The affection of his colleagues increased Dirksen's latitude for maneuvering. To an extent, senators indulged Dirksen—for example, in debate or negotiations—because they respected and liked him. Consequently, as time passed, he could point to the policy results of his accommodationist approach to minority politics.

Dirksen was self-conscious about his leadership, especially when it came to bringing along his GOP colleagues. He felt that patience and kindness were paramount:

You have to hear them out. You have to be careful not to be too precipitous or capricious in pointing out what the weakness of the other fellow's case may be, especially if he is on your side of the aisle, politically speaking. So that requires, I think, gentle discussion and a very gentle "oilcan" art, as I call it, so that the bearings never get hot.[61]

In sum, Dirksen centralized the minority leadership, albeit informally, under his dramatic, cajoling persona and capitalized on his productive ties to the Democratic leadership and all the presidents with whom he served. Beyond this, he offered new and meaningful roles to all the Republican senators who wished to participate actively. Ironically, much of his strength derived from the small size of the Senate minority. With only thirty-two or thirty-four senators, the Republicans could barely cover all the committees and subcommittees that were processing the activist Democratic agenda. Frequently, it was only on the floor that proposals were subject to close scrutiny from opponents, in part because of the potential for extended debate. With the elections of 1966, and especially 1968, Dirksen received reinforcements of energetic Republican senators, coupled in that latter year with the election of Richard Nixon. A new era had begun, and Dirksen was no longer the focal point of Republicanism in Washington.

Dirksen in Decline

Although 1968 brought a Republican resurgence in the Senate and Nixon's capture of the presidency, Dirksen's leadership strength had begun waning. The key components of his hold on power—his ties to the president, his encouragement of participation by all senators, his unwillingness to twist arms, his sense of the dramatic—worked to Dirksen's disadvantage during his last three years as leader. In addition, his health, never robust, began to suffer. Having always relied on his willingness and ability to outwork his peers, Dirksen increasingly found himself lacking the physical reserves he needed to accomplish all he wished—a decline most senators perceived.[62]

The Republican senators elected in 1966 and 1968 tilted the party's balance toward policy moderation. Senators such as Charles Percy (Illinois), Charles Mathias (Maryland), Edward Brooke (Massachusetts), Mark Hatfield (Oregon), and Bob Packwood (Oregon) were both more liberal and more independent-minded than most sitting Republican senators. They were reluctant to have Dirksen speak for them. Not only was the message different from what they might have preferred, but the style also rubbed them the wrong way. Even Dirksen's ties to the White House, essentially defined by his unstinting support for Lyndon Johnson's war, were viewed with mistrust.

Dirksen's centralized, personalized style also worked against him in the last few years, and especially in 1969. In 1968, when Johnson nominated Abe Fortas to be Chief Justice, Dirksen announced his early support for Fortas, despite the displeasure of many Republicans.[63] Michigan's Robert Griffin led the dissidents and rallied a firm majority of Republican senators around his position. Dirksen was forced to back off from his commitment to Fortas (and Johnson).

After Thomas Kuchel's (R-Calif.) defeat in 1968, Dirksen sought to move his good friend Roman Hruska (R-Neb.) into the minority whip position. As former secretary of the Senate William Hildenbrand reported:

He made no bones that he wanted Hruska to be the next majority leader. Some of the members said, you know, he ain't picking his successor.... So they voted against him. I think Dirksen was more surprised than anyone else that it turned out that way.... [The problem] wasn't a philosophical one so much as it was that the ties were so close that they just wanted some independence. The way to do that was to vote for [Hugh] Scott [R-Pa.].[64]

Scott defeated Hruska, 23-20, and for the remainder of his leadership never felt close to Dirksen. Even when the minority leader was hospitalized, Dirksen's friends made it difficult for Scott to function effectively.

Still, if Dirksen was not the force he once was, he retained the capacity, on occasion, to work hard and effectively. One former senator recalled that "he didn't have the vim and vitality that he once had, so there was some fall off in effectiveness.... [But] when he wanted to go to work, he could still do it, as well as ever. He was working on legislation right up to the time of his death."[65]

Finally, when Richard Nixon was elected president in 1968, Dirksen lost two key elements of his leadership. First, he no longer had a close and trusted friend in the White House. Nixon did not confer privately with Dirksen in the months before he took the oath of office.[66] One senator concluded that he saw Dirksen as "loyal to Nixon, but there was no close association with him,"[67] which was the norm for most Republicans. Beyond losing his ties to the White House, Dirksen also lost his status as the capital's leading Republican spokesman. Rather, he was now in the position of having to defend the president's program on Capitol Hill. Thus, in his last few months as minority leader, institutional and personal dynamics conspired to diminish Dirksen's power.

The Dirksen Leadership in Perspective

Any assessment of Dirksen as Senate leader revolves around two related questions. First, would he and his fellow partisans have been better served by offering clear, perhaps ideologically driven, policy alternatives to the Democrats' profuse initiatives of the 1960s? And second, did Dirksen's emphases on legislating, negotiating, and cooperating make him an effective leader?

"I Am a Legislator"

The MacNeil biography of Dirksen begins with the senator's flat statement: "I am not a moralist. I am a legislator."[68] Uncharacteristically parsimonious, this dual assertion defines the essence of the Dirksen leadership. During his tenure, Senate Republicans advanced few overall policy proposals of their own. In part, this stemmed from their one-third minorities, which gave them few opportunities to set the Senate agenda, especially with a pair of activist Democratic presidents. At least as important, however, was Dirksen's aversion to full-scale confrontation, as opposed to the regular give and take of Senate debate.

Dirksen sought to stake out as much common ground as he could on a given issue and then to expand that territory. As former senator Paul Fannin (R-Ariz.) pointed out:

Our legislation was more positive through his efforts than through those of any other person. He had the ability to bring people together, through compromise, through amendments that addressed their concerns. He could reduce inequities in legislation without upsetting the interests of any given senator.[69]

The absence of Republican alternatives bothered some senators. One legislator complained in the late 1960s: "We don't have [a Republican position]. Nobody has ever done it. I think it's a terrible mistake."[70] Still, the temper of the Senate minority of the 1960s was far more attuned to Dirksen's cooperative approach than to Senator Barry Goldwater's (R-

Ariz.) confrontational style. Goldwater's crushing presidential defeat in 1964 did little to convince Dirksen and his colleagues that presenting comprehensive alternatives was worthwhile. Dirksen "did not want to be tied to one position when negotiating in the majority-building process in the Senate," notes Charles O. Jones. Instead, "his style was one of remaining vague on an issue, or taking a position from which he could negotiate with the majority party, the president, and his own colleagues, and eventually accepting a compromise."[71]

Under Dirksen's leadership, Senate Republicans not only shied away from presenting comprehensive options but also voted in support of the president more than their House colleagues.[72] This was significant because, for Dirksen to negotiate effectively, he had to be seen as able to deliver. The 1964 Civil Rights Act exemplifies the Dirksen style of negotiation and compromise, especially when cloture came into play as a realistic possibility.

"The Most Powerful Member of the Senate"

Was Dirksen effective? Could he drive the process? According to contemporaneous interpretations, the answer is an unambiguous "yes." In part, Dirksen's power derived from the singular circumstances of the Democratic leadership. With Mansfield reluctant to lead energetically, with the death in 1963 of Senator Robert Kerr (D-Okla.), and with the weakening of the southern Democrats after the 1958 elections, any minority floor leader would have had the opportunity to act effectively. But it was Dirksen who seized the day with his flexible, accommodating, communicative style. MacNeil argues that "Kerr's death opened the way for Dirksen to become in his own turn the most influential man in the Senate, not merely the leader of the Republican faction there."[73]

Given his influence within the Senate, Dirksen could accommodate the interests of his Republican colleagues and cover them on tough votes. In the wake of the toughest vote of them all, on cloture for the 1964 Civil Rights Act, Senator J. Caleb Boggs (R-Del.) noted that despite his personal support for the bill, "there was a lot of opposition to the bill in my state. Dirksen was a wonderful leader. He was able to understand our problems and operated in such a way that made it easier for me to vote for cloture."[74]

Another Republican senator described Dirksen as "probably the most effective minority leader the party has had since it has been in the minority."[75] Ironically, his effectiveness was partly the result of Senator

Mansfield's unparalleled graciousness as majority leader. "We are in an extraordinary situation," one key Republican bluntly concluded in 1965, "We have a Majority Leader who is generous to the Minority, and a Minority Leader who is the most powerful member of the Senate."[76]

Such encomiums came not only from Republicans. Senator Joseph Clark (D-Pa.) proclaimed, with some bitterness, that in 1964 the civil rights bill "had become the Dirksen bill!"[77] Both Kennedy and Johnson frequently acted as if Dirksen were indispensable, to the extent of granting him numerous political favors and even, with Kennedy in 1962, scarcely lifting a finger to assist Representative Sidney Yates (D-Ill.), who could have given the senator a difficult reelection contest.

Finally, the press generally advanced the notion that Dirksen was a most effective senator. The height of journalistic recognition was reached in the wake of the 1964 Civil Rights Act, but many positive assessments came much earlier. The *New York Times* sang his praises in 1960,[78] and in a *Time* cover story in 1962 Dirksen was described as "the most effective G.O.P. floor leader in a line of succession that includes Oregon's Charles McNary [and all his successors]."[79]

Dirksen's effectiveness had distinct limits, however. He could operate with great leverage when Senate action required a two-thirds majority (cloture and treaties) or when he could affect the shape of legislation at the margins. But when he sought to strike out on his own, on constitutional amendments to allow for prayer in the public schools, for example, or to overturn the Supreme Court's reapportionment decisions, he could not muster adequate support. As MacNeil concludes, Dirksen's skills "brought him a personal power in the Senate that few men before him had ever matched. He could not, necessarily, dictate what the Senate would do, but he had the power when he chose to use it to decide what the Senate would not do."[80]

Dirksen in Retrospect

It is easy to see Everett Dirksen as the last of some mythical breed of Senate giants whose personalities allowed them great influence within the intimate confines of the upper house. Likewise, one can reasonably depict Dirksen as a unique figure whose talents were well suited to the Republicans' minority status in national politics. With his carefully tousled hair, his flair for the dramatic, and his close ties to a succession of presidents, Dirksen was surely one of a kind as a minority floor leader.

Still, viewed from the vantage point of the 1990s, he appears to be more of a transitional figure than he may have seemed to his peers.

The Floor Leader

With one foot planted in the past, as a midwestern Republican conservative, and one foot seeking firm ground in the changing political landscape of the 1960s, Dirksen helped to move the Senate floor leadership, along with Johnson and Mansfield, into the modern era. Like House leaders in the 1970s and 1980s, Dirksen realized that effective leadership could come only to the extent that he could convince his colleagues that it was worth their while to follow his direction. Although not as communicative or accessible as most of his successors, he contrasted sharply with the imperious Taft and Knowland. By ensuring that all Republicans had at least one good committee assignment, he placed all junior members in his debt, where he endeavored to keep them by granting favors and helping them in their campaigns. At the same time, Dirksen did not encourage—or even countenance—the independent, entrepreneurial style that became commonplace in the 1970s. His relations with an independent operator such as Charles Percy (R-Ill.) were consistently rocky. Dirksen correctly perceived that, if senators started to cut their own deals, his leverage with the Democratic leadership, the southern Democrats, and the White House would be severely limited.

In addition to accessibility and communicativeness, Dirksen's most notable contribution to the evolution of legislative leadership was his maintenance of a high public profile. As a result, criteria for selecting present-day floor leaders (such as George Mitchell or Bob Dole) include the ability to present oneself as an attractive, articulate public figure. With the "Ev and Charlie Show" and innumerable appearances on the Capitol steps, Dirksen set the standard here.

Finally, Dirksen's example of forging strong, trusting relationships with a range of key actors played an important role in shaping the subsequent leadership style of Senator Howard Baker, his protégé and son-in-law. Baker noted that in the late 1960s "I didn't have any clear view of how the leadership operated."[81] Rather, what came through was the importance that Dirksen placed on creating relationships in which one's word was a bond.

In short, Dirksen had a substantial impact on the floor leader's position, both through his general example (using the media) and through his specific effects on subsequent leaders, especially Baker. No single senator can be credited, or blamed, for the emergence of the modern floor leader's position. But Dirksen, along with Taft, Johnson, and Mansfield, conducted experiments and made adjustments that have greatly influenced the shape of the job today.

The Historical Figure

No assessment of Dirksen's leadership can be complete without at least passing acknowledgment of his impact on his time. It can reasonably be argued that Dirksen has been the most important minority party figure in the modern, post-1932 American legislative experience. He stood at the center of the civil rights battle and shaped the results of that legislative upheaval. He lent crucial support to Kennedy's Nuclear Test Ban Treaty. Less positively, albeit no less significantly, he offered continuing support for Johnson's prosecution of the Vietnam War.

Within the Senate, Dirksen demonstrated that there could be strong leadership without browbeating, that real affection could exist alongside tough legislative negotiations. However speculative, it is most interesting to note that in 1990 such students of the chamber as Howard Baker and Neil MacNeil could forcefully contend that a Dirksen would be able to provide effective leadership in today's fractious, individualistic Senate. We will never know, of course, but such a contention may represent the greatest praise of all for Dirksen's leadership.

NOTES

1. Neil MacNeil, *Dirksen: Portrait of a Public Man* (New York: World, 1970), 389.
2. "Dirksen 'Image' Admired by All," UPI clipping, Dirksen files, n.d., Dirksen Congressional Center, Pekin, Illinois.
3. "The Leader," *Time*, September 14, 1962, 27. The authorship is unattributed, but Dirksen's biographer, *Time* congressional correspondent, Neil MacNeil, wrote the piece.
4. EMD radio/tv script, April 16, 1961.
5. Roger H. Davidson, "The Senate: If Everyone Leads, Who Follows?," in *Congress Reconsidered*, 4th ed., ed. Lawrence C. Dodd and Bruce I. Oppenheimer (Washington, D.C.: CQ Press, 1989), 275.
6. William S. White, *Citadel: The Story of the U.S. Senate* (New York: Harper and Brothers, 1956), 21.
7. Donald R. Matthews, *U.S. Senators and Their World* (New York: Random House, 1960), 113.
8. Barbara Sinclair, *The Transformation of the U.S. Senate* (Baltimore: Johns Hopkins University Press, 1989), 28.
9. Matthews, *U.S. Senators*, 82.
10. Randall B. Ripley, *Power in the Senate* (New York: St. Martin's, 1969), 229.
11. See, among others, Ripley, *Power in the Senate*; James Sundquist, *Politics and Policy*

(Washington, D.C.: Brookings, 1968); Rowland Evans and Robert Novak, *Lyndon B. Johnson: The Exercise of Power* (New York: New American Library, 1966); and Ralph K. Huitt, "Democratic Party Leadership in the Senate," *American Political Science Review* 55 (June 1961): 331–344.

12. Huitt, "Democratic Party Leadership," 331–344.
13. Ibid., 344.
14. Alaskan senators joined the chamber in January 1959, and those from Hawaii in August of that year.
15. Randall B. Ripley, "Power in the Post–World War II Senate," in *Studies of Congress,* ed. Glenn R. Parker (Washington, D.C.: CQ Press, 1985), 308.
16. Sinclair, *Transformation of the U.S. Senate,* 42.
17. Steven S. Smith, *Call to Order: Floor Politics in the House and Senate* (Washington, D.C.: Brookings, 1989), 88ff.
18. See Sinclair, *Transformation of the U.S. Senate,* chap. 4; Kay Lehman Schlozman and John T. Tierney, *Organized Interests and American Democracy* (New York: Harper and Row, 1986).
19. The discussion of Dirksen's career is based on MacNeil, *Dirksen;* Edward L. Schapsmeier and Frederick H. Schapsmeier, *Dirksen of Illinois: Senatorial Statesman* (Urbana: University of Illinois Press, 1985); and Jean Torcom Cronin, "Minority Leadership in the United States Senate: The Role and Style of Everett Dirksen" (Ph.D. diss., Department of Political Science, Johns Hopkins University, 1973).
20. MacNeil, *Dirksen,* 73ff.
21. Howard Baker, interview with the author, February 5, 1990.
22. Schapsmeier and Schapsmeier, *Dirksen of Illinois,* 13; MacNeil, *Dirksen,* 31.
23. Louella Dirksen, *The Honorable Mr. Marigold: My Life with Everett Dirksen* (Garden City, N.Y.: Doubleday, 1972), 118.
24. Quoted in Schapsmeier and Schapsmeier, *Dirksen of Illinois,* 18.
25. Cronin, "Minority Leadership," 238–240. James W. Wadsworth, Jr. (R-N.Y.), came in first.
26. MacNeil, *Dirksen,* 88–89.
27. Ibid., 67.
28. Cronin, "Minority Leadership," 244.
29. MacNeil, *Dirksen,* 128.
30. Eisenhower's letter quoted in Fred I. Greenstein, *The Hidden-Hand Presidency* (New York: Basic Books, 1982), 79.
31. MacNeil, *Dirksen,* 134ff, and, generally, chap. 7.
32. Ibid., 147.
33. Ibid., 148.
34. *New York Times,* April 4, 1960, quoted in Cronin, "Minority Leadership," 307.
35. Cronin, "Minority Leadership," 326.
36. Ibid., 63.
37. Ibid., 64ff; see also Charles O. Jones, *The Minority Party in Congress* (Boston: Little, Brown, 1970), and Matthews, *U.S. Senators and Their World.*
38. Schapsmeier and Schapsmeier, *Dirksen of Illinois,* 131–132.
39. This remark was made during roundtable discussions held at the Brookings Institution in 1965, 245. Republican senators, Democratic senators, and staffs from each party met in separate groups. This material helped to shape much of Randall Ripley's *Power in the Senate.* Quotations drawn from these sessions are henceforth cited as Brookings Roundtable Transcripts. The author is grateful to the Brookings Institution and to Professor Ripley for providing access to these valuable documents. Participants were guaranteed anonymity.
40. Brookings Roundtable Transcripts, 250.
41. Ibid., 100.
42. Schapsmeier and Schapsmeier, *Dirksen of Illinois,* 131.
43. MacNeil, *Dirksen,* 188–189.
44. Charles McDowell, Jr., press release, March 14, 1963.

45. Stephen Hess, *The Ultimate Insiders: U.S. Senators in the National Media* (Washington, D.C.: Brookings, 1986), 122.
46. Ibid., 118–142. Only Robert Dole in the late 1980s replicated the Dirksen performance as minority leader. See Joe Foote, "House Members Don't Sell in Prime Time," *Roll Call*, March 15, 1990, 9.
47. Senator James Pearson, interview with author, November 20, 1989.
48. MacNeil, *Dirksen*, 186.
49. Ibid., 190.
50. From former secretary of the Senate William F. Hildenbrand, oral history interviews, Senate Historical Office, March 20–May 6, 1985, 63.
51. MacNeil, *Dirksen*, 312.
52. Pearson, interview with author.
53. Brookings Roundtable Transcripts, 626.
54. Ibid., 455.
55. Barbara Sinclair, *Majority Leadership in the U.S. House* (Baltimore: Johns Hopkins University Press, 1983).
56. Brookings Roundtable Transcripts, 270.
57. Pearson, interview with author.
58. See John Manley, *The Politics of Finance* (Boston: Little, Brown, 1970).
59. Quoted in Cronin, "Minority Leadership," 170, although she notes a tougher instance in a later discussion (364).
60. Personal interview with author, November 21, 1989. Interviewees were guaranteed anonymity.
61. Quoted in Cronin, "Minority Leadership," 356.
62. Ibid., 357ff.
63. See MacNeil, *Dirksen*, 332–336.
64. Hildenbrand, 89.
65. Personal interview with author, November 29, 1989.
66. Ibid., 343.
67. Personal interview with author, November 29, 1989.
68. MacNeil, *Dirksen*, 1.
69. Paul Fannin, interview with author, November 29, 1989.
70. Brookings Roundtable Transcripts, 267.
71. Jones, *Minority Party in Congress*, 168.
72. Ibid., 188.
73. MacNeil, *Dirksen*, 212.
74. Quoted in Charles Whalen and Barbara Whalen, *The Longest Debate* (New York: New American Library, 1985), 205.
75. Brookings Roundtable Transcripts, 270.
76. Ibid., 129.
77. Whalen, *Longest Debate*, 173.
78. Cronin, "Minority Leadership," 307.
79. *Time*, September 4, 1962, 27.
80. MacNeil, *Dirksen*, 270.
81. Howard Baker, interview with author, February 5, 1990.

CHAPTER 9

Mike Mansfield and the Birth of the Modern Senate

Ross K. Baker

T hat miracle of political engi-
neering, the Kennedy-Johnson ticket for the 1960 presidential election, had just been performed, when, wandering through
the crowds at the convention, a staff
member for Lyndon Johnson spied
Mike Mansfield, the Senate whip.
He approached the taciturn Mon-
tanan and announced grandly, "Well,
Senator, I guess you're going to be
the majority leader." Mansfield, looking glum, pulled on his pipe and
then said mournfully, "I don't *want*
to be majority leader."[1]

From most other politicians, such
an expression of unwillingness to
serve in an exalted post might be
viewed with suspicion as false mod-
esty, but with Mansfield the account
rings true. He never openly sought
power or position. But even if leadership was thrust on him, Mansfield
presided over one of the golden ages
of the U.S. Senate—a period that
revolutionized social relations in the
United States and witnessed the

*Mike Mansfield's quiet, egalitarian style of
floor leadership contrasted sharply with his
predecessor's ostentatious rule.*

high-water mark of American dominance of the international scene. But even Mansfield's greatest booster would not insist that he had brought any of this about. At the same time, however, Mansfield's most uncharitable detractor would not disparage his imprint as negligible.

The imprint is not self-evident, however. It requires interpretation, especially in the context of a nation undergoing great change and of a Senate in transition.

The Making of a Politician

Mike Mansfield was a child of the twentieth century, born in Manhattan to an Irish immigrant family on March 16, 1903. His mother died when he was six, and he was sent to live with his paternal uncle and his wife in Butte, Montana. The family was deeply devout and imposed on young Mansfield a stern discipline that evidently caused him at the age of eleven to run away from home for the first time. At school, he appears to have been an indifferent student. Finally, in 1917, he forged his date of birth on a U.S. Navy enlistment form and headed for boot camp at Newport, Rhode Island.[2]

Mansfield saw sea duty in the navy, but little of the world, so he signed up for a hitch in the marines after World War I and was assigned to a post in the Philippines. It was his first exposure to Asia, a part of the world with which he would be associated for his entire political life. In 1921, Mansfield's unit was dispatched to the port city of Tianjin, China, to protect American interests there in the wake of unrest in and around Beijing. Mansfield spent only six days in China, but the experience, as limited as it was, served in later years to give him credentials as a China hand.[3]

In the 1920s, Mansfield worked in the Butte copper mines, an experience that convinced him that only with a college education could he escape the hard life of a miner. He enrolled at the Montana State University in Missoula at the depths of the Great Depression in 1930, was graduated in 1933, became a teaching assistant in the history department, and wrote a thesis on U.S.-Korean relations for a master's degree that he earned in 1934.

During the latter part of the 1930s, Mansfield took his first steps toward political involvement by becoming active in the teachers' union at the university. His wife, Maureen, whom he had married in 1932, encouraged him to seek the U.S. House seat from Montana's First District.[4] He entered the Democratic congressional primary in 1940. The seat, which had changed hands several times, was being relinquished by Republican Jacob Thorkelson, who had been elected in the strong Republican year of 1938 but had lost his bid for renomination to Jeannette Rankin. Rankin's most likely challenger was Democrat Jerry O'Connell, who had himself lost the seat to Thorkelson in 1938. Mansfield finished third in the primary; and the victor O'Connell went on to lose to Rankin in the general election.

The Rankin victory strengthened the ranks of the Progressive-isolationists in the Montana congressional delegation. In fact, Montana senator Burton K. Wheeler was one of the preeminent figures in the efforts to keep the United States out of the conflicts in Europe and Asia. Mansfield had tried to get Wheeler's endorsement in the primary, but Wheeler rebuffed him even though Mansfield had privately secured the endorsement of the state's other Democratic senator, James E. Murray.[5]

With characteristic diligence and a sense of responsibility, Mansfield had attempted both to wage a vigorous campaign and to maintain his duties at the university teaching history and political science. He was well-liked by virtually everyone on campus, but some detected a quality in him that, later, his few detractors would criticize: "He tried too hard to be all things to all people," writes Charles Hood. "One former student remembered that [Mansfield] was skillful enough at 'fence-straddling' that he gave the impression that he agreed with both sides of a faculty controversy."[6] But Mansfield's ability to be ingratiating also enabled him to conduct successful grass-roots campaigns that involved a great deal of face-to-face contact with voters. This paid off for him in his second run for the House in 1942.

Jeannette Rankin cast the sole negative vote against declaring war on Japan on December 7, 1941, and declined to seek another term in 1942. In contrast to the 1940 race, Mansfield's opponents in the ensuing campaign enjoyed no advantage over him in name recognition. He easily defeated four rivals for the Democratic nomination and went on to defeat newspaperman H. K. Hazelbaker in the general election.

House Member and Asia Expert

Mansfield sought and obtained a seat on the House Committee on Foreign Affairs, a surprising choice for a Montana representative. He took his place along with another freshman who would leave his mark on American diplomacy, J. William Fulbright of Arkansas.

Though Mansfield's self-effacing demeanor is legendary, he proved to be a highly competent headline grabber. His floor speeches on the war in the Pacific were so effective that NBC and CBS asked him to deliver a radio address on the subject. Whether Mansfield advanced himself as a Far East expert or simply did not deny the credentials when they were attributed to him is a matter of interesting speculation. At the very least, by 1944 the mantle of expertise had fallen on him, and President Franklin D. Roosevelt asked him to undertake a fact-finding mission to China.[7]

Mansfield's trip to China and India, and his subsequent report to Roosevelt on conditions there, gave him indisputable credentials. But, although he relished his role as a foreign policy expert, he attended diligently to Montana matters, especially the effort to prevent the Army Corps of Engineers from raising the water level in Flathead Lake to generate hydroelectric power. In Washington, however, he was seen as a politician with an international outlook; he was even offered the post of assistant secretary of state by President Harry S. Truman.[8]

Mansfield declined the honor. He had his eye on the Senate, an ambition that meant a race against Republican Senate incumbent Zales Ecton in the 1952 election. Mansfield's challenge to the ultraconservative Ecton provoked intervention in the campaign by Senator Joseph R. McCarthy of Wisconsin, then at the height of his attacks on alleged Communist influence in government. McCarthy dispatched his aide, Harvey Matusow, to Montana. Matusow would later admit his job was to conduct a smear campaign against Mansfield. Brandishing bogus documents, Matusow expressed McCarthy's warning that if Mansfield were elected, "you might as well have an admitted communist in the Senate. It's the same difference."[9]

McCarthy's rage against Mansfield stemmed not only from the threat he posed to a McCarthy ally but also from Mansfield's association with the Roosevelt-Truman policy on China. The accusations against Mansfield resulted in the closest election victory Mansfield would ever experience—he defeated Ecton by five thousand votes.

Freshman Mansfield's Senate

A photo of three United States senators playing softball on a Georgetown athletic field captures more of the essence of Mike Mansfield the

This softball game offers a panorama of some of the eminent members of the Senate class of 1952; Henry Jackson, the earnest legislator; John Kennedy, the elegant charmer; and Mike Mansfield, the dutiful umpire.

senator than any speech or statement. Swinging with grim intensity at the blur of a softball is one member of the Democratic freshman class of 1952, Henry M. "Scoop" Jackson of Washington. Behind the plate as catcher, and using a battered fielder's mitt on his left hand, is another freshman, John F. Kennedy of Massachusetts. Dressed with informal elegance in Bermuda shorts, a white Oxford button-down shirt, and espadrille shoes, Kennedy would have been equally well attired for an afternoon of sailing. Behind Kennedy, serving as umpire, is a thin-lipped man whose outstretched arm indicates that he is calling a strike on Jackson. The umpire is Mike Mansfield. There is the panorama of some of the eminent members of the class of 1952: Jackson, the earnest legislator; Kennedy, the elegant charmer; and Mansfield, the dutiful umpire.

The Senate encountered by these three freshmen in 1953 was, for the Democrats, not an entirely happy one. A Republican president occupied the White House for the first time since 1933. The GOP had majorities, albeit slim ones, in both the House and the Senate—the latter's partisan breakdown was forty-eight Republicans, forty-seven Democrats, and one independent. One of the most conspicuous Democratic casualties was Ernest W. McFarland of Arizona, majority leader in the previous Congress, who had lost to newcomer Barry Goldwater. The loss of McFarland triggered a move on the part of Lyndon B. Johnson, Texas sophomore senator, for the post. Johnson's only competitor was Mansfield's Montana colleague, James E. Murray, who was being supported by Senate liberals. Although Mansfield might have been expected to support Murray, he was in fact one of Johnson's early supporters. Once elected, Johnson designated Earle Clements of Kentucky as party whip and proceeded to solidify his hold over the six new Democratic senators by assigning them major committees. Mansfield received a seat on the Foreign Relations Committee. When Clements was defeated in 1956, this solemn freshman senator was thrust suddenly into a leadership race.

On the Leadership Ladder: Mike Mansfield as Whip

There are several versions of how Johnson came to choose Mansfield as party whip in 1957. The most popular version is that Johnson's first choice, George Smathers of Florida, was unacceptable to Johnson's ally and fellow Texan, House Speaker Sam Rayburn. According to some accounts, Johnson had to settle for Clements as whip in 1953 after Rayburn had vetoed Smathers for what the Speaker regarded as unprincipled attacks on Claude Pepper in the 1950 Florida Democratic primary.[10]

Although Rayburn's displeasure may have prevented Smathers's selection in 1953, it is unlikely that Smathers would have been passed over again. For one thing, Smathers had been acting whip for most of 1956 while Clements was home in Kentucky trying to shore up his crumbling political base. Johnson was also personally fond of Smathers and had come to depend on him after his heart attack in 1955. Smathers was also a favorite of Georgia's Richard Russell, Johnson's mentor and confidant. Smathers, moreover, had some of the political characteristics that Johnson wanted for the impending struggle over a civil rights bill. What seems most likely is that Smathers simply took himself out of the race. Having served the hard-driving Johnson for the period of Clements's absence, he was simply worn out. As he explained it:

Frank Lausche [D-Ohio] came to me after Earle Clements had been defeated and said, "You've got to stay in there and be the whip. You're the only thing standing between us and rebellion." So I said "How about Mansfield?" and Lausche said, "I don't think Mansfield can stand up to Johnson and somebody's got to stand up to him." So I said, "I've been standing up to him so long that I'm bloody.[11]

A related explanation is provided by Harry McPherson, then serving as an aide to Johnson:

The fact that Johnson chose Mansfield said a lot about Johnson's sense of where the Democratic Party had to go if he was to become a national leader. If he had chosen Smathers, who was a favorite of Dick Russell's, it would have been the South's revenge for Appomattox. The Southerners would have been in control not only of most of the major committees but the majority leader and majority whip as well.[12]

Johnson was said to have considered Hubert Humphrey for the job of whip but concluded that the Minnesotan would be more useful as his emissary to the Senate liberals if he were not officially part of Johnson's leadership group. At Smathers's suggestion, Johnson turned to Mansfield, who also rejected his offer, saying he preferred to concentrate on his work on the Foreign Relations Committee. Johnson persisted, giving Mansfield the left-handed compliment that he would be the least objectionable candidate. "It was not a flattering argument," Mansfield said, "but after several meetings I finally lost my resolve against becoming whip."[13]

As whip to an activist floor leader, Mansfield had a limited role and even more limited visibility in the four final years of the Johnson leadership. Johnson haunted the floor, fashioned the meticulous bipartisan coalitions that characterized his narrow but significant victories in the period from 1955 to 1958. Johnson, with the energetic assistance of Bobby Baker, did not need or want an aggressive whip. What he needed, writes Harry McPherson, was "a reliable man who could manage the flow of legislation in his absence."[14]

If Mansfield was *primus inter pares* among the Johnson lieutenants, his primacy was infinitesimal. Hubert Humphrey was clearly Johnson's preferred nuncio to the liberal bloc of senators, who were persistent critics of Johnson and his wary approach to devising Democratic alternatives to legislative initiatives being issued by the popular Republican in the

White House, Dwight Eisenhower. But Mansfield also functioned as emissary to the liberals, sometimes for the unenviable purpose of bringing bad news. Johnson used him to convey his decrees after the Democratic triumph in 1958 that brought fifteen Democratic freshmen to the Senate and some factional wrangling.

Shortly after the election Joseph S. Clark of Pennsylvania sent Johnson a letter. It called for an end to the southern and western members' domination of the Democratic Policy Committee and the party's Steering Committee and urged an expanded role for northeastern and midwestern senators. Clark's letter was leaked to the press, and a distressed Johnson delegated to Mansfield the job of saying "no" to Clark. Mansfield did so in a letter dated December 9, 1958, instructing Clark to look to the "leadership and parliamentary skill of Lyndon Johnson" rather than to structural reform of the party committees.[15]

A Senate in Transition: From Johnson to Mansfield

The year 1958 saw an important series of changes both in the institution of the Senate and in the personal fortunes of both Johnson and his protégé Mansfield. Johnson's approach to the job of leadership for the first four years had been to push constructive but typically modest legislation with slender majorities. His legendary ability to assemble the necessary majorities (which gave him a reputation as a legislative magician) was based both on his own distinctive styles of persuasion and on the Senate's peculiar political configurations in the 1954–1958 period. He assiduously courted the elderly southerners who dominated the chairmanships and fashioned legislation to meet their approval primarily to prevent, writes McPherson, "Dick Russell from walking across the aisle and embracing Everett Dirksen."[16]

The need to refrain from estranging conservative southern Democrats like Russell became less acute after the election of 1958. That decisive event, for both Johnson and Mansfield, increased Senate Democratic majorities from forty-nine to sixty-four.

The number of Senate Democrats, impressive as it was, told only part of the story. Their composition had changed as well: southerners dropped from 42 percent to about 33 percent, and none of the fifteen freshman Democrats elected in 1958 was from the South. But the hardcore conservative southern Democrats had been shrinking for some time as nonsegregationists such as Tennessee's Albert Gore and Estes Kefauver were augmented by the likes of J. William Fulbright, George Smathers, Ralph Yarborough, and even Johnson himself, for whom opposition to racial equality was not an article of faith.

With great astuteness and calculation, Johnson had distanced himself from his conservative southern colleagues on some important civil rights votes and was advancing himself in the late 1950s as more of a national than a regional figure. But changes in the Senate's regional and ideological makeup were making his hard-driving leadership and calculated legislative centrism less attractive to his colleagues.

Mike Mansfield recognized this, observing recently that by the late 1950s:

> There was a feeling that the new senators were not being given the opportunity to act as much on their own responsibility as they would like. Lyndon Johnson was an extraordinary Majority Leader and had a style which was productive but, while he served in that capacity, the feeling of unrest was quite apparent among the younger and newer members and even among some of the older ones, as well.[17]

His inclusion on the Kennedy ticket therefore solved a number of Johnson's own problems. Although he certainly would have preferred to have been in the top spot, Johnson was rescued, in a sense, from his own certain decline as floor leader.

A New Leader for a New Senate

Whatever motives Kennedy may have had in choosing Johnson as his running mate, one very concrete benefit was that it removed Johnson from the Senate, where he would have constituted a rival power center. Kennedy knew Mansfield was in line to be floor leader and very much wanted him there. He phoned Mansfield shortly after the election to persuade him to allow his name to be placed before the caucus. Mansfield's notes of the conversation say, "I told [Kennedy] I didn't want to take it. He insisted that I take it—said he had talked it over with Johnson and others, and he wanted me to do it." Mansfield told Kennedy that he would consider it, but gave the impression of being so cool to the idea that Kennedy had Johnson make a follow-up call.[18]

According to Mansfield's notes of that conversation, it went this way:

> Johnson: Listen now, I want you to take this leadership. Everybody wants you to. Have you talked with Jack this morning? Did he tell you the same thing?

Mansfield: I don't want to do it, Lyndon, but I will think it over.
Johnson: Why?
Mansfield: I watched you too long and saw what happened.

Mansfield then suggested that Humphrey or Smathers might be preferable, and Johnson asked: "Do you think they can hold this party together? Now tell the truth." Mansfield replied with his own question: "Do *you* think I can?" Johnson shot back, "I know damn well you can."[19]

Johnson's motives for pressing Mansfield to take the job were not, however, prompted exclusively by solicitude for the party or the Kennedy legislative program. A few days after the victory of the Kennedy-Johnson ticket, the vice president—elect summoned Bobby Baker to his office to announce:

I'm gonna keep this office . . . and help Mike Mansfield and Bob Kerr and Hubert Humphrey pass the Kennedy program. It's gonna be just the way it was. Just between you and me and the gatepost, Bobby, I'm working it out with Mike and Hubert to attend meetings of the Senate Democratic Caucus. Maybe even preside over 'em. That way I can keep my hand in.[20]

So although Mansfield was undoubtedly first in line to succeed to the *formal* title of Democratic floor leader, Johnson was intending to remain de facto Senate leader.

Johnson knew well the limitations of the vice president's job—a point brought home to him in a meeting that took place during the transition. In that meeting, President-elect Kennedy reportedly entreated a still-reluctant Mansfield to take the job as floor leader. Praising Mansfield as "the best catalyst" for the Kennedy program, the president-elect plaintively announced: "I need you."[21]

Johnson, perhaps sensing that his own importance to Kennedy hinged on his mastery of the Senate, prevailed on Mansfield to introduce a resolution that would permit Johnson to preside over the caucus. Mansfield saw the request only as a call for an honorific role, but others viewed it as an unwarranted power grab by a member of the executive branch. Although only a few senators openly attacked the idea and the resolution carried by a 46-17 margin, the mood of the meeting was hostile. Johnson knew it and so did Mansfield. Johnson was hurt because the rejection came from those he once dominated; Mansfield was distressed because he knew he would appear to be no more than a front man for Johnson.[22] Mansfield's agreement to keep two key Johnson aides, Bobby Baker and Harry McPherson, strengthened this impression. It was assumed that they would work in tandem with Robert Kerr, the "uncrowned king of the Senate" and enable Johnson to run the Senate by remote control.

But there was little chance of this happening. Johnson had been rebuffed in his efforts to preside over the caucus; both Baker and McPherson realized that Mansfield was something totally new in the order of things:

Johnson was the ideal opposition leader; Mansfield would be the perfect team player. The Policy Committee staff and all the other paraphernalia of Johnson's leadership, swollen to serve as a shadow government in Eisenhower's time, could be reduced to a handful of mechanics.[23]

Although the staffs of the Democratic Policy and Campaign committees were more visible under Johnson, they had more authority under Mansfield. Some believed this created a power vacuum at the top. As Bobby Baker recalled:

Except for two or three hours each day, Mansfield disappeared to private haunts, there to read books and meditate. . . . I was not accustomed to that. . . . Senator Mansfield might not be available when consultations or decisions were required. Or he might suck his pipe and procrastinate rather than make decisions which would assist the flow of Senate business.[24]

Baker's jaundiced assessment of Mansfield is not surprising. Mansfield gets a more generous appraisal from another Johnson hand—one that gets very close to the kernel of Mansfield's influence as party leader in the ensuing sixteen years:

When [Mansfield] became majority leader in 1961, he announced that there would be few night or Saturday sessions, very little pressure on the members, and annual summer vacations. The response was what one might expect from boys in a prep school when an old tyrannical headmaster who believed in the redeeming power of work was replaced by a permissive young don. No more of Johnson's grinding, inexorable debates leading to a vote at 10 P.M. No more round-the-clock sessions, with their continual taste of ashes, their ache of boredom. It was like a holiday for a time, and it inspired cooperation out of gratitude.[25]

It was clear that the Senate was changing. Less clear, however, was how successful Mansfield's gentler approach would be in enacting the legislative program of the Democratic president.

Mansfield and the Kennedy-Johnson Agenda

John Kennedy faced a Democratic Congress whose leaders had, to a man, opposed his nomination. Sam Rayburn, Speaker of the House, and Mansfield were old Johnson supporters. The new Senate Democratic whip, Hubert Humphrey, had been Kennedy's rival in the 1960 Democratic primaries. But while Rayburn needed considerable stroking, Mansfield required no propitiation. In fact, he was so accommodating that when White House congressional liaison Lawrence O'Brien needed working space on Capitol Hill, Mansfield offered one of his conference rooms.[26] But despite the 65-35 Democratic margin in the Senate and the goodwill of Mansfield, the conservative coalition of Republicans and southerners was still intact, especially in the House.

That the Senate was, in general, a more relaxed and friendly institution did not help Kennedy's legislative program as much as the large Democratic margin might suggest. For one thing, Kennedy had provided no coattails for Democratic Senate candidates. The great Democratic surge of 1958 had abated. For the first time in the century, the party of an incoming president had failed to increase the number of its seats in Congress. The limited success of the Kennedy legislative program in the Eighty-seventh Congress may also be attributed to an inhospitable House of Representatives, still largely controlled by the conservative coalition of southern Democrats and Republicans. Success in the Senate did not ensure victory in the House. Even in the Senate, Kennedy strategists estimated that proadministration Democrats held less than 50 percent of the seats. This, combined with the certain use of the filibuster by southern members, prompted Mansfield to advise the president not to submit a civil rights bill in 1961. He also counseled Kennedy against intervening in the Senate to curb the use of the filibuster. Such an intrusion, he argued, would antagonize some friendly western senators.[27]

High on Kennedy's legislative agenda was a Medicare bill. After a fierce struggle in the Senate, the measure was tabled on July 17, 1961. Kennedy blamed this setback, in part, on Mansfield's "excessive pessimism, caution and delays," while others, such as biographer Theodore C. Sorensen, concluded that the president undercut his own effectiveness by being too deferential to senior members of Congress.[28]

By 1962, both Kennedy and Mansfield were more seasoned, and they developed a more personal relationship. According to one observer, it went beyond simple personal liking to a broader kind of kinship.

It occurred to me at the time that John McCormack was now Speaker, Mansfield was Majority Leader and JFK was president. And I had the strongest feeling that Mansfield was delighted by this.

I always thought there was a "we-ness" about Irish Catholics—I don't mean that in any conspiratorial sense—but in the same sense that when the old Texas crowd got together that there was a sense of "we-ness."[29]

But for all his personal affection for the president and even his ethnic pride, "Mansfield had no desire for the Senate or its members simply to become functionaries of the New Frontier. He considered it feasible to operate in a manner which testified to his loyalty both to the president and to the Senate."[30]

The Mansfield Style of Leadership

To talk of a Mansfield "theory of leadership" is, perhaps, to overformalize what was really more of an instinct. According to Edmund S. Muskie of Maine, who had abundant opportunity to observe the early Mansfield years:

Mansfield simply did not view the Senate as an instrument of its leadership. He felt that the way to make the Senate effective was simply to let it work its will. And he believed that the Senate would do just that. And he also believed that senators would rise to that responsibility if it was made clear to them that their responsibility was important.[31]

How did the Mansfield approach work with senators? His former colleague, Herman Talmadge of Georgia, provides an example.

I used to get to my office early every morning to work on my mail and get ready before committee hearings. One morning the phone rang (I guess it was about 9:15), and Mansfield was on the line. He said to me, "Herman, will you serve on the Watergate Committee?"

Of course it took me totally by surprise. I was not a candidate for the committee and had not requested an assignment to it.

I said, "Mike, you know my burdens are already very heavy. I'm chairman of a major committee. I'm vice-chairman of the Finance Committee. I'm number-two man on the Joint Committee on Taxation. I serve on the Democratic Policy Committee." And went on at some length about the heaviness of my burdens.

So he says, "Herman, will you serve on the Watergate Committee?"

And I replied, "Mike, since you put it that way, of course you must know I cannot refuse."

That was the way Mansfield operated. He didn't change a damn word or argue a damn bit. He just repeated the question as if I'd never even raised every objection I could think of.[32]

For some colleagues used to LBJ's energetic persuasive style, Mansfield's quiet persistence seemed curious—even upsetting. They felt the Senate was drifting and that the legislative process needed a more forceful hand. "I don't want to say that the Mansfield style was good or bad," observed Nevada's Howard Cannon, in politic fashion, "but it sure took a hell of a lot longer to get things out of Congress."[33]

Such comments, common among Johnson loyalists, emphasize a standard of legislative efficiency that was only one of Mansfield's goals. He strongly supported the legislative programs of the two Democratic presidents with whom he served, but was primarily devoted to strengthening the U.S. Senate as an assembly of equals. Mansfield rejected the concept of the Senate promoted by Johnson and publicized by journalist William S. White that, "The inner life of the Senate . . . is controlled by the Inner Club."[34] Rather, he believed (as Eugene McCarthy put it) that "there should be no particular groupings, no cliques, no inner circle among them, no establishment within the establishment."[35]

Party Structure and Function Under Mansfield

Mansfield's concept of leadership was reflected in his organization of the formal party apparatus of the Senate. Those who had chafed most conspicuously under LBJ's forceful leadership were particularly critical of his neglect of the Democratic Conference—familiarly known as "the Caucus"—as a forum for developing the party's legislative strategy. Mansfield, in contrast, saw the conference as a useful place both to get a sense of the Democrats' opinions and to iron out routine matters. The conference also allowed individual senators to expound their own views and positions to colleagues.[36] Using the conference in this manner accorded with Mansfield's vision of the chamber as a Senate of equals. But as the line demarcating the "inner club" from everyone else began to fade, so did the importance of the conference. What Johnson had initiated with his rule that every senator was entitled to serve on a major committee and what Mansfield advanced through his relentless insistence on senatorial equality was an individualism that eroded the caucus's power. By the end of Mansfield's career as leader, "caucus meetings attracted either small groups of senators who were already involved in a particular issue, or large groups of members who were wary of foreclosing their personal options in front of such a wide audience."[37]

Dramatic changes occurred in the other two principal party committees as well. Seats on the Steering Committee, which made Democratic committee assignments, and the Policy Committee, which drew up the legislative schedule, had been assigned by Johnson and were subject to only *pro forma* conference ratification. In 1961, however, the conference adopted a resolution, introduced by William Proxmire, that mandated regional and philosophical balance on all party committees. The resolution also required the Democratic floor leader to consult with other party leaders before recommending a member for service on a party panel. Interestingly, John Stewart observes that had the Proxmire resolution not passed, Mansfield would have discontinued Johnson's unilateral nomination practices.[38]

The Policy Committee was radically transformed from a panel whose function was to solidify support for policies already determined by the floor leader to one of ascertaining where members stood and then building a consensus. After determining the extent of agreement on a bill, Mansfield would draw up a schedule for floor debate. He would then delegate the job of resolving remaining minor or technical obstacles to the bill's principal proponents or opponents. Priority legislation sent up by the administration was invariably put on a fast track, and few bills were denied clearance because Policy Committee members opposed them.[39]

Equally dramatic were the changes in the Steering Committee, which came to be marked by diligent staff work and a sincere effort to bring individuals' requests for committee assignments into harmony with party needs, geographic and philosophical balance, and qualifications. In the few cases where staff recommendations were rejected, the committee labored to produce a consensus and then to ratify it by secret ballot. One can see Mansfield's deliberate effort to extricate the floor leader from decisions best made, in his view, collegially.[40]

Perhaps the least popular Mansfield reform concerned head counts on forthcoming legislation. Johnson had used the leadership staffs to gather all manner of intelligence, but Mansfield halted the practice of head counts, and the task fell to the congressional liaison staffs of the White House. This deprived the Senate leadership of advance notice about the outcome of votes. At the same time, Mansfield brought back little in the way of information to the Senate when he returned from his visits to the White House, a practice that prompted one student of the Senate to conclude: "A leader who dominates the flow of information can strengthen his hand. A leader who ignores the flow of information weakens his position."[41]

But here again, an egalitarian logic was at work. Although it is true that the absence of a tightly centralized head-count operation made it, as Stewart observes:

more difficult to receive advance warnings of potential trouble, and less information . . . about ways to resolve these difficulties once they were known, . . . the business of floor leadership became more of a collective enterprise and drew upon the talents of lesser party officers.[42]

As Edmund S. Muskie notes: "Mike Mansfield delegated his leadership to the Senate."[43]

Mansfield's conviction that the Senate needed to work its own will was also expressed in his scrupulous impartiality vis-à-vis the contests that produced his lieutenants. From 1961 until 1965 the majority whip, or deputy floor leader, was Hubert Humphrey, whose boundless energy and persuasive disposition gave him a prominence enjoyed by few whips. When Humphrey left the Senate in 1965 to become vice president, the Senate confronted, not a *diktat*, but a real choice.

Mansfield took no position on the contest waged in which Russell Long of Louisiana (the eventual victor), John Pastore of Rhode Island, Mike Monroney of Oklahoma, and, a last-minute protest candidate, Philip Hart of Michigan, all vied for the whip position. Again in 1969, when Senator Edward M. Kennedy decided to challenge Long, Mansfield gave no encouragement despite his affection for the Kennedy family and his dissatisfaction with Long's performance. Similarly, in 1971 he did nothing to dissuade Robert Byrd from ousting Kennedy.

Mansfield and His Lieutenants

Mansfield's laissez-faire approach magnified the importance of lesser party leaders and enabled them to be groomed for higher posts. Indeed, the four whips who served with Mansfield are recognized as senators of major importance: Humphrey (1961–1965), Long (1965–1969), Kennedy (1969–1971), and Byrd (1971–1977). Of the four, Mansfield was best served by the first and the last.

When Humphrey became vice president in 1965, Russell Long took up the duties of whip. But Long was second-ranking Democrat on the powerful Finance Committee and would accede to the chair in less than a year. Long's attention shifted at once from the duties of the floor to the demands of the committee room. His personal commitment to campaign-finance reform legislation was, moreover, not compatible with Mansfield's own priorities.

The Mansfield-Long relationship was strained. Mansfield considered Long inattentive to his work in the chamber and seriously out of step philosophically with himself and the Johnson administration. Twice in 1967 Long went public with major policy disagreements with the White House. Because Mansfield backed Johnson on both, Long's defiance was seen by Mansfield as directed at him as well.[44] For his part, Long considered Mansfield excessively cautious, overly solicitous of junior members, and unwilling to take on fights that the more combative Long might have tackled.

Long's preoccupation with his duties on the Finance Committee, along with his personal problems, meant that no one in the party's top leadership cared much about floor procedures. The task fell initially to four junior senators who sat on the Legislative Review Committee, a party panel that monitored minor bills for objectionable provisions. These four—Daniel Brewster of Maryland, Edmund Muskie of Maine, Philip Hart of Michigan, and Daniel Inouye of Hawaii—covered the floor in the absence of Mansfield and Long.[45]

This predominantly liberal group was, frankly, neither very interested in floor procedure nor particularly well versed in its intricacies. As Michael Foley observes:

Because of their orientation toward the public and their interest in diverse issue areas, the liberals were thought by some to be not only personally unable to debate a subject in depth, but unwilling to regard floor debate with the same respect as the conservatives.[46]

By 1967 and with the departure of Florida's George A. Smathers from the number-three party post of conference chairman, the responsibility for floor strategy devolved to Robert C. Byrd of West Virginia. Byrd's accession to the post and his mastery of floor procedures were emblematic of one feature of Mansfield's Senate—the prominence of conservative Democratic parliamentarians. With the arrival in 1969 of Alabama's James Allen, the Senate's two most effective floor tacticians until Mansfield's retirement were Byrd and Allen. Even while Russell Long continued to hold the post of whip, he encouraged Byrd to assume more of the responsibilities for floor strategy.

The greatest personal disappointment to Mansfield was Edward Kennedy, who in 1969 defeated Long for the whip post. While remaining scrupulously neutral in the Long-Kennedy contest, Mansfield was reportedly elated at the outcome. "Kennedy," Mansfield proclaimed, "is a link with the younger generation."[47]

But Mansfield's enthusiasm was short-lived. Like Long before him, Kennedy cared little for the drudgery of parliamentary combat and, like Long, was enveloped in personal problems. Responsibility for overseeing the floor continued to rest with Byrd.

But Mansfield's difficulties with his principal lieutenants in the late 1960s were eclipsed by the Senate's many successes. This was surely the most productive era in the recent history of the U.S. Senate. There was a vast outpouring of civil rights and social legislation despite a majority leader who cared little for the details of parliamentary procedure and whips who were distracted or impaired.

To acknowledge this strange concomitance of circumstances prompts us to wonder how it was possible. First, the presidential mandate delivered by the electorate in 1964 was stronger than any other in the twentieth century with the exception of that enjoyed by Franklin Roosevelt in 1936. Lyndon Johnson won with 90 percent of the electoral vote, while Democrats had a net gain of thirty-seven seats in the House and one in the already overwhelmingly Democratic Senate, making the Democratic Senate margin in the Eighty-ninth Congress 68-32 over the Republicans. This margin constituted the third-highest number of Senate Democrats in the twentieth century. Moreover, the conservative coalition of southern Democrats and Republicans had been battered by the diminishing percentage of Democratic seats from the Old South and by the small number of Republicans. Democrats in 1965 gave Johnson strong support irrespective of region. Pushing the unfinished agenda of the assassinated John F. Kennedy and advancing his own agenda aggressively, Johnson was less in need of a strong hand on the tiller of the Senate than presidents with less imposing majorities.

Mansfield himself was a natural ally both of Kennedy and Johnson. In fact, recent data show that Mansfield supported them more than any other majority leader sharing the chief executive's party identification. Only Howard Baker and Bob Dole in the Reagan years gave support approaching that which Mansfield provided the Democratic chief executives of the 1960s.[48]

But there was one legislative initiative confronting the Senate before the 1964 sweep whose outcome was by no means certain—the Civil Rights Act of 1964, passed by the House earlier in the year. The success of this effort was influenced profoundly not only by Mansfield's choice of strategies but also by his decision to turn over the day-to-day job of floor managing the bill to Hubert Humphrey. Mansfield's deferential but shrewd handling of the Republican floor leader, Everett Dirksen, also paid off handsomely.

Bipartisan Relations in the Mansfield Years

Mike Mansfield and Everett Dirksen could hardly have been more different: Mansfield was restrained, even introverted, while Dirksen was flamboyant, often to the point of theatrics; Mansfield's strong suit was his constancy, while Dirksen was positively protean; Mansfield was self-effacing while Dirksen basked in flattery. But antithesis can also imply complementarity, and in the effort to pass a civil rights bill in 1964, the yin and yang of Mansfield and Dirksen produced harmony and success.

Mansfield's decision to place the floor managing of the civil rights bill in Humphrey's hands was not merely a nod to the Minnesotan's long commitment to civil rights and a recognition of his effectiveness in debate. It also gave Mansfield a freer hand to deal with Dirksen and to strike the compromises needed to get the required sixty-seven votes to invoke cloture on what would certainly be a filibuster by southern conservatives.[49]

Mansfield's strategy on the civil rights bill serves as a model for an approach to contested legislation that would prevail throughout his time as leader. Mansfield rejected, as his successor Robert Byrd recounts,

President Johnson's plan to try to wear out filibustering southern senators by enforcing Rule 19, which limited each senator to two speeches during one legislative day. Johnson wanted to keep the Senate in session day and night to wear down the opposition, but Mansfield decided that the best strategy was to go for cloture and he began lining up the necessary sixty-seven votes. . . . This is why Everett Dirksen was so vital to this strategy. Mansfield needed enough Republican votes to compensate for the Democrats who opposed the bill—and a few others who opposed cloture under any circumstances.[50]

Johnson had believed for some time that the southern senators were vulnerable to concerted pressure on civil rights and that a combination of White House muscle and a determined Democratic leadership would easily nudge aside the southern conservatives. Eugene McCarthy witnessed a fascinating encounter earlier between Vice President Johnson

Leadership

According to this Berryman cartoon, the leadership of the Senate rests not with its floor leaders, Everett Dirksen (left) *and Mike Mansfield, but with the institution itself.*

and a group of Democratic senators, and his account illustrates strikingly the difference between the Mansfield and Johnson strategies.

It was early in '63. It was that period in which [Johnson] had nothing to do. We'd had the '62 election and we gained seats, and Lyndon figured we had the strength to put through a civil rights bill.

He got us one day about 5:30, and Johnson and Humphrey, and Muskie, and me, and Phil Hart, and Pat McNamara were talking. And in the course of it Lyndon said, "We ought to have a civil rights fight right now." I recall that the Kennedys had decided to finesse the civil rights issue through the '64 election, but Lyndon wanted to do it then.

He started down the list of southern senators and he began to tick off their various disabilities. He said, "Harry Byrd just got out of the hospital. Allen Ellender just went into the hospital. Dick Russell thinks he's got cancer of the throat, and then there are two or three others who just don't care—Fulbright, Russell Long, maybe Smathers."

He said that "there [are] only two of them who will fight on civil rights and are able-bodied. Mostly they're old and sick. You can break them down in two weeks. You can kill them."

McCarthy then drew the contrast:

It's inconceivable that Mansfield would have uttered those words. He would never say "Attack them when they're weak." He'd say, "Let them get out of the hospital." I also couldn't imagine him going to Kennedy and saying, "Let's hit them now because you've got all these old guys on the ropes."[51]

Johnson's assessment of the vulnerabilities of the southerners was undoubtedly astute. Indeed, a civil rights bill might have been passed a year or more earlier had his precepts been followed. It would have denied some political cover, however, to senators who were by no means segregationists and who simply needed to tell the people at home that they had fought the "good fight." One Johnson partisan who had the opportunity to observe both Johnson and Mansfield acknowledged the virtues of the latter's approach.

Mike Mansfield had the attitude that if he could get cloture, he'd pass the bill. If he couldn't get cloture, he'd just pass on to something else. I can't recall that he ever tried to wear people down by taking them around the clock. That didn't mean he wouldn't try more than one time to get cloture. He'd file several cloture petitions, but he realized that if he tried to wear out the opponents, he'd just as easily end up wearing out his own troops.[52]

Deprived of this face-saving device, southern opposition to the 1964 Civil Rights Act might have been fiercer than it was, but even with a more aggressive strategy with southern Democrats, the need to reach across the aisle was still there.

Mansfield's technique for securing bipartisan cooperation was to defer to Dirksen. As one who shunned the limelight, Mansfield felt comfortable doing this; as one who basked in it, Dirksen used his opportunities for visibility to the point where, as Neil MacNeil writes: "even Senate correspondents began to confuse Dirksen's functional role in the Senate as that of the majority leader, not the minority leader."[53] By deferring to Dirksen, Mansfield came under attack from his own Democratic colleagues. In 1963, Thomas Dodd of Connecticut assailed Mansfield's leadership on the floor of the Senate; the previous year, Wayne Morse had risen to question Mansfield's integrity. In both instances, Dirksen publicly rebuked the Democrats for their attacks on their own floor leader.[54]

Mansfield's legislative achievements suggest that his strategy was successful. So while President Kennedy complained of Mansfield's excessive solicitude toward Dirksen on the Nuclear Test Ban Treaty in 1963, the treaty was ratified only because Mansfield had prevailed on President Kennedy to reassure Dirksen about the state of U.S. military preparedness. And the center-stage role that Mansfield ceded to Dirksen in the fight for the 1964 Civil Rights Act was critical to its passage.

Mansfield made more than political alliances by reaching across the aisle. He also found his closest friend, George Aiken of Vermont, among the Republicans. McPherson described the relationship as "one of the few enduring simple friendships in the Senate."[55] In the Senate, however, no friendship is either wholly political or wholly personal. Charles Ferris recalls that Aiken was like a "vacuum cleaner of information on goings-on in the Republican conference."[56]

When Congress was in session, Mansfield and Aiken had breakfast together every morning, occasionally joined by a third senator, John Williams, Republican of Delaware. Typically, however, it was just Mansfield and Aiken. The friendship, which lasted twenty-five years, came about when the freshman Mansfield was pushing his tray down the Senate cafeteria line. An Aiken staff member spotted Mansfield heading for a table and a solitary lunch and invited him to join her and her boss for lunch. The staff assistant, who was later to marry Aiken, said the Mansfields and Aikens saw little of each other socially but described the two senators as drawn together by similar personal and political characteristics, observing simply: "It was just a very comforting relationship for two men in a very tough business."[57]

In his dealings with the Republicans, Mansfield's demeanor was little different from the one he used with Democrats. As Muskie recalled, "He did not believe in treating the Republican minority in a confrontational or hostile way, although he could certainly rise to the challenge."[58]

One issue, however, caused Mansfield to differ openly with his dear friend, disagreeing not on substance but on the proper approach to employ in reversing a policy that both men came to believe was ill-starred—the United States' military involvement in Vietnam. The Vietnam War posed for Mansfield the most agonizing dilemma of his years in public life, presenting him with the conflict between, on the one hand, his institutional role as the chief spokesman in the Senate for a Democratic president and, on the other, his profound conviction that the president had embarked on a dangerously wrongheaded policy.

Parting Company: Mansfield, Johnson, and Vietnam

In 1953, Justice William O. Douglas hosted a luncheon for U.S. senators who were interested in Asian politics. The guest of honor was a Vietnamese exile named Ngo Dinh Diem, who was living in a retreat house operated by the Maryknoll Fathers. Two guests who were most impressed by Diem were John F. Kennedy and Mike Mansfield.[59]

By 1962 Kennedy was president, Mansfield was majority leader, and Ngo Dinh Diem was president of the Republic of South Vietnam, a country in which twelve thousand American military personnel were serving officially in an advisory capacity. Increasingly, however, they were being drawn into the conflict against Communist insurgents.

Kennedy dispatched Mansfield to Vietnam to assess the political situation there. Mansfield reported to Kennedy on December 26, 1962, while the president was vacationing at Palm Beach. The two men spent several hours poring over the report, a pessimistic account that pointedly asked how much the maintenance of U.S. interests would be worth. A number of points in the report displeased Kennedy, but the senator reassured himself that "at least he got the truth as I saw it and it wasn't a pleasant picture that I depicted for him."[60]

Mansfield's position on Vietnam was remarkably consistent throughout the Kennedy administration. He argued that the United States had not really examined how Vietnam was vital to U.S. national interests, nor had it pondered the costs of propping up the pro-American government. He also believed that only Diem had the stature to lead the country. After Diem was assassinated in November 1963, Mansfield deplored privately the unexamined American policy in Vietnam and used every occasion to state his misgivings both to Kennedy and his successor, Lyndon Johnson. His respect for the presidency, however, and his conviction that the president had access to better intelligence information and advice than he had, caused Mansfield to back both men publicly. So, while urging Johnson not to escalate the war, he voted with the majority in the Senate for the Tonkin Gulf Resolution of 1964, which came to be interpreted by the administration as "the functional equivalent of a declaration of war."[61] Mansfield disputed this interpretation, but he did so with great discretion and restraint. Only with the advent of the Nixon administration in 1969 did Mansfield become actively involved with legislative efforts to reduce the United States' role in Southeast Asia.

This practice of not publicly breaking with the Democratic presidents while harboring serious misgivings about their Vietnam policies was agonizing for Mansfield and opened him to fierce criticism. His efforts to play the loyal Senate leader for the president clashed with his tragic vision of the conflict and thrust him into positions considered untenable by some.

He was chosen to lead a delegation there in 1965 in part because he was not a vocal critic of Johnson's Vietnam policy. His group consisted of senators Edmund Muskie, George Aiken, Daniel Inouye of Hawaii, and J. Caleb Boggs of Delaware. On their return, they issued a report entitled "The Vietnam Conflict: The Substance and Shadow." The report raised the specter of the war spreading to all of Southeast Asia, questioned the ability of Diem's successors to mobilize the South Vietnamese people, and warned that a massive infusion of U.S. troops would reduce even more in the eyes of the Vietnamese the conviction that the war was being fought on their behalf.

Two weeks after the Mansfield delegation issued its report, the Johnson administration submitted a request for more than $9 billion in new funds to prosecute the war. This provoked an effort on the part of some senators to debate Vietnam policy, and on March 1, 1966, Wayne Morse, an Oregon Democrat, offered a motion to debate the war on the floor of the Senate. As one senator recalled:

Senator Mansfield of Montana, the majority leader of the Senate, proposed to table the Morse amendment. This, I thought, was a surprising move on Mansfield's part, since the move of Senator Morse was clearly within the range of Senate rights and responsibility, and the Mansfield motion was clearly in the service of the Johnson administration. Mansfield's move was an attempt to silence the Senate on the issue, or if not to silence it, to cut off formal procedures; when the vote was taken, only five senators voted against the tabling motion.[62]

The Mansfield tabling motion eloquently summed up the terrible contradictions of his position—private remonstrations to Johnson and public demonstrations of solidarity with an increasingly beleaguered Democratic president.

His position won him little support among colleagues on either side of the Vietnam issue. On the one hand, Eugene McCarthy, who became identified with opposition to the war, said:

I never thought that Mike did as much as he should have in challenging the involvement in Vietnam. The Senate failed pretty badly in taking the responsibility for challenging the escalation of the war. Mike had been chairman of that special committee that went to Vietnam in '65 and filed a very negative report, but that's sort of where he left it.[63]

Russell Long, on the other, reflected: "One thing about him that did disturb me a bit was during the Vietnam War that Mike should have backed the president more."[64]

But there is a third position that perhaps approaches more closely the subtle rationale for Mansfield's position: if Mansfield had become an outspoken opponent of the war, Johnson would simply have written him off, banishing him as he had Frank Church and Wayne Morse. Thomas Eagleton, an antiwar senator, saw value in Mansfield's stance.

Mike did not develop that great antagonism with Johnson that Fulbright did. Fulbright became absolutely *persona non grata* with Johnson, as later on Stuart Symington did after Clark Clifford converted him to "dovedom."

It is just amazing to me that Mansfield didn't. It was a function of his personality, his style, the office that he held, and his conception of that office.

So, Johnson could say, "I can afford to break with Stuart Symington. I can even afford to break with Bill Fulbright, the chairman of the Foreign Relations Committee, but, my God, I can't afford to break with the man who succeeded me as majority leader."[65]

Johnson wanted the Democratic floor leader of the Senate to be drum major for his policy; Mansfield demurred. That he led no pep rallies for other teams won him little affection at the White House. Johnson aide Harry McPherson recalls that:

As [Mansfield's] active support was needed, his silence was almost as irritating to the White House as an exposed confrontation; it was not enough for a Democratic leader to look the other way as a line was being drawn in the dirt. . . . A party leader in the Senate was something more than a spokesman for his administration.[66]

McPherson's poignant recollection of an encounter between the two men captures the effect of the war on the relationship between Johnson and Mansfield:

One evening after a meeting, Mike Mansfield and Johnson walked out onto the drive there on the South Lawn of the White House. And Johnson put his hand on Mansfield's shoulder and said, "Mike, I just can't tell you what a difference it would have made to me to have had my majority leader backing me on this." Mike just nodded. It was a moment of anguish. Johnson nodded himself, touched Mansfield's shoulder again and walked back into the White House.[67]

Mansfield, Nixon, and Watergate

Richard Nixon's narrow victory over Hubert Humphrey in the election of 1968 was matched by a modest change in the partisan configuration in the Senate. The Republicans managed a net gain of six seats, which brought the partisan balance to fifty-eight Democrats and forty-two Republicans. Not since Zachary Taylor in 1849 had a first-term president faced a House and Senate controlled by the other party. This historical oddity was compounded by the fact that Nixon and his chief aides were relatively unknown to members of Congress. Evans and Novak write:

Despite his own four years in the House of Representatives, two in the Senate, and eight as the Senate's presiding officer, Nixon knew remarkably little about the workings of Congress and cared less. He had always had an inferiority complex about the Senate, which had not taken him into its mysterious inner club.[68]

Despite his general lack of interest in Congress, Nixon did attempt to identify key Democratic senators with whom he might work. The veteran Republican John Sherman Cooper of Kentucky recommended Mansfield, but he cautioned Nixon that if he really wanted to establish rapport with Mansfield, he would have to see him alone on a regular basis and would need to exercise discretion in publicizing reports of their meetings.

Little in the way of real rapport came of the Mansfield-Nixon breakfasts that the president held. The personalities of the two were ill matched, and Mansfield was not going to serve as Nixon's instrument in the Senate. Mansfield's own account of the meetings sound formalistic and bespeak of a restricted agenda:

I met with President Nixon on at least a once-monthly basis, sometimes two and three and, on one occasion, four times, and they were apart from the regular leadership meetings.

These breakfast meetings began with Nixon's first month in office. They were held at his request and they were all meetings just between the two of us, except for one, when Henry Kissinger was called in briefly and then left.

It was at those meetings that we began to discuss foreign policy matters and we initially started out considering ways and means of achieving a better status with the P[eople's] R[epublic of] C[hina], which eventually resulted in Kissinger's secret trip to Beijing, followed by Nixon's trip in February, 1972.

As far as domestic policy was concerned, we discussed it very little. As far as foreign policy was concerned, in almost all its aspects, we discussed it primarily in all our breakfast meetings.[69]

Although Nixon had asked for no specific mandate other than the hopeful vow to "bring us together," there was no question but that there were public expectations that he would move to terminate U.S. involvement in Vietnam. His decision in May 1970 to send U.S. troops into Cambodia, accordingly, set off a torrent of criticism in Congress. At the time of the Cambodia invasion, the Senate Foreign Relations Committee was holding hearings on an extension of the Foreign Military Sales Act of 1968 that had already been passed by the House. By a 9-5 vote, the committee voted to add an amendment proposed by Cooper and Church to cut off appropriations for the Cambodia operation.

Mansfield, no longer emotionally or politically tied to the White House, let the Senate work its will on the Cooper-Church amendment as it had learned to do on domestic matters. It was the Mansfield Senate in its fullest flower. It also drove the White House to distraction. "In the spring and summer of 1970," write Evans and Novak, "[Mansfield] permitted endless, unproductive debate on the Cooper-Church amendment to restrict future U.S. military operations in Indochina, thereby tying up Nixon's entire legislative program."[70]

While the Nixon administration battled antiwar senators over Vietnam, relations between the White House and the Democratic majority on domestic issues were not nearly so acrimonious. To be sure, two Nixon nominees to the Supreme Court failed to secure confirmation, but, in general, Mansfield's laissez-faire leadership enabled individual senators to make their own deals on domestic legislation with a White House that was by no means hostile to environmental, consumer, and welfare legislation. Mansfield's permissiveness provided an environment for increasingly individualistic senators to advance their own agendas. The Senate of one hundred policy entrepreneurs became the norm in the early 1970s. Far from standing in the way of his colleagues, Mansfield provided a hospitable setting for their freewheeling activities.

From 1967 to 1977, personal staff assigned to senators increased from around 1,750 to about 3,500. Part of this increase resulted from Senate action in 1975 providing each senator with a professional staff member for each committee assignment. Senators inclined to be aggressive and enterprising now had the wherewithal to pursue old projects and to develop new ones. The trend that began with the election of the class of 1958 now flourished in the egalitarian atmosphere of Mansfield's Senate.

With Nixon's reelection campaign in 1972, however, there emerged one of the greatest crises faced by American government in modern times, but also its greatest triumph—the Watergate affair and Nixon's resignation as president.

The manner in which the Senate investigated the burglary of the Democratic National Committee's headquarters at the Watergate complex in Washington, D.C., and the subsequent efforts by high officials to cover it up, was largely the result of Mike Mansfield's shrewd appraisal of the politics of the inquiry and the importance of the legitimacy of the committee that conducted the hearings. By the time that the Ninety-third Congress convened in 1973, Senator Edward Kennedy's Judiciary subcommittee was already holding hearings on Watergate. Mansfield felt, however, that the Senate's inquiry would be best conducted by a senator with no presidential ambitions. Given the jurisdictions of standing committees, the obvious choice would have been the full Judiciary Committee, chaired by James O. Eastland of Mississippi.

Mansfield had been in Montana during the 1972 election season campaigning for his colleague Lee Metcalf and was becoming increasingly disturbed by reports that Nixon campaign officials had attempted to discredit prominent Democrats through the use of "dirty tricks." On returning to Washington, he resolved to set the investigatory process in motion, but not with Eastland's committee because of the Mississipian's personal fondness for President Nixon.

At the beginning of the Ninety-third Congress in 1973, the Senate created a select committee on presidential campaign activities. It was this committee, rather than Judiciary, that Mansfield wanted as the engine of investigation. He wrote letters both to Eastland and to the man he wanted to head the new select committee, Sam Ervin, a conservative Democrat from North Carolina. In his letter to Eastland, he tactfully acknowledged that some aspects of Watergate properly came under the jurisdiction of the Judiciary Committee but pointed out that beyond them was "a cynical and dangerous intrusion into the integrity of the electoral process."[71]

To Ervin he suggested that he and Eastland meet and agree on a single investigatory instrument. He received no reply from Eastland for several days, and when Mansfield encountered him on the Senate floor, the Mississippian asked Mansfield what he wanted him to do with the Watergate investigation. "Give it over to Sam," Mansfield replied.[72]

Nixon regarded Mansfield's promotion of Ervin for the chairmanship of the select committee as an astute but highly partisan move by placing a morally unassailable Democrat at the head of the panel. Nixon wrote in his diary:

An indication of the fact that we are going to have a very hard four years is Mansfield's announcement that he wants Ervin's committee to investigate Watergate. Mansfield is going to be deeply and bitterly partisan without question.[73]

Mansfield chose the Democrats to serve on the committee with the same eye to propriety, legitimacy, and moral unassailability that characterized the establishment of the committee. He vetted the ranks of contenders for presidential hopefuls and weeded them out, even ruling out senators up for reelection. And, as the Talmadge interview reveals, he was relentless in getting the people he wanted.

Mansfield was equally diligent and astute in naming members for the 1975 select committee that investigated misconduct in U.S. intelligence agencies. Again, with an eye toward a chair of impeccable integrity, Mansfield settled on Philip Hart of Michigan, who, by then suffering from a terminal illness, declined the job. Another contender was Frank Church of Idaho who, according to one report, "almost knocked down Mansfield's door to get it."[74] But Church was known to harbor presidential aspirations, and Mansfield agreed only after extracting a pledge from Church that he would not launch a campaign for the nomination during the active phase of his committee's investigation.

Mansfield's work on establishing these two sensitive committees and assigning members to them is a good example of the majority leader at his most effective—working behind the scenes, scanning for possible political pitfalls, and pressing doggedly to get the right people on the committee, not with extravagant or eloquent arguments, but with the moral authority of someone who was universally respected.

Mansfield: The Man and His Legacy

Placing Mansfield's stewardship of the United States Senate into historical perspective, one cannot fail to be impressed with the sheer bulk of important legislation enacted in the years between 1961 and 1977. In addition to the colossal policy innovations—such as the Great Society legislation, environmental enactments, and the Civil Rights and Voting Rights acts—there were also benchmark institutional changes: the War Powers Resolution, the Budget Act, and the modification of Rule XXII that facilitated cloture would themselves have marked the Mansfield era as one of great achievement. This legislation was the product of many different senators. There was Muskie on budget reform; Cooper, Case, Church, Fulbright, Javits, and Morse on bringing the Vietnam War to a close; Mondale on modifying the filibuster rule; Bayh and Magnuson on lowering the voting age to eighteen; Humphrey and Dirksen on civil rights; and Kennedy on welfare. On only a handful of these matters was Mansfield deeply involved. His own interest in a more open attitude toward China and a lessening of the American military burden in the North Atlantic Treaty Organization (NATO) were not the subject of major legislative initiatives.

But Mansfield let "a thousand flowers bloom"—flowers that might well have blossomed without him but, then again, perhaps not so abundantly. His conviction that all senators were equal and his rejection of the "inner club" allowed the modern Senate of equals to emerge. So Mike Mansfield was good for individual senators. The more difficult question, however, is how good was Mansfield for the institution?

Much criticism of the modern Senate is, in effect, a commentary on institutional features that emerged during Mansfield's term as majority leader. The hyperindividualism, the ability of willful or obstructionist members to hold the institution hostage at times to their own petty interests, the hypertrophy of Senate staff and their assumption of unprecedented, even unwarranted, authority, are all developments of the Mansfield era.

But while it is true that debates often lagged and obstruction was tolerated—some might even say encouraged—his Senate was one in which brief service or unconventional style or philosophy never brought ostracism or marginality to a senator. There were no "nonpersons" in Mike Mansfield's Senate unless they chose that status for themselves. Neither was there a class of exalted supersenators except those whose wisdom or integrity caused their colleagues to search them out.

Mansfield understood that leadership in the modern Senate demanded novel resources. In an increasingly individualistic campaign setting in which candidates, not parties, were the central element, Mansfield grasped the value of political cover. This was manifested in his toleration of the filibuster. He allowed senators to posture and ingratiate themselves with voters who were less impressed by senators' party affiliations than by the quality of their advocacy on key issues. Mansfield gave senators that platform, and they used it—perhaps excessively.

He did not invent the modern Senate or fashion the modern U.S. senator with his own hands. He saw and understood change, and instead of expending his energies in futile efforts to avert it, he accommodated it and presided over an institution as internally democratic as at any time in history. He was less creative than he might have been, more permissive than he should have been, and not as attentive to the Senate's day-to-day business than many thought he needed to be. Nothing said on his behalf will ever convince Johnson votaries that Mansfield possessed any great leadership skills. But those who were first elected after 1958 esteem his shrewd comprehension of the changing rules of American politics; his adroit balancing between his loyalty to his one-time benefactor, Lyndon Johnson, and his tragic vision of the course of American policy in Asia; and, above all, his scrupulous honesty, fair-mindedness, and deep-seated belief in a Senate of equals.

NOTES

1. Booth Mooney, *The Politicians* (Philadelphia: J.B. Lippincott, 1970), 337.
2. In his excellent account of Mansfield's early years, Charles Eugene Hood, Jr., suggests that the stormy relations between Mansfield and his aunt have been the subject of a certain amount of "revisionism," but there seems to have been more than a thirst for adventure in young Mansfield's frequent attempts to run away from home. Hood also speculates that the stern Mansfield home, with its emphasis on duty, piety, and obligation, might well have affected Mansfield's attitude toward authority as an adult. Throughout his career, Mansfield was deferential to authority, accommodating, and nonconfrontational—traits often associated with a man who in his youth had come under the influence of a commanding and powerful woman. See Charles Eugene Hood, Jr., "China Mike: The Making of a Congressional Authority on the Far East" (Ph.D. diss., Program in American Studies, Washington State University, 1980), 55–74.
3. Ibid., 11–112.
4. Jim Ludwick, *Mansfield: The Senator from Montana* (Missoula, Mont.: Missoulian, 1988), 7; and Louis Baldwin, *Hon. Politician: Mike Mansfield of Montana* (Missoula, Mont.: Mountain Press, 1979), 14.
5. Hood, "China Mike," 193–194.
6. Ibid., 182.
7. At the core of Hood's treatment is the question of whether Mansfield puffed his own expertise on the Far East. At least some of the inflation was the fault of the media, ever vigilant for authoritative, quotable sources. Typically, the period of Mansfield's youthful sojourn in China as a marine was inflated from the actual six days to two, even three, years. Hood's conclusion seems to have been that if others were going to puff his credentials as a Far East expert, Mansfield would not be very energetic in pointing out their error.
8. Ludwick, *Mansfield*, 8.
9. Ibid.
10. Bobby Baker, *Wheeling and Dealing* (New York: Norton, 1978), 62. This version of Mansfield's accession to the whip position is also accepted by Rowland Evans and Robert Novak in *Lyndon B. Johnson: The Exercise of Power* (New York: New American Library, 1966), 98.
11. George A. Smathers, interview with author, May 16, 1989.
12. Harry McPherson, interview with author, August 21, 1989.
13. Quoted in Alfred Steinberg, *Sam Johnson's Boy* (New York: Macmillan, 1968), 450.

14. Harry McPherson, *A Political Education*, 2d ed. (Boston: Houghton Mifflin, 1988), 183.
15. Quoted in Evans and Novak, *Lyndon B. Johnson*, 199.
16. McPherson, *Political Education*, 130.
17. Letter from Mike Mansfield to the author, September 29, 1989.
18. Ludwick, *Mansfield*, 11.
19. Ibid.
20. Baker, *Wheeling and Dealing*, 134.
21. Steinberg, *Sam Johnson's Boy*, 547.
22. Evans and Novak, *Lyndon B. Johnson*, 307–308.
23. McPherson, *Political Education*, 183.
24. Baker, *Wheeling and Dealing*, 140.
25. McPherson, *Political Education*, 45.
26. Lawrence O'Brien, *No Final Victories* (Garden City, N.Y.: Doubleday, 1974), 132.
27. Theodore C. Sorensen, *Kennedy* (New York: Harper and Row, 1965), 342.
28. Ibid., 345–346.
29. McPherson, interview with author.
30. John G. Stewart, "Two Strategies of Leadership: Johnson and Mansfield," in *Congressional Behavior*, ed. Nelson Polsby (New York: Random House, 1971), 71.
31. Edmund S. Muskie, interview with author, June 22, 1989.
32. Herman Talmadge, interview with author, June 20, 1989.
33. Howard Cannon, interview with author, June 22, 1989.
34. William S. White, *Citadel* (New York: Harper and Row, 1956), 83–84.
35. Eugene McCarthy, *Up 'Til Now* (New York: Harcourt Brace Jovanovich, 1987), 55–56.
36. Stewart, "Two Strategies," 72.
37. Michael Foley, *The New Senate* (New Haven: Yale University Press, 1980), 187.
38. Stewart, "Two Strategies," 71.
39. Ibid., 73.
40. Ibid.
41. Randall B. Ripley, *Power in the Senate* (New York: St. Martin's, 1969), 93.
42. Stewart, "Two Strategies," 75.
43. Muskie, interview with the author.
44. Ripley, *Power in the Senate*, 94.
45. Robert L. Peabody, *Leadership in Congress: Stability, Succession and Change* (Boston: Little, Brown, 1976), 367.
46. Foley, *New Senate*, 163.
47. Peabody, *Leadership in Congress*, 131.
48. Jon R. Bond and Richard Fleisher, "Congressional Leaders and Presidential Success in Congress" (Paper delivered at the annual meeting of the Midwest Political Science Association, Chicago, April 13–15, 1989). Bond and Fleisher point out that on important votes, Mansfield supported Kennedy 100 percent of the time and that on all votes, his support of Kennedy was 87 percent. Mansfield was somewhat less supportive of Johnson, giving him 88 percent support on important votes and 77 percent on all votes.
49. Neil MacNeil, *Dirksen: Portrait of a Public Man* (New York: World, 1970), 213–238.
50. Robert C. Byrd, *The Senate, 1789–1989* (Washington, D.C.: U.S. Government Printing Office, 1989), 682.
51. Eugene McCarthy, interview with the author, June 20, 1989.
52. Russell Long, interview with the author, July 12, 1989.
53. MacNeil, *Dirksen*, 230.
54. Ibid.
55. McPherson, *Political Education*, 69.
56. Charles Ferris, interview with the author, August 14, 1989.
57. Lola Aiken, interview with the author, September 27, 1989.
58. Muskie, interview with the author.
59. Arthur M. Schlesinger, Jr., *A Thousand Days* (Boston: Houghton Mifflin, 1965), 321.

60. Mike Mansfield, interview, June 23, 1964, 24, Oral History Project, John F. Kennedy Library.
61. Nicholas Katzenbach, then under secretary of state, used this phrase in testimony before the Senate Foreign Relations Committee.
62. McCarthy, *Up 'Til Now*, 184.
63. McCarthy, interview with the author.
64. Long, interview with the author.
65. Thomas Eagleton, interview with the author, July 7, 1989.
66. McPherson, *Political Education*, 74–75.
67. McPherson, interview with the author.
68. Rowland Evans, Jr., and Robert D. Novak, *Nixon in the White House* (New York: Random House, 1971), 106.
69. Letter from Mike Mansfield to author, September 29, 1989.
70. Evans and Novak, *Nixon*, 107.
71. Theodore H. White, *Breach of Faith* (New York: Atheneum, 1975), 230–231; and Byrd, *Senate*, 704–705.
72. White, *Breach of Faith*, 230–231.
73. Richard Nixon, *RN: The Memoirs of Richard Nixon* (New York: Grosset and Dunlap, 1978), 773.
74. Quoted in Loch K. Johnson, *Season of Inquiry* (Chicago: Dorsey, 1988), 15.

APPENDIX

SENATE MAJORITY AND MINORITY LEADERS, 1913–1991

SENATE MAJORITY AND MINORITY LEADERS

Congress		Party Ratios	Majority Leader	Minority Leader	President
63d	1913-1915	D51 R44 I1	John W. Kern (D-Ind.)	none	Wilson
64th	1915-1917	D56 R40 —	Kern	none	Wilson
65th	1917-1919	D53 R42 —	Thomas S. Martin (D-Va.)	Henry Cabot Lodge (R-Mass.)	Wilson
66th	1919-1921	R49 D47 —	Henry Cabot Lodge (R-Mass.)	Thos. S. Martin (D-Va.)/ Oscar Underwood (D-Ala.)[a]	Wilson
67th	1921-1923	R59 D37 —	Lodge	Underwood	Harding
68th	1923-1925	R51 D43 I2	Lodge/	Joseph T. Robinson (D-Ark.)	Coolidge
69th	1925-1927	R56 D39 I1	Charles Curtis (R-Kan.)[b]	Robinson	Coolidge
70th	1927-1929	R49 D46 I1	Curtis	Robinson	Coolidge
71st	1929-1931	R56 D39 I1	James E. Watson (R-Ind.)	Robinson	Hoover
72d	1931-1933	R48 D47 I1	Watson	Robinson	Hoover
73d	1933-1935	D60 R35 I1	Joseph T. Robinson (D-Ark.)	Charles L. McNary (R-Ore.)	F Roosevelt
74th	1935-1937	D69 R25 I2	Robinson/	McNary	Roosevelt
75th	1937-1939	D76 R16 I4	Alben W. Barkley (D-Ky.)[c]	McNary	Roosevelt
76th	1939-1941	D69 R23 I4	Barkley	McNary	Roosevelt
77th	1941-1943	D66 R28 I2	Barkley	McNary	Roosevelt
78th	1943-1945	D58 R37 I1	Barkley	McNary/	Roosevelt
79th	1945-1947	D57 R38 I1	Barkley	W. H. White, Jr. (R-Maine)[d] White	Roosevelt/ Truman
80th	1947-1949	R51 D45 —	W. H. White, Jr. (R-Maine)	Alben W. Barkley (D-Ky.)	Truman
81st	1949-1951	D54 R42 —	Scott W. Lucas (D-Ill.)	Kenneth S. Wherry (R-Neb.)	Truman
82d	1951-1953	D48 R47 I1	E. W. McFarland (D-Ariz.)	Wherry/ Styles Bridges (R-N.H.)[e]	Truman
83d	1953-1955	R48 D46 I2	Robert A. Taft (R-Ohio)/ Wm. F Knowland (R-Calif.)[f]	Lyndon B. Johnson (D-Tex.)	Eisenhower

Congress	Years				Majority Leader	Minority Leader	President
84th	1955–1957	D48	R47	11	Lyndon B. Johnson (D-Tex.)	William F. Knowland (R-Calif.)	Eisenhower
85th	1957–1959	D49	R47	—	Johnson	Knowland	Eisenhower
86th	1959–1961	D64	R34	—	Johnson	Everett McK. Dirksen (R-Ill.)	Eisenhower
87th	1961–1963	D64	R36	—	Mike Mansfield (D-Mont.)	Dirksen	Kennedy
88th	1963–1965	D67	R33	—	Mansfield	Dirksen	Kennedy/ Johnson
89th	1965–1967	D68	R32	—	Mansfield	Dirksen	Johnson
90th	1967–1969	D64	R36	—	Mansfield	Dirksen	Johnson
91st	1969–1971	D58	R42	—	Mansfield	Dirksen/ Scott	Nixon
92d	1971–1973	D54	R44	12	Mansfield	Hugh Scott (R-Pa.)[g] Scott	Nixon
93d	1973–1975	D56	R42	12	Mansfield	Scott	Nixon/ Ford
94th	1975–1977	D61	R37	12	Mansfield	Scott	Ford
95th	1977–1979	D61	R38	11	Robert C. Byrd (D-W. Va.)	Howard H. Baker, Jr. (R-Tenn.)	Carter
96th	1979–1981	D58	R41	11	Byrd	Baker	Carter
97th	1981–1983	R53	D46	11	Howard Baker, Jr. (R-Tenn.)	Robert C. Byrd (D-W. Va.)	Reagan
98th	1983–1985	R54	D46	—	Baker	Byrd	Reagan
99th	1985–1987	R53	D47	—	Bob Dole (R-Kan.)	Byrd	Reagan
100th	1987–1989	D55	R45	—	Robert C. Byrd (D-W. Va.)	Bob Dole (R-Kan.)	Reagan
101st	1989–1991	D55	R45	—	George Mitchell (D-Maine)	Dole	Bush

[a] Underwood became minority leader on April 27, 1920, filling the vacancy caused by the death of Martin on November 12, 1919. Gilbert M. Hitchcock (D-Neb.) served as acting minority leader in the interim.

[b] Curtis was named minority leader on November 28, 1924, filling the vacancy left by the death of Lodge on November 9, 1924.

[c] Barkley became majority leader on July 22, 1937, filling the vacancy caused by the death of Robinson on July 14, 1937.

[d] McNary died on February 25, 1944, and Wallace H. White, Jr. (R-Maine), was named minority leader shortly thereafter.

[e] Bridges became the minority leader on January 8, 1952, filling the vacancy caused by Wherry's death on Nov. 29, 1951.

[f] Knowland was named majority leader on August 4, 1953, filling the vacancy created by the death of Taft on July 31, 1953. Taft's seat was filled by a Democrat, Thomas Burke, on November 10, 1953, changing the party divisions in the Senate to 48 Democrats, 47 Republicans, and 1 Independent, thus giving control of the Senate to the Democrats. Knowland remained "majority leader;" however, until the end of the 83d Congress.

[g] Scott became minority leader on September 24, 1969, filling the vacancy left by the death of Dirksen on September 7, 1969.

CONTRIBUTORS

Donald C. Bacon is a project director and coeditor of the *Encyclopedia of the United States Congress*. He has been a Washington, D.C.-based writer and editor for thirty years. His career in journalism includes stints as an editor of *U.S. News & World Report*, staff writer of the *Wall Street Journal*, and political columnist of the Newhouse Newspapers. He is the author of *Congress and You* and coauthor of *Rayburn: A Biography* (1987), which was selected as "Book of the Year" by the *Washingtonian* magazine and as "Best Biography" by the Texas State Historical Commission.

Ross K. Baker is professor of political science at Rutgers University. He served as special assistant to Senator Walter F. Mondale and on the staff of Senator Birch Bayh. He was a speechwriter in the presidential campaign of Senator Frank Church in 1976. From 1982 to 1983 he served as consultant to the Democratic Caucus of the U.S. House of Representatives. He is a regular contributor to the *Los Angeles Times* and the *Atlanta Journal and Constitution*. His books include *Friend and Foe in the U.S. Senate* (1980); *The New Fat Cats* (1989); and *House and Senate* (1989).

Burdett Loomis is professor and chairman of the Department of Political Science at the University of Kansas. He is author of *The New American Politician* (1988) and *Interest Group Politics* (1990). In 1984 he directed the Congressional Management Project, designed to increase management capabilities of members of Congress. He is currently preparing a book on state-level policy making, tentatively entitled *Overtures, Deadlines, and Endgames: A Year in Political Time*.

Robert W. Merry is executive editor at Congressional Quarterly. He began his career at the *Denver Post*, where he covered the Colorado Senate and local politics. In 1974 he became a political reporter for the *National Observer* and in 1977 a Washington correspondent for the *Wall Street Journal*, where he covered Congress, national politics, and the White House. In

1987 he joined Congressional Quarterly as managing editor of the *Weekly Report* and other congressional publications. In January 1990, he was promoted to his current post.

Steve Neal, a political writer and columnist for the *Chicago Sun-Times,* was White House correspondent for the *Chicago Tribune.* He is the author of *McNary of Oregon: A Political Biography* (1985). His previous books include biographies of Wendell Willkie and Oregon governor Tom McCall and a study of the Eisenhower presidency. A frequent contributor to *American Heritage* and the *Nation,* he is currently working on a biography of Abraham Lincoln. As a journalist, he has won awards for investigative and in-depth reporting.

Walter J. Oleszek is senior specialist in the legislative process for the Congressional Research Service of the Library of Congress, where he has worked since 1968. He has served on the staffs of various Senate and House panels dealing with committee and institutional reorganization. He assisted the House Rules Committee in the development of the Legislative Reorganization Act of 1970 and the Senate Special Committee that reviewed the operation of the Senate committee system in 1976 and 1977. The author of five books on Congress, he is an adjunct faculty member at American University.

Donald A. Ritchie is associate historian in the U.S. Senate Historical Office. A former president of the Oral History Association, he currently serves as a council member of the Society for History in the Federal Government. Among his publications are *James M. Landis: Dean of the Regulators* (1980); *Heritage of Freedom: History of the United States* (1985); and *Press Gallery: Congress and the Washington Correspondents* (1991).

Howard E. Shuman has been professor of public policy at the National War College since 1985. From 1982 to 1984 he was visiting senior lecturer at the University of California at Santa Barbara. He served as administrative assistant to Senator William Proxmire from 1969 to 1982. Previously he had been administrative and legislative assistant to Senator Paul Douglas. He is the author of *Politics and the Budget: The Struggle Between the President and the Congress* (1988).

William C. Widenor is professor of history at the University of Illinois at Urbana-Champaign. Before taking his Ph.D. at the University of California at Berkeley in 1975, he spent eight years in the U.S. Foreign Service. He is the author of numerous articles and reviews, and of *Henry Cabot Lodge and the Search for an American Foreign Policy* (1980), which in 1981 won the Organization of American Historians' Frederick Jackson Turner Prize for the year's best first book in American history.

INDEX

All committee references are to Senate committees except where otherwise indicated. Democratic and Republican party committees are cited under the specific party names.